The Greek World 479–323 BC

SIMON HORNBLOWER

Methuen

London and New York

First published in 1983 by
Methuen & Co. Ltd
11 New Fetter Lane, London EC4P 4EE
Published in the USA by
Methuen & Co.
in association with Methuen, Inc.
733 Third Avenue, New York, NY 10017
© 1983 Simon Hornblower

Typeset by Activity, Salisbury, Wilts, and
printed in Great Britain by
Richard Clay & Co. Ltd
Bungay, Suffolk

British Library Cataloguing in Publication Data

Hornblower, Simon
  The Greek world, 479–323 BC.—(Classical
  civilizations)
  1. Greece—History—To 146 B.C.
  I. Title   II. Series
  938   DF214

  ISBN 0-416-74990-9
  ISBN 0-416-75000-1 Pbk

Library of Congress Cataloging in Publication Data

Hornblower, Simon
  The Greek world, 479–323 BC.

  (Classical civilizations)
  Bibliography: p.
  Includes index.
  1. Greece—History—Athenian Supremacy, 479–431 B.C.
  2. Greece—History—Peloponnesian War, 431–404 B.C.
  3. Greece—History—Spartan and Theban Supremacies,
  404–362 B.C.   4. Greece—History—Macedonian Expansion,
  359–322 B.C.   I. Title.   II. Series.
  DF227.H67 1983   938   83-13062
  ISBN 0-416-74990-9
  ISBN 0-416-75000-1 (pbk.)

To Hector Catling

Contents

List of maps

Preface and acknowledgements

This book is dedicated to Hector Catling, Director of the British School at Athens (BSA). By inviting me to lecture in 1979 and 1981 to courses held at the BSA on the Greek city-state, jointly organized by the BSA and the Department of Education and Science, and attended by sixth-form teachers, he made me think about many of the topics discussed in the present book. He also, both at Athens and on the sites we visited (in Attica and the neighbouring city-states) taught me much not just about Mycenaean Greece — his own speciality — but about Greece of all periods.

I am grateful to the general editor of this series, Fergus Millar, for his original invitation to write this book, and for encouragement and comments since. The book has been much improved by his general and particular criticisms, made at the penultimate stage. My wife Jane has also read and commented very usefully. John Roberts of Eton College read a draft of chapters 1–3, for which I am also grateful, as also to Susan Sherwin-White and Robin Seager for comments on particular chapters and to Robert Parker for reading the proofs.

I have frequently, too frequently it may be felt, referred to other things I have written, especially to my book *Mausolus*, Oxford, 1982, my additions to the *Athenian Empire* LACTOR edn 3 (1983), and my forthcoming chapters (iii and xi[a]) on Persia and on Asia Minor in the *Cambridge Ancient History*, edn 2, vol. vi. I have also drawn on a forthcoming (1984) book of mine on *Thucydides* (London). The reason is simply to save space by not repeating references or arguments given more fully in those places.

SIMON HORNBLOWER

Oriel College Oxford

21 February 1983

Abbreviations

(see also p.294 for titles of periodicals)

Arch. Reps = *Archaeological Reports*, booklet issued annually with *Journal of Hellenic Studies (JHS)*.

CW = M. Crawford and D. Whitehead (1983) *Archaic and Classical Greece, A Selection of Ancient Sources in Translation*, Cambridge (disappointing, especially on the non-literary evidence for the fourth century).

Syll.³ = W. Dittenberger (1915–24) *Sylloge inscriptionum Graecarum*, Leipzig, edn 3.

FGrHist. = F. Jacoby, *Die Fragmente der griechischen Historiker*, 15-vol. collection of the fragments (i.e. quotations by other ancient authors from) of Greek historians whose works do not survive complete. 'Fragments' are cited thus: *FGrHist*. 328 Philochoros F 119 means fragment no. 119 of Philochoros, who is historian no. 328 in Jacoby's numbering.

Fornara = C. W. Fornara (1977) *Translated Documents, Archaic Times to the Peloponnesian War*, Baltimore, Ma.

Hicks and Hill = E. L. Hicks and G. F. Hill (1901) *Greek Historical Inscriptions*, Oxford.

Hill² = G. F. Hill (1951) *Sources for Greek History 478–431 B.C.*, revised edn by R. Meiggs and A. Andrewes, Oxford.

IG = *Inscriptiones Graecae* (1873–) Berlin.

ML = Russell Meiggs and David Lewis (1969) *A Selection of Greek Historical Inscriptions to the End of the Fifth Century B.C.*, Oxford.

Michel = Ch. Michel (1900–27) *Recueil d'inscriptions grecques*, Brussels.

OGIS = W. Dittenberger (1903–5) *Orientis Graecae Inscriptiones Selectae*, Leipzig.

SEG = *Supplementum Epigraphicum Graecum* (1923–).

Tod = M. N. Tod (1946 and 1948) *Greek Historical Inscriptions*, vols i² (superseded by ML) and ii (the standard collection of fourth-century inscriptions).

WV = J. Wickersham and E. Verbrugghe (1973) *Greek Historical Documents, The Fourth Century B.C.*, Amsterdam.

op.cit. = the work already cited.

s.v. = entry under. So Suid. s.v. Pericles means the Byzantine lexicon called the Suda or Suidas, ed. A. Adler, entry under Pericles.

Σ = scholiast or ancient commentator on an ancient author. The most important and frequently cited in this book are: Σ Pindar in Drachmann's 3-vol. edn, published by Teubner; Σ Aischines, ed. Schultz; Σ Demosthenes, ed. Dindorf in vols viii-ix of his edn of Demosthenes, now reprinted by Arno, London. So Σ Aischin. ii.31 means the scholiast on Aischines, speech ii paragraph 31, which is to be found on p. 289 of Schultz's edn.

Note also the following Greek or Greek-derived words used in the text:
arche = rule, empire
ekklesia = political assembly
helot = member of the servile population of Sparta
thete = the lowest property-class of citizens at Athens; the fleet was manned predominantly by thetes
hoplite = heavily-armed infantryman; under the name *zeugites*, the second lowest property-class at Athens
polis = city-state
phoros = tribute
chora = territory, often as opposed to the *polis* which exploited it
pentekontaetea = the 'fifty years' c. 480–430
(*see also remarks prefaced to the index*).

1 Xerxes' legacy

By the end of the period covered by this book, 'the Greek world' will include everything between Italy and India. The westward expansion of hellenism, that is the Greek way of life, had long ago been achieved, in the eighth- and seventh-century colonizing phase of Greek history, when Greeks settled in Italy and Sicily. The eastward expansion had also *begun* several centuries before 479. Thucydides, the great fifth-century Athenian historian, speaks (i.12) of the Greeks in this early phase as occupying Italy and Sicily on the one hand, and Ionia (western Turkey) on the other, and treats them as comparable operations. That was not quite accurate in that western colonization after 750 was much more highly organized than the earliest settlement of Greeks in the east. But there was another and for our purposes more important difference: Carthage, the strongest non-Greek power in the west, mostly left the Greeks in Italy and Sicily alone; but when the Persian Empire moved up to the west Mediterranean coast in the sixth century, a movement of conquest which established firm imperial institutions (chapter 6), the presence of this solid power halted for two centuries the natural tendency of the Greeks, 'brought up in the company of Poverty' (Hdt. vii.102), to colonize eastwards in numbers. There is an essential qualification to this. The evidence of inscriptions (see p. 8), and of archaeology — for instance the sixth-century Persian king Cyrus' tomb at Pasargadai in Iran (D. M. Stronach, *Pasargadae*, 1978) — has shown that individual Greek craftsmen were in great demand from Persian patrons, and moved freely within Persian territory. Herodotus, the fifth-century Greek historian of Persia, was one famous beneficiary of this freedom; so were the Greek mercenary soldiers who found new opportunities with Persian employers after 431. Moreover, on many pages of this book, including the last page of all, we shall show that the fourth-century Persian satraps (governors) in the Mediterranean region were specially active agents of hellenization, and *that* meant importing

1

Greece and the Aegean

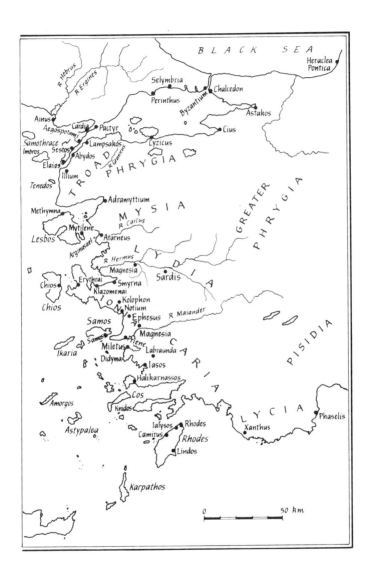

Greeks from the islands and mainland. It is nevertheless true that it was only when Alexander the Great conquered the Persian Empire *c.*330 BC that the full-scale colonization of the east could be resumed, with the city-foundations of Alexander himself and of the hellenistic age generally, so that the two hundred years between Cyrus and Alexander can be seen as an interruption in a single process of *eastern hellenization achieved by the formal settlement of whole new Greek communities*. One main message of this book is that Alexander continues or resumes processes which had already been started or interrupted earlier, and to get that message across it will be necessary to investigate many parts of the Greek world other than the central city-states of the Greek mainland. That is because it is often those 'peripheral' places which anticipate future developments most clearly.

Even by the end of the *first* half of this book, the end of the fifth century, 'the Greek world' already has an impressive regional spread, and covers very different types of terrain, although Alexander's conquests are still three-quarters of a century away. In this first, fifth-century, half of the book the political and cultural narrative will be punctuated by regional chapters whose purpose is to introduce the main cities and areas of the classical Greek world: Italy and Sicily; Cyrene, Africa and Egypt; Persia and Asia Minor; Macedon, Thessaly and Boiotia; Corinth; Sparta; and finally Athens. Then, in the second, fourth-century, half of the book, a unified narrative is offered, which takes the earlier regional discussions for granted. It is one main aim of this arrangement to bring out the way in which the attractions exerted by certain regions determined the policies of other Greek states over long periods. For instance, there is the Thessalian theme. From the time of King Kleomenes of Sparta *c.*500 BC to that of Philip II and Alexander the Great of Macedon, other Greek states tried to get control of Thessaly in central Greece. The *reasons* for this are given, all at once, in the 'Thessaly' chapter (chapter 7); but the *stages* of the struggle for Thessaly are distributed over the whole book. Another example might be Sicilian interference, or the fear of it, in the affairs of Greece proper. The permanent importance of such themes helps to connect the fifth century to the fourth, and it is another main aim of the book to bring out the closeness of that connection between the two centuries: even in terms of the history of Athens, who lost the 'Peloponnesian War' of 431–404 to Sparta, the end of that war represents only a light break in continuity. For instance, Athenian imperial aims revived very soon indeed after 404.

The phrase 'cultural and political narrative' was used above. It is a feature of this book that 'non-political' history is not separately discussed, except for a centrally placed chapter on the effects of the Peloponnesian War (which, by advancing professionalism in many areas of activity, changed military, social and cultural life more than it did political; cp. what was said about Athens at the end of the preceding paragraph). This interwoven presentation means that many strictly non-political topics are discussed less fully than the student whose prime interest is in, say, art or archaeology will wish. But there is an outweighing advantage. The argument of this book proceeds, where possible, by the simultaneous marshalling of *all* available kinds of evidence — not just the literary sources but the evidence of inscriptions, archaeology and art. This has been done in the belief that the relegation, in a text-book, of 'cultural and social life' to a distinct section of the work (usually at the end), is unfaithful to the facts of life and so of history, where change happens on all fronts at once. *That* is the advantage of interweaving political with other kinds of history.

The sources thus used (about which a word must be said in conclusion) are cited in brackets in the text; they are sometimes quoted as well as cited — not as often as would have been ideal, but where space is tight the desire to *illustrate* the story must sometimes yield to the simple need to *tell* it at intelligible length. Modern books and articles are referred to by notes, collected at the end of the book. The long and exceptional first note to the final 'Alexander' chapter, to which attention is here specially drawn, reflects the peculiarly tricky source-problem of Alexander's reign.

So frequent an insistence, expressed by the bracketed ancient references, on the primacy of the ancient evidence is deliberate. A text without such running references to often conflicting source-material would certainly provide the suspension making for an easier ride over the potholes and bumps of ancient history. But the potholes and bumps — gaps or contradictions in the evidence, and such deliberately placed obstacles to understanding as the utterances of orators with cases to plead — provide shocks which arguably ought *not* to be absorbed: like any other shock-absorber, the bland synthesis achieves comfort only by protecting one from the uneven surface of reality, and the historian — unlike the car-passenger of this metaphor — ought to want to get as close to that uneven reality as he can.

Now for the sources themselves: first, literary.

There are three surviving full-length histories by contemporaries or near-contemporaries of the events they describe. First, *Herodotus*, who described the wars between Greece and Persia of 499–479, and the prehistory of Persia and Greece before the clash. He is so rich a source that he often needs to be used even by the modern historian whose *starting*-date is 479. Second, *Thucydides*, whose immensely detailed but at the same time highly selective history of the Peloponnesian War of 431–404 is prefaced by an account of Athenian expansion 479–439 which is the most valuable literary account of that vital but poorly documented topic that we have. Third, *Xenophon*, who wrote a *Hellenica* ('Greek Affairs') covering the period from 411 to 362. This is a vivid, personal and partisan work of reminiscence, written from too Spartan a viewpoint (its author was an Athenian but his sympathies were with the Spartans, among whom he spent much of his adult life), and with an often strange distribution of attention. In addition there is Xenophon's *Anabasis* which describes his participation with the 'Ten Thousand' (an army of Greek mercenary soldiers) in an expedition in 400 against the new Persian king in support of a rival claimant. All three authors are translated in Penguins: G. Cawkwell's revisions of the two Xenophon books are very useful. (The Alexander historians are discussed in n. 1 to chapter 18.)

In addition we have books xi–xvi of the 'Library' (a universal history) of *Diodorus of Sicily*, a writer of the Roman period whose value for the classical Greek historian is that he drew for the years 479–340 on an earlier 'universal history', by the fourth-century BC writer *Ephorus*. This (together with inscriptions, see p. 8) can be used to correct Xenophon and fill in some of his many gaps, since in the fourth century Ephorus represents a tradition independent of Xenophon; for the fifth century, by contrast, Ephorus/Diodorus is usually less valuable because it does often represent a source already available to us in its original form, namely Thucydides, but rearranged so as to treat the achievements of individuals one by one. (This is why Diodorus went to Ephorus not Thucydides: Diodorus likes to moralize, and could accommodate his moralizing more easily to history treated as a series of connected biographies, in the 'Ephoran' manner.) There is a Loeb translation of Diodorus.

Other historians do not survive either complete or in 'digested' form like Ephorus, but only in isolated quotations by later writers. Such 'fragmentary' historians, as they are called, include the fourth-century *Ktesias* (who wrote about Persia) and *Theopompus* (who wrote about Philip). *Plutarch*, a biographer writing in the Roman period, drew on such writers abundantly, as well as on the surviving historians, and is thus immensely valuable to us. (All Plutarch's relevant Greek *Lives*, except the important *Artaxerxes* which is in a Loeb translation, are translated in the Penguin volumes *The Rise and Fall of Athens* and *The Age of Alexander*.)

The *Oxyrhynchus Historian* (HO or Hell. Ox.) deserves mention separately from both 'surviving' and 'fragmentary' historians. This is an extended but incomplete section of a fourth-century historian, found on papyrus at Oxyrhynchus in Egypt. It covers events of the 390s, and is high-grade material. It has an additional interest and importance in that it can be shown that Diodorus' version of events around the turn of the fifth and fourth centuries closely follows the reliable Hell. Ox. where the two can be compared. This means that Ephorus, whom Diodorus used, himself used Hell. Ox., and this discovery has had the effect of forcing a revision of scholarly judgements of Diodorus' general worth, as against Xenophon's, as a source for those years. The revision has invariably been in Diodorus' favour. So books xiii–xiv of Diodorus have merits greater than the books which come after them, and far greater than the books which come before. There is no complete translation of Hell. Ox., except for the very good section on the federal constitution of Boiotia, translated in J. M. Moore (1975) *Aristotle and Xenophon on Democracy and Oligarchy* (extracts also in WV).

The writings of Athenian orators survive only from the late fifth century onwards, when they become an important source for both the political and the social historian. *Andokides'* first and third speeches (*On the Mysteries* and *On the Peace*) illuminate key events in Athenian history of 415–404, and in Greek history of 392, respectively. The fourth-century orators include *Lysias* and *Isaios*, who in English terms are a politically involved 'common-law' barrister and a 'chancery' barrister, that is, the one covers all variety of topics, the other specializes in estates and wills. Lysias was a *metic*, i.e. not a national of Athens but resident there. He was actually from Syracuse in Sicily (see p. 200). Finally (to omit some minor figures) there is *Isokrates*, a professor and pamphleteer rather than an orator, whose more ephemeral writings will be used in this book, but whose chief importance and influence in history lies beyond the chronological scope of this volume and may be mentioned here: it is that he formulated an ideal of rhetorical education as a training for *life*, which dominated Greco-Roman educational practice. This worldly programme was opposed to the 'pure research' programme of Plato. The argument is of enduring importance: in a comparable nineteenth-century debate, the 'Isokratean' position was held by the worldly Benjamin Jowett, the 'Platonic' by the pure scholar, Mark Pattison. *Demosthenes* (384–322), the greatest of the Athenian orators, and his contemporary *Aischines* are prime evidence for Athenian society, and for Athenian reactions to the securing of power over Greece by Philip II of Macedon. All these writers are in Loeb translations; see also the Penguin *Greek Political Oratory*, containing a number of important short speeches, W. R. Connor, *Greek Orations* (similar), and the Penguin *Demosthenes and Aischines* (Dem. xviii, xix; Aisch. ii, iii).

Finally, two works of or attributed to *Aristotle*, the *Athenian Constitution* and the *Politics*. The first, abbreviated *Ath. Pol.* (and perhaps not an authentic work of Aristotle) has an account of the historical evolution of its subject as well as a descriptive analysis; the *Politics* is a much longer treatise on political thought, the first of its kind. Its scope is not confined to Athens, and though a work of theory it has a wealth of illustrations from actual Greek history and practice. There is a Penguin of the *Politics*, soon to be joined by one of the *Ath. Pol.* by P. Rhodes. The *Old Oligarch* (see p. 153), falsely attributed to Xenophon, is a right-wing pamphlet about Athens and her democracy, dating from the 420s; translated in the Loeb Xenophon or Moore, op. cit.

The non-literary evidence is that of coins, archaeology and above all inscriptions (see pp. x–xi for abbreviations and translated collections). Most of the important inscriptions are decrees and other documentary records carved (nearly always) on stone, many but not by any means all* coming from Athens which as a democracy believed in making its records permanently visible 'for anyone who wished to see' (Andokides i. 83), and which made its magistrates strictly and publicly accountable for their actions, especially in the financial sphere. That is why there are so many *financial* records on stone, a fact which is specially useful to us because ancient literary writers tended to disdain such matters for stylistic reasons. (See also p. 94 for the reasons for the absence of inscriptions from Corinth.) It is above all the constant flow of finds of new inscriptions ('epigraphic' finds) which means that

---

*Asia Minor, especially after 400 BC, is another rich and rewarding source.

ancient history would not be a static subject, even if the perspectives of modern students of ancient history were not constantly changing — as they are. The great modern French epigraphist Louis Robert (*Epigraphik der klassischen Welt*, 1970, p. 21) has called inscriptions the ancient historian's 'fountain of youth'.

In 480/79 BC the United Greeks defeated a Persian invasion led by King Xerxes. A little later, in 476, at the Olympic Games (games of high prestige held at Olympia in the western Peloponnese, and open to all Greeks) there were victorious participants from Sparta, Argos, Aigina, Mytilene, Thasos, Italy and Sicily, competing in the presence of the Athenian Themistokles (Plut. *Them.* xvii.4) who had done much to bring about the defeat of Persia in the recent wars. The Theban poet Pindar, who specialized in the writing of odes celebrating victorious athletes and the owners of victorious chariot-teams, wrote no less than five odes for victors in these games of 476.[1] All this was an impressive display of Greek psychological unity: Olympia was always to be associated with panhellenism, which means the consciousness of Greek unity (cp. p. 200 for Lysias in 384). But in the centuries after Alexander the Great, Italy, Sicily, Athens, Sparta and Thebes are poorly represented among Olympic victors: instead we find Macedonians and Asiatic Greeks. Panhellenism, which had been a brief possibility just after 480, had failed. Macedon now rules the subject Greek world.

The *poleis* or city-states of mainland Greece, after their Persian triumphs, did not, then, stay united to form a single nation: panhellenism had been brought into being by the fear of foreign invasion, and as that fear receded, so did the reality of panhellenism. But the ideal (or the illusion) of panhellenism survived in oratory and became an inescapable part of Athenian public life. Moreover, since ancient education was primarily a training for public speaking, and a way of transmitting the teacher's own techniques and values,[2] the theme was surely taught and travestied from schooldays upwards. But, likely though all this is, the precise content of fifth-century oratory must — since, by accident, nothing survives earlier than Antiphon and Andokides late in the century — be a matter for inference and no more. (The speeches in a historian as idiosyncratic as Thucydides cannot be taken as representative of ordinary practice.) More securely known are the preoccupations of artists and architects: thus, the Parthenon frieze contains a double reference to the defeat of the Persian Empire, both in form (the long procession of human

beings is a deliberate reminiscence of the Reliefs of the Tribute-Bear-
ers on the Apadana at Persepolis) and in content (the 192 sculptured
figures and their horses represent the 192 dead heroes of the battle of
Marathon).[3] More crudely, the column blocks of the old Parthenon,
victim of the Persian sack of the city, were embedded in the side of the
Acropolis: the message is 'that is what the Persians did'. Nor was this
interest confined to Athens: Artemisia of Halikarnassus, a squadron-
commander in the fleet of Xerxes which Athens destroyed at Salamis,
was not only an object of fascination to the Athenian readers of
Herodotus and Aristophanes (*Lysistrata* 675, etc.) but was depicted in
a fifth-century building at, of all places, land-locked, Athens-fearing
Sparta.[4]

The repulse of Persia may not have created a Greek nation-state,
but it remained psychologically potent, which was to make it easy for
Philip of Macedon (or his historian Kallisthenes) to develop the
notion of a new Persian War to avenge the outrages of Xerxes, a
century and a half before. The hellenistic historian Polybius regarded
this as a mere pretext (iii.6), and he was right. But, considered purely
as propaganda for Athenian consumption, the 'revenge' motif was
shrewdly conceived; did not the prayers which opened meetings of the
Athenian popular assembly regularly include disparagement of 'the
Medes', i.e. Persia? (Ar. *Thesm.* 337, 365). If Athens in the event
failed to respond to the cry of 'crusade' that was only because her
suspicion of Philip and Alexander was even greater than her hatred of
Persia or her greed for Persian territory in Anatolia.

Persia was something else for the Greeks: a point of reference. A
common enemy did more than supply themes for the makers and
manipulators of Greek public opinion; it gave the Greeks, if not a
word for themselves (they had that already), an added awareness that
they were Greeks, and that 'Hellas', their word for their country, was
more than just a geographical expression. The transition in attitude
can be traced. The *Persians* of Aeschylus, produced in the 470s,
balances shades of literary light and dark in its handling of Greeks and
Persians, and this *chiaroscuro* effect might be thought to imply that
Persia and Greece are being presented as a pair of opposites. But the
detail of the play does not allow this conclusion. On the contrary,
Aeschylus does not treat the Persian Wars as fought with the intention
of liberating Greece as a whole, but as a series of victories by separate
Greek states. Thus the battle of Salamis, though it contains phrases
like 'children of the Greeks', was, in the Aeschylean account,

designed to free *Athenian* tombs and hearths, and the battle of Plataia
was won by the *Dorian* (that is, the Spartan) spear (lines 403–4; 817).
So the picture here is fragmented. But Herodotus, writing, perhaps,
in the 440s, does speak of Greek liberation from the barbarian
(vii.144.3). Herodotus, indeed, did much to promote the conception
of Greece as a unity. Like so many of the great historians of antiquity
(or of more recent times), he was an exile from his native place — he
came from Halikarnassus (Bodrum) on the south-western coast of
what is now Turkey. Moreover, his father's name Lyxes is not Greek
but Karian.[5] This alien origin, and therefore disinterest towards
neighbourly rivalries among the mainland Greek states — together
with the gift for intellectual organization of an anthropologist and an
epic prose-poet — may have been what enabled him, in a remarkable
passage, to group the Greeks under certain unifying categories. The
Greeks, he says (viii.144), are a single race because of common blood,
common customs, common language and common religion. It would
be hard to improve on this formulation. It is likely enough that
Herodotus was helped to it by the great event of the Persian Wars
themselves, but that does not reduce the originality of the thought.

So Persia gave the Greeks their identity, or the means for
recognizing it. This, in the long view, is what gives the year 479 its
importance, and makes it a suitable moment to begin a history of the
classical Greek world. Many considerations, it is true, can be urged
against this choice of date. It is, for example, not an artistic watershed:
it is wrong to draw a line at the Greek naval victory of Salamis, near
Athens, and treat what comes before it as 'archaic' and what comes
after as 'classical'. By 479, Pindar and Aeschylus were established
poets, and tragedy was an established medium, Greek vase-painting
and architecture (like the temple of Aphaia at Aigina, datable to about
the year 500) had taken a fresh turn *before* the Persian Wars, and the
same is true of sculpture — a female statue known as the 'Sulky Girl'
(Acropolis 686), long thought to be of 'classical' date and style, may in
fact be earlier than the destruction of Athens in 480.[6]

Again, 479 does not represent anything like a decisive political
break. Sparta's control of her allies, through the Peloponnesian
League, was uninterrupted, and though the development of the
Delian League (chapter 2) as such postdates the Persian Wars,
Athens (who was already a democracy in 506) had a prehistoric role,
which she never forgot, as colonist of Ionia. She had taken the first
historical steps towards overseas expansion as long ago as the late

seventh and early sixth centuries, with the establishment of an outpost at Sigeion, near Troy, at the mouth of the Hellespont. Equally momentous was the securing of the island of Salamis, offshore from Attica. The wresting of the latter from Megara, and the installation there of Athenian settlers with specified military obligations (ML 14 = F 44B) made possible the exploitation of the Piraeus harbour (which Salamis dominates) instead of the open, and less satisfactory, anchorage at Phaleron — near the site of the modern Helleniko airport. By these means Athens had, by 500, secured the two ends of the grain-route from south Russia, via the Black Sea. This was a source of food on which she was certainly drawing by the time of the Persian Wars (Hdt. vii.147). And under the sixth-century Peisistratid tyrants, Athenian interests had been extended to include the Chersonese (the modern peninsula of Gelibolu), again on the way from the Black Sea, where the Athenian Miltiades established a colony. His family's enemies at home called it a tyranny: this was, undoubtedly, a vigorous, state-sponsored and commercially motivated venture. Again, Athens controlled the island of Lemnos soon after 500: this too was Miltiades' doing (Hdt. vi.137ff., confirmed by two inscriptions, IG i^2 948 and *Weickert Festschrift*, 7ff. 'The Athenians [dedicated this] from the spoils from Lemnos': *c*.500 BC). So Athens, even before the Persian Wars, already counted for something in the Aegean world beyond Attica.

Finally, the Persian Wars did not alter the *social* structure of the Greek World: chattel slavery, the development of which accompanied and was caused by the rise of the self-determining *polis* (with its doctrine of the land-owning citizen, *polites*, for whom the personal performance of 'servile' tasks was an affront, and who therefore needed slaves to do his work for him)[7] was well established by 480, like the *polis* itself. This can be shown to be probable by a single instance. Chios, which had by 550 borrowed from Solon's Athens the advanced idea of a second Citizen's Council (ML 8 = Fornara 19), is also supposed to have led the Greek world in the use of chattel slavery. As to other forms of dependent labour, the serf population of Sparta (the Messenian *helots*) had been finally subjugated no later than 600, and other cities and regions — Argos, Sikyon, Krete, Thessaly — had similar exploited classes (Stephanus of Byzantium, entry under 'Chios'). So too in Greek Asia Minor, the change after the 470s from Persian to Athenian control (which was anyway far from complete) did not affect the status of the barbarian serfs who tilled the territories of the cities there, like the *Pedieis*, i.e. plainsmen at Priene (Syll.³ 282). Nor were the Persian Wars long enough or destructive enough — contrast the effects of the Hannibalic Wars on third- and second-century Italy — to produce serious social consequences in Greece, like the deracination of the peasantry. That might have led to a massive increase in slave-labour.[8]

'Xerxes' legacy' is not to be sought in some social and economic catastrophe; and it is not even likely (unlike the Peloponnesian War: see chapter 11) to have included an abrupt adjustment of the balance in Greece between town and country. Thus, to take only Athens, it is now known that in about the year 500 only one-quarter of Athenians could claim urban origins.[9] (This fact is ascertainable from their 'demotics', that is their indications of deme origin, such as Demosthenes 'Paianieus', the man from Paiania. A *deme* was a local unit, a village defined as a political entity by two things, the right to send a councillor to the Council of Five Hundred, and the possession of an identifiable body of demesmen.) This low proportion of one-quarter bears out Thucydides' view that most Athenians were country-dwellers till the Peloponnesian War (ii.14ff). But it is in itself surprising: if the vocabulary of Kleisthenes' constitutional reforms of the late sixth century meant anything, with its division of the citizen-tribes into three groups of *trittyes* or thirds (city, coastal, inland), it should have meant that roughly 33⅓ per cent of the population of Attica belonged to each area. But now it is clear that it did not. Elsewhere in Greece, too, agriculture remained overwhelmingly predominant — though this is easy to state, plausible to believe but impossible to prove, as is neatly shown by the curious fact that, of all the funerary epigrams from the Greco-Roman world, only a handful refer to work in the fields.[10] Yet for most people this must have been almost the whole of life.

It is arguable, therefore, that neither culturally, nor politically, nor socially, did the Persian Wars inaugurate marked change. But they are decisive for Greek *morale*; and this is where we began, with panhellenism, which deserves if anything does, to be called Xerxes' legacy.

Why, then, did panhellenism remain only a concept (to be revived by Xenophon and Isokrates in the fourth century, but only as a name for the plan to conquer Persia)? Its practical failure is unexpected, given the solid if suspiciously shared achievements of 480/79, and the intellectual awareness, voiced by Herodotus in the passage already cited, that the Greeks had, potentially, so much in common. The answer must be sought in another Greek concept, the divisive and destructive — but untranslatable — concept of *phthonos*: jealousy, malice, rivalry, envy, grudge. It was this which prevented the Greek states from coalescing into something like a nation-state, or subordinating themselves to Athens or Sparta in perpetuity, as the Italian peninsula was to be subordinated to Rome; equally, it was *phthonos* which caused Athens and Sparta to deny their citizenship to allies and outsiders, and thus ensured (as Romans could later see) that both their hegemonies were short-lived. Nor was this merely Imperial Roman hindsight: to the Greek Polybius, writing as early as the second century BC, the Athenian Empire of the fifth century seemed a mere flash in the pan (vi.43). To explain this, it will be necessary to show that *phthonos* accompanied the Athenian Empire, or *arche*, from the beginning.

2 *Phthonos* (envy) and the origin of the Delian League

'The border of Attica used to be at Eleutherai, but when Eleutherai became attached to Athens, Kithairon, instead, became the border with Boiotia. Eleutherai was not forced to join Athens in war; she did so because she wanted Athenian citizenship, and out of hatred (*echthos*) for Thebes.' That is how the second-century AD geographer Pausanias (i.38) describes Eleutherai, one of the outlying places of Attica. The passage is precious for the understanding which it provides, and assumes, of Greek political life. Athenian citizenship (the geographer does not need to explain) conferred enormous positive benefits: the restriction to citizens of the right to own land is fundamental to the economic history of Athens.[1] Equally powerful, however, is assumed to be dislike of a near neighbour, in this case Thebes. In the same spirit Herodotus (viii.30) had sought to explain why Phokis had taken the Greek side against Persia in the Great War: it was, he says, because of hatred (*echthos* again) for the Thessalians next door. 'If the Thessalians had backed the Greeks', he adds cheerfully, 'I think that the Phokians would have *gone over to the Persian side*' (the word for that is 'medise').

Greek history is full of petty disputes about small strips of land: in 351, Demosthenes (xv.17) was to list 'wars about partition of land or boundaries' among the dissensions which make democracies go to war against each other. Such wars (he rather absurdly implies, but his argument requires it) are of small account compared with wars against oligarchies, which are commonly fought with one's freedom or very political existence as the issue. Disputes about bits of land could be of very long duration: the prize must go to a dispute between Samos and Priene which began in the eighth century, was the immediate cause of the Samian revolt from Athens in 440, and was finally settled by the Roman Senate in 135 BC, after Lysimachus, one of the successors of

15

Alexander, and the hellenistic state of Rhodes had both tried their hand at arbitration or adjudication.[2]

It is usual to explain such disputes, among mainland Greek states at least, by reference to the small size of the territories of the Greek *poleis*, never well enough off for good land, and each with its own alluvial plain hemmed in by mountains. All of this certainly encouraged Greek particularism — it is not for nothing that the peninsula gave its name to the concept of 'balkanization'. But it hardly explains why, say, Miletus in Asia Minor, with its rich hinterland,[3] or the west Greek states (like Sybaris and Kroton in Italy, who hated each other) with their large, fertile agricultural holdings, should have behaved exactly like the more cramped Greeks of the homeland. Perhaps, like the idea of the *polis* itself, *echthos* for a near neighbour was something the Greeks took with them when they emigrated.

On the level of practical politics, the principle that my neighbour's enemy is my friend explains much about Greek history in the fifth century. For instance, the Corinthians had been for several centuries friendly towards the Athenians, because of a common dislike of Megara, the state which separated them geographically. Thus we shall see (p. 38) that Corinth, shortly before the Persian Wars, made Athens a loan of twenty ships. This loan was for Athens' use against the island state of Aigina, and is a further illustration of the principles governing neighbourly hostility: Corinth and Athens were united in *phthonos* against Aigina as long as the latter was the most powerful sea-state in the Saronic Gulf. Trouble — the so-called 'First Peloponnesian War' — began between Corinth and Athens only in the late 460s, by which time the independence of both Megara and Aigina, subjected to Athens in 457, was precarious. That is, good relations between Corinth and Athens depended on shared hostility towards the minor states which lay in between, by land or sea. When those minor states ceased to exist, or were annexed by one side or the other, the neighbour's neighbour became just a neighbour, and an enemy instead of a friend.

This feeling, that the *polis* next door was another world, explains the failure of the Greeks to develop a common legal system; there is no such thing as 'Greek law'.[4] A fifth-century inscription makes the point clearly: Oianthea and Chaleion, two towns in Lokris (central Greece) some six miles apart, agreed what rules should apply in cases of unjust seizure. The treaty provides that citizens of the one state who reside more than a month in the other shall be subject to the legal procedure of the host state. That is, a journey of six miles meant that different jurisdictions would prevail (Tod 34 = Fornara 87). Similarly, citizens of fifth-century Knossos on Krete were not allowed to possess land at Tylissos, a place also, as it happens, just six miles distant (ML 42 = Fornara 89). The principle that foreign nationals might not possess land was therefore by no means confined to Athens. It means, incidentally, that the large-scale possession of overseas properties by individual rich Athenians in the time of the empire (p. 30) was legally indefensible,[5] as well as merely unpopular for more obvious reasons with the allies.

The great classical instance of *phthonos* was between Athens and Sparta. Their rivalry, after the Persian Wars, was permanent. As late as the 350s Demosthenes, in his speech for the Megalopolitans (Dem. xvi) could appeal to the Athenian instinct to keep Sparta weak — although Sparta's capacity to do damage anywhere had ended with her loss of Messenia more than a decade before. (Attitudes were frequently slow to adjust to changed reality: even Polybius, as we shall see, p. 169, could praise Philip II of Macedon for his invasion of the Peloponnese in 338, because 'by humbling Sparta, he allowed the Peloponnese to breathe again': xviii.14. Equally anachronistic, as applied to Sparta in the time of Philip — but equally indicative of the enduring *phthonos* felt towards her.) But how far the rivalry between Athens and Sparta, however permanent it may have been, dominated everyday life and thinking (in either place) is not clear. Thucydides, in his introduction to the main Peloponnesian War of 431–404 BC, says that Spartan fear of Athenian power was not spoken of openly at Athens, and he must have meant something by this, although he goes straight on to make a speaker from Corcyra openly allude to exactly that fear (i.23; i.33). Perhaps the tension was overt only at certain moments and in certain theatres. In any case, normality of relations even between enemies might persist, in some departments of life, to a degree surprising to modern eyes. A good example is the way in which Corinth, as a recent scientific study of the composition of Greek coinage reveals, got one-third of the silver for her coins from the Athenian mines at Laurion in south Attica throughout the fifth century till 431, although Athens and Corinth fought a protracted war in the middle decades of that century (the First Peloponnesian War).[6] This is chiefly to be explained by the absence in Greek war and diplomacy — at least before the Athenian decrees passed in the 430s against Megara (p. 91) — of the notion of economic sanctions.

There were other complications, which compel us to modify the simple picture of Greek politics as an opposition of state against neighbouring state, or of ideology against ideology. One such complication was the relative respectability of admiration for the politics and lifestyles of other states or political systems. The earliest and most extreme example of this is medism, the name given to pro-Persian attitudes in Greece or Asia Minor before, during and for several decades after the Persian Wars. Medism is admiration for autocracy among a people who had all got rid of their own autocrats. The essentially Athens-centred character of the literary tradition in the fifth century, with its strong democratic dislike of Persia (p. 10), means that medism can be mistaken for a fundamentally unGreek sort of treachery. But sympathy for Persia was not so irrational. Her attraction was that she did not force her doctrines of government on her subject-peoples (chapter 6). For some Greeks, like Xenophon, irritated by 'troublesome demagogues' (*Hell.* v.2.7), the support of a distant Persian king, or a congenial local satrap, was preferable to the interference of Athens or Sparta, both of whom made a habit of installing types of government favourable to themselves (Thuc. i.19; Ar. *Pol.* 1307) and of choosing the people to run them. More positively, fondness for a Persian lifestyle was by no means unthinkable.[7] Very early in the Achaemenid Persian period, one Pytharchos from the Greek city of Cyzicus is said to have been befriended by Cyrus the Great; that was long known from literary sources, but now the signature of a man called Pytharchos has turned up at Persepolis, 'I am (the property? the signature?) of Pytharchos' (Fornara 46 — perhaps a *descendant*, judging from the letter forms, rather than Pytharchos himself). A little later than Cyrus' friend, there is reason to think that Herakleitos of Ephesus, the philosopher, may have admired the Persians as 'warlike fire-worshippers.'[8] Certainly, the Persian element at Ephesus was very strong: the priest of Artemis there bore the Iranian name Megabyxos down to the Roman period. Further south, in Halikarnassus, Herodotus was called 'barbarian-lover' by Plutarch. This is hardly surprising in view both of Herodotus' own Karian blood (p. 11) and of the cosmopolitan character of Halikarnassus, where the Iranian name Megabates is attested in the fifth century (ML 32 = Fornara 55).

The Greek population of the Persian-held hinterland of Asia Minor included expatriates from the mainland. Themistokles in exile was the most famous of these; but there were others, like the 'medisers'

Gongylos of Eretria and Demaratos ex-king of Sparta. Their descendants were still there in the fourth century (Xen. *Hell.* iii.1.6) and even in the third, by which time their families had intermarried (Syll.^{3} 381: 'Demaratos son of Gorgion'. Xenophon gives Gorgion as a name in *Gongylos*' family.) And another pocket dynast, Hermias Tyrant of Atarneus, was also linked to the others by a marriage tie (Sextus Empiricus *Adv. Math.* i.158). These dynasties were settled in Anatolian fiefdoms (i.e. lands gifted in a feudal way, cf. p. 67), where they presumably occupied land in the territories which had once been enjoyed and exploited by the cities of the coast, with their servile work-force (p. 12). This change in ownership was not trivial. Such enforced erosion of city-territory, to make room for Persian favourites (not all of whom were Greeks: there were Hyrkanians from the Caspian, settled in Asia Minor[9]) should be added to the grievances of the Ionian Greeks who revolted from Persia in the 490s. This Greco-Iranian society has left cultural traces which will be looked at later (chapter 6). Here, it is only the political aspect that needs stressing: it is easy to see the flight to Persia of the Athenian General Themistokles in the 460s as a pure act of treason. But what of King Agesilaus in the fourth century, who was leader of a war against Persia — and 'guest-friend' (*xenos*) of the Persian satrap Mausolus? And what of Herodotus himself, who managed to admire Athens and Persia impartially? Or of the Greco-Iranian culture in fifth- and fourth-century Lycia? Some Greeks and 'culture-Greeks' in the classical period found it possible to cultivate Persian values and Persian friendships; and to judge them traitors to hellenism is to treat adhesion to the standards of Athenian democracy as the only criterion of Greek political behaviour. Certainly, the resident medisers were a fundamentally undemocratic force in western Anatolia, whose influence more than once affected the history of the Greek struggle for power in the Aegean area. But it is unhistorical to treat them as less than or other than Greeks.

In Greece itself there were expressions, analogous to 'medism', which described attitudes of partisanship towards other Greek states. A late fifth-century inscription from Thasos reveals that the oligarchic government then in power confiscated the property of six men because of *attikismos*, support of Athens (IG xii.8.263). And Thucydides (iv.133) speaks of 'attikisers' at Thespiai in Boiotia, whom the neighbouring Thebans punished for their politics: the separatist tendencies of such individual Boiotian states, which for so long kept Boiotia weak, often combined with pro-Athenian and anti-Theban leanings. As early as 519, Boiotian Plataia had been recommended by King Kleomenes of Sparta to attach herself to Athens (rather than to Sparta, for whose help Plataia had originally appealed). Plataia took the advice — and thereby weakened the position of Thebes, a consequence the likelihood of which cannot have escaped Kleomenes (Hdt. vi. 108).

Again, there were Spartan sympathizers at Athens and Athenian sympathizers at Sparta. If their operations have left more historical traces than 'square pegs' elsewhere, that is only because Athens, the best-documented city of ancient Greece, was the place these people veered to or from. Their names tell us much about the sympathies of their parents at least. Thus the name Alcibiades was borne by a famous Athenian — but it was also hereditary in the family of the Spartan magistrate Endios, alternating father-son father-son with Endios' own name. And Athenaios the son of Perikleidas was one of a team of Spartan ambassadors sent to conclude the peace which presaged the Peace of Nikias: his father Perikleidas, too, had been an Athens expert, who had brought an appeal from Sparta to Athens in 465 for help against their revolted helots (Plut. *Kimon.* 16). The similarity of Perikleidas' name to that of the great Athenian Pericles is, however, fortuitous: the two men were contemporaries, so neither can have been named after the other. But the name of Pericles, the fourth-century ruler of Limyra in Lycia, is surely a gesture towards Athenian *paideia* (culture, education). On the Athenian side, Kimon called his son Lakedaimonios, 'Spartan', a neat parallel to Athenaios, 'Athenian'. Themistokles' children included an Asia, a Hellas, an Italia and a Sybaris — a gazetteer of Athenian fifth-century aspirations. One might compare the Victorian imperialist Napier, a governor of the Ionian islands, who called a daughter 'Cephalonia'.

On a deeper level, Spartan resistance to change found admirers at Athens. One was the idealist philosopher Plato, whose aim was to construct a theoretical society which would be (unlike the states Plato saw around him: p. 154) both inoculated against the causes of civil dissension and impervious to foreign attack. (When Plato wrote the *Republic*, in the mid-fourth century, Sparta actually satisfied neither condition: there had been deep *helot* trouble in 399 — p. 191 — and Sparta had been defeated at Leuktra in 371 and then invaded. Perhaps what impressed Plato was Sparta's survival — for survive she did — of such shocks.) Sparta had other Athenian admirers too, the men who in the 450s wanted to 'put an end to the democracy and pull down the Long Walls' (Thuc. i.107), and their descendants, the young men[10] who led the oligarchic revolutions of 411 and 404; or men like Kritias (whose epitaph praised him for having briefly 'restrained the arrogance of the accursed *demos*'). These 'lakonisers' were called the 'Cauliflower Ears' because like the Spartiates they went in for violent physical exercise (Plato *Protagoras* 342b) — an activity which in early Greece had aristocratic overtones.

Whatever the political aims of the Spartans Perikleidas and Athenaios, it is safe to assume that they did not include 'putting an end to the *Spartan* way of life'. The most drastic possibility open to Spartiates with political vision was to free helots and create the possibility of more dynamic military strategies using this extra manpower. King Kleomenes, Pausanias the Regent and the late fifth-century general Brasidas (p. 100) all had plans of this kind, which Brasidas actually carried out. The helots thus liberated were called the *neodamodeis*, new people, a word which must mean that they were integrated in some sense into the *damos* or people. That (so more conservative Spartans feared) would in the long run have redefined and widened the *damos*, weakening the monopoly on power of the few full Spartan citizens, and would indeed have damaged the Spartan way of life. There was another way: to round up the more spirited helots and liquidate them, as was done to 2000 of them at some time in the fifth century (Thuc. iv.80, cp. pp.100, 221).

'Square pegs' remained few, however. For most Athenians and Spartans, the great period of *phthonos* began as the Persian Wars ended (not that the wars themselves had been free from tensions).

'Thus the Athenians built their walls and restored their city immediately after the retreat of the Persians.' That is Thucydides' summing-up of an episode which marked the tangible start of Athenian independence from Sparta (i.89f.). The rebuilding of the walls of Athens, devastated by the Persian sack, is said to have been unwelcome to Sparta: an assertive act. In protest, she sent ambassadors to Athens to complain; but these were detained while Themistokles went to the Peloponnese to lull Spartan suspicions while the walls were hastily built — 'from whatever materials came to hand', Thucydides says, and a patch of wall which can be seen near the Dipylon Gate confirms him. When the rebuilding work was complete, Themistokles tore off the mask and told the Spartan detainees that Sparta must henceforth treat with Athens 'as with a state which knew how to consult her own interests and the general good' — the first hint of imperial pretensions. The Spartans concealed their anger, not least (Thucydides claims) because 'the enthusiasm which the Athenians had shown in the Persian Wars had created friendly feelings between the two cities'.

But that is precisely the difficulty: how friendly *were* feelings between Athens and Sparta after the Persian repulse? The problem matters because it must affect our judgement of the circumstances in which Athens began her league; and therefore of the history of the next fifty years. The difficulty is this: Thucydides constantly writes as if Sparta acquiesced in the formation in 478/7 of the Delian League (the name given to the organization of Greek states under Athenian leadership, whose common treasury was on the island of Delos in the centre of the Aegean Sea). He does this not merely when putting defensive speeches into the mouths of Athenian speakers — that would not be surprising — but in his own considered narrative (i.95, end). There is, however, other evidence which suggests that Sparta's 'acceptance' was forced on her.

First, there is Thucydides himself, whose account, though it generally implies that Sparta yielded the hegemony gracefully, contains puzzles. Straight after the Athenian wall-building Thucydides describes a joint Athenian, Peloponnesian and allied expedition, which captured Cyprus and Byzantium. This was led by Pausanias (Regent for the under-age King Pleistarchos). His behaviour, however, 'resembled a tyranny rather than a military command', and the *echthos* so caused drove the allies into the arms of Athens. Pausanias was summoned home in disgrace to stand trial.

It all seems too easy, and too black and white. In Thucydides' version, the warmth felt by Athens and Sparta for each other gives way to *echthos*, all as a result of the pride of one young and still not very experienced[11] Spartan, whose conduct was anyway disapproved by his home government. The suspicion arises that Sparta had other reasons for relinquishing her supreme position, and that she did so against her will (otherwise why did she send the Cyprus-Byzantium fleet out at all?). This suspicion deepens when one consults sources other than Thucydides.

Herodotus, in one of his rare glances forwards to events after the Persian Wars, remarks casually that the insufferable behaviour of Pausanias was the *pretext* which enabled the Athenians to 'snatch the hegemony' from Sparta (viii.3.4). There is no suggestion here that

Sparta gave way to Athens willingly. Herodotus also records (vi.72) an expedition led by the Spartan King Leotychidas to Thessaly in 476 (see p. 81). This shows that expansionist ambitions were still alive then.

Then there is Aristotle's *Athenian Constitution*. This says (xxiii.2) that the Athenians took the hegemony, 'the Spartans being unwilling', *akontōn Lakedaimonion*. Aristotle is saying explicitly (see Lysias xii.63 for an exactly parallel use of *akontōn*) that Athenian hegemony was contrary to Spartan wishes.[12]

Another fourth-century item may be relevant: Arrian, using sources close to Alexander the Great's own time, records a rebuff delivered to Alexander by the Spartans in 336. He makes them say (*Anabasis* i.1.2) that it was the Spartan tradition to lead, not to follow the lead of others.

The truth, however, may be that Thucydides was neither completely wrong nor completely right: that is, opinion at Sparta was split. This leads to the third piece of anti-Thucydidean evidence, namely Diodorus. At xi.50 he gives, under the year 475, details of a debate held at Sparta, on the question whether to dispute the hegemony with Athens. The date could be earlier than Diodorus says,[13] in which case this evidence might be relevant to Spartan morale at the beginning of the Delian League (winter 478/7). The younger Spartans, on this account, itched for the money which a Spartan naval empire would bring (a nice comment on the supposed absence of coined money in Sparta); but the elders and people were dissuaded by an elder called Hetoimaridas, who warned that it was not in Sparta's interests to bid for control of the sea. This does not look like invention: Hetoimaridas is otherwise unknown, so that the detail of his name at least is circumstantial; and although the opposition of young and old Spartans was to recur in 432 before the Great Peloponnesian War, that does not exclude similar opposition in the 470s, since patterns can recur in Spartan history (and in human psychology).

Finally, we come back to Thucydides, and a phrase describing a *second* voyage out by Pausanias, after his trial (p. 22). Thucydides says that Pausanias went out 'ostensibly to conduct the Greek War, but really to open negotiations with the (Persian) king' (i.128). What does 'Greek War' mean here? The phrase 'Persian War' means 'the war against Persia'; so might not 'the Greek War' be a war fought *against* Greeks? That is, we might have here a reference to open hostilities between Athens and Sparta. This argument is ingenious,[14] but does not work. The main difficulty with it can be seen only by looking at the context, which concentration on the two words 'Greek War' may obscure. There is surely a contrast between Pausanias' *avowed* aim (to fight Persia) and his *real* aim (to do a deal with her).

But the 'Hetoimaridas debate', supported as it is by other evidence, shows that some Spartans were prepared to go to war with Athens, rather than see her take over the leadership of Greece. What then did Hetoimaridas mean when he said that a 'struggle for the sea' was not in Sparta's interests?

The answer lies partly in the steps Sparta would need to take to assemble a permanent navy: she could no doubt get timber by buying or bullying, she had a harbour at Gytheum where traces of docks have been found,[15] but she could not provide the hundreds of rowers required except by finding some equivalent of Athens' 'naval mob' of poor citizens who served as rowers, and *that* meant using helots — always a politically sensitive proposal (p. 21). But perhaps the older, warier, Spartans were thinking less of the future than of the present and the past. Here there was plenty to alarm them: the suggestion of a speaker in Plato's *Laws* (698) of a Messenian War (that is, helot trouble) at the time of the battle of Marathon is not supported by much other evidence — though see ML 22 = *JHS*, lxix, 1949, pp. 26ff. and commentary. But Sparta certainly had other problems. Her league, the 'Peloponnesian', had started when she allied herself in the mid-sixth century with Tegea, in Arkadia, to the north of her. But Tegea was now restless, as a macabre incident shows. The state diviner Hegesistratos of Elis, in trouble at Sparta after the Persian Wars, escaped from confinement in the stocks by slicing his foot off at the ankle, and somehow hobbled over the border to Tegea, which, Herodotus says, *was on bad terms with Sparta at the time*. And Leotychidas, whose Thessalian expedition collapsed, also fled to Tegea (ix.37; vi.72 with p. 81). The coinage confirms that some Arkadian cities were, about now, beginning to regret having submerged their identity in the Peloponnesian League: a federal Arkadian coinage, bearing the word ARKADIKON or an abbreviation, was struck in the decades immediately after the Persian Wars, and should therefore be connected, not with the earlier intrigues (p. 26) of King Kleomenes — the older view — but with secessionism in the 470s BC.[16]

Two individuals loom, from the fog that is Peloponnesian history in this period, as specially responsible for compounding Spartan difficulties. One is Pausanias the Regent, whose second and final disgrace was due to the suspicion that he was tampering with the loyalty of the helots (p. 21): 'and it was true', Thucydides adds. The reason is presumably that Pausanias, enterprising rather than (as in the official version) treacherous, planned to supplement Sparta's supplies of manpower by drafting helots into the army. That showed foresight: there had been 5000 citizen hoplites at the battle of Plataia in 479, a decent total, but even if the precise proportion of helots to Spartiates given by Herodotus, namely 7:1 (ix.28), is exaggerated, the imbalance was probably already big enough to cause unease.

The other individual is Themistokles of Athens, who had gone to the Peloponnese after his ostracism (a kind of 'banishment by plebiscite' for ten years, without forfeiture of property or taint of criminality). He stayed at Argos, and visited other places in the Peloponnese. (Themistokles was the hero of the Persian Wars, but seems to have realized sooner than most Athenians that the enemy had changed and was now not Persia but Sparta: see p. 21 on the 'walls' episode). His stay in the late 470s falls at a suspiciously active period in Peloponnesian politics. Elis in the west, perhaps already democratic even before the Persian Wars,[17] moved further away from Sparta in 471/0, when she synoikised (that is, her village-communities formed themselves into a single *polis*: Diod. xi.54). Though synoikism is not, by itself, either 'democratic' or 'oligarchic',[18] such a concentration of resources meant that for the future Sparta would find Elis harder to coerce. Themistokles could have been behind this. And since his base was Argos, it is natural to look for signs of the revival of an aggressive Argos. The signs are there by the end of the 460s, when Argos allied with Athens; but even earlier, perhaps in 469, Argos had fought against Sparta at Tegea (Hdt. ix.35) and took advantage of Sparta's helot problems in 465 to destroy Mycenae. Moreover, the undated synoikism of the Arkadian city of Mantinea was the work of Argos (Strabo 337) — or perhaps should we say Argos and her energetic guest Themistokles, and put this event in 470 alongside Elis?[19]

It is an interesting question why Spartan leadership inside the Peloponnese went sour at just this period. Motives in the dissident cities were no doubt mixed. First, Spartan leadership may not, in 470, have seemed the inevitability it had been in 550, since Athens had now emerged as a major Greek power on a par with Sparta. (The increase in Athenian prestige after the Persian Wars, and its eventual result, the Peloponnesian Wars, can thus be seen as another bequest from Xerxes' legacy.) Second, the old Peloponnesian troublemaker Argos was in very low water in the first thirty years of the fifth century (the battle of Tegea is the first evidence of an improvement). The decline of Argos may have made the smaller Peloponnesian states ask themselves what, or who, Sparta was supposed to be protecting them against. Finally, the Spartan king Kleomenes had been engaged in the 490s in some kind of deal with the Arkadians (Hdt. vi.74) which perhaps encouraged Arkadian thoughts of a looser Spartan rein. When this came to nothing and Kleomenes fell, opinion against Sparta may have hardened.

So when, in late summer 478, the allies asked the Athenians to be their leaders, Spartan chagrin was probably mixed with relief. Athens now assumed the command, and fixed which of her allies were to provide money, and which ships, for the war against Persia. 'A pretext', Thucydides says (i.96.1) 'was to exact reparation for what they had suffered, by ravaging the Persian king's land.' Pretexts imply that the motive given is not the whole story. Here, scholars have assumed that Thucydides must be saying *either* that Athens' real but concealed motive was to impose her will on her allies, *or* that her real but concealed enmity was with Sparta not Persia.[20] If one has to choose between these two, the first explanation must be right: the following chapters go on to list the step-by-step extension of the empire. If so, the implication of 'pretext' is that Athens consciously and cynically planned her empire from the first, and that is disturbing: first, because it implies they could predict the future, and second because other sources imply idealism. Thus Aristotle's *Athenian Constitution* (xxiii.5) describes the dropping of lead weights into the sea — a sign of solidity, solemnity and permanence; and Herodotus, speaking of the defection of Ionia from Persia after Mykale (ix.105) treats it as a second Ionian Revolt, and that, on the analogy of the 499 revolt, meant liberation. (Again, liberation from 'the Mede' is given as an original aim of the league by Thucydides' speakers, e.g. iii.10.4, but they have a case to plead and cannot be trusted.) So there is misleading Thucydidean hindsight in the word 'pretext'. This conclusion can be avoided in only one way: 'pretext' could be taken to imply, not that Sparta, or the allies of Athens, were the 'real enemy', but that *leadership* (Thucydides has just used the word) was something that appeared to the Athenians *desirable absolutely*, with no implication that they designed the empire from the start. They had a pretext for leadership ('a', not 'the' pretext: the indefinite article lessens the degree of hypocrisy), namely the war against Persia.

No elaborate conditions were imposed on league members. Aristotle's *Athenian Constitution* says that they swore 'to have the same friends and enemies', a formula which no other source gives, but which is respectably fifth-century, being found at Athens in the 420s (Tod 68: alliance with Bottiaia in northern Greece), and at Sparta at the same period, in a newly discovered treaty with the Aitolians (SEG xxvi.461; published in 1974). The allies also pledged not to refuse to serve in league campaigns (this could be and perhaps was used as a device for preventing exit from the league) and not to make 'private wars' on other league members (Thuc. vi.76). Most important was the undertaking to provide ships. Some allies provided money instead, to a total of 460 talents, Thucydides says (but this total is incredibly large).[21] The Athenian Aristides assessed the amounts.

There was a single league assembly in which Athens had only one vote — though small states could be relied on to follow the leader. A single assembly is clearly implied by a phrase in an allied speech in 428: 'the Athenians *led us on an equal footing* at first' (Thuc. iii.10.4). The same speech calls the allies 'equal in votes', *isopsephoi*, and though this word *can* mean 'equal in decision-making influence', that cannot be true here because the word *polupsephia*, 'multiplicity of votes' (no other meaning is possible), occurs a few lines earlier, so the suffixes ought to mean the same thing in both nouns. The allies, then, were 'equal *in votes*' to each other and Athens. It was different in the fourth century (p. 212) when Athens, eager to please, set up a two-chambered system.

The extent of league membership at the beginning is given by no ancient source. (After 454 one-sixtieth of the annual tribute from the allies was made over to the goddess Athena, and records survive of these small payments, inscribed on stone: the so-called Athenian Tribute Lists — an inaccurate name, because the actual 'tribute lists' do not survive.)

The islands of the central Aegean joined straight away — Delos after all housed the league treasury, and her neighbours in the Cyclades must surely be counted in. So must the large offshore islands to the east, Samos, Chios and Lesbos; presumably they brought with them their possessions on the Anatolian mainland, their *peraiai* (p. 199). Far to the south-east, Rhodes and even some cities on half-semitic Cyprus may have been original members.

Of the mainland parts of north Greece and Asia Minor, Thrace east of the River Struma remained Persian-held for the time; but some cities of the Chalkidike peninsula were in the league in 478. This is likely because in 421 they were made to pay the 'tribute of the time of Aristides' (Thuc. v.18) — unless, implausibly, this formula is shorthand for 'payment at an early, i.e. low level' with no implication about early membership.

In Asia Minor, Herodotus' comparison (p. 26) with the first Ionian Revolt of 499 means that most of coastal Ionia joined this second revolt; and since places in Karia to the south, and the Aeolid to the north of Ionia participated in the 499 revolt, they joined Athens in 478. But here as elsewhere places further inland stayed out, as did the Greeks in the west (Italy and Sicily; but cp. IG i^3 291: western 'tribute' c. 415).

There was much goodwill towards Athens when she assumed the leadership. She (unlike preoccupied Sparta) offered hopes of liberation from Persia for the *polis* dwellers of western Asia, and protection for the islanders (the Turkish coast is clearly and menacingly visible from the big eastern islands, which then as now were afraid they would be suddenly overwhelmed from the hostile mainland). A hundred years later, however, when Athens started a Second Naval Confederacy, there was no stampede to join. The experience of the Delian League had made Athens' former subjects canny.

Something, clearly, went wrong. It is easy to criticize attempts to search literal-mindedly for the point at which the 'league' became an 'empire', and it is true that there is something odd about speaking of the 'harsh' imperialism of a later (420s) politician like Kleon, as if imperialism is ever soft. But there was a change: the Athenians' own vocabulary is one pointer. At some time in the fifth century they began in their inscriptions to use the formula 'the cities which the Athenians rule', and it is not absurd to try to date the change (the answer: the early 440s, see IG i^3 27^{22}); nor, having dated it, are we committed to saying that there was nothing which we should call Athenian 'rule' before then.

Part of the trouble, though, is admittedly a gap in the evidence. There are hardly any Athenian inscriptions before c.460, but several dozen decrees after that. This cannot easily be explained, any more than can the absence of surviving forensic (i.e. law-court) oratory before the Peloponnesian War. A better approach is to accept that the machinery of control was instituted gradually, and to look at its structure rather than its development.

The administrative and political checks on the allies were numerous and ubiquitous: they consisted of several hundreds of Athenian officials, governors, 'supervisors' (*episkopoi*) — and garrisons. Sometimes garrisons were sent at the request of the democratic party in the 'host' city, as by Corcyra in *c*.410 (Diod. xiii.48), and this can be seen as part of Athens' policy of supporting democracies. There were exceptions, though, like Boiotia and Miletus, where as the fifth-century writer nicknamed the Old Oligarch tells us she tolerated oligarchies (from the tribute lists we can add that the league membership included Karian dynasts with very unGreek names like Pigres and Sambaktys. It would have taken a long time to explain the notion of democracy to these feudal philistines). In any case, the idea (which goes back to Thucydides) that the 'democrats' generally favoured Athens is too crude. A sharp distinction between *demos* and oligarchs, between few and many, existed in the urbanized central zone of Greece within a fifty-mile radius of the Corinthian Canal; but elsewhere, especially in the agricultural north, these divisions did not exist to anything like the same extent, and here Athens was hated and feared.[23] In any case, even at Samos where a *demos did* exist, it is possible that Athens backed a propertied regime instead (Thuc. viii.21, contra Diod. xii.28 and perhaps ML 56).

Judicially, Athens' control was tight. Foreign defendents were obliged to come to Athens to be sued there (ML 31 = Fornara 68),[24] the disadvantages of this to them were not just expense of travel and politically motivated hostility, but uncertainty about the actual law. The large, undirected, juries of classical Athens hindered the development of exact law. One consequence of the concentration of law-suits in the metropolis of Athens was that subject states lost the power to inflict the death penalty (Antiphon v.47; ML 52 = Fornara 103).

Economic coercion also made use of the law: in the fourth century, and quite possibly in the fifth as well, there were rules prohibiting Athenian citizens from carrying corn elsewhere than to Athens, and from lending money on ships bound elsewhere than to Athens (Dem. xxxiv.37; xxxv.51). There were also more direct tactics: an Athenian inscription of 428 mentions 'guardians of the Hellespont' (ML 65 = Fornara 128) who controlled the passage of corn from the Black Sea.

Nor was this just a war measure: a 10 per cent levy (at the Hellespont?) is mentioned in a decree of about 434/3 (ML 58 = Fornara 119). Above all there was the tribute,[25] up to thirty talents from the highest payers (Aigina, Thasos) and nowhere a light burden, being carefully adjusted to capacity to pay. Antiphon's speech *On the Tribute of Samothrace*, of which only a fragment survives (see Loeb, *Minor Attic Orators*) shows the kind of arguments a subject-city would use; 'ours is unproductive rough land, much of it uncultivated ...' and so on.

Territorial encroachment was the most resented abuse of all, as is proved by the specific renunciations in the 'charter' of the Second Athenian Confederacy of 377 (Tod 123). For the lower classes the empire meant *cleruchies* (grants of land on territory still possessed by allies) or colonies (similar grants on evacuated sites). For the upper classes it meant that they did not have to pay for the fleet, an enormous benefit. (Ar. *Pol.* 1304b shows that in states where the rich had to foot the bill for the navy without being cushioned by tribute, social revolution could result. His example is fourth-century Rhodes.) More positively, it meant the possibility of estates overseas,[26] like those in Thasos, Abydos and Euboia, attested in inscriptions (ML 79 = Fornara 147D), one of which is worth the staggering sum of over eighty talents (half a million drachmai, at a time when one drachma represented a day's wage for a skilled workman). Some of these properties could, it is true, have been properly acquired by marriages to foreign heiresses, but most were, from the allied point of view, completely illegal (p. 17). All this meant that rich and poor Athenians were agreed about the desirability of having, running and policing the empire; a solidarity which ended only when the state reserve of 1000 talents was used up in 411 (Thuc. viii.15), and there was no more tribute. (See further p. 145, 172.)

Religious interference took no doctrinal form. But Athena, like the Athenians themselves, was a property-owner. Her precincts are attested by boundary-stones on Kos, Samos, Aigina and Euboia (Hill[2] B.96). They are just another form of expropriation.

Against this treatment there was no redress for the allies, apart from knowing influential contacts at Athens. Athens lacked what Rome later provided, a system of extortion law and courts — though even at Rome it was hard to get justice or even an advocate.

The positive advantages to the allies of subservience to Athens included security from Persia (a protection which was at most times no more than propaganda, and anyway covered only cities which were vulnerably placed) and from piracy. There may even have been allies who, when they visited the buildings, like the Parthenon, on the Athenian Acropolis and its south slope, thought that their tribute had been splendidly, and not altogether selfishly, spent. In any case, their views are irrecoverable.

3 Athens imposes her will

The new Athenian alliance had little to fear from the Persians in the years immediately after its formation. The initiative passed to Athens. Her first naval success was to expel Pausanias from Byzantium (he had avoided conviction after his recall to Sparta, and had returned to Byzantium). The Athenian campaigns which follow — the capture of Eion in northern Greece, on the River Struma, and of the island of Skyros, north-east of Euboia, both in 476/5 — were the work of Kimon, son of Miltiades the victor of Marathon. Miltiades' last operation (in 479) against the island of Paros, in the Cyclades, can be seen as an attempt to move on to the offensive against Persia after the defensive stand at Marathon. Paros had been a failure; but Miltiades' son Kimon pursued a similar line in the 470s and 460s, showing that he saw himself as the heir to his father's policies as well as his debts (for which see Plut. *Kim.* iv). But the similarity goes further: Miltiades had been a great figure in the early colonial days of Athens: his pocket principality in the Chersonese was in the van of Pisistratid expansion (for good relations between the tyrants and Miltiades in the 520s see the archon-list ML 6 = Fornara 23, belying Herodotus: Miltiades had held high office under the tyrants). In a sense, such sixth-century conquests are the beginning of Athenian imperialism. So Kimon's campaigns, which culminated in the victory over Persia at the River Eurymedon in Pamphylia, show continuity not just with Miltiades the enemy of Persia but with Miltiades the founder of an overseas Athenian Empire. This was very self-conscious imitation, as is proved by the peculiarities of some epigrams which celebrate the family's achievements: a surviving pair commemorates the Persian victories in the strange order Salamis-Marathon;[1] it was perhaps Kimon himself who thus sought to remind Athenians, in verse, of his father's great battle, just as painters were to remind them of it by their *Marathon* in the Painted Stoa built in the middle of the fifth century: Oinoe, a deme close to Marathon, was the title of one of the subsidiary hoplite engagements depicted.[2] Not that Kimon was the only Athenian statesman who sought to recall Marathon specifically: the 192 horsemen of the Parthenon frieze, begun after Kimon's death and completed as late as the 430s, may depict the Marathon dead, who numbered just 192, and who were given heroic honours. That would justify the presence of horses on the frieze, since cavalry competitions were a feature of funerals for heroes.[3]

Kimon's attack on Skyros was done on orders from the oracle of Apollo at Delphi; and Kimon perhaps put up a thank-offering in the sanctuary there (see Plut. *Theseus* xxxvi and the inscription at *Revue Belge*, xxxiv, 1956,542). Athenian interest in Delphi meant interest in central Greece, and control of land as well as sea. Themistokles, as well as Kimon, perceived the political value of a friendly or at least neutral Delphi: in about 478, when Sparta tried to expel the medising majority from the Delphic Amphictyony (the federal organization which decided the sanctuary's affairs), it was Themistokles who opposed them, arguing that to get rid of the medisers would make the Amphictyony unrepresentative of Greece: more bluntly, it would make a present of Delphi to Sparta (Plut. *Themistokles* xx).

On that occasion Themistokles carried his view; but (Plutarch says) the Spartans took against him from that moment, preferring to advance Kimon instead. This is simplified and implausible (how could the Spartans exercise influence over Athenian politics?) but the grain of truth is that Themistokles was indeed out of favour at Athens by the end of the 470s, when he was ostracized (Diod. xi.54). Perhaps we should not look for too deep a political explanation: ostracism was for the man whose leadership had been rejected — which might happen for reasons of style rather than content — and whose disapproving presence was an obstruction and a reproach. Shortly before Themistokles fell, Aeschylus (in 472) produced a play, the *Persians*, which reminded the audience of how Themistokles had deceived King Xerxes at the time of the battle of Salamis. From a poet whose plays elsewhere show sympathy with Themistoklean policies (p. 37), this must be a topical not a nostalgic allusion — a contribution to a debate about whether Themistokles should stay or go. The play was financed (see Syll.[3] 1078) by the young politician Pericles, who cannot have been indifferent to its pro-Themistoklean content. That Pericles' maternal relatives, the noble family of the Alkmaionidai, were enemies of Themistokles (as they certainly were) is no objection to this view: Pericles' father had already distanced himself from the Alkmaionidai by the time of his ostracism in 484 (*Ath. Pol.* xxii, where his politics are distinguished from those of his Alkmaionid kinsman Megakles).

Themistokles' friends were, however, either too young (like Pericles) or too powerless (like Aeschylus, who, as a poet, had to put his points obliquely), and he was ostracized. His activities in the Peloponnese may have been provocatively anti-Spartan (p. 25); in any event, he was forced to look for a permanent home in the king's Asia. He was condemned to death in his absence (469) and arrived in Persia as late as 465, eluding *en route* an Athenian fleet which was besieging Naxos.

It will not do to paint Themistokles as Kimon's opponent on the issue of foreign policy principles — that is, as a medising Sparta-hater — and thereby to seek to explain his ostracism in 471: it is now certain that very many *ostraka* were cast against him in the early 480s when his patriotism was not in question. And the logic of Themistoklean imperialism was perfectly compatible with the expansion of Athenian power in the Aegean for which Kimon was responsible, and which ultimately roused Kimon's friends the Spartans to make war on Athens, in 431.

That expansion had continued, after Eion and Skyros, with the coercion of Karystos on Euboia, and the suppression of the revolt of Naxos, the largest island of the Cyclades, which attempted to revolt in the early 460s. Individual Athenians felt no compunction at this tightening of the screws: an Athenian father of about this time called his son Karystonikos, shamelessly exulting in the 'Victory over Karystos', and the name Naxiades, which occurs in the same inscribed casualty-list (ML 48) can be similarly explained.

The Athenians did not, however, lose sight of the Persian War which, in accordance with the propaganda of 478, was still going on throughout the 470s. Soon after Naxos, Athens undertook a big aggressive campaign in the south-eastern Aegean, under Kimon's leadership; this was perhaps in response to allied discontent at the way the league was turning into a machine for policing its own members. The Persian fleet put out from Cyprus and was defeated in Pamphylia (southern Asia Minor) at the battle of the River Eurymedon. This brought in new allies, particularly from inland Karia, and new revenue. Returning from this success, Kimon was obliged to deal with a major allied revolt, that of Thasos, an island in the north Aegean, rich in minerals. It may indeed have been the news from Thasos which turned Kimon back from seeking further conquests after the Eurymedon victory. Ancient states did not much practise 'economic policies' in our sense, but they liked to control their own sources of corn, and of silver for the purpose of coining. So, because of the silver mines which it controlled, Thasos was — considerations of league discipline apart — too important to be allowed to slip the leash (465).

At last Sparta began to stir. When Thasos, under siege by Kimon, appealed to her for help, she offered 'secretly' (but the offer was evidently everybody's secret at Athens) to invade Attica and thereby to relieve Thasos indirectly: Thuc. i.101. (Thuc. i. 99–117 is the main source for the years 479–440.) This was a clumsy piece of diplomacy: the offer was not implemented, though Thucydides is sure that it was sincere. It cannot have pleased Kimon, the Spartans' friend, any more than it pleased politicians of more obviously radical complexion. But the same year, 465, saw the biter bit: instead of forcing Athens to abandon an overseas operation to deal with a problem nearer home, that is, a Spartan army menacing the Attic border, Sparta was herself forced to welch on the Thasos offer, because she had to deal with a revolt of the helots at Ithome in Messenia. This coincided with an earthquake — for a superstitious Spartan, a sign of divine disapproval, which might well make the helots, who were surely experts in the psychology of their oppressors, hope that Spartan nerve might give.

Unable to cope alone, the Spartans called on Athens for help. The inconsistency is striking: unwilling to see Athens put down Thasos, a rebel subject, Sparta nevertheless calls on the Athenians to join her in putting down her own rebel subjects. Kimon's prestige was still enough to get help voted, though he had first to beat back a prosecution for bribery over Thasos by Pericles. What happens next is a cardinal moment in fifth-century Greek history.

The Athenians, 4000 hoplites (Aristophanes, *Lysistrata* 1143) and their commander Kimon were sent home by the Spartans, who feared what Thucydides, echoed by Plutarch, calls their *neoteropoiïa*, their subversive tendencies. This rebuff led to a shift in Athenian domestic policies — the ostracism of Kimon — and to a switch to an audaciously anti-Spartan stance in foreign affairs — alliances with Argos and Thessaly and the acceptance of the adhesion of Megara. During Kimon's absence, the democratization of the Athenian constitution was taken a stage further: the Areopagus, the upper council in the Athenian state, composed of ex-archons, was deprived of its political and legal functions, other than those which concerned a few cases of homicide. These powers, which the reformers Ephialtes and Pericles tendentiously represented as 'usurped privileges', were given to the council of 500 and to the People i.e. the Assembly and the law-courts. Just what was redistributed in this way is obscure, but the Areopagus almost certainly lost its prospective control of magistrates through the *dokimasia* (testing of qualifications for office) and its retrospective control of magistrates through the system of *euthuna* (examination of accounts after their year of office). Also, the nine archons lost their first-instance jurisdiction to the popular law-courts. Finally, the punitive powers of the 'Kleisthenic' council of 500 were defined for the first time. (*Ath. Pol.* xxvf.; archons: see index.)

In Plutarch (*Kim.* xv) Kimon tried to reverse these changes on his return from Ithome. This has created a temptation to explain the passing of the radical reforms by pointing to the absence of the 'conservative' Kimon and his 4000 'conservative' hoplites. But this is wrong, for several reasons. First, the Athenians who were dismissed from Ithome for 'subversive tendencies' were not the Athenians who were at that moment overturning the Areopagus but precisely Kimon and 'his' hoplites (but we have no right to assume that he chose them personally; four thousand are a lot of people to know by name). So they were not conservatives at all. Second, a related point, the class of hoplites (technically, the 'zeugite' class) and the class of thetes (the lowest of the four census-ratings introduced by Solon in 594) were not opposed groups:[4] on the contrary, both classes stood to gain from the demotion of the Areopagus. (It is relevant that the archonship was not open to the zeugites till 457, to the thetes *informally* some time after that date, *formally*, never. Both, then, were politically underprivileged groups in 462.) Third, we should ask *who* ostracized Kimon? He was ostracized after his return by an 'electorate' which certainly included the 4000 hoplites he had brought back from Ithome, who went on to fight the Spartans hard over the next decade and a half of warfare (the First Peloponnesian War, see further p. 39). Kimon, therefore, was dumped by (among others) his own troops of a few months before — he was, after all, the man who had got them into the Ithome mess. Kimon (remember Thasos after all) may not have been very well pleased with the way his Spartan friends had treated him, but that did not save him. Fourth, and finally, the rejection of the Athenians by the Spartans makes more sense if the Ephialtic reforms are seen as part of a process rather than as an event, that is, if the qualities which the Spartans feared were gradually manifesting themselves over the whole thirty-year period, 487–457.

The process begins with a reform of 487, the introduction of the lot instead of election for the archonship. This must instantly have lowered the prestige of the archonship, and therefore of the Areopagus, which was recruited from former archons. No oligarchy ever reforms itself willingly from within, and almost the only Areopagite with the necessary combination of prestige and radical views to have brought about such a reform is Themistokles. Hence the *Ath.Pol.*'s statement that Themistokles helped Ephialtes overthrow the Areopagus, which is crudely impossible on the dates, may not be completely valueless. It could be an abridged version of an intelligent original discussion of the Ephialtic changes, which went 'Themistokles, by introducing the use of the lot for the archonship in 487, prepared the ground [actually; not necessarily by far-sighted intention] for Ephialtes' attack on the Areopagus in 462'. Incidentally Aeschylus, who supported Themistokles in the *Persians* of 472, and supported the reform of the Areopagus in the surely topical[5] *Eumenides* of 458, a play which also praises the new Argive alliance of 460, is thus consistent in his politics. Finally, the new limitation on the first-instance jurisdiction of the archons is not likely to have replaced the old system at a stroke; a decree for Phaselis (ML 31 = Fornara 68) in which an archon still has substantive powers could thus date from a little *after* 462 — but not much.

To return to Plutarch's account, we must still explain why Kimon's opponents waited, as they evidently did, till the cat was away. The answer is not difficult, if we remember that each meeting of the Assembly was different in composition from all others; personal oratory and ascendancy, not party organization, decided the issues, and that is why the absence of Kimon mattered so much: he would have given his usual speech on the 'special relationship' with Sparta, urging that nothing be done to the Athenian constitution to which oligarchic Sparta would take mortal offence. Again, this makes sense only if it is allowed that Kimon had, for several years already, had his rivals: Pericles had prosecuted him for bribery, though the charge was withdrawn. That looks like a young man's demagogy (cp. Julius Caesar's prosecution of Dolabella, or the way Cicero avoided taking prosecution briefs after his youthful attack on Verres). Pericles' next logical step was to get a power-base. So, to outdo Kimon, who threw his orchards open to the Athenian public, Pericles introduced pay for juries. The final step was the Ephialtic reforms. So Kimon's rivals, Pericles and Ephialtes, were not political newcomers in 462. Here, as elsewhere in Greek history, the temptation to have one politician off the stage before his 'successor' arrives, as in a well-constructed old-fashioned play, is delusive. Pericles overlapped with Ephialtes, and both with Kimon; and for a while it may have seemed feasible to operate Kimonian politics alongside those of his more radical competitors.

By making an alliance with Megara, Athens was clearly seeking to secure herself from a lightning invasion from the west — the threat which had been made at the time of Thasos. The alliance with Megara did not, however, automatically produce a state of war between Athens and Sparta;[6] on the contrary, the *polis* which really suffered from Megara's change of loyalties was Corinth: Thucydides dates from this moment the emphatic hatred, *sphodron misos*, which Corinth felt for Athens. This was a new factor in Greek politics; previously Corinth had been friendly towards Athens, partly for the standard reason that Greeks tended to be friends with their neighbours' enemies (p. 16). Thus the quarrel between Megara and Corinth, which drove the former to detach herself from the Peloponnesian League in 461 and join Athens, was originally over boundary land. *That* was a quarrel which went back to at least 720 BC, when the athlete Orsippos of Megara, more famous as the first man to run nude in the Olympic Games, 'freed' some borderland from the Corinthians (Hicks and Hill, no. 1).

Corinthian friendliness towards Athens lasted, as we have seen (p. 16), throughout the archaic period and into the classical, i.e. as long as Megara was an independent power, capable of causing trouble for both Corinth to the west and Athens to the east: Megara's tyrant Theagenes helped Kylon try to become tyrant of Athens in the late seventh century and, in the early sixth, Megara fought Athens hard for possession of Salamis. Fellow-feeling between Athens and Corinth, occasioned by Megara, is traceable as far back as the time of the Cypselid tyrant of Corinth, Periander: called on to arbitrate between Athens and Lesbos over the possession of Sigeion on the Hellespont, he awarded it to Athens. That cannot have pleased the Megarians or their daughter-cities in the region, like Byzantium. Then it was a Corinthian who, in the late sixth century made a speech (Hdt. v.92) which saved Athens from invasion by Spartans who wanted to reinstate the Pisistratid tyrant Hippias. Finally, Corinth lent Athens twenty ships for her war against Aigina (vi. 89). Here we have a maritime application of the same principle which, by land, determined Corinth's attitude to Athens and Megara; Corinth's policy was to strengthen whichever of Athens or Aigina looked the weaker, so as to prevent the stronger from controlling the Saronic Gulf. Stories in Herodotus of Corinthian-Athenian rivalry in the Persian Wars go back, not to 480, but to the 450s, when Herodotus was gathering his material and when the First Peloponnesian War was on. So Corinth tended to favour Athens against Megara by land and Aigina by sea. That all changed when Athens threatened to absorb Megara and Aigina — which was the position at the end of the 460s: Athens subjected Aigina in 458/7. Incidentally the pattern was to be repeated thirty years later: when under the Thirty Years Peace (446) Megara returned to the Peloponnesian League, and Aigina regained some kind of autonomy, Corinthian hostility towards Athens abated, only to revive in the mid-430s when Athens once again began to pressurize Megara, by the 'Megarian Decrees', and to infringe the autonomy of Aigina (Thuc. i.67).

Corinth, then, not Sparta, was most nearly affected by the rapprochement between Athens and Megara in 460 and, consistently with this, it was Corinth rather than Sparta who fought Athens hardest in the war which now broke out, the First Peloponnesian War, of 460–446.[7]

The first engagement of the war, that at Halieis, a port in the Argolic Gulf, was certainly fought between Athens and Corinth, plus Epidaurus, alone. Moreover a sea-battle which followed, off Kekryphaleia, a small island between Aigina and Epidaurus, and some fighting on Aigina itself and in the Megarid, were conducted by 'the Peloponnesians', who are mentioned several times. Nowhere in Thucydides' account is it safe to think that this expression includes the Spartans, and in the operations in the Megarid the Corinthians, and only the Corinthians, are mentioned by name on the Peloponnesian side. A newly discovered fifth-century inscription (recording an alliance between Sparta and a people called the Erxadieis in Aitolia: SEG xxvi.461) suggests that Sparta normally had the obligation to help her league allies if they were attacked ('if anyone marches against the Erxadieis with warlike intent, Sparta is to help with all possible force'); that she did not intervene to help Aigina is the measure of her lack of will to fight. (For another occasion when Sparta put her league obligations second to self-interest, in 425 BC, see p. 133.)

In all these engagements Athens was conspicuously successful, the more remarkably so since she was involved, from perhaps 459, in a distant adventure requiring much manpower, an Egyptian revolt from Persia. The violence and confusion which Diodorus (xi.71) says marked the end of Xerxes (465) and the accession of Artaxerxes, who acquired the throne by murdering his elder brother, led Egypt in the south of the empire and Baktria in the east to revolt in the hope of freedom. Of the Baktrian revolt nothing is known except that the satrapy was recovered by aid of a providential wind, presumably a sandstorm blowing from the Turkish steppes. In Egypt the rebel leader was Inaros, a Libyan chieftain, who applied (?460) to Athens for help. He was doing quite well even without it: he had already defeated and killed the satrap Achaimenes, Xerxes' brother (Hdt. iii.12; vii.7). When the message arrived, Thucydides says, the Athenians 'were just then engaged in an expedition against Cyprus with two hundred ships of their own and of their allies'. But they let themselves be diverted to the Nile Delta and there holed up the Persians in the 'White Castle'. The mention of Cyprus is interesting because it shows that Egypt was not mere opportunism: the decision to attack Persia in strength on Cyprus had already been made. A tribal casualty-list (ML 33 = Fornara 78) confirms this: it starts with Cyprus and Egypt, in that order. The Cyprus expedition shows that, even after ostracizing Kimon, the Athenians were happy to follow up Kimon's Eurymedon victory. In other words, the 'Themistoklean' policy of aggression towards Sparta did not exclude 'Kimonian' war on Persia.

What Athens wanted from Egypt is not stated by the sources, which are very bad; but Egypt was a supplier of corn to other states, from biblical times to the Roman Empire. This landed wealth of Egypt was, later in the fifth century, exploited by rentier Iranian landowners who include Queen Parysatis of Persia herself, Darius II's wife: their demands are preserved in Aramaic on leather documents bought in Egypt in 1943–4 and now in the Bodleian Library in Oxford. That quoted below, p. 64, refers to the rent paid on Egyptian domain land to a Persian absentee overlord.[8] To cut the Persian nobility off from such sources of revenue would be a good way of avenging the Persian attempt to satrapize Greece in 480, and to farm Attica and Euboia as royal estates. But the negative motive is not the whole of it; Athens was anxious about her own supplies of grain in the mid-fifth century, and benefited in 445/4 from a massive gift of corn — 30,000 medimnoi, or a million and a half daily rations — from an Egyptian prince 'Psammetichos' (Philochorus F 119 = Fornara 86). It may be right to guess that Athens' ambitious foreign policy of this period, which includes diplomacy with a non-Greek town far in the interior of Sicily (ML 37 = Fornara 81, an alliance with Segesta in 457), was forced on her by the need to seek alternative supplies of corn, because her usual overseas sources had for some reason become precarious.[9] They were the Black Sea and Thrace. Now in the Black Sea region the dynasty, which had come to power after the Persian Wars, ruled a principality centred on Pantikapaion until 438, when they were succeeded by a new one founded by one Spartokos (Diod. xi.31). Unfortunately we know nothing about the predecessors of Spartokos, nor can archaeology help much, and we cannot say whether dynastic troubles in the 450s might have caused shortages on the Athenian grain market; the seizure of power by the Spartokids is too late to be relevant. Thrace looks more plausible: there, the new kingdom of Teres and his son Sitalkes was in being by mid-century. Such new sources of political energy may well have made the Athenians look hungrily away from their old markets to Sicily and Egypt. That is not a complete explanation for Athens' *continuing* preoccupation with Sicily, which culminated in the great expedition of 415, but may be relevant to the first contacts. Nor, to argue from the other end, was the Sicilian alliance of 457 without precedent in Athenian thinking: Themistokles called two of his children Italia and Sybaris, and had special ties with the island of Corcyra, whose importance for Sicilian trade was noticed by Thucydides (i.36). It has recently been suggested[10] that another major motive for fifth-century Athenian interest in the west was the desire for the abundant shipbuilding timber of southern Italy (cp. Thuc. vi.90.3 and p. 57 below).

At first the Athenians and Inaros were brilliantly successful, as revolts from Persia often were, initially — before the Great King had had time to mobilize a feudal force from nothing. At first he tried bribery, sending his agent Megabazos to Sparta to get them to create a diversion in Greece by invading Attica. Though nothing came of this, it is of interest because it anticipates the 'Cold War' methods by which Persia sought to infiltrate Greece in the second half of the century. When the full Persian army did arrive, perhaps no earlier than 456, Lower Egypt was still in the control of the rebels, though Upper Egypt, with its garrison of Jewish colonists at Elephantine, held out. The numerical imbalance was not too great, even with the large Greek contingent: the Persians swept up Greeks and Egyptians into a small island in the Nile Delta called Prosopitis. The entire Athenian fleet of 200 ships, plus a relieving squadron of 50, was annihilated (454). This poorly documented affair does not come within the scope of Thucydides' detailed narrative, but his summing up, 'few out of many returned home' (i.110), specifically anticipates the use of that precise phrase about the disaster in Sicily (vii.87). Such a shattering of great imperial hopes was the material from which 'tragic' history could be written (though Athenian recovery after both Egypt and Sicily was quick); but Thucydides, who never explores the same theme twice, reserves the full treatment for books vi–vii.

The few survivors got home via the friendly Greek state of Cyrene to the west. Though there is no reason to think that the kings of Cyrene had actually helped Inaros at the beginning of the revolt, the fall of the Persian-backed Cyrenaean monarchy at about this period can be attributed to the infectious restlessness of Egypt next door,[11] cp. below, p. 61.

Meanwhile the war in Greece was more evenly matched and fought. As long as Corinth led the Peloponnesians, Athens had the best of it, though she was sufficiently alarmed to build the Long Walls, which secured communications between Athens and her harbour city of Piraeus: in future, Spartan invasions would not cut Athens off from the sea (Thuc. i.107). But in 458/7 a large Spartan army crossed into central Greece, ostensibly against Phokis in support of Doris, Sparta's 'mother-city'. (That is an allusion to the Dorian Invasions, in the period after the collapse of the Mycenaean states; the newcomers were supposed to have entered the Peloponnese after a stay in the central Greek region known in historical times as Doris.) The Spartan force, 1500 of 'their own' hoplites, was strikingly big, even if 'their own' included an element of, say, half drawn from the 'perioikic' communities, that is, the Peloponnesian areas which were under Spartan control but not actually enslaved as was Messenia. If the rebel helots at Ithome were still maintaining their siege (465–455 are the dates Thucydides implies) this use of manpower was reckless indeed; so perhaps the text is wrong and the Ithome dates are really 465–460. In any case, Sparta was evidently up to something big; unable, after disciplining Phokis, to return overland — the Athenians now possessed Megara, it must be remembered, also Pegai, a strategically useful port on the Corinthian Gulf — they decided to wait in Boiotia for a while. The Athenians came out and fought them at Tanagra

(457); the Spartans first won but then lost decisively to the Athenians under Myronides at Oinophyta two months later. What was happening, and why did the super-powers collide just here and just now? The full story is given by Diodorus: the Spartans' hope was to establish Thebes as a counterweight (*antipalon*, xi.81.3) to Athens. Athens, for her part, could not allow a strong, centralized and hostile Boiotia to the north of her. (The position can be compared to that in 404, when the Spartans hoped to make Attica, this time, a docile satellite, Xen. *Hell.* ii.4.30, *oikeia kai piste*; Thebes and Corinth wanted Athens to be utterly destroyed sooner than see her turned into a Spartan puppet. Or we might compare the way Philip II kept Phokis intact in 346 rather than make a present of it to Thebes.[12] Such considerations constantly determine policy in Greek history.) If this means attributing to Athens an uncharacteristic desire for *land* empire, we should not hesitate to do so — Thucydides (i.111) after all records an expedition to *Thessaly* as well; and if any individual was responsible it was surely Pericles, whom Aristotle (*Rhetoric* 1407) quotes as saying that the Boiotians tended to 'cut each other down' — that is, they were weak because internally divided. This was surely an argument for getting involved in Boiotia, because it was too weak *to resist effectively*, rather than an argument for leaving Boiotia alone, because it was too weak *to make trouble for Athens*.[13] A recent land survey of Boiotia reveals a much higher density of urbanization and population than had previously been suspected, cp. below p. 84 for this; why not help ourselves, the Athenians must have said, to some of that good soil — cheaper and less dangerous than planting colonies in Thrace where they might be and sometimes were overwhelmed by the natives.

With the free hand in Boiotia given her by Myronides' victory at Oinophyta, Athens, exceptionally, is said to have supported the oligarchs there (*Old Oligarch* = Ps.Xen. *Ath. Pol.* iii.11). This is probably not quite the ideological paradox it sounds: it just means that she supported the politicians and parties in fragmented Boiotia who would tend to *keep* Boiotia fragmented, that is, the Thebes-haters, the local men who wanted to be big frogs in small and separate Boiotian ponds. That such people could be called oligarchs is not surprising, since their aim was to keep power in their own irresponsible fingers. Athens, then, was not doctrinaire in the methods she used to further her interests on the mainland. Religious propaganda could also be exploited: an inscription (IGi³9) shows that Athens, probably in the

450s, made an alliance with the Amphictyonic League, in other words, she was continuing Themistokles' policy of trying to win influence at Delphi. Delphi by land was to be what Delos already was by sea, a religious focus for Athenian imperialism.

By sea Athens had forced the submission of Aigina, and the general Tolmides sailed in triumph round the Peloponnese (both 456). Then came the Egyptian catastrophe. But the rapid sequence of the events which follow proves that Athens' morale remained buoyant even though 250 of her ships were at the bottom of the Nile Delta. One lesson Athens had learnt, not to overreach herself with warfare in two theatres. So a truce was made with the Spartans (451) which, as Thucydides describes it (i.112), need not have been motivated by more than Athens' commonsense desire to deal with her enemies one by one. A big expedition was sent to the eastern Mediterranean, the direct cause of which was the return from ostracism of Kimon, shortly before 451. Such an expedition takes time to mount, and there cannot have been much of a gap between the Egyptian failure and the decision (?453/2) to return to Cyprus. Moreover, Athens showed no loss of grip when dealing with refractory league members in the east Aegean in 452. (See ML 40, 43 for her intervention against medisers in Miletus and Erythrai.) But Kimon's death on Cyprus, after some glorious victories, ended that pha.e of aggressive Athenian activity, and the Athenian Kallias arranged a peace with Persia.

The end of the Persian War did not bring to an end the Athenian Empire, though the existence of the confederacy was now harder to justify. There were also other reasons why resentment of Athens should have intensified in the late 450s: for instance, this was the period of the first cleruchies (settlements of Athenians on allied territory abroad). Thus a cleruchy was imposed on Andros in 450, perhaps on Euboia too, since tribute from these islands drops after 450, one sign of a cleruchy: loss of land brought mitigation of tribute.[14] Only Athenian citizens could profit by allotments of land as 'cleruchs' (literally, 'allotment-holders') and it may be more than chance that the qualifications for Athenian citizenship are more closely defined at just this moment (451): citizen descent was now required on both sides (*Ath. Pol.* xxvi; Philochorus F 119 = Fornara 86). The intention of this law is in doubt;[15] the idea that it was specifically directed against Kimon, whose mother was Thracian, fails because Kimon is now thought to have died as early as 451,[16] too early for the law to have touched him. Part of the idea may have been a selfish desire to limit citizenship to as few people as possible, now that it brought greater material advantages.

The ideological disillusionment after the Peace of Kallias, inside an empire that had lost its *raison d'être*, is noticeable even in our desperately thin historical record. The great rectangular block on which are inscribed the one-sixtieth fractions of the allied tribute which were 'paid' to the goddess Athena has room for one fewer annual list than the available years, and the most likely solution from a technical point of view is that no one-sixtieth was paid to Athena in 449. Some unusual explanation is called for. The idea that Athens actually remitted all tribute that year can be dismissed — there is no other good evidence for an easing up in the way the empire was run. Either the money was earmarked for some special project like the building of the temple to Athena Nike, goddess of victory, a way of saying 'we have won the war against Persia' or else Athena was refused her one-sixtieth part, for symbolic reasons, the other fifty-nine sixtieths being paid in the usual way. The payment to Athena was the *aparche*, the 'firstfruits' in a religious sense. By not giving this to Athena, the Athenians were tactfully declining to cream off the best for the national goddess, thereby showing that all tribute that was collected was needed for utilitarian purposes.

Though there were grumblings in the league, Athens was now formally at peace, for the first time since the Persian Wars, having settled her differences both with Sparta, provisionally, and with the Great King. Her only clash with Sparta was indirect, at Delphi (448). Sparta had taken Delphi out of Phokian control; Athens intervened to give it back to the Phokians, and that was that. In other words, Athens was still holding to the idea of a central Greek, religiously based land empire. This would need diplomatic adjustment soon.

The immediate cause of the Thirty Years Peace with Sparta was Athens' extreme vulnerability in 446. First, Athens lost Boiotia in a rising which ended in an Athenian defeat at Coronea. The rebels were helped by exiles from Euboia, which may imply a concerted plan, because Euboia revolted next, encouraged by the Athenian reverse in Boiotia. Also, the Euboian cleruchy may actually and ironically have accelerated the revolt it was designed to prevent — because cleruchies had a garrison function; but if the cleruchy was installed as early as 450 it cannot have been an immediate grievance.[17] Finally, during Pericles' absence on a punitive expedition to Euboia, Megara revolted, and the Spartans invaded Attica, reaching Eleusis and the

Thriasian plain. Pericles returned from Euboia, and then marched straight to the Megarid (as an inscription, supplementing Thucydides, reveals: ML 51 = Fornara 101). Mysteriously the Spartan king Pleistoanax now withdrew, thereby puzzling and enraging his compatriots, who fined him (Thuc. ii.21): he went into voluntary exile in Arkadia. The Athenians could now return to Euboia, which they subdued (*katestrepsanto*, a strong word). 'Not long after, the Athenians made a peace with the Spartans and their allies for thirty years, giving up Nisaia, Pegai, Troizen and Achaia, their possessions in the Peloponnese' (Thuc. i.115.1). The unrecorded item in this narrative must be that the terms of the final peace were *agreed in principle* by Pleistoanax and the Athenians when the former was still at Eleusis. (See too Fornara 104: bribery of Pleistoanax.)

The Thirty Years Peace meant, for Athens, the end of the central Greek land empire, the end of the plan to control Delphi through the Amphictyony, the end of the Athenian outposts in the Peloponnese. Nevertheless, the peace was an Athenian triumph because it allowed each side to keep what it possessed when the treaty was signed (Thuc. i.140) and thus acknowledged Athens' empire by sea. The proof of this can be seen only by anticipating the events of the next ten years, during which she sent colonies to the west — to Thurii in Italy (Diod. xii.10ff.) but for this venture see p. 57 below: *not* simple 'imperialism' — and to the north, to Brea in Thrace (ML 49 = Fornara 100; ?446) and to Amphipolis in 437 (Σ Aischin. ii.31). Pericles also led an expedition to the Black Sea (early 430s?), a display of Athenian power to make the corn-route safer (p. 41). Most important, Athens enjoyed a free hand in the east: Kolophon on the Asiatic mainland was coerced in *c*.446 (ML 47 =Fornara 99). And when Samos revolted in 440, the Peloponnesian League let Athens get away with savage reprisals. Sparta voted for war against Athens on this occasion in her own chamber, thereby getting Samos on to the Peloponnesian League agenda; the Corinthians voted for peace in the second, decisive meeting, composed of the whole league (Thuc. i.40). Corinth could afford to be indifferent to the vengeance Athens took against Samos; Megara was what mattered to Corinth, and Megara was now back in the Peloponnesian camp. As for Sparta, perhaps her first vote was merely a warning shot, and her *second* was for peace; she was publicizing her own resolve to abide scrupulously by the terms of the Thirty Years Peace:[18] Samos was 'possessed' by Athens in 446 and so she had a right to keep it. Another point of view would be that the peace guaranteed autonomy for both sides' allies (Thuc. i.67.2), an autonomy which Athens was infringing on Samos. With Samos, Thucydides ends his account of the *pentekontaetea*, before the fifty years were up, and ignoring the early 430s. This is deliberate, an emphatic full close to the story of Athenian growth and the fear it inspired in Sparta. Samos was the last major violation of autonomy which Athens was to get away with.

4 Italy and Sicily in the 'Fifty Years'

In 479 BC Gelon, tyrant of Syracuse, displayed himself unarmed before his people and made a speech in justification of his career (Diod. xi.26). The crowd hailed him, Diodorus says, as 'benefactor, saviour and king'. The interest of this triple acclamation is that it sounds emphatically and oddly hellenistic (cp. OGIS 239,301, etc., inscriptions of the Seleucid and Pergamene kingdoms). Now Diodorus' Sicilian narrative here is taken from the third-century BC historian Timaios of Tauromenium (Diodorus also used the fourth-century Ephorus, and his extensive use of these two writers makes Diodorus the main source for west Greek political history in the classical period.) But Diodorus himself probably added the titles used of Gelon; in the same way he regularly gives his early Egyptian pharaohs the hellenistic royal virtues. Diodorus' information then was possibly false; but his insight is correct.

The tyrants of classical Sicily did indeed behave like the kings of hellenistic Greek history, intermarrying (with a vengeance: they practised polygamy), shifting populations around (Gelon's transfer of capital and population to Syracuse), and building on a heroic scale. They anticipated the hellenistic taste for theatre: Dionysius I brought his bride from Italian Lokri in a warship decorated with gold and silver; Plutarch's *Life* of Demetrius has a splendid account of the cortège in which the third-century king Antigonos Gonatas brought back by sea to Macedon the funeral casket of his father Demetrius. The Sicilian tyrants also look backwards to the archaic age of mainland Greece: Gelon's appeal to the Syracusan populace is demagogy of a kind that recalls Pisistratus of Athens, as does his demand for a bodyguard. So Plato, who wrote about both the Athenian family of Pisistratus and the tyranny in fourth-century Sicily, spoke (*Rep.* 566b) of the 'tired old tune', the tyrannical demand for a bodyguard; for the relevance of this to Sicily see p. 187. Aristotle too (*Pol.* 1305) mentions Pisistratus and Dionysius I in the same breath. And intermarriage is something which had characterized the age of the tyrants,[1] epitomized by the party given by Kleisthenes of Sikyon for his daughter Agariste's suitors (Hdt. vi. 126ff) — but there are also marriage links between the Kypselids of Corinth and both the families of Miltiades of Athens and of the Egyptian king Psammetichos. The Sicilian tyrant Hiero married the daughter of Anaxilas of Rhegion; and Gelon and Theron of Akragas married each other's daughters. These parallel developments in east and west were not quite independent: Herodotus says (vi.131) that a man from Sybaris and another from Siris, both Italian towns, were among Agariste's suitors at Sikyon; and some of the poets patronized by the western Greeks had experience of mainland monarchy — Pindar and Simonides both wrote for Sicilian patrons: Pindar composed the Tenth Pythian, his earliest poem, for the Thessalian Thorax of Larisa, and Simonides had been patronized by Polykrates of Samos and Pisistratus of Athens in turn.[2] Plato wanted tragedians banned because they were 'singers of the praises of tyranny' (*Rep.* 568b).

The Sicilian tyrants did not, however, take the personality cult as far as the successors of Alexander. Their dedications are no less assertive; but like Kypselos, whose name originally stood on the Corinthian treasury at Delphi (Plut. *Mor.* 400e), they identified themselves with the state, or put themselves on a level with it: they did not openly claim to rule it. So Gelon's thank-offering after the battle of Himera, in which he defeated the Carthaginians, just reads 'Gelon son of Deinomenes the Syracusan'; similarly the bronze helmet found at Olympia, dedicated by Hiero after his victory at Kyme — 'Hiero son of Deinomenes and the Syracusans' (ML 28–9 = Fornara 54, 64). And none of the Sicilian tyrants before Agathokles (end of the fourth century; he was also the first Sicilian to call himself *basileus*, king) put his own name on his coinage — contrast the HIΠ- issue of Hippias of Athens (B. V. Head (1911) *Historia numorum*, Oxford, edn 2, p. 377), admittedly a coinage struck in exile at Sigeion, *c.*500 BC, but one which shows that the idea of a coin with an individual's name on it was at least thinkable that early.

Gelon of Syracuse had left his younger brother Hiero in charge of Gela. On Gelon's death in 478 Hiero took over Syracuse, and another brother called Polyzalus married Gelo's widow Damareta, who was a daughter of Theron the tyrant of Akragas, cp. above. (It was Polyzalus who dedicated the famous 'Charioteer', a bronze statue

Italy and Sicily

celebrating a victory at the Pythian games of 474 at Delphi.) Theron's son Thrasydaios, who ruled Himera as his father's 'proconsul', and the disgruntled Polyzalus, formed a brief alliance against Hiero. The alliance between Hiero and Theron looked like breaking up, but by 476 friendship was renewed, Polyzalus pardoned and Pindar was able to write victory odes (Olympians i and ii) for both Theron and Hiero in the Olympic Games of 476. This moment is perhaps the high point of the Sicilian tyrannies, judged by what Greeks regarded as glorious. Theron died in 472 and his son Thrasydaios did not keep the power long. The Syracusan tyranny lasted for a few more years; Hiero was even able to install his son Deinomenes as ruler of a new city of Etna, built to house the population of Katane and Naxos, ousted some time in the 470s (cp. Diod. xi.49). Pindar wrote the Third Pythian in 474 and referred in it to Hiero 'of Etna', to flatter the tyrant's pride in the new foundation. By 467 Hiero was dead, and his son Deinomenes' rule, like that of Thrasydaios, was brief.

External policy was equally brilliant: in 480 Gelon defeated Carthage off Sicilian Himera, and in 474 Hiero defeated the Etruscans at Kyme (ML 28,29).

The crude facts about the tyrannies are easily stated; it is harder to get at the truth about what the tyrannies were like. The archaic tyrants of old Greece and of classical Sicily, the hellenistic kings and the Roman emperors, attracted the same kinds of stories. Herodotus' Samian tyrant Polykrates was brought a present of an enormous fish by a fisherman and a good story was attached — but Suetonius' Tiberius and Juvenal's Domitian were also brought large fish to which good stories were attached; again Tarquin in Livy i and Herodotus' Thrasybulus of Miletus both recommend 'pruning the tallest poppies', i.e. eliminating noble dissidents. This kind of thing, what has been called the 'roving anecdote', makes it easy to recognize the tyrannical or other *type*, hard to get at the truth about an individual. Nor are such stories necessarily false: life may deliberately imitate literature (cp. p. 268 on Alexander and the Homeric heroes), and life may imitate life — Domitian reading Tiberius' notebooks to get ideas. But by looking back at the archaic phase of Greek history and forward to later autocrats, as we have done with the Sicilian tyrants, we can remind ourselves that the democratic interludes of Greek history were not merely short but untypical — in Syracuse, Macedon, Cyrene and satrapal Asia Minor one-man rule was normal for much of the period 479–323 BC.

In Syracuse, however, as in some other of the Greek states of the west, tyranny alternated with periods of self-determination. (The word 'democracy' should perhaps be avoided because the kind of *demos* or people who did the ruling is often precisely what we need to know, and do not.) The history of the Greek west cannot, however, be written like that of truly democratic Athens; for one thing, there are virtually no politically informative inscriptions. (And the western Greeks tended to make their dedications at the nearest of the Greek sanctuaries of the mainland, Olympia, rather than creating or patronizing a big cult centre of their own.) Fifth-century Italy and Sicily did produce historians, like Hippys of Rhegion, or Antiochus and Philistus of Syracuse, the 'Sicilian Herodotus and the Sicilian Thucydides'; even Dionysius I, tyrant of Syracuse from the late fifth century to 367, wrote history as well as the tragedies and comedies for which he was, as we shall see, more famous.[3] But of Hippys' work on Italy only a few quotations survive, and these are about foundation myths of places, or physical curiosities. Antiochus was used by Thucydides for Sicilian antiquities at the beginning of his book vi, but not for fifth-century history, though he went down to 424. Philistus was rated high in antiquity, but forty-one of the seventy-seven surviving quotations are all from the same late geographical dictionary. The important surviving narrative, as we have noticed already, was written by Diodorus, himself a Sicilian, writing in the Roman period. He came from Agyrium in the interior, not far from Etna. (Diodorus' universal history is weighted towards Sicily in the classical period, conspicuously so in book xiv which covers 404–387; this is no doubt partly because he was Sicilian himself.) Philistus may have influenced the tradition which survives in Diodorus more than is now obvious; he was an adviser of Dionysius I and was exiled by that tyrant's son Dionysius II. No later writer could afford to ignore so well-placed a source.

Diodorus' account of Gelon is not hostile; but he treats the fall of the tyrannies at Syracuse (467) and Akragas (472) as welcome events, the beginning of 'democracy'. He saves himself from inconsistency by criticism, in each case, of the harsh rule of a son and successor (Thrasydaios at Akragas and Deinomenes at Syracuse); but as with the fall of the tyrannies of old Greece there are deeper causes. Deinomenid policy at Syracuse had been successful in creating wealth and with it a prosperous agricultural class, which could not be excluded from office forever. Things were similar in other of the big cities of Sicily. Diodorus' narrative of Sicily at this time is in a way superior to that of Thucydides, who in his introduction to the Athenian expedition against Sicily in 415–413 undertakes to explain his view that Athens was biting off more than she could chew. We expect some account of Sicilian civilization and resources, some description of the fortifications of Syracuse, the temples (an index of prosperity) of Akragas, or the revenues derived from the subjugated interior; something, in fact, like Herodotus book ii, about Egypt, which introduced the invasion by the Persian king Kambyses. Instead we get from Thucydides a dry list of founders and foundation-dates for the various Sicilian cities. Diodorus, by contrast, gives a fine idea of the size and wealth of the Sicilian cities. Of Akragas, which put up more temples in the fifth century than any other Mediterranean city except Athens, Diodorus says (xi.25; cp. xiii.81) 'her revenue was derived originally from the large indemnities levied against Carthage after Himera. She subsequently derived much revenue from exporting goods from her hinterland to Carthage.' (He goes on to describe how swans came to settle in the public lakes of the city.) There is an important point here: ancient accounts of Greek relations with Carthage often treat her as a barbarian power whose dealings with the Greeks were uniformly hostile. This passage of Diodorus rightly emphasizes that in times of peace there were benefits in having a rich neighbour like Carthage. But our sources do not for the most part interest themselves in times of peace — the impression from Diodorus' own narrative is that Dionysius did little but fight wars against Carthage; but Carthaginian aggressiveness, like Persian, was exaggerated by 'crusading' Greek historiography and poetry. The other (modern) extreme, that of denying that there was such a thing as Carthaginian imperialism, is equally unsatisfying: from Plato onwards, Greeks spoke of Carthaginian *eparcheia*, a compound of *arche* = rule or empire, in Sicily; and the Carthaginians imposed tribute, *phoros*, on Greek cities which fell into their power (e.g. Diod. xiii.59: Selinus).[4] But for most of the fifth century Carthage's relations with the Sicilian Greeks were co-operative and good; and her fourth-century quiescence in the reign of Dionysius II, who did not provoke her, is striking.

Democracy, then, in Syracuse, Akragas and elsewhere, meant the rule of a prosperous agricultural class, which did not necessarily regard Carthage as an enemy, or benevolent co-existence with Carthage as a sin. One might compare the position of Anatolian 'medisers' (p. 19). In about the middle of the fifth century Syracuse introduced the radical-seeming device of *petalism* (which like Athenian ostracism was a way of getting rid of prominent enemies, except that olive 'petals' i.e. leaves, not sherds, *ostraka*, were used); but we should not be deceived. This had no very radical consequences: it was dropped after a few years, Diodorus says (xi.87), because too many of the prominent citizens were thereby discouraged from engaging in political life. Syracuse was not a naval empire but relied like Akragas on the exploitation of an agricultural interior, worked by the subjugated natives, the Sikels. The conditions for establishing and consolidating Athenian-style democracy were absent. But there *were* present all the ingredients of *stasis*, civil strife. Athenagoras, the Syracusan demagogue, is made by Thucydides (vi.29) to say that Syracuse 'is only rarely in a state of internal peace'. This was because Syracuse was a multi-racial society. Constant immigration to this relatively new country (cp. p. 57 on Thurii) and population transfers meant that the citizen body of many west Greek communities was more fluid than the states of old Greece: this is the 'mixed rabble' of which Thucydides speaks (vi.17, in the mouth of Alcibiades). But the old *Gamoroi*, the 'land-holders', at Syracuse kept up their Dorian loyalties, occasionally sending numerically small but often in the event significant contributions to Sparta in her struggles at home in the fifth and fourth centuries (see too p. 187 for the way the favour was returned). And outside in the *chora* or hinterland, and virtually ignored by Thucydides, were the 'true blacks',[5] the Sikel peasants or serfs. The Athenian expedition against Syracuse was thus, as we shall see, not altogether hopeless in its aims, which certainly included the manipulation of the hatred of these groups for each other. (A later writer, Polyainus i.43, speaks of a slave uprising at Syracuse during the Athenian operations of 415–413, cp. p. 141.)

We should imagine similar conditions at other places for which we have no such extended literary record as exists for Syracuse or even Akragas. At Kamarina, Psaumis, a private citizen, used his money to help rebuild the city, refounded in *c*.460 after its destruction by Gelon in 484. (West Greek cities oscillate between prosperity and obliteration, justifying all Pindar's insistence on the mobility of fortune: Olympian xii is his frankest hymn to Fortune, *Tyche*, and is addressed to a Sicilian victor, Ergoteles of Himera.) The fifth Olympian praises Psaumis who 'builds well-founded houses, grown with speed like the tall branches of a forest, bringing his city's people from the harsh bonds of their distress into the light of day'. These few lines, written probably in the 450s, illustrate how much of Sicily's wealth was in private ownership and how much was expected of its possessors. (For parallels one must wait till the hellenistic age, when again citizens step in to underwrite their impoverished cities.)[6]

Elsewhere there is not even the clue of a sentence in Pindar to show who was behind some great construction: Segesta, for instance, a long way over in the interior of the west of the island, had a fine fifth-century temple, the expenses of whose construction can only have been met (given the position of the city) from agricultural wealth, that is, from the product of the labour of the native Sikels. (Not that Segesta was itself a Greek community: the Segestans were *Elymiots*, that is, natives, of some kind not yet understood, although the scribblings from their vases are in Greek letters, *Kokalos*, 1967, pp. 233ff. and their architecture was Greek. Cp. *Arch. Reps*, 1981–2, p. 105 for Attic pottery penetrating between 580 and 420. The resulting wealth made possible the issue of splendid coinages (K. Jenkins (1976) *Coins of Greek Sicily*, edn 2, for illustrations): the coinage of Segesta copies some famous Syracusan types such as the river-nymph Arethusa, but also depicts the local goddess Segesta (*Arch. Reps*, 1981–2, p. 105). If Segesta was a Greek-barbarian hybrid, so too was Selinus, whose architecture includes a mixing of the 'Doric' and 'Ionic' architectural orders (*Arch. Reps*, ibid., p. 102). This would have been disapproved by purists. The same thing is found at fourth-century Labraunda in Karia, where culture is equally hybrid.

In about the middle of the fifth century the Sikels found a leader, Duketios. He established himself in the heart of Sicily, near Etna, about 449, and it took several years and several expeditions by Syracuse to dislodge him. He was finally taken prisoner but got away from Sicily by pleading the status of a suppliant; later he returned and was killed. This curious story is of interest because it is rare in classical (as opposed to hellenistic or Roman) Greece for an oppressed group to find a leader with the capacity to defy organized city-state forces. The Duketios episode is a measure of the submerged resources of the native Sikels (Diod. xi.76–xii.29 *passim*).

Sicilian wealth and power was coveted both by outside powers and by Syracuse, the greatest *polis* of Sicily down to Roman times. Of the outsiders, Carthage established herself permanently in the west of the island; the classical wars were fought about where to draw the line of boundary. The other outside power was Athens, whose interest in the west allegedly began with Themistokles, who called one of his daughters Italia. In 457, when she was already fighting on two fronts, in Egypt and in the first Peloponnesian War, Athens made an alliance with Segesta (ML 37). Later orators were to castigate the Athenian Assembly for making alliances with any state which offered itself, and it is hard to see what good Athens hoped for from Segesta in 457. But this alliance was followed by others, with more accessible cities, Leontini on the east coast of Sicily, and Rhegion on the straits between Italy and Sicily, on the Italian side (ML 63–4), probably in about 443. By this time the other power with ambitions of hegemony in Sicily, Syracuse herself, had probably begun to coerce her neighbours in an organized way. Diodorus (xii.30) speaks of her massing troops and resources with a view to conquering all Sicily: it was not only under her tyrants that Syracuse's foreign policy was expansive. Whether Athenian involvement in Sicily and support of the Ionian, or rather non-Dorian, cities there was the cause of Syracusan expansion, or whether the Athenians were reacting in alarm to Syracusan aggressions against Athenian friends, is hard to say, so gappy is the narrative. (And such questions are always among the hardest to answer even where evidence is full.) But though Athens' diplomatic interest in the west goes back so early, it seems that Syracuse's aims of conquest long preceded and are independent of any serious commitment of men or money by Athens.

Of fifth-century Italy, no consecutive history can be written. Diodorus' sources were less interested in it than in Sicily, as was Diodorus himself: he gives the Roman consuls and even some episodes of Roman history like the Decemvirate, but does not help much with the Greek cities which are our present concern. Some later biographies survive of the Pythagoreans who settled in Italy, and these describe the oligarchic governments and even federations of cities which they established, but the details cannot be trusted: 'saint literature' is notoriously fanciful, and these are hellenistic treatises whose authors had ideas of their own about the theory of kingship; these have probably contaminated the biographical material beyond salvage.

In the extreme south Italy's history follows, naturally, a Sicilian pattern: we saw that Anaxilas of Rhegion married into the Syracusan tyrannical house, and he practised the same kind of aggression against the neighbouring Greek states as his Sicilian contemporaries. An attempt to annex nearby Epizephyrian Lokri was put a stop to by Hiero in 478. Lokri too has a Sicilian rather than an Italian flavour in the fifth century: a Lokrian, Agesidamos, was the only Italian to receive a victory ode from Pindar (Olympian x). One event in Greek Italy, however, is fully described, in the early chapters of Diodorus' book xii: the foundation of Thurii, on the exceptionally fertile site of the former Sybaris in southern Italy. Sybaris had been destroyed by its neighbours the men of Kroton in 510 BC; the mid-fifth-century recovery, organized by Athens, coincides with an attested corn-short-age in mainland Greece: an Egyptian pharaoh, in revolt from Persia, gave Athens 40,000 sacks of corn in the 440s. It looks then as if Thurii, which contained colonists from states other than Athens, including some Dorian ones,[7] was an overseas enterprise of an archaic type — a response to a temporary food crisis. Thurii was thus not a straightforward piece of Athenian imperialism. However, there was certainly an imperialist aspect: as we have seen (p. 41) one of Athens' motives for western involvement was the abundant shipbuilding timber of southern Italy, and timbers from, precisely, Thurii are mentioned in an Attic inventory of the late fifth century (IG i³ 386 l.100). But Thurii, as a mixed foundation, was a victim of her own mixed loyalties, and contained both pro- and anti-Athenian elements (for an expulsion of the latter group see Thuc. vii.33). Accordingly, we find Thurians helping now Athens, now Sparta, in the Peloponnesian War (ib. vii.57.11; viii.35.1. Local tensions: ML 57).

Elsewhere in Italy colonization continued in the fifth century: Siris was refounded by Tarentum in the 430s, under the name Herakleia (Diod. xii.36.4). The Italian states advertise their prosperity in buildings like the fifth-century temples at Paestum (Posidonia), which are comparable in size to those at Akragas, but are on a higher artistic and technical level. The main independent cultural contribution of southern Italy in this period lay, however, in the sphere of philosophy: fifth-century followers of Pythagoras of Kroton, the mathematical and metaphysical theorist, formed themselves into ascetic cult-communities and became involved — sometimes violently — in the politics of the Italian *poleis*. Among these Pythagoreans was Lysis of Tarentum, who was to be the teacher of the Theban statesman Epaminondas, but attempts to link Theban politics with Pythagorean philosophy are not convincing.[8] Another, more austerely intellectual, centre was Elea, which gave its name to the Eleatic school whose most famous representatives (Zeno, who is not the same Zeno as the fourth-century founder of Stoicism; and Parmenides) addressed themselves to philosophical problems of being and identity.

In conclusion, Italy and Sicily suffered from the same divisions and neighbourly jealousies as Old Greece, jealousies made more dangerous by racial friction and the threat of native risings (cranky philosophical activists did not help). And yet (p. 16) the geography of Italy and Sicily did not, as it did in mainland Greece, impose these divisions[9] — there was, for instance, no shortage of good land for corn and cattle as the ears-of-corn coinages of Metapontum and Siris in southern Italy, or the Thurii bull, remind us. But the colonial Greeks of the west, like colonials in all periods, inherited and exaggerated the classic attitudes of their race; in particular, the governing feeling that as Pindar put it 'it is better to be envied than pitied' (Pyth. i.85). Pindar's poetry, celebrating the values of old aristocratic Greece, did not have to be adapted much for west Greek consumption.

5 Cyrene, Africa and Egypt in the fifth century

In the year 474 BC, Polyzalos, brother of Pindar's patron Hiero, won the four-horse chariot-race in the Pythian games at Delphi. In the same year Telesikrates of Cyrene in north Africa, another colonial Greek city, won the foot-race in the same stadium (Σ Pindar Pyth. = vol. ii, p. 220 for the dates). Pindar celebrated that victory in his Ninth Pythian ode. These are more than coincidences: there was much that Greek Sicily and Greek Cyrene had in common, patronage of Pindar being only the most obvious and symbolic link. Pindar wrote two more odes for victors from Cyrene, the Fourth and Fifth Pythians (462); both were for Arkesilas IV, hereditary 'Battiad' king of Cyrene (descended from Battos, the original founder in c.630). And here is another link: at Cyrene, as at the Syracuse of Gelon, Hiero and Polyzalos, monarchy survived from the sixth century, when most of the cities of old Greece got rid of their tyrants, into the fifth.[1] Again like Syracuse (which co-existed with Carthage), Cyrene co-existed happily and for decades with a great non-Greek power, Persia. The conquest of Egypt and Cyrenaica as far west as Euesperides (not far from Benghazi) by the Persian Kambyses did not entail the overthrow of the Battiads, nor did it interrupt the cultural traffic of Dorian Cyrene with Ionian Attica. This leads to the final area of resemblance to the great cities of the west, namely social structure. Cyrene, like Syracuse, was culturally cosmopolitan, so that for instance its art owes a clear debt to Athens, witness the bronze head from the mid-fifth century, in the style of Phidias (Chamoux, *Cyrene*, plate xxiv, 3–4); it was multi-racial, so that the sixth-century reformer Demonax allowed one tribe for the native 'dwellers round about',[2] as well as one for the old Greek settlers and one for new arrivals (Hdt. iv.161, cp. 159.4). Moreover, native names like Alazeir occur at Cyrene (Hdt. iv.164

59

with *Sammlung Gr. Dialekt.-Inschr.*, 4859); Bakal is another native name, attested in a late fourth-century decree of Ptolemy I from which we derive much of our knowledge about the early hellenistic city (SEG ix.1, line 81; M. Austin (1981) *The Hellenistic World*, no.264 for translation, but omitting the names at the end). So there was intermarriage with natives, something also implied by Pindar (Pythian ix), who describes how Telesikrates' ancestors competed for the daughter of Antaios the Libyan giant (and cp. Callimachus Hymn 2.85ff.) (These natives, however, probably did not usurp citizenship in any numbers.) And the population, like Syracuse, had a backbone of old-established Dorian Greek farming families (Rhodians and Spartans as well as the original Therans). Neither at Syracuse nor at Cyrene did the native element, which consisted partly of nomads (*JRS*, 1978, p. 224), much influence the quality of Greek culture, except that the need to impress the Libyan locals may have had something to do with the long survival of the Battiad kingship.[3] Things were very different in, say, Anatolian Ephesus or Halikarnassus (pp. 18f.). Cultural cosmopolitanism at Cyrene meant that its connections ran across to the rest of the Greek world, not down to the natives whom the Greek colonists had displaced or overrun. (The *georgoi* at Josephus, *Jewish Antiquities*, xiv, 115 may be native serfs.[4] If so, they would correspond to the native serf labourers of Persian Asia Minor, and Bakal and Alazeir would correspond to the far fewer *privileged* Anatolians who achieved honour and office under the Achaemenid satraps.) Nor did Egypt, which is after all a long way to the east of Cyrene (Athens being nearer to Cyrene than is the Nile) make much impact except in a few points of ritual. Thus the women of Cyrene abstained from veal (Hdt. iv.186) in deference to the rules of Isis worship. (See too p. 62 on Ammon.)

In Cyrenaica, then, the social and economic pattern was agricultural, and to a degree which was thought remarkable even in a world not familiar with alternatives to agricultural economies (p. 13). Like Thurii or Metapontum, Cyrene issued coinage which depicted the riches of its soil, in the form of the plant Silphium. This mysterious drug has not been identified by botanists, but from the time of Solon to that of Caesar it was to Cyrene what sherry is to Spain. Silphium was used as a vegetable in cooking, as fodder for cattle and, most important, it was supposed to be a cure-all, for infection, indigestion and so on, rather like comfrey in the modern herbarium. It was a royal monopoly, and an earlier King Arkesilas is depicted on a Spartan vase of the mid-sixth century supervising his officials as they weighed it on a man-size balance (Chamoux, *Cyrene*, plate vi. But one theory says the substance here depicted is not Silphium but wool).

For Pindar, Cyrene was the place of many sheep (Pyth. ix.6), and the equestrian successes of Arkesilas and Timokrates were won on the famous bay horses of Cyrene. (For a virtuoso charioteer from Cyrene who showed off before Plato, see Lucian *Dem* 23.) By the third quarter of the fourth century the cavalry commanders of the 'solo horsemen' and 'four horsemen' form an officer class with political privileges (SEG ix.1). (See, however, further p. 62 on the political vicissitudes of the fourth-century city.) The landowners, like the land-holders or Gamoroi of Syracuse, were a feudal nobility who were not always on easy terms with their kings. In the fourth Pythian (293ff.) Pindar pleads with Arkesilas for one of these nobles who is out of favour, a 'pollarded oak-tree' — cp. the tyrant's maxim about 'pruning the tallest poppies' on p. 51; and in the late sixth century when the balance of strength was the other way, Arkesilas III had been forced out of the country to Samos. The lifestyle of a Cyrenaean aristocrat was centred on his *pyrgos* (Hdt. iv.164; Strabo 836), a word found in Asia Minor and Attica (Xen. *Anab.* vii.8; *JHS*, 1947, 68ff., cp. chapter 11, n.11) to describe a fortified estate, which in Asia Minor and no doubt in Cyrene was run in irresponsible baronial fashion. These aspects of Cyrene — a monarchic government supported or occasionally subverted by horsebreeding aristocrats — recall two other places whose hospitality Pindar sampled early in his career, Thessaly and Macedon.

In the fifth century there were only two kings of Cyrene before the monarchy fell some time before *c.*450, Battos IV 'The Fair' and Arkesilas IV;[5] in about the middle of the century, Cyrene freed itself from the never very oppressive control of Persia, perhaps following the lead of the Egyptian revolt. Perhaps, too, there is a link between the internal revolution and the rejection of Persia.[6] (End of Persian control: Thuc. i.110, help given without reprisals to Athenian refugees from Egypt; end of monarchy: Σ Pind. Pyth. = vol.ii, p.93; Aristotle F 611.17 = Hill *Sources*[2] p.42.) When Arkesilas IV had succeeded Battos IV is unknown, but Pindar addresses him as a young man in 462. In 460, two years after his success at the Pythia, Arkesilas achieved the crown of human ambition by winning the chariot-race at Olympia, fulfilling Pindar's prayer at the end of the Fifth Pythian. By the middle of the century Arkesilas was himself on the run, fleeing from Cyrene via Euesperides to the west, where he was assassinated.[7]

Pindar knew (none better) how to celebrate a victorious horse in the literal sense, but rarely backed a political winner: clients of his, or their families or their states, came to misfortune in Athens, Sicily, Aigina and Cyrene. The monarchy in Cyrene had been a splendid and successful anachronism; the 'democracy' which ousted it (Arist. loc.cit.) made no such splash in the world beyond Africa. That 'democracy' was probably an oligarchy of a narrow enough type. Thereafter till the end of the century Cyrene virtually disappears from the record except that a Cyrenaean individual helped Athenian survivors of the Sicilian disaster of 413 (IG i^3 125; Dem. xx.42; p.143; but see Thuc. vii.50.2 for state help by Cyrene to Sparta in 413). Political disorders in 401 (Diod. xiv.34) forced the oligarchs at Cyrene to compromise with their opponents (i.e. set up a 'mixed' constitution and share power more widely). A real 'Kleisthenic' democracy, i.e. one modelled on Athens, was established in perhaps 375 (Arist. *Pol.* 1319b). In this period the coinage improves in quality and increases in volume; and the Treasury of Cyrene at Delphi was built. But the cavalry class was back in power by the third quarter of the fourth century (SEG ix.1), after overthrowing the Kleisthenic democracy as Aristotle says. It was this regime which sent a gift of 300 horses and five four-horse chariots to Alexander the Great (Diod. xvii.49), and sold off Cyrene's corn to the Greek world in time of shortage (Tod 196).[8] This inscription names Athens, Corinth, Thebes and Alexander the Great's mother Olympias as recipients. Cyrenaean generosity on this occasion was still being recalled in the Emperor Hadrian's time, in the second century AD (*JRS*, 1978, p.113, l.19 with p.117).

Arkesilas IV is called king of many cities by Pindar. These certainly included Euesperides, near but not identical with Benghazi, Barke and Taucheira (Tocra), both to the west; and Antipyrgos (Tobruk) to the east: Barke certainly issued coinage modelled on Cyrene's after 480 (British Museum, *Catalogue of the Coins of Cyrenaica*, p.clxviii). Only at Tocra has archaeology confirmed a substantial Greek presence in the fifth century, but even here the Persian period is impoverished compared to what went before.[9]

One consequence of the Persian presence in Cyrenaica was to bring the Egyptian oasis of Siwah, with its oracle of Ammon, into closer touch with Cyrene; Zeus Ammon, as Pindar calls him, features on the reverse of Cyrenaean coins issued after 480. The great period of the spread of new, especially Egyptian, oriental and Thracian cults was the fourth century (chapter 13), but it is worth remembering that Kroisos (Hdt. i.146) in the sixth century, and the Athenian Kimon in the fifth (Plut. *Kim.* xviii), had already consulted the Ammon oracle.

Egypt itself had been penetrated by Greeks as early as the seventh century, when Ionian and Karian mercenaries were hired by the Saite pharaohs. Egyptian knowledge of Anatolia went back much further: the Greco-Karian city of Pedasa, just north of Halikarnassus, is mentioned in the Gazetteer of Amenhope (twelfth century BC). After Egypt was conquered by the Persian king Kambyses in 525 BC the Greeks and Karians lost their old employers; but it is certain from several pieces of evidence that they stayed on under the new management, as distinct ethnic groups, surviving until and beyond the Macedonian takeover in 331. In the first place, Herodotus (ii.61), discussing Egyptian customs, specifically mentions 'the Karians who *are* in Egypt': the historian wrote this in the mid-fifth century. Second, recent excavations at Saqqara, the burial-place of Egyptian Memphis, have produced Karian graffiti of the classical as well as the archaic period. Third, Greeks in the fourth century and later are described in written sources and inscriptions as coming from Naukratis, which was the old port of trade between the Greeks, with their silver to sell, and the xenophobic Egyptians with their more stagnant economy — but a surplus of wheat. (For money of Jawan, i.e. Ionia = Greece in Egypt at the end of the fifth century, see *Brooklyn Aramaic Papyri*, no.12.)

Over the centuries these Greeks and Karians intermarried with the natives, so that in hellenistic times people called 'Karomemphites' and 'Hellenomemphites', obvious results of miscegenation, are attested in Memphis.[10] These Greeks and Karians had garrisoning jobs in the Persian period, the enemy being presumably the native Egyptians. Another well-documented foreign garrison in Egypt (this time directed against trouble from the south as well as subversion from inside) was made up of contingents of Jews stationed in Upper Egypt at Edfu (Elephantine), at the Third Cataract of the Nile. The evidence for this group is a set of letters on papyri (A. Cowley (1923) *Aramaic Papyri*, Oxford). The most interesting of these is from the Persian king himself, regulating the details of the Jewish passover. It dates from 419 BC (Cowley, no.21): it stipulates the days of unleavened bread and gives instructions for abstinence from beer and work. This document is astonishing proof of the religious tolerance, and attention to detail, shown by the kings of Persia.

Egypt revolted from Persia three times in the fifth century, proving that these Greek and Jewish garrisons were needed. A revolt in 483 was put down straight away. The third and most successful revolt began in 404 and gave Egypt independence till the 340s (there was a brief final revolt in the 330s). In between fell the revolt of Inaros, a Libyan prince, 462–452, whose final defeat entailed the defeat of an Athenian force of 200 ships, sent to help Inaros during the First Peloponnesian War (see p. 42). Persia's vigorous actions to recover Egypt are in proportion to what was at stake. From the fifth-century period of Persian control between c.450 and 404 there survive leather documents (G. Driver (1957) *Aramaic Documents of the Fifth Century BC*) which show that much of the best land in Egypt was parcelled out among absentee Persian landlords, who include the Persian queen Parysatis herself, the wife of Darius II (ruled 424–404). Here is an extract from a letter written by an indignant rentier to his bailiff (Driver, no.x):

> (In regard to) that domain which has been given to me by my lord in Egypt — they are not bringing me anything thence ... let a letter be sent ... to instruct one named Hatu-basti, my officer, that without fail he collect the rent on those domains and bring it to me...

When in the next century Alexander the Great, after winning the battle of Issos in Cilicia, turned south against Egypt rather than going immediately east towards the Iranian centre of the Persian Empire, his decision, as we shall see, was strategically sensible; what is surprising is that the Persians surrendered so quickly, not trying to defend Egypt at all, although economically Egypt probably mattered more to the Persian upper class than any other satrapy.

In the late 330s, after Alexander had entered and taken over Egypt, his officer Peukestas son of Makartatos put up what is the earliest Greek documentary papyrus from Egypt. It was published in 1974 and is cited on p. 277. It is the first drop of a deluge of such material, which makes social life in Egypt in the centuries after Alexander better known to us than any other part of the ancient world. But Greek knowledge of Egypt, and the Greek presence there, already had a 300-year history when Peukestas put up his notice. It is not surprising that in the mid-fourth century the shape of the Pyramids should have influenced the architecture of an otherwise Greek building like the Mausoleum at Halikarnassus; or that the cult of the Egyptian Isis should have had worshippers at fourth-century Athens (Tod 189, line 44 and p. 178).

6 Persia and Asia Minor

The Jewish garrison at Elephantine (p. 63) exemplifies the mixed racial and cultural character of the Persian Empire:[1] it was a garrison of Jews, stationed in Egypt, commanded by Iranians, owing allegiance to Persia, recording its business in Aramaic, on a site whose name is Greek (the 'place of ivory'); finally, among the names identified in its papyri is a Chorasmian from north of the River Oxus in Afghanistan. Ease of travel was one of the benefits brought by an empire as large and stable as the Persian, which after the conquests of Cyrus, Kambyses and Darius I in the second half of the sixth century extended from Thrace to modern Afghanistan and from the Caspian Sea to the Persian Gulf and the Third Cataract of the Nile. The eastern travels of Herodotus, who moved freely across the two thousand miles separating Babylon from Cyrene, were made possible by Persian indulgence and protection, in much the way that the evangelism of St Paul was facilitated by the Roman Peace. Some Greeks admired Persian methods (p. 18); even Plato, who thought that Persians suffered, as from a disease, from an excess of tyranny which made them congenitally weak, could call their empire a 'solidly based system' (*Laws* 685 where the reference is to Persia). Herodotus' *History* can be seen as a sermon on the text that Greeks and Persians, even in their great period of conflict, gradually came to value each other's qualities:[2] at first (Hdt. i.153) Cyrus the Great scoffs at the Greeks who come together in a market-place to cheat each other; by the end, the exiled Spartan king Demaratos is shown (vii.104) lecturing a clearly impressed Xerxes on the subject of Spartan deference to law.

The Persian Empire, then, was not uniformly hated or despised by Greek writers. Nor did Greek interest in Persia cease after the fifth century:[3] apart from Plato, several fourth-century commentators had good things to say, like the Oxyrhynchus Historian (xix Bartoletti), who comments on the way Persian commanders deliberately withheld payments from (Greek) mercenaries; this would put them more in their power. The two most interesting items, in view of recent archaeological finds, are, first, a remark of a fourth-century historian, Herakleides of Kyme (*FGrHist.* 689F 2), who says that the Persian king pays his soldiers in food, dividing the meat and bread equally, and that this corresponded to the money which Greek employers paid to their mercenaries. Herakleides goes on to speak of them as the king's 'fellow-diners'. And, second, there is a sentence in Plutarch's *Life* of Artaxerxes (chapter iv) about the revolt of the younger Cyrus (for which see p. 184): 'some say that he revolted because he was not given enough rations.' The publication in 1969 of the Persepolis Fortification Tablets makes all this intelligible: the tablets record payments of large quantities of food — grain, sheep and so forth — to Persian grandees like 'Parnaka', the Pharnakes who is named by Herodotus (e.g. viii.126). Thus (PF 6581): '10 sheep, entrusted to Harbezza, Parnaka received for rations. At Persepolis and Tenukku. Third month, for a period of 5 days, in the 19th year. Basaza wrote (the text). Mannunda communicated its message.' Now to eat ten sheep in five days a man needs a lot of help. The rations given to Parnaka were surely intended to support a large household, of a feudal type; in fact a household of what Herakleides called 'fellow-diners'. That satraps as well as the king had their entourage of fellow-diners is proved by Xenophon's *Anabasis* (i.8.25) which says that Cyrus the Younger had his 'table-sharers', and by Diodorus' description (xvii.20) of the 'kinsmen' of the satrap Spithrobates, who fought with him at the battle of the Granikos in 334. (This item comes from Kleitarchos, who was interested in Persian institutions, cp. F 5; not surprisingly since he probably grew up in Persian-held Ionia, which as with Herodotus, Ephorus and Herakleides must have helped determine his literary bent.)

Feudalism is a system of loyalty in return for benefits, usually land. In that general sense Achaemenid Persia was feudal. The satraps often revolted from the Great King, but when Alexander invaded, they fought to repel him. Greeks found these attitudes hard to understand; accustomed to connect one-man rule with harsh policing, they imagined that the Persian Empire must have been held down by a system of institutionalized controls — garrisons and garrison-commanders — and touring royal armies and officials, King's Eyes and King's Ears, and so on (Xen. *Oec.* iv.6; Isok. iv.145). These (it was thought) watched for signs of revolt among satraps. There is *some* evidence for all of this; but a recently discovered inscription from Xanthos in Lycia (SEG xxvii.942 = *Mausolus* M9) shows the satrap, Pixodaros, not the king, appointing a garrison-commander.

The benefits received by the satraps were too great for any of these checks to be necessary. What were those benefits?

For the immediate entourage, the kinsmen or table-sharers of the king, splendid maintenance was one benefit. These were the feudal followers whom Herakleides had in mind. There is not much other evidence for any kind of standing army: the classic historians of the fifth century speak of the Ten Thousand 'Immortals', but that word is now thought to be a mistranslation of an Old Persian word meaning 'followers', which takes one straight back to feudalism.

But for most of the king's vassals, who did not inhabit the Iranian heartland, the benefit took the form of gifts of land like medieval fiefs, in return for which the man 'enfeoffed' was expected to maintain a levy of troops. Such were the troops who fought Alexander at the Granikos. In the late fifth-century Babylonian satrapy 'bow land' and 'chariot land' were given away on condition that the owners for the time being paid for soldiers or cavalry. The system goes back to the sixth century, when the founder of the Persian Empire, the great Cyrus, presented seven cities in northern Anatolia to Pytharchos (see p. 18; *FGrHist*. 472.F 6 for the grant); and Persian 'gift-giving', commented on by Thucydides (ii.97), continued through the time of Themistokles (i.138) down to the eve of Alexander's arrival. Arrian (*Anabasis* i.17.8) mentions 'Memnon's Land' in the Troad, whose possessor was a Persian general (and see further p. 71 for Persians or Persian favourites settled in Anatolia). Such generosity was at the expense of the Greek cities of the coast, and helps to explain why they revolted from Persia again in 479 (Hdt. ix.105, treating their adhesion to the new Delian League as a second 'Ionian Revolt'), as before in the Ionian Revolt of 499. The Ionian cities were however less prosperous as a result of choosing Athens not Persia; monumental building there declines in the fifth century.[4] There is not much evidence for active hellenization outside old Greek centres like Halikarnassus, Smyrna and Ephesus; though some progress is made at inland Anatolian sites like Etrim (the Syangela of the Athenian Tribute Lists, later hellenized as 'Theangela'): objects like a Panathenaic amphora made in Athens *c*.420, and red-figure pottery, attest the same penetration of Greek influence. But this kind of thing does not speed up till the time of the fourth-century satraps.

The explanation of Greek discontent under Persian rule is not, then, economic. (Miletus, which had led the original 490s revolt, is said by Herodotus to have been at her greatest prosperity then.) Instead a psychological cause is needed. That cause is simply a preference for freedom, *eleutheria*. In other words, those Greeks who did not profit, as did Pytharchos, Themistokles or Memnon, from the Persian presence, preferred self-government to good but alien government. It would be wrong to be too sentimental about what 'freedom' meant to Greeks; Thucydides (iii.45.6) makes a speaker use the phrase 'freedom, or rule over others', and similar uses can be found in Greek authors from Herodotus (i.210) to Polybius (v.106). In modern times Sir Isaiah Berlin has distinguished between two 'kinds of freedom', freedom from something and freedom to do something. Greeks valued the second kind, which included freedom to oppress and dominate, at least as much as the first.

In what ways did the Persian Empire restrict the freedom of its subjects? The two most obvious and irksome are subjection to satraps and extortion of tribute, including personal military service.

First, what was a satrap? He was a Persian provincial governor, whose powers had few limits provided he stayed loyal. Satraps led contingents from their satrapies in the great battles against Greeks or Macedonians of which we hear in Herodotus or the Alexander-historians; they also levied troops for less grand operations. Thus we hear of 'those who muster in the plain of Kastollos' (Xen. *Anab.* i.1.2; 9.7). Satraps usually had the military authority where the satrapal authority was divided, as it sometimes was (see p. 281); and such divided commands could enable the king to keep an eye on the ambitious. In diplomacy with subject or foreign peoples, satraps were supposed to refer everything to the Great King (Diod. xv.41.5), but there is nothing to imply deference to the king in inscriptions like Mausolus' treaty with the Pamphylian city of Phaselis, or his grant of political privileges to the Kretan city of Knossos (H. Bengtson (1975) *Die Staatsverträge des Altertums*, edn 2, vol. ii, 260, J. Crampa (1972) *Inscriptions of Labraunda* 40 = *Mausolus* M 7, 10). In the sphere of finance, satraps were supposed to forward tribute (Thuc. viii.5).

The presence of such a satrap, then, was the first affront to local freedom. How oppressive the satraps were in reality is a question which can be answered only by looking at the second area in which Persia impinged, tribute and military service.

Personal service, and the obligation to lead one's own retainers, is essential to a military system like the Persian. Herodotus says that a rich Lydian called Pythios tried to get his son exempted from the draft by entertaining the king magnificently; but the king had the young man sliced in half and made the army march between the pieces (Hdt. vii.27f.). The punishment oddly resembles the Roman way of purifying an army after some pollution: did the Achaemenids, who, as Darius' Behistun inscription proclaims, ruled by the grace of Ahura Mazda, regard military conscription as a religious duty? Later, it was possible to pay for somebody else to carry a pike for you; like the Athenian Empire and the Peloponnesian League, the Persians found such a system more convenient and perhaps, in dissident satrapies, more secure. But the result was, by the fourth century, an excessive use of Greek mercenaries, which weakened every part of the Persian army except the cavalry arm: see p. 280 for the performance of Iranian cavalry at Issos and Gaugamela.

In finance, the crude picture in Herodotus' list of the Tributes (iii.89ff.) and depicted on the reliefs at Persepolis — huge quantities of bullion brought by subject peoples — must be modified by the fourth century. By then the satraps in Asia Minor (which is the best-attested cluster of satrapies) allow the *poleis* to grant citizenship and tax exemption on their own initiative, provided the Great King gets his tribute (*Mausolus* M 5, 8, 13, with formulae anticipating hellenistic grants). Whether Asia Minor is untypically sophisticated, we cannot be sure; the picture there at least is that Persia did not suppress local autonomy (see further pp. 199f.). And the tendency towards appointing natives rather than Iranians as satraps after 400 gave a chance to humbler men who could rise as their masters rose; *Mausolus* M 9 shows the satrap appointing two Karians to office in Xanthos. Much of this evidence is from the satrapy of Karia, and though the satraps there certainly enjoy unusual latitude, there is no denying them their full status as satraps as a new, erroneous, theory has it:[5] the matter is put beyond doubt by the Aramaic text of the great trilingual inscription found in 1974 (see the full text in *Fouilles de Xanthos*, vi, 1979) which refers to Pixodaros as satrap in Karia; moreover a scholion on Demosthenes *Peace*, which may go back to Theopompus (who was certainly the source of other Hekatomnid material in the Demosthenes scholia, cp. F 299), calls Mausolus satrap of Karia, quite simply.

That one language of the Xanthos trilingual inscription of 1974 is Aramaic, the Persian bureaucratic script, is a reminder that there were Persians in numbers settled in classical Anatolia. The new, native-born administrators did not displace these Iranian settlers but imitated and co-operated with them. A strong Iranian presence throughout the period 479–334 is indicated by chance literary references, such as Herodotus, who refers not only to Persian individuals at Sardis before the Ionian Revolt from Persia of the 490s, but also to Persians being given the land round Miletus *after* the revolt (v.101; vi.20). Or there is Xenophon, who describes (*Anabasis* vii.8) the rich feudal estate of the Persian Asidates in north-west Asia Minor at the beginning of the fourth century. The 'territory' of Tithraustes, a Persian name, in Hellespontine Phrygia, is mentioned by a papyrus dealing with the events of the Social War of the 350s (*FGrHist*. 105, cp. p. 243). But here it is epigraphy which has added most strikingly to our knowledge: as early as Herodotus' day there had been Persians with names like Megabates at Halikarnassus (ML 32), and new inscriptions from fourth-century Labraunda, a sanctuary in Persian-held Karia, attest the Iranian proper names Phrathethnes and Ariarames (*Inscriptions of Labraunda* 77; 28). In the late fourth century Bagadates and Ariaramnes, two more, obvious, Persians, are honoured at another Karian sanctuary, Amyzon (J. and L. Robert, 1983, *Amyzon*, i. p. 97). As late as the Roman period we find a man with the splendid name Marcus Antonius Bagoas (Keil and Premerstein, *Zweite Reise in Lydien* no. 10; this man must have got the Roman citizenship from Mark Antony, but Bagoas is a Persian name). Further north there are Persian names in the Pontic region (*Studia Pontica* iii, 1910, nos 1; 98). Another inscription, published in 1975 (*Comptes Rendus, Académie des Inscriptions* (*CRAI*), 1975, p. 308) regulates points of Zoroastrian ritual, and stands in the name of Droaphernes the (Persian) governor: it is interesting evidence of religious syncretism, i.e. fusion, that a religious text of this kind should be promulgated in *Greek*, i.e. there were Greek-speaking Zoroastrian converts at fourth-century Sardis. That may also be the implication of the phrase 'Gods of the Greeks and Persians' at hellenistic Tabai in Karia (*CRAI*, 1978, p. 281).

Persian values also made themselves felt at native satrapal courts: a recently published *Greek* verse inscription from *Lycian* Xanthos, put up by a local dynast, echoes *Persian* educational ideals ('riding, shooting and speaking the truth', Hdt. i.136) when it speaks of:

> what wise men know,
> archery, virtue, and hunting on horseback — this I know
> also
>
> (SEG xxviii.1245, lines 14f.)

The dynast in question is called Arbinas: he is certainly a Lycian but it is thought that the form of the name is Persian. Such Persian names survive in local nomenclature till Roman times: the priests of Artemis at Ephesus went on being called Megabyxoi for centuries after 330; or we might compare the place-name Maibozani, recently attested (*JRS*, 1975, p. 65, line 10, with p. 73: a Roman inscription from Ephesus of the first century AD). This same place Maibozani, which is an Iranian name, has recently yielded a dedication to 'Persian Artemis', i.e. Anahita (*Bulletin de correspondance hellénique = BCH* (1982) p. 372). And cp. the new early hellenistic attestation of a 'Median Artemis', S. Sherwin-White (1982) *ZPE* xlix, p. 30; Persian Artemis/Anahita is well-attested in hellenistic Lydia, cp. Keil and Premerstein *Erste Reise in Lydien*, pp. 25, 43, 52; *Dritte Reise*, p. 64; and especially K. Buresch, *Aus Lydien*, pp. 66ff., cp. 117ff. Archaeology confirms the picture: the so-called 'pyramid tomb' at Sardis is in fact certainly the monument of a Persian; 'pyramidal stamp seals' of Persian type have been found in Asia Minor (*Iran*, 1970, pp. 19ff.); at Sardis excavations have uncovered a relief depicting *both* Cybele and Artemis/Anahita (G. Hanfmann and N. Ramage, *Sculpture from Sardis*, 1978, no. 20); and Greco-Iranian *stelai* (funerary pillars) from the satrapal capital of Daskyleion in north-west Anatolia are sometimes carved in Aramaic, indicating the Persian nationality of the customers for whom they were executed (*Rev. Arch.*, 1969, 17ff., 195ff.). From the same site, Daskyleion, come *bullae* (seals) also inscribed in Aramaic (*Anadolu*, 1959, pp. 123ff. For excavations at the 'fine hunting and fishing country' — cp. Xen. *Hell.* iv.1.15f. — of Daskyleion see *Arch. Reps*, 1959/60, 34f.). But it must be repeated that this extensive social penetration by Iranians does *not* seem to have destroyed local autonomy or opportunities for office-holding by locals: thus the Amyzon inscription mentioned above certainly honours Iranians, but one of the *archontes* (magistrates), has a Karian name (Panamyes) and so does Hyssollos the 'Treasurer of the Gods' and the 'mountain guard' Paes son of Panamyes. (See additional note, p. 322.)

This was the Persian Empire with which the Greeks dealt — large, catholic and not mountainously tyrannical towards the local communities, at least in its later phases. The internal history of Persia and its kings is harder to reconstruct, because there is no native Persian historiography. Xerxes, the invader of Greece in 480, died in 465 and the long reign of Artaxerxes I began, lasting till 425. It was he who ended the war with Athens, or perhaps turned the hot war into a cold one (because satraps continued to subvert Athenian-supported democracies in Anatolia): after the Persian recovery of Egypt in the 450s Athenian aggression against Persia was checked, except for a brief campaign in Cyprus at the end of the 450s. The resulting Peace of Kallias of 449 did not, however, affect the diplomatic position of *Sparta*, and it is easy to be misled by the Athens-centred character of the written sources and forget that Sparta and Persia were technically at war right down to 412 BC.[6] This is not just an historical curiosity, although for much of the fifth century Sparta and Persia had no attested dealings. The word 'attested' is important: there was certainly more to-ing and fro-ing between Persia and Greek states than is recorded, especially on a change of ruler. For instance, Argos, in perhaps the later 460s, needing protection against Sparta after concluding an alliance with Athens, sent to Persia for reassurance of friendship from the new king, and got it (Hdt. vii. 151). Sparta wanted help in the Peloponnesian War, and sent more than one delegation (Thuc. iv.50); the difficulty was that Persia insisted that Sparta recognize that Asia Minor was Persian property, and this Sparta, for domestic reasons to do with the Peloponnesian League, could not do (pp. 102, 127).

Artaxerxes I was succeeded in 424 by Darius II after an anarchic interval. Under Darius the Lydian satrap Pissouthnes revolted, and the Athenians supported this revolt which was continued by his bastard son Amorges (see p. 139). That support ended the Peace of Kallias, and Persian intervention in Greek affairs is now stepped up (413). Support of Amorges and its ultimate consequence, the defeat of Athens in the Peloponnesian War, is however a story we shall resume later.

7 Macedon, Thessaly and Boiotia

At Vergina in 1977 the Greek archaeologist Manolis Andronikos, excavating the royal Macedonian graves of the fourth century BC at Vergina, found a bronze tripod dating from the early fifth century. This was an heirloom from the time of King Alexander I 'Philhellene' as he was later called; it was perhaps a prize won at the Olympic Games as described by Herodotus (v.22). Alexander had to argue with the authorities before they would let him compete, but he convinced them that he was descended from the royal house of Argos. He came first equal in the foot-race. This incident raises for the first time a question which is still being debated two and a half thousand years later: were the Macedonians Greeks?[1] The orators and propagandists of the fifth and fourth centuries do not help for they contradict each other. For the fifth-century sophist Thrasymachus Archelaos was a barbarian, and Demosthenes could call the Macedonians 'barbarians' as at xiv.3, where Philip is the 'common enemy of the Greeks'. It has also been acutely pointed out that the title 'philhellene', which was perhaps first given to Alexander I by writers of the fourth century, actually implies a *denial* that he was Greek. But the Macedonian kings could be regarded as more Greek than their Macedonian subjects. Isokrates (v.139) clearly implies that Philip, as a descendant of Herakles, is Greek. The argument is the same as that used 150 years before by Alexander I — and just as impossible for us to test. What is clear is that Macedonians wanted to be thought Greek. When Philip in 346 settled the Third Sacred War, he was (personally; not the Macedonians as a race) admitted to the Delphic Amphictyony, the body which managed the prestige sanctuary at Delphi; and so he gained admission to the Greek fraternity. Alexander the Great also found Greek culture valuable if only as a way of patronizing his Macedonian peers: he remarked to a Greek fellow-feaster (Plutarch *Alex*. li) that the Greeks seemed to walk among Macedonians as demigods among wild beasts.

Language and inscriptions help more. Greek was to the language of the Macedonians as cultivated speech to a boorish patois. Unlike the Illyrians (Polyb. xxviii.8.9 on the Illyrian *dialektos*), Greeks were intelligible to Macedonians without an interpreter, though a Macedonian commander who wanted his troops to understand him immediately would speak 'in Macedonian' (Plut. *Alex*. li, papyrus in *GRBS*, 1978, 227ff.). Little is known about how Macedonian Greek was spoken, except that for instance Philip was pronounced Bilip. No Greek-Macedonian interpreters are recorded for Alexander's expedition, though hardly any interpreters of any kind are, so this is not significant; but Alexander's education, at the hands of Aristotle, and his reading — Xenophon, Euripides, and especially Homer — shows him thoroughly imbued with hellenism at the cultural level. (For more on this see chapter 18. Bilip: Etymologicum Magnum 179.)

There is much less evidence for the fifth century than for the fourth, when Philip and Alexander attracted attention to Macedon, but recently discovered gravestones show that by 400–350 Macedonians had good Greek names (which they were given in the *fifth* century, of course) like Xenokrates, Pierion and Kleonymos (M. B. Hatzopoulos and L. D. Loukopoulos (1980) *Philip of Macedon*, plates 109–10 on pp. 206–7).

Classical Macedon was however organized in a manner unlike that of the Greek states who dominate the history of the period — that is, Sparta, Athens and the cluster of *poleis* round the Isthmus of Corinth. In Macedon the *ethnos* or tribe was what mattered; there was not much urbanization before the Peloponnesian War. There *were* Greek cities in the north Aegean but many were colonies from seventh-century Euboia and Corinth. (This meant that till Philip II's time Macedon was short of good harbours.) The organization by *ethnos* not *polis* was not completely foreign to Greeks: Thucydides (iii.94) calls the Aitolians 'a large *ethnos* living in unwalled villages'. From at least the middle of the seventh century[2] the Macedonians had been ruled by kings, whose relationship to their subjects was basically feudal, resting on loyalty and consent: they ruled 'by law and not by force', as Arrian says (*Anab*. iv.11.6); and from Amyntas' early fourth-century alliance with the Chalcidians (Tod 111, quoted in full at p. 205) we see that 'the Macedonians' are interchangeable with 'Amyntas', and this shows that the Macedonian monarchy was not an unlimited autocracy. As to feudalism, an inscription (Syll.[3] 332) shows Philip II giving away a hereditary lease, and Greek city land at Amphipolis was doled out to Macedonians (Arrian *Indike* xviii, cp. Tod 150). As with the Persian kings, military service was expected in return. Arrian (*Anab*. i.16.5) mentions grants of freedom from 'land tax, personal service, and other dues', all probably very old institutions, though the phraseology of Arrian's source looks early hellenistic.

The fifth-century kings of Macedon, and indeed those of the fourth century till Philip acceded in 359, imported Greek culture —Pindar wrote a poem for Alexander I in the 490s — while keeping at spear's length the Greeks who were actually manufacturing that culture. Alexander I Philhellene had medised (below) in the Persian Wars; philhellenism, not for the last time, does not imply letting Greeks have their way politically. The Macedonian royal house was deeply involved with Persia: Gygaia, the sister of Alexander I, was given in marriage to a Persian called Boubares, and they lived off the revenues of a Phrygian city given them by the Persian king (Hdt. viii.136). This must have happened about the middle of the fifth century.

When Xerxes invaded, Herodotus has nothing to say about resistance by Macedon, and this is one of the strongest arguments for thinking they medised. In the 470s Alexander gave refuge to Themistokles when he was on the run to Persia, a tangibly anti-Athenian act. Alexander was probably right to think, as he evidently did, that he would be better off if Persia rather than Athens ruled the Aegean: within a decade of the establishment of the Delian League, Athens began the expansion in the north, and the attempt to settle Amphipolis, on the River Struma, which at certain times in the next century and a half dominated her foreign policy to the exclusion of all else (Thuc. iv.102; Σ Aischin. ii.31). In perhaps 478 Alexander had captured the so-called Nine Ways near Amphipolis, probably an attempt to counter the Athenian conquest of Eion, also near the mouth of the Struma (p. 32). But Alexander could not hold it against the Edoni, local tribesmen, which may have given the Athenians the idea that they could move in and plant a colony (465). The Athenian attempt was a fiasco, 10,000 Athenians were killed[3] and Athens turned to Egypt and Sicily where she was sure of at least some local support. Not till the early 430s, at the acme of her power, did she manage to establish a presence at Amphipolis, and its capture by the Spartan Brasidas in 424 was one of her most damaging losses in the Archidamian War, the responsibility, if not the fault, lying at the door of the historian Thucydides, who was commanding in the area.

Why did the place matter so much? One reason was timber; triremes need many different kinds of wood,[4] and plenty of it (for Greek anxiety on this score see Tod 111, quoted on p. 205). Attica could not satisfy the needs of a standing navy, and inscriptions show that Athens got cypresses from Knidos in Asia and Karpathos in the Dodecanese (Tod 110, now known to be fifth-century not fourth). But Thucydides (iv.108) also mentions 'other sources of revenue' from Amphipolis, which may include corn as well as money. Thucydides also underlines the strategic importance of the place: an enemy like Sparta, if she held Amphipolis, could strike at Athens' north Aegean allies, provided that Thessaly allowed a safe passage to the Struma area. And if the north Aegean panel of tribute-paying allies succumbed to attack or subversion, the Hellespontine corn-route would be at risk.

Alexander's interests and those of Athens were thus opposed (which did not stop him from minting copiously in coinage designed for easy trade with Athens),[5] and the opposition was inherited by every Macedonian king till Philip, who ended it by seizing Amphipolis for good. But no king of Macedon before Philip could afford to provoke Athens to outright invasion. That meant that Macedon had to flirt from time to time with Sparta or whoever looked the strongest counterweight to Athens after Persia had recoiled from the Aegean in the mid-fifth century. But Sparta needed Amphipolis too, as the doorway to the north Aegean, Thrace and eventually the Hellespont, cp. above. And Sparta, who normally had no fleet of her own and no naval tradition, could not attack any other Athenian tribute-district *except* the 'Thraceward Region'. So Spartans at Amphipolis were not much more attractive from the Macedonian angle than Athenians. Therefore Athens and Sparta must be played against each other, and their troops preferably used, not against *each other* (which might end in a definite result), but against Macedon's frontier enemies.

For it is a prime fact about classical Macedon, and one that explains why so large and rich a country counted for so little until so late, that she was a frontier province of the Greek world; beyond lay Illyrians, Dardanians and Thracians, and beyond *them* the drifting pre-Celtic populations of central Europe, undisciplined fighters but unlimited in manpower. There is some justice in the way Macedon, who had thanklessly insulated Greek culture from these destructive outsiders

and nomads for so long, should finally, in the persons of Philip and
Alexander, have taken over that culture by diplomacy and conquest.

The great practitioner of the 'balancing strategy' was Alexander I's
successor Perdikkas, who ruled *c*.452–413. He changed sides nine
times in his reign. His attitudes are best illustrated by this typical
passage from Thucydides (iv.83: 424 BC; the details of the
diplomacy are irrelevant):

> Then, too, the envoys whom Perdikkas had sent to Sparta had
> given the impression, while they were there, that he would bring
> into the Spartan alliance a great number of the places on his
> borders; and on the basis of this, Brasidas thought himself
> entitled to consider the wider implications in dealing with
> Arrhabaios. Perdikkas, on the other hand, replied that he had
> not brought Brasidas there to act as an arbitrator in the
> differences that existed between him and Arrhabaios; his
> function was simply to destroy those enemies whom he,
> Perdikkas, pointed out.

Perdikkas' diplomacy was subtler than just pitting Athens against
Sparta and conversely: before the great Peloponnesian War broke
out he shrewdly persuaded the Greek cities near Olynthus to
coalesce into a federation; this was an act designed to weaken the
greater confederacy of the Delian League, since Athens' policy
(Thuc. iii.10–11) was always to keep her subject allies disunited. (See
i.58 for Olynthus.) Near the end of his reign Perdikkas may even have
made an alliance with Argos, who after the Peace of Nikias in 421
again starts to take an individual line on foreign policy.

The Macedonian king during the second half of the Peloponnesian
War was Archelaos, 413–399. Thucydides praises him highly in
general terms (ii.100), but Macedon was only a secondary theatre in
the Decelean and Ionian Wars, so that he does not figure very much in
the narratives of Thucydides or his continuator Xenophon. In 410
Athens under Theramenes helped him to capture Pydna (p. 175); and
for his part Archelaos allowed Athens to export timber and oars from
his kingdom (ML 91). The old balancing strategy of Perdikkas could,
it seems, be shelved now that Athens was so much weaker: Archelaos
could afford to give and receive real benefits.

Thucydides' praise of Archelaos, written not long before the latter's
death in 399, tells how he built forts and straight roads, and
reorganized the army, both infantry and cavalry arms, doing more for

it than all his eight predecessors put together. This is a rare example of Thucydides adopting the criterion of physical *erga* or constructions to measure a king's greatness, something Herodotus had done regularly (cp., for example, iii.60 on Samos). Archelaos' court indeed recalled some of the archaic tyrants, strong men and patrons of the arts like Polykrates himself. Archelaos gave a home to the Athenian poets Euripides and Agathon, and the painter Zeuxis executed animal mosaics at Pella, the new capital. Athenian pottery has also been found at Pella, for instance (*Arch. Reps*, 1981–2, p. 36) a vase depicting a contest between Athena and Poseidon. (The move from Aigai to the more central Pella looks forward to hellenistic times: cp. p. 211; also p. 48 on the way Sicily too simultaneously shows 'archaic' and 'hellenistic' features. It might be better to call the 'democratic', classical period of Greek history the anomaly.) At Vergina, later in the fourth century, the quality of recently discovered fresco-painting suggests an established tradition which might go back to Archelaos' time;[6] and continuity is also suggested by Pliny's statement (*Natural History* xxxv.62) that Zeuxis gave Archelaos a painting of Pan, who was to be patron deity of the third-century Macedonian king Antigonos Gonatas (see the coin illustrated as frontispiece to W. Tarn (1913) *Antigonos Gonatas*).

When Archelaos died he had begun an intervention in Thessaly which, had it been carried through, might have pre-empted Philip's operations in the 350s. As it was, Macedon was to endure, after 399, one of its most anarchic phases, a story which will be resumed in a later chapter.

Pindar wrote the first poem of his career (Pythian x) for a Thessalian patron in 498:

> Happy is Sparta; blessed is Thessaly.
> For from one ancestor has each its king,
> Sprung from great Herakles valiant in battle.

This opening[7] places Thessaly straight away in the centre of Dorian Greek culture; the Aleuad dynasty in Thessaly is treated as a branch of the house of Herakles, that is, it is grafted on to the Dorian Peloponnesian tree. By the order of words the poet even hints that Thessaly is *more* fortunate than her sister Sparta.

The rulers of Thessaly, then, resembled the Macedonians in asserting blood-ties with Dorian Greece. Thessaly's claim to be considered as Greek was racially no worse than Macedon's; Simonides had performed there before Pindar, and in 460 Thessaly was to produce an Olympic victor called Agias. *Polis* life was further advanced there — Pindar speaks of 'the cities' of the Aleuads — and Greek inscriptions go back to earlier dates (extant ones start *c*.550, L. H. Jeffery (1960) *Local Scripts of Archaic Greece*, p. 98, no. 1, a sacred law; and Pausanias (x.16) says that a statue dedicated by a Thessalian called Echekratidas was the first dedication ever made at Delphi). But, like Macedon, Thessaly was ruled 'dynastically'; a fourth-century monument to Daochos, ruler of Thessalian Pharsalos, says that he ruled 'by law not force' (Syll.[3] 274), a claim echoed exactly by Arrian about the kings of Macedon (see p. 75). There were, however, important differences: there was always a king, or claimant king, of Macedon; but there was not always a *tagos* of Thessaly (their word for ruler over the four great districts or *tetrarchies* of Thessaly.). Thus a fifth-century Thessalian inscription uses the phrase 'whether under a *tagia* or in an *atagia*', that is, whether there is or is not a *tagos* (Syll.[3] 55 and *ZPE*, 1980, p. 272).

At other times the great houses of the cities of Thessaly, the Echekratids of Pharsalos, the Skopads of Krannon, the Aleuads of Larisa, co-existed, feuded and intermarried: thus a sixth-century Skopas had a mother called Echekrateia, and Pausanias' Echekratidas (above) was from Larisa not Pharsalos. It is even arguable that we should just speak of a clannish 'Heraklid aristocracy' and not subdivide further.[8] At the bottom of the scale were the *penestai*, serfs. (But it has recently been pointed out that occasional use of these as cavalrymen means they cannot have been a wholly depressed class.[9]) In between was the cavalry-owning class proper, who took slowly but eventually to ideas which could be described as democracy (p. 83). A *demos* in the Athenian sense hardly existed.

Again and again in the fifth and fourth centuries the other Greek states tried to get a hold on Thessaly. Thessaly was important for several reasons. First, there is Thessaly's enormous fertility and wealth (Xen. *Hell.* vi.1 is the key text). Thessaly always struck visitors as awesomely rustic, an impression confirmed by small items like the title of the eponymous magistrate in Syll.[3] 55, the 'warden of the forests'. Second, a related point, Thessalian cavalry was the best in Greece: Xerxes had heard this (Hdt. vii.196) and held a gymkhana there to see for himself (actually the Thessalian horses were defeated by Xerxes' own). And from a fourth-century Athenian alliance (Tod

147) we see that 'cavalry' (*hippeis*) was the name of a class of Thessalian magistrate. (See further p. 266 for Thessalian cavalry in Alexander's time.) Third, control of Thessaly was a valuable asset strategically — it opened the way to the north and thus eventually the Hellespont, cp. p. 77 on Amphipolis; Xenophon (*Hell.* vi.1.11) shows awareness of the connection between Thessaly and Macedonian timber. Fourth, central Greece, and in particular Boiotia, was not well off for harbours, but Thessaly had Pagasai, the ancestor of the modern Volos, still a port of economic importance. Fifth, for historical reasons, whoever controlled Thessaly controlled the Delphic Amphictyony, an international committee which could impose fines for religious offences, usually trumped up, and generally exert a practical moral ascendancy of an enjoyable kind over the Greek community. Moreover, the Thessalians by tradition held the presidency of the Amphictyonic Council (Syll.[3] 175) which could be useful when it came to putting a motion.

Sparta's designs on Thessaly and central Greece date from the time of Kleomenes I of Sparta (in the late sixth and early fifth centuries): Pindar's bracketing of Sparta and Thessaly is not random, but may celebrate a deal between Kleomenes and the Thessalian Aleuads. Soon after the Persian Wars, as we saw on p. 24, King Leotychidas of Sparta led an expedition to Thessaly, and ended the *tageia* of the Aleuads; at about the same time, Plutarch says, there was most unusually a Spartan fleet at Pagasai, whose strategic importance we have just noticed, and the Spartans tried to get control of the Amphictyony (see p. 33; Plut. *Them.* xx). Then in 461 (p. 35), a year of decisive foreign policy choices all over Greece, Thessaly allied with Athens (Kimon called a son Thettalos, so perhaps he was responsible, though note Plut. *Kim.* xiv.4: Kimon says that *he* has never toadied to the Thessalians).

Who if anyone was tagos in Thessaly in these years? Probably as a result of Leotychidas' intervention of 476 the tageia had passed from the Aleuads, Pindar's hosts. The next tagos was probably Echekratidas of Pharsalos (see Thuc. i.111). But in between we should imagine a gap in the tageia: Plutarch (*On the Malice of Herodotus*, xxi) says that Leotychidas '*ended* the tyranny' (temporarily); and if Echekratidas was a Spartan nominee whose tageia went right back to 476 his Athenian alliance is harder to explain. Echekratidas' son Orestes (note the name Orestes, assertively anti-Dorian — it was the name of Agamemnon's son in a famous myth about pre-Dorian Greece — and perhaps a hit at Aleuad pretensions) was thrown out by 454 by an anti-Athenian (or simply anti-Echekratid, or even more simply anti-Orestes) party; Athens failed to restore him (Thuc. i.111). There was certainly plenty of anti-Athenian feeling, for some Thessalians fighting for Athens at the battle of Tanagra in 457 (p. 42) changed sides (Thuc. i.107; Diod. xi.79). But the alliance with Athens must have been renewed before the beginning of the Peloponnesian War when Thessalians fought on the Athenian side again (Thuc. ii.22). Sparta did not abandon her aims in Thessaly; in 426 the Spartans founded a colony at Herakleia in Trachis, which commanded the Thessalian border (p. 131); and later in this book we shall follow this thread of Spartan policy further still (see p. 153 and chapter 14, p. 186).

In the twenty-seven years *c.*440 to 413 the tagos was Daochos of Pharsalos.[10] But this was not a period of straightforward centralized rule. As we shall see, one of the effects of the Peloponnesian War was to intensify political activity and pamphleteering. We hear of a visit to late fifth-century Thessaly by Gorgias of Leontini, the celebrated orator and sophist, and of actual interference by Kritias (p. 83). Gorgias is quoted by Aristotle (*Pol.* 1275b) as sneering at 'manufactured Larisans', which implies that citizenship and power was being further extended. In 404 Xenophon (*Hell.* ii.3.4) records a defeat of the Larisans by Lykophron of Pherai, who 'wanted to rule all Thessaly'. This man is in fact what the archaic Greek world would have called a *tyrannos*. Thessaly had now reached the stage of development that the Isthmus states — Corinth, Megara, Sikyon — were at in about 650 BC. At that time Thessaly, like Boiotia and Sparta-Messenia, had an abundance of agricultural land, plenty of horses and few towns, that is, little opportunity for peasants to exchange grumbles and for subversive foreign notions to penetrate. Urbanization and tyranny are connected, and both are consequences of trade (which spreads ideas and causes dissatisfaction among the rich but politically excluded). Herodes (p. 305, n. 1) shows Thessaly *exporting* corn to her neighbours (xvi). Recent archaeological finds (see e.g. *Arch. Reps*, 1979–1980, p. 40: city defences at Pharsalos) show that the Thessalian wealth commented on by Plato (*Meno*) and Xenophon (*Hell.* vi.1), was being used by the fourth century to modernize Thessaly, and especially its *towns*. So the old-fashioned horse-rearing aristocrats, in their baronial castles at places like Amphana, had their rivals. Jason of Pherai, a descendant of

Lykophron (and called tyrant by Diodorus (xv.60.1) without equivocation) was certainly rich (Polyain. vi.1.2ff.). Lykophron's tyranny had a popular base; Xenophon (*Hell*. ii.3.36) relates how shortly before Lykophron came to power the Athenian Kritias tried to establish democracy and arm the penestai. The unrest looks like the precursor to Lykophron's seizure of power. Urbanization was the cause: the Thessalian cities do not start to mint coins till the fifth century and this implies the beginnings of political self-consciousness after prolonged backwardness.

This incident of late fifth-century history is not trivial: Lykophron's own tyranny did not last long; he was opposed by an old-style *dynastes* (Diod. xiv.82), Medius of Larisa. Lykophron turned to Sparta for help. But Medius and the anti-Spartan coalition in the Corinthian War of the 390s checked him (cp. chapter 14 for these events, specifically p. 187 for the expulsion of Spartan influence from Pharsalos, a Spartan garrison-point in the early 390s). But Jason, as we shall see, was a statesman of stature in the Greece of the 370s, dealing on equal terms with the Athens of the Second Athenian Confederacy and the Thebes of Epaminondas. He failed too, removed by assassination; but the failure goes deeper: Macedon succeeded where the tyrants of Thessaly did not, precisely because the polis life in Thessaly, which on the economic level made possible the rise of a tyranny, prevented one man from imposing his authority permanently like an Archelaos or a Philip; that was because on the political level the word polis implied what it had not implied in 650 BC: self-determination.

The geography of Boiotia might to a shallow observer seem to suit her for naval hegemony. That was the view of Ephorus at least, who said (F 119) that Boiotia, situated on three seas (probably he meant the Corinthian Gulf and the Euboian straits north and south of Chalkis) was made by nature for *thalassokratia*, rule of the sea. But a contour map will show how hard that would have been: the Corinthian Gulf ports, at the ends of deep valleys, have no mutual communication, and the eastern harbours are not much more accessible.[11] Mycenaean Boiotia had indeed been open to the greater world, much more so than in classical times: in the Thebes Museum there are stirrup jars proving commerce with Minoan Krete, and there is even some lapis lazuli from Afghanistan, evidence of a Hittite connection. Dark Age

Boiotian emigrants to Anatolia are responsible for Boiotian-type place-names like Erythrai and Mykale in Asia Minor (though the red, *erythros*, soil of Boiotian Erythrai and the red stone of the Ionian city make the name physically appropriate for both). In the historical period Hesiod's ancestors, emigrants from Boiotia, settled in Kyme in the Asiatic Aeolid. But Boiotia was not a major colonizing state because — and this is the fundamental fact about her — her soil was good, something which strikes any traveller who crosses Mt Kithairon into Boiotia from Attica, and there was plenty of it, especially in the two plains to north and south controlled by Orchomenos and Thebes respectively. The Oxyrhynchus Historian says that classical Boiotia could put out paper forces of 11,000 infantry and 1100 cavalry, and the high density of population which this implies for the fourth century gets some confirmation from a recent Boiotian land survey round the Teneric plain west of Thebes (*Arch. Reps*, 1981–2, p. 27). Polybius' comment on the low birth rate in late *third*-century Boiotia (xx.6) is in strong contrast.

The character of Boiotian political and social life was the consequence of these agricultural riches: insularity. However amenable to overseas influence Boiotia may have been in the prehistoric period (p. 83), classical, fourth-century and hellenistic Boiotia was in many respects deeply conservative and introverted. This is well-illustrated by the plentiful funerary monuments of hellenistic Boiotia, which retain features, such as the simple naming of the dead man without patronymic, which in other parts of the Greek world had long given way to more sophisticated formulae; and Boiotia retained her local script till the age of Epaminondas in the fourth century.[12] A similar conservatism marks the techniques used by Theban vase-painters, who avoid foreshortening and make no attempt to achieve three-dimensional realism, thus lagging behind Attic rivals.[13] It is also perhaps a sign of Boiotian isolation that there were no tyrants in archaic Boiotia, and that by the Persian Wars Thebes, then the first city of Boiotia, was controlled by a *dynasteia*, an irresponsible family government (Thuc. iii.62). Plataia, however, the main state south of the River Asopos, always looked towards Athens and her democracy: the connection actually went back to 519 BC when Kleomenes of Sparta told Plataia to attach herself to Athens (p. 20, and cp. p. 19 on Thespiai and *attikismos*).

With oligarchy went federalism (though the connection was not a necessary one, since in the fourth-century league we find *democratic* institutions). Federalism was Boiotia's great contribution to politics. Boiotia's reputation for philistinism was a joke with which other Greeks never got bored, but neither in the visual arts[14] nor in literature (Hesiod, Pindar) does the reality match the label 'Boiotian swine', a gibe recorded by Pindar himself. (One suspects that Boiotia's real misfortune in this respect was mere proximity to Athens.) And there were fine Boiotian historians: Kratippos and Daimachos of Plataia are only names, but the Oxyrhynchos Historian, who was surely a Boiotian, deserves in some ways to be put beside the Athenian Thucydides, whose continuator he was. Finally, in the late fifth century Epaminondas was a pupil of the Pythagorean Lysis of Tarentum.[15]

Federal Boiotia probably began in the sixth century (there are Boiotarchs at Hdt. ix.15 — 479 BC — whom there is no special reason to write off as an anachronism by the historian) and the league was never dissolved in the fifth,[16] despite the disgrace and demoralization caused by Theban medism in the Persian Wars, and despite a decade's loss of independence to Athens, in Boiotia as a whole, between 457 and 446. In the Persian Wars, however, the Boiotian League had evidently not ordered a general policy, because Plataia and Thespiai fought for the Greeks whereas Thebes medised, a stain she was never to wipe out. In 367 Pelopidas at Susa, asking for a peace treaty from Artaxerxes II, even reminded him of Thebes' traditional friendship with Persia.

Boiotian history from 479 till the First Peloponnesian War of 460–446 is not recoverable, though something can be done with the coins. Tanagra tried to replace Thebes as informal hegemon of the league in mid-century, but it was on Thebes that Sparta's plans centred in the First Peloponnesian War. The central Greek states, Doris and Phokis, quarrelled in 459 and Doris appealed to Sparta; with this stage Boiotia probably had nothing to do.[17] Sparta disciplined the Phokians, but found herself in a trap. The Spartan army moved into Boiotia, crossing to Tanagra in the east, dangerously near to Oropus and Attic territory. Athens could not ignore this, and an indecisive battle (Tanagra) followed by a decisive one (Oinophyta) gave Athens control of Boiotia till 446 (see p. 43 for her 'land empire' ambitions, and for Sparta's desire to set up Thebes as a counterweight to Athens).

Athens was expelled from Boiotia in 446, and the Boiotian League was perhaps reorganized now; in a valuable description the Oxyrhynchus Historian (chapter xvi) gives the system essentially as it was in the 440s, though for instance he takes account of Plataia's destruction in

427, after which Thebes took her votes. There were four councils in each of the constituent cities, membership of which was oligarchic in the sense that there was a property qualification (Ar. *Pol.* 1275a25), although the members got expenses for attending, something usually found in 'democratic' states. There were also four federal councils of 135 members, which were themselves sub-councils of a big federal council of 540; one of these sub-councils prepared the business for the others, a job which probably rotated. A citizen of, say, Thespiai was also a citizen of federal Boiotia, in something of the way that in Attica demesmen of, say, Sounion were also Athenians. Both systems gave a kind of proportional representation: the number of councillors which each Attic deme sent yearly to the Council of Five Hundred depended on its population (p. 112); and the number of federal councillors in Boiotia supplied by the cities depended on the size of the city and its territory. The allocation was achieved by a sophisticated system of groups or units comprising one or more cities.[18] So, Tanagra provided one Boiotarch or federal magistrate, and 60 councillors, Orchomenos two Boiotarchs and 120 federal councillors. After Thebes swallowed up Plataia in 427 she controlled four Boiotarchs and 240 councillors. Orchomenos was the only state in Boiotia other than Thebes which had any natural claim to rule all Boiotia; Tanagra's brief attempt was possible only in an unusual period when Thebes after her medism was in temporary discredit. The reasons for Orchomenos' special role were geographical: she controlled the northern plain and Thebes the southern; and also historical: Mycenaean Orchomenos had counted for at least as much as Thebes, and Orchomenos still had pretensions to lead Boiotia in the eighth century. But though Orchomenos was favoured in the 447 arrangements, it was Thebes and Thebes alone who issued coinage (an indication of political leadership within Boiotia) from then till the King's Peace of 386.

Despite some similarities with Kleisthenic Attica, Boiotia differed in that there was no great popular assembly made up of thousands; still more important, Theban control of Boiotia was not as obvious and inevitable as Athenian control of Attica. The Theban citadel, the Kadmeia, does not master or menace the Boiotian skyline like the Athenian Acropolis; and there were always places like Orchomenos and even Tanagra which envied Thebes' leadership. Equally, there were others such as Plataia or Thespiai which looked to Athens instead. Since the end of Athens' archaic war with Eleusis it would have been absurd for any deme of Attica to think of rivalling Athens.

Thebes, by contrast, even in the time of her hegemony, would have to destroy her rivals in order to claim to speak for Boiotia. However, it was precisely the lack of consensus about Thebes' — or anybody else's — leadership which in the fifth century led to federalism of so unusual and developed a kind, and which gave Boiotia the cohesion, and the manpower, to defeat Sparta at Leuktra in 371.

8 The eve of war

Control of Boiotia, and the central Greek land empire generally, was lost to Athens in 446 as part of Pericles' deal with Pleistoanax. But her command of the eastern seas was unimpaired, as is proved by the free hand she enjoyed in suppressing revolt on Samos in 440/39. Thucydides narrates the events of the next decade not as part of the 'Fifty Years', to which they strictly belong, but as part of the sequence of events which immediately caused the great Peloponnesian War. The Fifty Years, in the historian's causal scheme, were the underlying cause of the war, which Thucydides saw as the process of Athenian aggrandizement which struck fear into Sparta. This is the 'truest cause' of Thuc. i.23, a famous and deeply original statement which is the first conscious attempt to develop a theory of historical causation: 'The truest cause', he says, 'was one not much admitted at the time: it was the growth of Athenian power, which frightened the Spartans and forced them to war. But the publicly alleged reasons were as follows...' and Thucydides goes on to give them: quarrels between Athens and Corinth over Corcyra and Potidaia. Elsewhere in book i (chapter 118) Thucydides closes the *Fifty Years* by speaking of Athens' power 'rising to a peak plain for all to see', and of Athens 'encroaching on Sparta's allies'.

Even if we accept, as we should, that Thucydides is right about the 'truest cause' (and in the passage last quoted he comes near to running together true cause and alleged reasons, so we should not try to separate them too sharply), there is still a major problem: what weight should we give to the various instances of encroachment? Historians have quarrelled about that since Thucydides and perhaps before (for there is some reason to think that he was writing to correct what he saw as error, notably about the Megarian decree, for which see p. 91).

First, there is an episode which Thucydides mentions neither in the *Fifty Years* nor as an 'alleged reason' in book i; but it has a claim to be mentioned, because it is clear interference with the colonial empire of

Sparta's ally Corinth. It is the alliance made with Akarnania by the Athenian general Phormio, mentioned (though not dated: see p. 6) by Thucydides in a backward-looking reference (ii.68) when describing routine operations of the year 429 BC. Now Akarnania, in north-west Greece, was a Corinthian colony which kept close links with the mother city: the Akarnanians put the winged horse Pegasus, the emblem of Corinth, on their coins in the fifth century. Phormio's alliance was hardly, given the distance of Akarnania from Athens, the considered policy of the Athenian Assembly — the general just made it on the spot — and may have been mere opportunism, for Athens made many alliances which never came to anything and were not expected to. But it would be useful when Athens next got involved in Italy or Sicily, where another Corinthian colony, Syracuse, was growing richer and stronger. (It is also relevant to Athenian fears that, as Livy tells us under the year 431, Carthage now encroached in Sicily for the first time, iv.29.8 with R. M. Ogilvie (1965) *Commentary on Livy i–v*, Oxford.) So Phormio's action in making the alliance, though only a pawn penetration, was an offensive move against Corinth deep in her own, Adriatic, side of the colonial chess-board; and it was perhaps defensively conceived with an eye to a further-flung Corinthian colony, Syracuse. All this makes it unlikely that the alliance ante-dated 440, when Corinth, for whatever reason, voted *against* war with Athens over Samos (p. 46), i.e. when surface relations were still good. But equally, the alliance should not be dated too late in the 430s, because then it would have cried out for mention at some point in the book i narrative, where the immediate 'alleged reasons' for the war are rehearsed at length. A date c.439 or 438 is best.

Later in the 430s Athens renewed alliances with two other western cities, Leontini and Rhegion (ML 63 and 64 = Fornara 124–5, cp. p. 56 for the original alliances). Thucydides was right (ii.7 and ML, p. 173) to imply that in the west, sides *had already* been taken when the war broke out.

Corinth's north-western interests were threatened more directly by the affair of Corcyra, which is one of the two 'alleged reasons' which Thucydides does describe fully. A quarrel between Corcyra, a daughter-city of Corinth, and Epidamnos, a daughter-city of Corcyra herself, led to the first open clash, the battle of Sybota, between Athenian and Peloponnesian League ships (433): Epidamnos had appealed over the head of Corcyra to the 'grandmother' Corinth, while Corcyra asked for, and got, help from Athens. The Corinthians sent a delegation to Athens to try to prevent the second of these appeals from succeeding. One of their complaints against Corcyra is specially revealing: the Corcyreans, they say, 'do not pay us appropriate respect as their mother-city'. This theme, the ties between city and colony, and the ways they were reinforced, weakened or broken in the great war, is important to Thucydides, and it is not accidental that it occurs thus early.

The second and other 'alleged reason' was to do with Potidaia, another Corinthian colony, this time in northern Greece, on the westernmost claw of the crab-like Chalcidic peninsula. Again, Corinthian control was tight: Corinth sent out a magistrate annually to govern Potidaia, an *epidamiourgos* (Thuc. i.56). (This very Roman-looking institution has another Dorian parallel, the man sent by Sparta every year to govern the offshore island of Kythera. The office was called *Kytherodikes*.) Despite this, Potidaia paid tribute to Athens, who in 433/2 demanded that Potidaia should send home the Corinthian magistrates and pull down part of her walls. Corinth sent help to Potidaia, the Athenians sent a besieging force, and so Corinth and Athens clashed for the second time.

Thucydides does not tell us all we need to know about these encroachments on Peloponnesian League allies, and there are other encroachments which he scarcely mentions at all. (We have seen one, the Akarnanian alliance. Others are discussed below.) Still on the first of these two categories, more can be said about Potidaia from the Athenian Tribute Lists. Athens raised Potidaia's tribute from six to fifteen talents as early as the period 438–434,[1] which means that she was pressurizing Potidaia ('encroaching' on allies of the Peloponnesians) much earlier than Thucydides implies.

Then, in the category of encroachments which Thucydides barely mentions, there is Aigina. One of the complaints against Athens was that Aigina 'was not autonomous as the treaty required' (Thuc. i.67.2). What treaty was this? Perhaps it was the Thirty Years Peace of 446; or perhaps there was a special arrangement with Aigina, who may have had her autonomy guaranteed individually, though she certainly paid tribute to Athens. Tribute payment could be compatible with autonomy, because 'autonomous but tribute-paying' is to be the status of some cities in the north after the Peace of Nikias (Thuc. v.18). The infringement of Aiginetan autonomy perhaps affected their legal rights — they may have been forced to bring cases to be heard at Athens. But anyway this looks like a grievance of standing.

Most important was Megara. Thucydides' reticence about the decrees passed against Megara in the 430s, perhaps early in the decade, is one of his most famous silences, comparable to his omission of the peace of Kallias. His silence about Megara is not complete: Pericles is described as telling the Athenians that they will not be going to war over a trifle, if they refuse to rescind the Megarian decree as the Spartans demand. It is, he says, a 'test of your resolution' (i.140). Again, the Corinthians (i.42) urge the Athenians to remove the 'previously existing suspicion on account of the Megarians', where 'previously'[2] is more likely to refer to the early 430s than to Megarian behaviour *c.*460, which was not something Athens could do much about now. (See also the passages cited below.)

The Megarian decree, passed in ostensible punishment for the cultivation of some sacred land, barred the Megarians from the *agora* (the social, political and commercial meeting place of Athens) and from the harbours of the Athenian Empire (Plut. *Per.* xxix; Thuc. i.67; 139). This punishment has an obvious appropriateness to the crime, because Plato in the *Laws* (871a) recommends that murderers, another category of 'polluted' offender, be excluded from the 'harbour and the agora', and in Athens itself boundary stones saying 'I am the boundary of the agora' demarcate the area not to be entered by the polluted. This does not,[3] however, prove that the exclusive or even the main purpose of the decree was religious, i.e. not political or economic. First, there is a point of logic: sanctions may take a religious form but have a political or economic purpose and effect. Second, the Plato analogy needs looking at more closely. True, the occurrence of the phrase about 'harbours and agora' is striking, but what Plato says is that the murderers should not be allowed to *pollute* the *temples* or the agora or harbours, etc. That is, the religious aspect is specifically stressed by Plato, much more so than any version of the Megarian decree; if the Megarian exclusion was primarily religious, it is very strange that the exclusion does not extend to the obvious *religious* meeting-places and events, that is temples and sacrifices. (As in inscriptions, e.g. Syll.[3] 1016 from fourth-century BC Iasos in Karia: 'let him be excluded from the sacred place'.) Third, though the agora certainly *has* a religious aspect — Kleisthenes probably purified it and banned burials there when he gave it new political importance[4] — it also, and equally certainly, was a place where ordinary commerce was carried on, thus Demosthenes (xviii.169) mentions the wicker booths set up for trading there. Fourth, the evidence from

Aristophanes' play the *Acharnians*, performed in 425 (lines 515ff.) is overwhelming: an elaborate parody of the Megarian decree is *immediately* followed by the statement that the Megarians were starving slowly. It is perverse to dissociate the two passages conceptually and insist that the starvation refers to routine annual invasions of the Megarid. Finally, it is no use trying to escape by saying that ancient trade was not carried out by the nationals of ancient states but by non-citizens, so the Megarian decree cannot have injured Megarian trade: the generalization about ancient trade should be corrected to read 'ancient *Athenian* trade', which is what nearly all our information is about. Nor can we say that Megarians could have got nationals of other states to act as middlemen. Who would wish to carry, or to buy, polluted goods? Certainly not the pious Spartans.

So the Megarian decrees had economic effects, and were surely intended to. Of course the Athenians took good care not to be wrongfooted morally: hence a religious aspect was needed for the punishment of an ostensibly religious offence. After all *spondai*, meaning literally libations, was the Greek word for treaties, like the Thirty Years Peace, which would have been broken by unprovoked coercion of Megara. But the Megarian decrees were seen, with justification, as Athenian aggression, and Corinth, remembering the 460s, must have thought Athens was up to her old intrigues. What Athens presumably wanted, for pollution *could* be got rid of, was for the Megarians to vow an expensive building or pay some humiliatingly large fine (thus acknowledging Athenian ascendancy), for the 'chief malefactors', i.e. the anti-Athenians, to be hounded out, and for Megara to be quietly absorbed into Athens' sphere of influence.

The final items indicating Athenian warlike preparations rather earlier than Thucydides implies are the Athenian decrees moved by Kallias (ML 58) which show that the temple treasures of the demes were moved from exposed positions in Attica to the Athenian Acropolis; the decree is as early as 434.

It seems then that for much of the 430s war looked imminent, and to that extent Thucydides, who under-reports the earlier stirrings and expansion, should be corrected. But his general picture of Athenian expansion, forcing the Spartans to war, stands.

The Spartans subsequently felt guilt at having started the war: there is a revealing sentence in Thucydides (vii.18) which says that they came to think they had lost the war of 431–421 because 'they themselves had sinned' when the Thebans attacked Plataia when the 'libations' were still in force. Certainly the Athenians were technically justified in accepting the neutral Corcyra as an ally, despite Corinthian claims that the Thirty Years Peace provisions about neutrals did not envisage their being enrolled by one side to the intended detriment of the other (as if international treaties usually have anything to say about the future state of mind of the signatories! See i.35, 40). To express the awkwardness of the Spartan position Thucydides uses awkward language (i.88): the Spartans voted, he says, that the 'libations' had been broken and took a decision for war not so much because they were persuaded by the arguments of their allies as because they were afraid of the growth of Athenian power. This is strictly illogical: the growth of Athenian power could never be a reason why the 'libations' had been broken. What Thucydides means is that the Spartans were immediately responsible for the breaking of the treaty/libations — but that Athenian dynamism was behind it all.

9 Corinth

When Thucydides spoke of the allies who urged Sparta to go to war, he was thinking of Corinth above all. Our evidence for the organization and internal politics of classical Corinth is meagre, and out of proportion to the city's importance. There are good reasons for this: first, Corinth was an oligarchy, and in oligarchies, unlike democracies such as Athens after 462, magistrates are not accountable to the same extent and there is less need to put up inscriptions. Second, Corinth was sacked by Lucius Mummius in 146 BC with Roman thoroughness, not to rise again for a century. Perhaps inscriptions were among the casualties. (It may also be relevant that Corinth, as recent finds show, used lead for public inscriptions at early dates: *Arch. Reps*, 1975–6, p.8. Lead is more easily reused than stone, and texts more easily effaced.) Third, and less depressing than the first two, Corinth is not completely excavated (most of what the modern visitor sees is Roman) and there is still hope that the classical agora may produce evidence of the kind we want; though to get it, the excavators (the American School in Athens) will need permission to dig under the main square of the modern town. For the moment, classical Corinth, like archaic Chalkis and for the same reasons, has much to say but stays silent. Fourth and last, Corinth inspired little history-writing: Aristotle's *Constitution of the Corinthians* does not survive, nor does Theopompus' *Korinthiakos* (T 48); apart from that there are only hellenistic prose versions of the archaic Corinthian poetry of Eumelos, and hellenistic treatises on the Isthmian games, which were held nearby. If Pindar in the Thirteenth Olympian meant anything at all by saying that the Muses breathed sweetly over Corinth, he was not referring to his own day but perhaps to that of the Corinthian Arion who invented the dithyramb. Corinthian philistinism, more real though less notorious than Theban, is part of something deeper and more disturbing: she had no ideology to offer, nothing that is like Athenian *paideia* or Spartan *agoge*, 'culture' and 'discipline' respectively. Actually the charge of lacking those two qualities was levelled against *Thebes* (by Ephorus: see F 119), but even Thebes had a decade of hegemony; Corinth never. This is not fortuitous.

Corinth was always, however, important. This importance was partly strategic: by walling off the Isthmus (land narrows) of Corinth, as was done in the Persian Wars and again in the hellenistic period, the Peloponnese could be turned into an island, or a tortoise with its head tucked in, as the Roman commander Flamininus put it. Polybius (xviii.11) called Corinth and Chalkis the handcuffs of Greece, and the importance of Corinth to Macedon, which this comparison indicates, goes back to 338 when Philip II made Corinth the physical centre of his new Greek league (though whether the meeting-chamber has been identified on the ground is disputed). There were military reasons, too, for Julius Caesar's choice of refounded Corinth as the site of a colony and the Roman capital of Greece, *colonia laus Julia Corinthi*: even in Caesar's day, the Roman colonies had military or policing functions. Corinth controlled both the north-south route joining the Peloponnese to central Greece and the east-west haulage passage[1] on the site of the modern Corinthian Canal. Corinth's peculiar position created *two* prosperous harbours, Lechaion in the west and Kenchreai in the east. A further strategic asset was the colossal citadel, the Akrokorinth, which is very hard to take by storm: its most famous capture, by Aratos of Sikyon in the third century, involved treachery. The Akrokorinth dominates the Isthmus region, and it is one reason why Aratos' home city of Sikyon just west of Corinth was never more than a second-rate power. As Plutarch says (*Aratos* xvi) of the Akrokorinth: 'it hinders and cuts off all the country south of the Isthmus from intercourse, transits, and the carrying on of military expeditions by land and sea, and makes him who controls the place with a garrison sole lord of Greece.'[2] The Akrokorinth has its own water supply, the Peirene spring, which meant that the inhabitants could stand long sieges.

All this makes it hard to see why Mycenaean Corinth was of no consequence; the answer is probably just that, unlike Attica and the Argolid, it lay off the main routes of Mycenaean penetration. But by Homeric, i.e. Dark Age, times its natural epithet was already 'the wealthy', as Thucydides noticed (i.13). Partly this was the result of Corinthian trade and craftsmanship; Herodotus (ii.167) says that the Corinthians despised craftsmen less than did other Greeks (note the negative formulation) and a recent survey of Corinthian territory confirms the exceptional variety of goods manufactured there.[3] Corinth was also famously cosmopolitan: its prostitutes gave it a reputation somewhere between nineteenth-century Paris and Post-Second World War Saigon: 'not everybody has the wealth to go to Corinth' the proverb said, and those who did go there might be unlucky and take away more than pleasant memories, judging from the terracotta penises still visible along with models of other parts of the body in the Corinth Museum — dedications by sufferers from venereal disease (see also *AJA*, 1941, 442f.).

It is, however, a mistake to pigeon-hole Corinth as just a city of traders, craftsmen and luxury. On the contrary Corinth was very rich in agricultural land, as no one who has climbed to the top of the Akrokorinth can doubt. The old quarrel between Corinth and Megara was about borders; by the end of the archaic period Corinth had absorbed most of this frontier zone of good arable land, so that Strabo (380) can say of Krommyon, which is halfway to Megara, that it 'was once Megarian but is now Corinthian'. Nor was this a purely archaic problem: the border trouble with Megara in the 460s may reflect population pressure in the Corinthia.[4] A further sign of the importance of agriculture to Corinth is the quantity of fertility offerings to Demeter the corn-goddess — again these can be seen in the Corinth Museum.

The politics of Corinth reflect the prosperity of its agriculture and commerce. The Corinthians celebrated the fall of the Bacchiad tyrants in the sixth century by building the great temple of Apollo — and also by reorganizing and strengthening their tribal system. The Corinthia, the territory of Corinth, was by now large: it included the lonely cul-de-sac of Perachora in the north, as well as the territory towards Megara in the north-west, towards Sikyon in the west and Kleonai to the south. The new system is a blend of tribal and geographical: there are now eight tribes and three geographical groupings (perhaps Corinth city, the northern districts of Perachora and the Megarian border, and the southward extension towards Kleonai and Argos).[5] In Kleisthenic Athens and in the Cyrene of Demonax (see p. 59), as also in the Rome of Servius Tullius, such tribal changes, compromises between the criteria of family descent and physical residence, were a way of coping with new claimants to citizenship; and perhaps the same is true of Corinth, which needed to enfranchise immigrant craftsmen and the population of freshly incorporated and conquered areas, thus strengthening the citizen body. (The military aspect of Kleisthenic-type changes should never be forgotten.) It is remarkable that this reform, which is so like that at democratic Athens, was the work of *oligarchs*, showing that there is nothing *distinctively* democratic about Kleisthenes' tribal changes, although Herodotus says Kleisthenes introduced the tribes and the democracy, in that order (vi.131).

What Athens and Corinth had in common was perhaps the immigrant craftsmen who had been drawn to the cities in the salad days of their respective tyrannies. But Corinth went oligarchic, Athens democratic. Why was this? Perhaps Sparta, who helped to eject the Cypselids, and tended to favour oligarchies, was better able to influence Corinth, which was closer than Athens; or perhaps the explanation is just that 506 is much later than 585 when the Cypselids fell. Classical Corinth possessed some of the ingredients of Athenian-type democracy: she had what for Athens was a great catalyst of naval democracy, a colonial empire (in the north-west and north-east), comparable to Athens' possessions before 500 at Sigeion, the Chersonese and on Euboia at Chalkis. Her geographical position, like Athens', was accessible to outside influences and radical thinking. She even had, by the classical period, Long Walls running down to Lechaion harbour, like those which joined Athens to Piraeus; and she had a decent-sized navy: the Corinthians lent twenty ships to Athens before the Persian Wars and contributed forty in the Persian Wars themselves, and they had one hundred and twenty ships at Sybota (p. 89). But by the mid-fifth century the oligarchs' grip was tight.

That did not change till the Peloponnesian War, one effect of which was to erode the Corinthian middle class.[6] A recent archaeological find is illuminating: one Corinthian fishmonger, whose Carthaginian amphoras and exotic western Mediterranean merchandise (the scales of the fish can be identified) show that his was a high-grade shop, went out of business in the early years of the Peloponnesian War, perhaps as a result of the Athenian blockade of the Corinthian gulf (*Arch. Reps*, 1978–9, p.10). Corinth suffered badly from the war: in a naval building programme in 413 BC she provides only fifteen ships (to which should perhaps be added another twenty-five operating in the Corinthian Gulf).[7] The political result was longer delayed, but equally startling: in the 390s, by an amalgamation unthinkable half a century before, Corinth merged with Argos to form a single, *democratic*, anti-Spartan state. Corinth, which had done so much to bring on the war by urging on Sparta, was more damaged by it, and more permanently, than any other city.

10 Sparta

At the beginning of the Peloponnesian War the Greek world looked to Sparta as liberator (Thuc. ii.8).

Sparta, a small city on the River Eurotas (see map 1), at this time controlled a larger continuous stretch of land than any other single Greek city: in fact, most of the southern Peloponnese. Lakonia proper, the territory of the city of 'Lakedaimon' (the correct name throughout antiquity for what only the poets called 'Sparta'), included the large and fertile district between the Parnon mountain range to the east and that of Taygetos to the west. But since the eighth century the Spartans had also ruled Messenia, the western half of the southern Peloponnese, beyond Taygetos, an even larger and more fertile district. The subjugated population of Messenia tilled the land as serfs, *helots*. The helots are directly responsible for Spartan military supremacy in Greece: a great revolt (the Second Messenian War) in the seventh century caused Sparta to impose on her citizens a strict military discipline, the *agoge*. This gave her primacy in the Peloponnese and a reputation for invincibility beyond: in Diodorus of Sicily's universal history, only three of the remarkable human phenomena of Greek history are regularly called invincible, *aniketos*. They are Alexander the Great; the Silver Shields (a Macedonian *corps d'élite* of the early hellenistic period); and the Spartans up to the date of their defeat at the hands of the Thebans at Leuktra in 371. The other word habitually used by Diodorus (reflecting Ephorus; cp. ML 95 and Lys. xxxiii.7) for pre-Leuktra Sparta as a physical entity is *aporthetos*, unravaged, and that was true (and most unusual for a Greek *polis*). This was partly thanks to Sparta's protected geographical position. Invincible and unravaged, Sparta was the natural power to be invoked by the Greek world as liberator in 431.

'Liberator' was a role familiar to her: in the sixth century she had posed as a political giant-killer, putting down tyrannies in mainland Greece and even on the islands. She did not abandon this policy even after the debacle at Athens, when her deposition of the anti-Spartan[1]

Pisistratids in 510 resulted in a regime even more vigorously hostile to herself, which she tried and failed to overthrow in its turn. The evidence for the continuance of the policy into the fifth century comes from Thessaly, where Leotychidas had put down the *tagos* in the 470s (p. 81). The interventions of Sparta outside her borders after the 470s were erratic: she seems not to be able to make her mind up whether to be an imperialist power or to be Little Sparta. One reason for this was the fear of revolt by her helots (p. 21), who certainly outnumbered full Spartan citizens many times over. Thucydides, an acute social historian when he wants to be, remarks that 'most of the dealings between the Spartans and their helots were of a precautionary character' (iv.80), and tells a suitably laconic story of two thousand specially manly helots who were garlanded and led round the temples as if they were about to be given their freedom; *they were never seen again and nobody knew what happened to them.* Xenophon's story of the revolt of Kinadon (*Hell.* iii.3) is more detailed but hardly more chilling. He describes a conspiracy in the early 390s of helots, who together with the other inferior classes outnumber the full Spartan citizens, at a casual count in the agora, by four thousand to forty. This revolt was suppressed with total ruthlessness. One phrase of Xenophon's, about the helots wanting to 'eat the Spartiates raw', is no less memorable for being an echo of Homer (*Iliad* iv.35).

The link between cautiousness in foreign policy[2] and fear of helots is manpower, dealt with more fully on pp. 21ff. Adventurous Spartan generals — Kleomenes, Pausanias the Regent, Brasidas, Lysander — tried to get extra soldiers from the nearest source, their own country's helots. But the home government always resisted this simple but dangerous solution, passing up chances to expand territorially if that meant the helots could stab them in the back — or eat them raw. Roman experience suggests that these fears were rational: one cause of the Social War of 91–88 BC was Roman military dependence on her allies; this dependence was not recognized and rewarded by extra privileges such as citizenship, so the allies turned their fighting experience against Rome herself. Sparta did, theoretically, have categories of enfranchised helots, *neodamodeis* (and there were other halfway groups, p. 221). But they were few. Anyway such selective enfranchisement was itself no more than a cynical way of heading off despair, what modern political scientists call 'repressive tolerance'.

Rome, it has been said, suffered from a 'neurosis of fear' in her external relations.[3] The same could be said of Sparta and her internal relations (which as we saw affected external relations too). One form this took was xenophobia. This should not be exaggerated: the Spartan Lichas (Thuc. viii.39) has the Cyrenaean patronymic Arkesilas (cp. too p.189f. for Pharax and Lysander); and a remarkable passage in Herodotus (ix.76f.) makes Pausanias the Regent in 479 BC acknowledge a *xenia* (guest-friendship) with a man from Kos in the Dodecanese. What Pausanias actually says is that Hegetorides, the *xenos* in question, 'is bound to me by closer ties of friendship than anyone else in that part of the world'. This implies that Pausanias had other such *xeniai*. (This *xenia* directly anticipates that between the early fourth-century Spartan king Agesilaus and the Persian satrap Mausolus, not to mention the fusion policies of Alexander: see p. 193.) It is odd, and neatly illustrative of the contradiction in Spartan attitudes, that Herodotus can say of the Spartan-led Greeks in the same period that Samos 'seemed to them as far away as the Rock of Gibraltar', while telling elsewhere in his book of a Spartan, son of Archias, who was called Samios because of his father's Samian links (viii.132; iii.55). But by comparison with Athens, Sparta was certainly xenophobic. An excellent comparison of Athenian and Spartan habits and philosophy is given by Thucydides, in the mouth of Pericles (ii.39): 'our city is open to the world, and we have no periodical deportations in order to prevent people observing or finding out secrets which might be of military advantage to the enemy.' Thucydides writes with feeling: he complains in his own person in book v (68) of the secrecy with which the Spartans conduct their affairs, which meant that no one knew how many Spartans there were at the first battle of Mantinea in 418.

Whether to use or repress helots, then, was one Spartan dilemma, which helps explain the vicissitudes of Spartan foreign policy. But the Peloponnesian War, and the propaganda of liberation, created another more special dilemma. 'Liberation' meant taking the initiative, breaking up the Athenian Empire.[4] But that would cost money. Spartan finances look pathetically primitive: an inscription (ML 67 = Forn. 132: 390s), recording contributions to the Spartan war fund, includes gifts of *raisins*: no six-thousand-talent reserve, or regular allied tribute such as Pericles boasts of in Thucydides' narrative (ii.13). Moreover, since Sparta depended on personal service from her allies, she had to consult them constantly, whereas

Athens had a freer hand, because she had stopped holding congresses of *her* allies well before the beginning of the war. That Spartan deference to allied feeling was indeed a matter of necessity not sentiment is shown by her peace proposals to Athens in 425: in Thucydides' account (iv.20) the Spartans say that if Athens and Sparta do a deal the rest of Greece will do them honour. This is diplomatic language for joint hegemony and a proposed sellout of the Peloponnesian League.

Eventually (Xen. *Hell.* v.2.21) the Spartans did copy Athens and go over to a system of contributions of money not men; but that was in the 370s. In the fifth century there was for a Greek state only one major source of income apart from taxing one's own citizens or allies: Persia. And this is where the special dilemma comes in: Persian finance might be available for the defeating of Athens, but not for the 'liberation' which Sparta's allies wanted, because the liberation envisaged included the freedom of the Greeks in the Persian king's Asia.[5] This explains the Persian king's response to Spartan requests for financial help in the 420s, that he could not understand what they wanted. He understood perfectly well, but was waiting for them to make up their minds whether they wanted money or a claim to Asia Minor. They could not have both. So Sparta could not please both her allies and Persia, yet she needed them both. Eventually she plumped for Persian help, but at a time (412) when her potential critics inside the league were less effective (cp. p. 97 on Corinth). Even so, she returned to Asia in the 390s, proving Alcibiades right (viii.46) when he told the satrap Tissaphernes that Sparta would be a less convenient ally than Athens if and when the war ended, because Sparta comes as a liberator. Athens by contrast was an unblushing imperialist and would respect Persia's imperialist ambitions. It is hard to believe that Thucydides when he wrote these words had not lived to see at least the Spartan Derkyllidas' Asian expedition of 400.

Here then were two of the disabilities, helot problems and money problems, produced by the Spartan system. A third disability lay in her constitution: Sparta had no satisfactory apparatus for decision-making and the formulation of strategy. The government of classical Sparta had most of the disadvantages of monarchy, oligarchy and democracy. The kings (there were two of them) were exposed to the standard temptations of autocratic power without the constitutional invulnerability which such power generally confers: men like Kleomenes I and Pausanias the Regent were statesmen of stature, and the hostile literary tradition should be adjusted accordingly; but their private tastes and temperaments certainly helped cause their fall, if only by giving ammunition to their critics. Nor did the kingship make for singleminded action on the battlefield: Sparta found ways of getting round the more obvious difficulties of dual command, but a king could always be brought to book by the oligarchic element (the *gerousia* or council of elders, which was responsible for political trials) or by the democratic — the Assembly, which could fine a king and limit his powers (cp. p. 161 for Agis in 418). The gerousia had the oligarchic failing that it was accountable to nobody, and its supposedly judicial decisions were sometimes (as e.g. over King Pausanias in 403, p. 183) politically warped. The Assembly, which was a kind of democracy, though a rather small, special and elite one, was liable to the bad democratic habit of rapidly overturning its own or its advisers' decisions: so for instance Thucydides (vi.89ff.) implies that a single speech by Alcibiades was enough to make the Assembly reverse a decision not to help Syracuse in 414. The right to hear ambassadors, and other foreign speakers like Alcibiades, was an important prerogative of the Assembly, and it is here that Spartan foreign policy must have taken some of the dramatic about-turns attested in the classical period — though technically the Assembly could only decide and not debate (Ar. *Pol.* 1273); debate was supposed to be reserved for the gerousia which very occasionally is found actually debating, as in the Hetoimaridas Debate of the 470s (see p. 23).

The five *ephors*, magistrates, gave a preliminary hearing to ambassadors too, and had some powers of *euthuna* (review of conduct engaged in by officers of state). But being annual they would be open to reprisals if they threw their weight around too much.[6]

From all this it should be clear that the conduct of war and foreign policy left too much to chance and personal axe-grinding. Aristotle called the kings 'hereditary generals' and an incompetent or even average king could do a lot of damage in a short while — like Kleombrotos who lost the decisive battle of Leuktra in 371 but was not catastrophically inept. Kings who showed independence risked the fate of Pleistoanax, exiled in 446 — most unfairly, because Sparta ratified his provisional settlement with Athens, which became the Thirty Years Peace (p. 46). The number of kings who came to grief in the fifth century is staggeringly high,[7] and this must have had a deterrent effect on kings who contemplated taking initiatives. (The two most famous Spartan 'initiatives' of the fourth century, Phoebidas' capture of the Theban citadel the Kadmeia, and Sphodrias' raid on the Piraeus, were both the work of competitively minded private individuals: pp. 207, 209. King Agesilaus' reaction in both cases was roughly 'Spartan interests, which are all that matters, mean that we need soldiers like that': Xen. *Hell.* v.2.32; 4.32. A very Spartan remark in its insular nationalism, but also a good comment on the conformity which was evidently far more usual than such reckless behaviour.)

As we shall see in chapter 13 the Greeks, even the militarily professional Spartans, did not develop a system comparable to the Roman *imperium militiae* or the dictatorship, which are both ways of relieving a commander from the normal political constraints on decisive action. Nor was the *agoge*, or rigid training system,[8] a good way for the kings, or anybody else, to learn initiative; great Spartan successes like the first battle of Mantinea (418) are put down to Spartan *gnome*, 'resolution', almost 'guts' — rather than leadership. There is little sign of experimentation in these spheres: Lysander's radical solution of an elective kingship got nowhere (p. 156) and the system of decarchies, young Spartan 'proconsuls' first heard of in 423 (Thuc. iv.132) when they are sent to govern cities in the north, became the most hated of Spartan institutions. As for war policy, Spartan censorship and secrecy could not conceal the rivalries and back-biting: jealousy, *phthonos*, felt for Brasidas by the 'leading men' of Sparta caused him to be starved of supplies (iv.108), and Pleistoanax's supporters waited twenty-six years to get him recalled in 420, which they did by bribing the oracle in the best archaic tradition. And Thucydides describes no sharper conflict than that between the aggressive Spartan Sthenelaidas (i.86) and the more cautious King Archidamus; for the supposedly more 'open' society of Athens he records only the views of Pericles and an anonymous delegation which does not contradict him.

It is not, then, surprising that Spartan indecision, so manifest in 446 and again in 440 over Samos (p. 46) should persist through the 430s. At the beginning of book iii, when describing the revolt of Lesbos in 427, Thucydides says that the Lesbians 'had been wanting to revolt even before the war, but the Spartans had been unwilling to receive them into alliance'. This shows a Spartan caution which is at variance with their previous bellicosity over Samos.

Sparta, for all these structural shortcomings, was a great power, and calculations about the outcome of the war, as well as delight that she was prepared to play the liberator, must have caused the Greek world generally to favour her over Athens (p. 99). Delphi is a good barometer: the oracle said (Thuc. i.118) that Apollo would fight on the side of the Spartans whether they invoked him or not. Discerning Greeks like Thucydides (i.10) knew that the relative splendour of the physical remains of Sparta and Athens was no index of their real strengths: suppose, he says, that the city of Sparta were to become deserted, future generations would find it hard to believe that the place, an old-fashioned, higgledy-piggledy collection of villages, was really as powerful as it was represented to be; whereas if the same were to happen to Athens, one would think that she was twice as powerful as she really was. The central fact about Sparta was indeed, as Xenophon saw (*Lakedaimonion Politeia* i.1), her way of life, her *epitedeumata*.[9] Pericles in the Funeral Oration was to try to meet this appeal head on, by drawing damaging contrasts with Athenian *epitedeumata*. Nevertheless we shall see that it is even more obviously true of Attica than of Sparta that it is her physical environment which determines her history.

11 Athens

When a city rules an empire, a historian with any curiosity will ask
whether the imperial city was specially geographically favoured from
the first. Rome, for instance, was sited on the first crossing of the
River Tiber, controlling the route from Latium to Etruria; Corinth
was a colonial power in the archaic period thanks largely to her
position on the Isthmus (p. 95); and explanations of the greatness of
Byzantium, from Polybius book iv to Gibbon, have begun with
geography. Sparta, as we saw, is an exception (in that human factors
— the *agoge* — were even more important than geographical), but
Athens is not. Her natural advantages were enormous.

In the first paragraph of the first chapter of his *Description of Greece*,
Pausanias mentions the silver mines of Attica, at Laurion in the
south-east. And Xenophon, at the beginning of his *Revenues*, lists
Attic silver — alongside Attica's natural produce and her central
position by land and sea — as one of her three great advantages. That
silver had helped to finance the fleet which won the battle of Salamis,
but it was important under the empire too: the building accounts of
the Propylaia, the ceremonial gateway to the Acropolis, dated 434/3,
record payments from the treasurers of a Laurion silver mine as well
as from the *Hellenotamiai*, the treasurers of the Delian League (ML 60
= Fornara 118B). This neatly sums up the sources of wealth, external
and internal, which paid for the great Acropolis building programme.
Still later, the Laurion mines surely helped to subsidize the
Peloponnesian War: they are neglected by Thucydides in his
statement of Athenian finances (ii.13), but they feature in an
inscription (IG i³ 90) of 424/3. The Peloponnesians ravaged the mine
district in 430 (Thuc. ii.55), but it is hard to destroy a mine without
explosives, and it was not till the Spartans envisaged setting up a fort
on Attic territory at Decelea (p. 142) that there could be talk of
seriously damaging Athens' mining revenues (vi.91).

The other product native to Attica, and important for her economy,
was the olive, Athena's tree in religion and myth. From the

olive-branch, modern languages have derived a synonym for 'peace'; the reason is that the olive is the product *par excellence* of peaceful cultivation, because it takes fifteen to twenty years to mature, and the destruction of olives was always the first task of an invading army. The great olive oil benefactions of the hellenistic age, when the oil was used to lubricate the skins of participants in the gymnasia of the eastern Greek cities, are an index of profound peace. It was remarkable that in the Archidamian War the Peloponnesians abstained from destroying those Attic olive trees which were regarded as sacred to Athena (Androtion F 39). All Greek states needed olive oil, not just to do the work of modern soap and artificial light, but as the equivalent of fat in the cooking and preparation of food (butter was for barbarians). In 'thin-soiled' Attica (Thuc. i.2) the olive was unusually important: its deep roots could penetrate the subsoil and get into the rocks,[1] enabling the tree to thrive where other plants could not. Grain and orchards do flourish in, for example, the Marathon plain, the market garden of modern Athens, but the inability of Attica as a whole to feed a large population gave the olive an additional role as an export, to be sent to south Russia to pay for Ukrainian corn.

All this concerns Athens' produce, not her position. But the geography more than the geology or the botany of Attica were to determine Athens' future. Her geographical advantages were not as obvious as those of Corinth, Rome or Byzantium, but Athens owed to them much of her success and sometimes her survival. Xenophon was right to insist on them.

First, Athens is surrounded by a barrier of mountains, her first line of defence:[2] working clockwise from Eleusis in the west, Mts Aigaleos, Parnes, Pentelikon and Hymettos run round the city, imagined at the centre of the dial (the best place to get an impression of this is from near the Philopappos Monument on the Hill of the Muses). Parnes, to the north, turns into Kithairon, which guards north-west Attica. With some artificial help — the old Pisistratid strong point at Eleusis (p. 110), the fortresses planted along the Kithairon–Parnes range (p. 128), and the fourth-century 'Dema Wall' which closes the Aigaleos–Parnes gap — this was massive natural insulation from land attack.

These fortifications deserve a word: much of what survives is of fourth-century date, for a good reason:[3] in the fifth century Athens had her fleet, and that was the chief instrument of her classical imperialism. But the common assumption that Pericles' war strategy meant the total evacuation of Attica neglects the evidence for fortifications in his time, not all of which, surely, were abandoned in 431 (see further p. 128). With that qualification it is true that Attica, from dates earlier than Themistokles, looked to the 'wooden walls' of a famous oracle delivered to Athens in the Persian War: the phrase referred to the fleet (Hdt. vii.141).

The second, then, of Athens' geographical blessings is her prime naval position (which is really what Xenophon had in mind). Athenian activity by sea was nothing new in the fifth century. In Mycenaean times, Thorikos on the east Attic coast was importing the black volcanic glass called obsidian from the island of Melos, a reminder that there was and is a good little harbour nearby at Laurion; Attic submycenaean and geometric pottery has been found as far away as western Asia Minor;[4] and the archaic Athenian colonies at Sigeum and the Chersonese, and the sixth-century cleruchies on Salamis and Euboia, foreshadow the fifth-century empire.[5] In part it was geography which made this possible. The carrot-shaped Attic peninsula dangles into the Aegean towards the Cyclades islands; there are more than a hundred miles of hospitable Attic coastline, with plenty of good harbours from Skala Oropou in the north-east, past Laurion, just mentioned, round Sounion with its dockyards. Those which survive are hellenistic,[6] but classical Sounion was fortified too (Thuc. viii.4). Then comes Phaleron, and the best harbour of all, the three-bayed Piraeus, safe to use only after Athens had taken Salamis, opposite, from Megara in the days of Solon.

Third, the Acropolis of Athens — a feature which, like some other masterpieces of nature or art, is so familiar that it is hard to see it with fresh eyes — was an inevitable centre for the *synoikism* or concentration of Attica from a plurality of villages into a *mia polis*, 'one city'. ('Athens' is a plural noun in Greek; one might compare other such synoikised places, like Philippi.) The Athenian Acropolis, defensible, symbolically overbearing, and provided with its own water supply, goes far to explain why Dark Age Attica did not remain like Keos or Euboia, a coalition of small states.

Instead, Athens became a *mia polis*, and the political life of Attica was dominated by Athens. Dominated, not monopolized: the obvious physical impressiveness of the remains in the city, and its consequent attraction for archaeologists, can easily lead, and has led in the past, to a neglect of the *deme*, the local population centre. This has been changing, as more work is done on the Athenian Council (*Boule*) of 500 members, lists of whom have been turning up since the Americans began to excavate the *agora* in the 1930s. The Council of 500 was drawn from the demes in proportion to their population (see p. 112) and it is now known (for instance) that in the time of Kleisthenes no more than one-quarter of known Athenians can be attributed to city demes.[7] We would have expected the fraction to be approximately one-third, because Kleisthenes divided Attica into three, not four: city, coast and inland. Thucydides (ii.14–16) was right to say that it was only with the Peloponnesian War that the real migration from country to city took place. It does not follow from this that country voters in the Periclean Assembly outnumbered city voters 3:1 because, as Aristotle noted (*Politics* 1318), farmers tended to stay away. But it *does* prove, and this is important, that many citizens of Attica may have looked to their deme first and their city second. Thus Thucydides says (ii.16) of the evacuation of Attica that the Athenians took it so badly because it was *like leaving one's polis*; this is on the face of it a paradox because they were going *from* their country demes *to* the polis.

Another reason why the relation of demes to city is now seen differently, and why demes now seem more important, is simply that more archaeological work has been done on deme sites. In general, the further from Athens you go, the more impressive the remains become. This surely suggests that in the more distant demes — Eleusis with its great sanctuary and fortifications, or Rhamnous and Sounion with their temples of Nemesis and Poseidon (ML 53 = Fornara 90B for the treasury accounts of Rhamnousian Nemesis) — the city's magnetic pull was less strong than in a deme close to the city, like, say, Kolonos. A deme like Sounion or Thorikos had many of the attributes of a city-state: there were deme liturgies: Michel *Recueil d'inscriptions grecques* no. 151, from Aixoneis (liturgies were the arrangements by which individuals financed the cultural life, and even the military defence, of their communities — a blend of self-advertisement and taxation). The city deme Kollytos put on a play by Sophocles, namely the *Oinomaos* (Dem. xviii.180); Lamptrai (IG ii^{2}1204) politely inscribes its gratitude to a man of Acharnai, only thirty kilometres away across Mt Hymettos. Yet the man is treated like a man from another *polis*. From Sounion comes a splendidly illuminating decree of the demesmen, which reads: 'It seemed good to the men of Sounion: since Leukios has given the demesmen land to build an *agora*, three men are to be chosen straight away to measure an area not less than 2 plethra by 1, so that there shall be broad space for the men of Sounion to *agorazein*' ...(the last word is untranslatable: 'carry on all the activities usual in an agora' is accurate but too prosaic; there is also the sense of 'promenading oneself': Syll.³ 925). The formulae ('it seemed good', 'straight away') are aped from 'city' terminology (and note the deme *agora*, something normally characteristic of a *polis*, cp. p. 66) — or should we say that the city aped the demes? After all, *euthunai*, compulsory accounts presented by magistrates, are an institution known from deme government (IG i³42, Skambonidai) before they appear in the city.

Rich deme evidence comes from Eleusis, one of the proudest and most important of the deme sites, partly because of its sanctuary to Demeter and Kore where the cults of the great Eleusinian mystery religion were performed, partly because of a too often forgotten feature of the place: its defences. The Pisistratids, who as we saw (p. 99) were on uneasy terms with Sparta, had blocked off the main land route from the Megarid and the Peloponnese by enclosing Eleusis with a mudbrick wall. In the fourth century, as we learn from inscriptions (e.g. Syll.³ 957), the 'defence of Eleusis' was the charge of detachments of the young conscripts called *epheboi*; and Eleusis, Panakton and Phyle are mentioned together as the main fortresses of Attica in a hellenistic text (Syll.³ 485). (Dem. liv., *Against Conon*, gives in its opening paragraphs a brilliant snapshot of the vexations of life under canvas in such a frontier posting — actually Panakton — including hooligans from the next door tent emptying chamber-pots over you.) Eleusis' importance is reflected in the honours she confers, like a miniature polis: in Syll³ 1094 (cp. Hdt ix 73: Sparta honours Decelea) two foreigners, Thebans, are granted preferential seats at the sanctuary spectacles and — a very interesting phrase — 'freedom from the taxes over which the Eleusinians have control'. The phrase quoted is hardly attested elsewhere except as a fourth-century and hellenistic Asia Minor formula, used by the cities under the Persian and Seleucid kings and satraps. 'Taxes over which the city has control' implies a contrast with royal taxes, which the city is not competent to remit; the phrase thus signifies and asserts autonomy, albeit limited, in fiscal affairs, enjoyed by indulgence of a sovereign. In the fourth-century east, the sovereign is the satrap; for Eleusis, the sovereign is the city of Athens. Classical Eleusis, then, though only a deme of Attica, behaves something like a hellenistic polis, with *amour propre* but curtailed freedom. Another deme with more than purely parochial status was Piraeus, whose demarch was a state appointment (*Ath. Pol.* lviii).[8] Today likewise Piraeus' importance makes it much more than a mere annex of Athens and it has its own political traditions, regularly voting communist.

Again, the visitor to Thorikos, if taken there blindfold from the real city-state of Euboian Eretria, might well find it hard to tell the two apart, and might think that he was in another place with the same independent status: there is a fortified acropolis, a theatre and a temple — just as at Eretria. But Eretria was a polis which could wage war on Xerxes of Persia if it chose, and it did. Belgian excavations at Thorikos have added to the total of known deme inscriptions: a sacred calendar, published in 1975 (SEG xxvi.136) shows what a remarkably full religious life the deme enjoyed; the inscription lists no fewer than forty-two separate gods or heroes, including the local deme 'hero' called Thorikos.[9] Another such religious calendar, from the deme of Erchia, is headed 'the greater demarchia' (SEG xxi.541 = Sabben–Clare and Warman, *Culture of Athens*, LACTOR no. 234), and these words probably refer to the duties of the deme magistrate or mayor, the *demarch*. This man combined many of the jobs of parish priest, village policeman, eponymous magistrate (Fornara 90B, the Rhamnous accounts) and even collector for the inland revenue: the debtor Strepsiades in Aristophanes' *Clouds* is bitten by a 'demarch under the bedclothes' (line 37), and demarchs collected the *eisphora*, a capital tax.[10]

For the citizens of Attica (at least in classical times: it is remarkable, and sad in its implications for the vitality of deme life, that deme decrees are rare after the fourth century) deme routine was more immediate, though no doubt objectively less important, than what happened on the Pnyx. One interesting section of the new Thorikos text is the reference at the end, just before the stone breaks off (as so often with Greek inscriptions, at the most interesting point) to *elections* at deme level, something we should like to know more about (see further p. 119).

On the most miniature scale of all, smaller even than the demes, were the Attic *komai* or villages; even these had their *komarchs*, though about these officials virtually nothing is known.

Some inhabitants of Attica perhaps did not bother much with either deme or polis politics: the country house below the cave of Pan at Vari (the ancient deme of Anagyrous), whose remains were cleared and studied by the British School at Athens and published in 1973, gives an impression of self-sufficiency — there is copious archaeological evidence for bee-keeping at the Vari villa — and peace, a long way from the speechmakers of the Pnyx. That peace might be disturbed (as in Dem. xlvii, *Against Euergos*) by pirates, local rowdies or litigants seeking what is nowadays politely called a 'remedy by self-help'; in which case the answer was to take refuge inside the fortified central *pyrgos* or tower, whose foundations are still a feature of the Vari site.[11]

All this shows that Attica was far from being just a city with territory round it, but was a compromise between a centralized state and a federal one. The compromise is symbolized by Lysias' mention (xxiii.3) of 'the barber's shop by the Herms in the Athenian *agora* where the demesmen of Decelea congregate' — an evocative phrase which evidently described a well-known social phenomenon, since it is almost exactly reproduced in an inscription from Decelea (Syll.[3] 921, lines 63–4). That need for compromise arose from a feature shared by much of the Greco-Roman world: ancient states, being reliant on agriculture, faced a permanent struggle to prevent civic assemblies from being dominated by the urban population; Rome solved this by eventually allowing *dual* citizenship — that is, citizenship both of Rome and of the home community whose constitution would be modelled, in a municipal way, on that of often faraway Rome. Attica after Kleisthenes, which allowed a man to be loyal to and to participate in the affairs of his deme, and also to join in making the city's decisions, was another such attempt to reconcile city and countryside. The main bridge between the two was the Council of 500 members, appointed annually from the demes in proportion to their population — so for instance Eleusis was allowed to send eleven councillors to the city, and the great deme of Acharnai sent twenty-two, while some tiny demes like Pambotadai and Sybridai took it in turn to send a single councillor, each sending one every other year. (After 431, rural demes were less 'representative': p. 109.)

The demes were organized into three groups (or *trittyes*), coastal, inland and city, and these were artificially aggregated into bigger units called tribes, *phylai*: a *trittys* of coastal, a *trittys* of inland and a *trittys* of city demes went to make up one of the ten tribes of Attica, each of which sent fifty councillors to Athens. In each tribe, as we have seen, there were a number of coastal, a number of inland and a number of city demes, roughly sixteen or seventeen of each type going to make up a *trittys* (only in the tribe to which Acharnai belonged was this system modified, because twenty-two out of fifty councillors is already well over a third). This system was devised not just with political but with military arrangements in view, and this is another way in which city and countryside were brought together: the demes and *trittyes* were often arranged along, and clustered at the ends of, the strategic highways of Attica, thereby making for easy mobilization, with the *agora* of Athens as the place of muster.[12] An example is the string of demes from Tribe Five, Akamantis, which run Thorikos-Kephale-Prospalta-Sphettos and thence to the city; the section from Thorikos to Sphettos is along an arterial road, which by Kleisthenes' dispositions was enclosed first within the coastal, then within the inland *trittys* of Akamantis. The road-building of the Pisistratids in the sixth century was what made this possible. Roman Italy again provides an analogy: the roads built by people like Aemilius Lepidus in the first half of the second century physically facilitated the political and cultural unification of Italy in the course of the next 150 years.[13] Finally, the 'deme judges' (again an originally Pisistratid invention) dispensed a justice which was uniform for all Attica, but they travelled round the demes on a kind of assize circuit; they too must have been agents of unification. (They had been suspended after the fall of the tyranny in 510, but for their re-creation in the year 453 see *Ath. Pol.* 26.3.)

Symbolic of the unification of Attica — but also of the importance of the demes — was the commissioning of the same architect, a top man, to design temples of Nemesis at Rhamnous, of Poseidon at Sounion, of Ares at Acharnai and of Hephaistos at Athens. Nemesis was suggestive of vengeance, specifically for the assaults on Greece and its temples by Persia (cp. Fornara 90A: Pausanias), and the site was geographically appropriate because the Persians had landed in 490 not far away at Marathon; Poseidon meant rule of the sea, and a temple to him at Sounion was a fitting piece of arrogance, visible far out in the Aegean; Ares was the god of war and Acharnai was the most warlike deme and the one with the most manpower (Thuc. ii.19); while Athens herself, with her five-figure total of metics,[14] is audaciously presented as the smithy of Hephaistos. This huge fourfold piece of political iconography,[15] comparable as imperial propaganda to the Great Exhibition in London of 1851,[16] was executed we should remember by a single hand and was therefore surely centrally

Demes of Attica

commissioned; but it is equally significant of the proud standing of the demes that they were chosen as the vehicle for this glorious Attica-wide religious boasting.

Centralization, along with a recognition of the demes as objects of loyalty, affection and even cult (witness deme 'heroes' like 'Thorikos'), goes back to Pisistratus, who started the worship of Artemis of Brauron on the Athenian Acropolis, but without suppressing her cult at Brauron itself. Fifth-century Athens followed Pisistratus' example consciously: he had swivelled the Eleusis Hall of Mysteries round so as to face the city of Athens; in the 420s Athens inscribed a great decree regulating the offering of first-fruits to Eleusis by her own demes, by the cities of the empire, and by others of the Greeks (ML 73 = Fornara 140). Pisistratus had made Eleusis a symbol of the unity of Attica; for the fifth-century Athenians it was that, and a symbol of Athens' rule over a united Aegean as well. In the same spirit Athens purified Delos in 426 — as Pisistratus had done in the previous century:[17] control of Delos, the birthplace of Apollo the father of Ion, helped to justify control of *Ionia*.

Kleisthenic and post-Kleisthenic Athens, then, owed to Pisistratus the idea of centralizing Attica without draining away deme autonomy; but in the Kleisthenic arrangements, which lasted until the Macedonians suppressed Athenian democracy in 322, that principle was used not just in the sphere of religion, but formally and politically, in the arrangements for selecting the 500-strong Council by lot (for more on this see p. 119).

The Council (*Boule*) was not, however, the sovereign body: *that* was, or was supposed to be, the Assembly (*Ekklesia*), open to all Athenians — or rather to all free, male, adult citizens. (Any discussion of Athenian democracy should quickly define the word 'democracy': the voting *demos* was an elite group from which slaves, women and the allies were all excluded.) *Pay* was given after *c.* 403: *Ath. Pol.* xli.

The following paragraphs will try to test whether or not the Assembly *was* sovereign. Attendances of *c.*6000, out of a male population in 431 of about 40,000, could be accommodated on the Pnyx, the open-air meeting-place, and that total was regularly reached in the fourth century,[18] as we know from the very many attested grants of citizenship, for which a quorum of 6000 was required. Recorded debates are sophisticated (naturally: much of our evidence is from a sophisticated historian, namely Thucydides), but voting techniques were not: there was no counting of votes at all[19] (something which would have taken several hours when the agenda was as crowded as that given at the beginning of Demosthenes' fiftieth speech of 362 BC), and the 'consensus' was determined by a show of hands, which tellers then adjudicated, in a fashion no more precise than that of a modern shop-steward who 'counts' a sea of hands at a trade union mass meeting. (This should be remembered when we read Thucydides and Aristotle on what the latter called the 'childish' Spartan way of taking decisions, 'by shouting not voting'.)[20] What perhaps helped to keep things relatively orderly and even solemn was the custom of offering prayers at the beginning of the meeting. Attending the Assembly was, like most things the ancient Greeks did, a religious act.

That the Assembly was sovereign over the Council is true enough as a generalization, but it represents the conclusion of most modern interpretation, rather than the ancient theory. At the trial of the generals after the sea-battle of Arginusai (p. 150), who were tried collectively and thus in defiance of the constitution for failing to save survivors, the mass of the people shouted (Xen. *Hell.* i.7.12) that 'it would be monstrous if the people could not do what it wanted'. But a thinking participant like Socrates (with a following in the Assembly) found this incident difficult to stomach, and so inasfar as the passage contains a statement of constitutional principle, it ought not to be pressed. Again, the orators (as at Dem. lix.88) imply the sovereignty of the *demos*, but oratory is not reflective political science. A celebrated passage of Aristotle's *Politics* (1313b38) proves less than is sometimes assumed.[21] What Aristotle says there is that the *demos* would *like* to be a *monarchos*, an autocrat, he does not quite say that it is. Nor does the *Athenaion Politeia* say more than that on certain matters the *Boule* does *not* have the final decision (xlv), which is less than a direct and triumphant assertion of the Assembly's sovereignty. For a speaker in Herodotus (iii.82) the trouble with democracy is, not that the *demos* is itself the *monarchos*, but that democracy leads to real monarchy, the ascendancy of one man. Which need not refer only to Pericles, though the historian cannot have forgotten him.

The practical workings and relations of Council and Assembly will be a better guide. The surprising conclusion they suggest is that the Council was more of a brake on the sovereignty of the Assembly than is usually supposed.[22]

First, did the Council stick to its main constitutional job, which was to prepare business for the assembly (*Ath. Pol.* xlv)? Two inscriptions from the early fourth century show that it did not always do so (Tod 103, 108 = WV 7, 11): they have the unusual opening formula 'it seemed good to the Council'. The normal formula is 'it seemed good to the Council and People', indicating that the decree had been prepared for the Assembly ('the people') by the Council, and was then voted on by the Assembly. The two unusual inscriptions, just referred to, were evidently passed by the Council on its own sole initiative, and did not reach the Assembly: they record an alliance with Eretria, and honours for Dionysius I of Syracuse. The Eretrian alliance arranges for the Council to choose ten men to go to Eretria, and there is a similar provision in a document from the year 367 (Tod 137 = WV 39): *the Council* is to choose a herald to make a protest to the Aitolian League (cp. also Aisch. ii.19). Again, a story in Thucydides (v.45) shows that the Council hears foreign ambassadors before the Assembly does (Alcibiades persuades a Spartan delegation, after their first audience, which was with the Council, to deny at their later audience with the Assembly that they had full powers to treat with Athens). So the Council had control both of outgoing and of incoming diplomatic traffic. Finally, the Council even negotiated in secret from the Assembly: Demosthenes (ii.6, with Theopompus F 30a) mentions a secret pact made in the 350s between the Athenian Council and Philip II of Macedon to exchange Pydna, which Athens held, for Amphipolis; and the continuous text of the Oxyrhynchus Historian begins with the sailing of a trireme under one Demainetos to the south-east Aegean 'not on the instructions of the people', but after Demainetos had unveiled his plans in secret to the Council.[23]

Second, the judicial powers of the Council were greater in practice than the official limit, a five-hundred-drachma fine: Aristophanes speaks as if the proposal to execute the poet Euripides was a Council matter (*Thesmophoriazusai* 1.79), and in the 360s the Council put to death a political assassin on the island of Keos (Tod 142 = WV 44). As a member of an allied community he perhaps deserved no consideration.

Third, the power of any 'probouleutic' body (that is, one which prepares business for a larger sovereign meeting) will be enhanced the more often it, and the less often the sovereign body, meets. The Council was exempted from meeting on the sixty or so annual festival days, but not on the monthly ones;[24] this adds up to a large number of meetings (*c*.300) held per year. The Assembly on the other hand met only four times in each *prytany* (tenth part of the year, i.e. a bit longer than a month); extra meetings could no doubt be called (though the word usually taken to refer to such meetings, *sunkletos*, may just mean a meeting called at short notice).[25] This imbalance, in the number of sessions held by the Council compared to the Assembly, must have made it easier for the Council to usurp executive powers. Finally, if the generals had the authority to summon, or to prevent the summoning of, the Assembly, that was a further limitation on the Assembly (see further p. 120).

Fourth and finally, the social composition of the Council — which had a tendency to be more upper class than the Assembly, and to be drawn more from the traditionally, almost professionally political families — must have inclined it to play the master not the servant. Theoretically, the Council should have been a cross-section of the people socially (as we have seen it was geographically): its members were appointed by lot, they served only for a year at a time, so that the Councillors should not have felt themselves to be a cohesive hereditary body like the old Areopagus or the (semi-hereditary) Roman Senate, and they could not serve more than twice in their lives. In fact, however, the Council's composition was not random, as two kinds of evidence show: evidence for the high social class of individual members,[26] and evidence that it was possible to get on to the Council in a given year if you wanted to.

As to the first, it is not surprising that poorer citizens, especially those from more distant demes, found it hard to walk in to the frequent meetings of the Council (though the argument from distance should not be overstated: Andokides (i.38) mentions an early morning walk of twenty miles from Laurion to Athens as nothing special). In the developed democracy there was pay for attending the Council, but ironically it is not attested before Thucydides' account of how the oligarchs of 411 (temporarily) brought it to an end (viii.69). Perhaps it started about the mid-fifth century. As to the second kind of evidence, which shows you could intrigue your way onto the Council, this is a puzzle: was the lot then ineffective? The facts though are clear: Kleon in the fifth century and Demosthenes in the fourth are found on the Council in specially exciting years for foreign affairs, 427 and 346, the years of the Mytilene Debate and the Peace of Philokrates respectively (pp. 130, 253). And father and son teams are found serving together, presumably by arrangement. Somehow, then, the operation of the lot could be evaded. Here, as with Council pay, the date of the introduction of the lot is relevant: the first attestation is again surprisingly late, and is anyway indirect. It is the regulations imposed on the Asia Minor city of Erythrai in *c*.450 BC (ML 40 = Fornara 71) which included a Council appointed by lot; Athens would hardly have exported such an institution before she had one herself. The change from an elected Council at Athens to one appointed by lot was perhaps part of the 'Ephialtic' set of reforms (pp. 35ff.). So for its first half-century, after Kleisthenes, the Athenian Council was an unpaid elected body, something which gave it an elite character which it may never wholly have lost.

But it is from *after* the change that we have evidence for Councillors like Kleon and the fourth-century Athenian Demosthenes whose year on the Council fell at improbably convenient moments for their political careers; this makes one suspect corruption, a suspicion strengthened by Aischines' direct accusation that Demosthenes bribed his way onto the Council in 346 (iii.62). Unless this means actual ballot-rigging, it must refer to bribing people *not* to put their names forward at deme level for the ballot for the Council; the candidate who 'eagerly put his name forward' according to Lysias (xxxi.33) is evidence that this stage of the process was voluntary. (That there were actual preliminary deme *elections* to determine which names went forward to the ballot is unlikely[27] given that fourth-century Attic oratory, of which a great deal survives, is wholly silent about such elections — although the new Thorikos text, for instance (p. 111), shows that there were *some* elections at deme level.) Alternatively Aischines' charge of 'bribery' could refer to vaguer but still politically valuable arrangements whereby the habitués of the ancient equivalent of the left-wing coffee-shop in a deme agreed to put forward no candidates in one year provided the right-wing coffee-shop held back the following year. There is no evidence for precisely that kind of deal, but a little imagination will show how the system could be 'worked' in favour of individuals, and such working of the system could certainly be described as 'bribery' in the elastic vocabulary of Athenian political abuse. The final way of getting on to the Council in a given year was by being an *epilachōn* or stand-in, and that may explain some instances of 'carpet-baggers', i.e. political adventurers who offered themselves as Councillors for demes other than their home deme. But Aischines expressly excludes that explanation for Demosthenes.

The Council then was not quite a 'cross-section' of Athenians, but contained disproportionately many rich, determined politicians; and lobbies, political dynasties or mafias could perpetuate themselves over the years despite the restrictions on re-election (so the contrast with, for example, the Roman Senate is not after all total). Little explicit literary evidence confirms this view of the Council; there is for instance nothing in the pamphlet called the *Old Oligarch*, written in *c*.425, although in other contexts it does comment on the influence at Athens enjoyed by the wealthy and well-born. There is only a remark in Plutarch's *Alcibiades*, where he is recounting the story of the double-crossing of the Spartan ambassadors (p. 117): Alcibiades (xiv.8) urges the Spartans to go before the Council because it is more 'moderate and kindly' than the People, that is the Assembly. (But since Plutarch is, in this section of the *Life of Alcibiades*, so heavily dependent on Thucydides, who omits that item, it may represent Plutarch's own addition rather than an independent fifth-century source. In Plutarch's day, tension between Council and Assembly was a fact of Greek city life.) On the other hand there is a remark of Lysias (xxx.22) who says that when times are hard the Council listens more readily to prosecutions of the rich; this suggests class solidarity between the Council and the poor on the one hand against the rich on the other.[28]

So much for the Council. There were other restraints on the right, or ability, of the Assembly to 'do what it wished'. The most important was the panel of the ten generals. The generals were the only important magistrates to be elected normally one from each of the ten tribes, elected by the people as a whole. There were no limits on re-election. That the Assembly could depose and fine them at no notice, as happened to Pericles himself towards the end of his life, shows that the Assembly was theoretically and actually master. But, as with the Council, that generalization must be qualified. Thucydides (ii.22) says that Pericles, as general in 431, 'did not summon the Assembly', and though this may have been just an exercise of personal authority, there is another passage (iv.118.14), from a faithful transcript of an Athenian decree, which gives the generals power to summon, and perhaps by implication the power to prevent the summoning of, the Assembly. Certainly the generals had direct access to the Assembly, and could propose motions: one inscription (Syll.[3]132) opens with the formula 'by the motion of the generals'. Even if such inscriptions were non-existent rather than just rare, it would be no more than commonsense to guess that generals in the field must have enjoyed great executive latitude, especially in wartime — more latitude than was compatible with the exercise of detailed control, and so of full sovereignty, by the Assembly. For instance when in *c*.438 (p. 89) Phormio made an alliance with the Akarnanians in north-west Greece (Thuc. ii.86) it is inconceivable that he awaited approval from Athens. Of course if he made the wrong decision he could pay for it by loss of his command, as we have seen, or even with his life, as happened to Timagoras, the ambassador who accepted humiliating terms at a peace conference in 367 (Xen. *Hell.* vii.1.38; p. 229). But often a general must have been left to his initiative. This was partly because of difficulties of communications: ancient Greek diplomacy was conducted on foot for the most part, and runners rather than mounted dispatch-riders were used for urgent messages.

As for naval campaigning, much of it was done at a great distance. So Demosthenes (Thuc. iv.2.4: this man is a fifth-century general, not the famous fourth-century politician) is explicitly told to use his fleet round the Peloponnese 'as he thought fit'; he took Pylos with it (p. 132), an act which Thucydides implies was more extempore than it really was, but which was nevertheless not something specifically authorized by the Assembly. And most striking of all, the three generals in Sicily in 415 (Thuc. vi.47ff.) debate strategy as if all the options are wide open. Only Nikias mentions their specific brief from the People to proceed against Selinus, and his views do not prevail. There was anyway ambiguity about that brief, because (vii.11) the same Nikias alludes in a letter to the Assembly to a brief to proceed against Syracuse: same phrase, different object. The other part of the explanation for the initiative tacitly granted to generals is the need for confidentiality and secret co-ordination between geographically separated forces. Thucydides, unusually, mentions a security breach (iv.42): advance intelligence about an Athenian attack had reached Corinth via Argos. If that kind of thing had happened very often, Athens would have lost the war much sooner than she did. An example of the kind of executive pre-arrangement, which must have happened more often than we are told, is the way in which Demosthenes (iv. 89) with the fleet went to Siphai, Hippokrates was to march on Delion. (It went wrong, but that is not the point.) Or there is Nikias who (iii.91) sails from Melos to Oropos on the Boiotian border, thence to Boiotian Tanagra, to meet Hipponikos coming from Athens. (In none of this do the geographical or military details matter, which is why the background has not here been explained: what matters is the *constitutional* issues raised.) Finally, iv 90 shows that generals *called out troops* off their own bat.

We should like to know how much of this kind of thing was discussed openly on the Pnyx by the Assembly, and how much or how little communication *between* generals was centrally re-routed from the *strategeion*, the generals' office, in the *agora*. But it is noticeable that such information is commoner in those sections of Thucydides' narrative (books iii and iv) which date *from years when he himself was a general* and had privileged access to the deliberations in the *strategeion*. This might imply that Thucydides knew more than the Assembly did.[29] It might also imply (what in wartime is plausible at any period of history) that the executive, in the shape of the panel of the generals, a tight group of only ten at maximum allowing for absentees, gained power at the expense of its larger and more unwieldy constitutional master, the Assembly. And though the Archidamian War accelerated this process no doubt, Athens was at war, or Athenians were on campaign, like Phormio in Akarnania, virtually every year of the pentekontaetea.

We must now consider the role of the 'demagogues', and the way their rhetorical and other skills enabled them to manipulate the Assembly and so detract from its sovereignty.

The generals were not the only officials or individuals, the extension of whose power tended to erode that of the Assembly. In the fifth century, the complex business of running an empire threw up the 'demagogues', to us a word of political disparagement but not much specific content. By contrast, the Athenian demagogues, the 'leaders of the people', had definite and valuable, though not constitutionally recognized, functions within the Athenian state. First, there was no public prosecutor at Athens, so like the Roman informers, the *delatores*, men like the demagogue Kleon took it on themselves to bring prosecutions for such offences as peculation of public money. More important, it was necessary that somebody should be acquainted with the details of imperial finance, and the Athenian constitution, like that of Rome in the republic, had no provision for a civil service, and like the Roman Senate, the Athenians governed and legislated as amateurs. Rome eventually, under the empire, looked to a newly and specially created bureaucracy from former slaves of the Emperor and from free men of sufficient rank; Athenian public slaves never progressed beyond low-grade secretarial jobs. Instead, much detailed work was done by demagogues.

There was surely nothing very new[30] about these more profes-
sional-looking politicians, though they scarcely feature in the sources
before Pericles' death in 429. The nature of those sources is part of the
explanation: no comic play survives in anything like complete form
earlier than the beginning of the Peloponnesian War, and Thucydides
for artistic reasons (like Tacitus delaying the introduction of Sejanus
until the opening of the second half of his six 'Tiberian' books), delays
the introduction of the arch-demagogue Kleon until Pericles is off the
stage for good. Yet we know that Kleon was not only a vocal opponent
of Pericles' war strategy, i.e. was politically active in Pericles' lifetime
(Plut. *Per.* xxxiii), but may have contracted an advantageous political
marriage as early as the year 440.[31] (This makes it hard to draw any
line between old and 'new', i.e. post-Periclean, politicians in terms of
social standing; similarly we now know that the later and much-vili-
fied demagogue Kleophon was the son of a man high enough up the
social ladder to have served as a general: ML 21.)

Nor are the political techniques of the politicians of the 420s
specially new. Kleon, in Aristophanes' *Knights*, is represented as a
'lover of the demos', but *Philodemos* occurs as a proper name in a
casualty-list of as early as *c.*460 (ML 33 = Fornara 78); more
important, Kleisthenes in the sixth century had taken the demos into
partnership, as Herodotus puts it, and Pericles in the 460s had won
over the people with jury pay. (Thucydides never saw Pericles at his
demagogic debut, or he might have felt less dismay at the look of the
great man's successors: ii.65.) A strange story in Plutarch (*Moralia*
806), about Kleon, at the beginning of his career, summoning his
friends, his *philoi*, and renouncing their friendship, has been taken to
show that Kleon took his role as 'people's friend' more seriously than
his predecessors; but this embarrassing-sounding scene is hard to
visualize, and is of doubtful historicity, being attributed to no source,
reputable or disreputable. Worse, the story is provably false: the
decree (ML 69 = Fornara 136) which enacted the raising of the tribute
in 425 was moved by Thoudippos — who we know from Isaios (ix)
was Kleon's own son-in-law and so a *philos*. So much for abandoning *philoi*. As for oratorical technique, *Ath. Pol.* (xxviii) says that
Kleon was the first to raise his voice and use theatrical gestures — as if
all politicians earlier than Kleon spoke in a monotone with their arms
rigidly at their sides! But there are anyway other anecdotes which for
what they are worth trace the origin of political professionalism to
dates earlier than Kleon: a Byzantine lexicon called the Suda, for

instance, makes Pericles the first to take a written speech into court, while for Cicero (Brutus 46) oratory developed in the 460s, as a result of the fall of the tyrants in Sicily, an event which prompted litigation about landownership. *Something*, however, must lie behind the feeling in the literary sources that politicians like Kleon were different, and perhaps the difference should be sought in the new and larger audiences assembled on the Pnyx as a result of the evacuation of Attica in 431. Faced with an audience which included Dikaiopolis, the main character in Aristophanes' *Acharnians* (see lines 1ff.), farting and grumbling as he watched the Spartans put a match to the combustible parts of Attica, a speaker might well need to invent cruder techniques. But there was crudity in Athenian politics before Kleon.

On the positive side though, these politicians got things done, and got them done in detail[32] (the use by Kleon, then absent from Athens, of his son-in-law Thoudippos to move the complex reassessment decree of 425 implies efficiency and a refusal to trust to luck. For Kleon's connection with the decree — Thoudippos is not the only evidence — see p. 137). Not only Kleon but the equally detested figure of Hyperbolus (detested, that is, by Thucydides and Aristophanes) looks a little different and more respectable when tested against documentary evidence, just as radio broadcasts of puerile exchanges in the House of Commons ignore the work on Select Committees on which most MPs spend most of their time. For instance there is a long, sober and sensible-looking decree about the cult of Hephaistos, moved by Hyperbolus (IG i^{3}82); and the Argive alliance of *c*.418 (IG i^{3}86) can be interpreted as an expression of Hyperbolus' determination to use allied tribute for the unofficial war being fought in the Peloponnese[33] (p. 139). Hyperbolus was a failure but not a fool. These men, like the generals, were at the mercy of the Assembly — whose composition changed with every meeting — but knowledge is power, and their skills, and factual grasp of routine information, could not be overthrown except by superior skill and superior grasp, though they were unusually vulnerable by reason of their prominence to the irrational weapon of ostracism, which destroyed Hyperbolus. Only once does Aristophanes play on the possibility that the demagogues, for all their 'philodemos' pretensions, were actually an undemocratic force: in the *Wasps* (715ff.) '*they* (the demagogues) insincerely promise to give you, that is the people, corn doles, and even to hand over Euboia to you'. Nowhere else is an 'us-them' mentality so clearly expressed; but their technical proficiency and factual command of state business must have enabled such men to acquire great and even lasting power — again, at the Assembly's expense, despite their need to pose as agents of the popular, that is of the Assembly's, will. For Plato in a marvellous metaphor (*Republic* 488) *Demos* was a huge, deaf old sea-captain, drugged and overpowered by ignorant riff-raff who take over the wheel themselves — true, except for the word 'ignorant'. Ignorance was not a fault of Kleon, or Hyperbolus.

In the fourth century, Athenian democracy was curtailed in ways harder to resist than a Hyperbolus, who could simply be got rid of: the institutionalized power of the men who administered the various state funds grew in the course of the fourth century, and as such people got above themselves Athens became a less democratic place than it had been in the fifth century.[34] The most important fund was the *theoric*, from which pay was given for attendance at festivals. This move towards efficiency and specialization affected most departments of state; thus five of the ten generals have distinct functions by about 350: general in charge of overseas hoplite expeditions, general appointed for the defence of Attica, general for the Piraeus and so on. And we hear for the first time of permanent salaried architects. (But note that, despite what has been said in this paragraph concerning the administration of *funds*, the fact that there was less political pay in the fourth century also helped to dilute the democracy.)[35]

But these fourth-century 'apparatchiks', the men of the age of Eubulus (p. 245), were not the first Athenians to gain power by boring work on committees. And this leads to the last and perhaps greatest check on popular sovereignty in the age of Pericles, namely Pericles himself. Pericles' position is (*almost* everywhere: see p. 126 on finance) described by Thucydides as if his authority depended solely on charismatic qualities of leadership, but this cannot have been the whole of it. We know, for instance, that he was president of the commission for the building of the great statue of Athena by Phidias, and of that for the Lyceum (Philochoros F 121 and 37), that he was on the Parthenon commission (Strabo 395), and that he was responsible in an elected capacity for the Odeum (Plut. *Per.* xiii). All of that is relevant to Thucydides' description of Athens under his regime as 'ostensibly a democracy, but actually one-man rule'. Pericles, no less than Kleon, was proof that knowledge, even or especially routine knowledge, is power, and it is that which makes Pericles the greatest demagogue of them all. Only Pericles, of all the speakers in Thucydides, is allowed a speech about anything so detailed and unethereal as war finance, namely at ii.13, where Pericles' self-imputed capacity to 'understand what was needed and to expound it' (ii.60) is better illustrated than anywhere else in Thucydides. The confidence of Pericles' exposition is magnificent; but did he after all 'understand what was needed'? The first ten years of the Peloponnesian War, to which we now turn, were to show that he did not, and that Periclean democracy — which was based on the power of money ('hail in due apportionment of *wealth*' say the chorus of Aeschylus' *Eumenides* to Athens, line 996) and on the admiration of that power — was more precarious than Pericles had allowed. In more concrete terms, Pericles' confidence in Athenian resources was superb but misplaced: his war policy put Athens into the red, and it was the demagogues, with their 'undemocratic' technical expertise, who got her out of it. Thucydides must have perceived this, without necessarily endorsing the extreme views which he gives two of his speakers: Alcibiades who said that democracy was acknowledged folly; and Kleon who said that a democracy was incapable of running an empire (vi.89; iii.37).

specially sacred areas like Marathon and Decelea (Diod. xii.45; Hdt. ix.73) — and then only initially.

On the positive side ('not adding to the empire ...') Athens did not refrain from adventurous overseas campaigning even in Pericles' lifetime — a big ravaging operation against Epidaurus in the east Peloponnese (ii.56, cp. vi.31) was a good way of keeping manpower occupied and out of Athens during the plague, and despite its size does not imply that Periclean strategy was incoherent. And the references in the first book of Thucydides (122;142: speeches by Pericles and the Corinthians) to *epiteichismos*, i.e. the establishment *by both sides* of permanent occupied positions in hostile territory, need not be anachronisms on the historian's part (although the *epiteichismos* technique did not come into its own till the Athenians took Pylos in the west Peloponnese in 425). In other words, responsible Athenian opinion, already in 432/1, envisaged taking and holding strong points in the Peloponnese. But that notion falls short of 'extending the empire'.

The second question is, who after Pericles' death in 429 was responsible for any departures from his policy? Thucydides (ii.65.7) says there were such departures, but the passage is sweeping and unhelpful: it is not clear if it refers only to the running of the Archidamian War, that is the ten years 431–421 — which as we shall see was not noticeably 'unPericlean' — or to the whole war, especially the expedition to Sicily, 415–413. If the latter, the reference to 415 is a strange leap in time from the immediate context of ii.65, which is Pericles' death. But probably the second view is right, Thucydides' perspective in 404, after which date he wrote the passage, having become foreshortened. In any case the Sicilian expedition was not initially misconceived (cp. p. 142 on ii.65.11), so even taken as a judgement on the whole war Thucydides' verdict at this point cannot be accepted. We must ask the question for ourselves, were there any departures from Pericles' strategy? For that enquiry a factual framework is required. We have no guide other than Thucydides' *History* (for Diodorus see p. 6), and great though Thucydides' authority is, we must remember that his choice of material is determined by two warring motives: the desire to record everything that happened, and the desire to 'write up' selected incidents because they illustrate a theme he thinks important.[9]

The first invasion of Attica by the Spartans, the Athenian Plague, and the beginning of the siege of Plataia by her Boiotian neighbour

Thebes, are the main events of Thucydides' war narrative up to the death of Pericles (ii.1–65). The rest of the second book describes in detail some naval fighting on the Corinthian Gulf between the Peloponnesians and the forces of Phormio the Athenian. Thucydides' object here seems to be to fix in our minds salient features of naval warfare rather than to insist on the importance of the events described (see chapter 13, p. 157 for the precise tactical points involved here). Book iii opens with the revolt of Athens' ally Mytilene (cp. p. 136), and this is made to alternate with the continuing story of Plataia.

It has often been noticed that the actual military importance of the fall of Plataia, when it happened, was small, and it seems that Thucydides' aim in juxtaposing Plataia and Mytilene is to contrast Athens' desertion of her faithful ally Plataia (for she did nothing to help her) with her speed and severity in dealing with Mytilene: although the original decision to execute all male Mytileneans and enslave the rest was modified (the result of the celebrated Mytilenean Debate between Kleon and Diodotus the advocate of clemency), Mytilene was still punished with a harshness no less exemplary because not taken to the extreme. The strong language of Antiphon (v.79) on this subject is exaggerated but shows that Mytilene was thought of as having paid heavily. There is also a — more obvious — comparison between Athenian and Spartan methods: Sparta the liberator listens to the arguments of Thebans and Plataians and decides on severity — in Spartan interests; Diodotus successfully pleads for leniency over Mytilene — in Athenian interests (though we may suspect that Thucydides has suppressed speeches which appealed to compassion, since he does say that their original decision came to seem savage to the Athenians).

The third great set piece in book iii after Mytilene and Plataia is the description of the revolution at Corcyra (427), a highly generalized and paradoxical piece of writing. But there was more straightforward campaigning to be recorded: in the same year as Corcyra, Athens sent a first expedition to Sicily, partly to help Leontini in the name of friendship — but partly also to stop grain being exported from there to the Peloponnese and to see if 'affairs on the island could be brought under Athenian control'. This ambiguity of motive, a conservative and a radical, is to recur in Thucydides' narrative of the great Sicilian expedition of 415.

In 426 we find Sparta setting up a colony (iii.92) at Herakleia in Trachis just south of Thessaly, a foundation on a massive scale, designed to throttle Athens' passage to the north (this looks forward to Brasidas' operations and shows, p. 128, that he did not quite have a monopoly of adventurous thinking), and to cut Athens off from Euboia where so much food was kept, in the form of grain or on the hoof (ii.14). The passage is worth quoting in full, both because of the importance of the main issue it raises, namely Spartan ambitions in central Greece, compare p. 82; and because it is Thucydides at his historically perceptive best: as with the causes of the war as a whole (chapter 8) he gives both the surface cause or pretext, in this instance an appeal from the people of Doris and Trachis against their neighbours the Oitaians, *and* the profounder causes, that is the underlying Spartan strategy in terms of Thrace and Euboia. We should note also the way in which even so obviously and specifically anti-Athenian a wartime project is submitted to Apollo at Delphi for his approval, like any normal colonizing venture. Here is the passage (Thuc. iii. 92–3):

> After hearing the ambassadors, the Spartans decided to send out the colony, since they wished to help both the Trachinians and the Dorians. Also it seemed to them that the new city would be well placed for the war against Athens since it could be used as a naval base directed against Euboea, with the advantage of a very short crossing, and it would also be useful as a position lying on the route to Thrace. There was every reason, therefore, why they should be enthusiastic about founding the place.
>
> First of all they consulted the god at Delphi, and, when they had received a favourable reply, they sent out settlers from Sparta itself and from other cities in the Spartan area; they also called for volunteers from other parts of Hellas, with the exception of the Ionians, the Achaeans, and some other peoples. The founders of the city and leaders of the expedition were three Spartans: Leon, Alcidas, and Damagon. So they established and fortified anew the city now called Herakleia...

Two final points: Diodorus (xii.59) adds that there were as many as 10,000 colonists — a huge but round and perhaps not trustworthy total. Second, the shrewd assessment by Thucydides of the real reasons for the colony may have something to do with the specially privileged position he held in these middle years of the Archidamian

War, when he was party to what was being said in the councils of the ten generals (cp. p. 122). We may contrast the earlier, Athenian, expedition against Epidaurus (ii.56) which is *not* explained though it too was on a big scale. Here the historian perhaps could not draw on the conversations of his militarily more experienced seniors.

If the size of the Herakleia venture is puzzling compared to what was achieved by it[10] (Thucydides goes on to put its relative failure down to Thessalian hostility) it is nevertheless of importance as a large and impressive link in the chain of Spartan interest in central Greece, which began with Kleomenes in the sixth century (Hdt. vi.108, early involvement with Plataia; cp. p. 81 on Pindar's Tenth Pythian as evidence for Kleomenes' Thessalian contacts), goes down through Leotychidas in the 470s, and continues well into the fourth century: a Spartan harmost (v. index) Herippidas was sent to deal with internal trouble at Herakleia in the 390s (Diod. xiv.38). To return to the Peloponnesian War: it is likely that Herakleia was lost after the Peace of Nikias, but that Sparta recovered it before 413.[11] In other words its retention by no means ceased to be official policy after the 'adventurous' Brasidas was dead, just as its foundation had preceded his period of prominence.

Finally in book iii, there are Demosthenes' operations in north-western Greece in Aitolia against the Ambraciots. The loss of 120 men 'in the flower of their youth, the best men lost in the whole war' (iii.98) made Demosthenes fear to return home without retrieving this Aitolian failure, which he later felt he had done after winning successes in co-operation with Athens' Akarnanian allies (cp. p. 89 for this alliance). The use of light-armed troops was the most portentous feature of this fighting, anticipating the *peltasts*, the light-shield bearers, of the more impoverished fourth century (p. 163). Here as often, Thucydides' treatment is not purely narrative but 'diagnostic', that is he isolates and stresses the features which seem to him to explain some general phenomenon whose significance may be developed later (at iv.30, Demosthenes at Pylos is explicitly said to have learnt the lesson of Aitolian guerilla tactics).

With book iv (425–423 BC) the pace accelerates, and Thucydides perceptibly begins to accord a greater role to chance over planning, to *tyche* over *gnomē*. Demosthenes' seizure of Pylos is the first real piece of *epiteichismos* (p. 129) and is treated by Thucydides as an inspiration of the moment. This cannot be quite right: the exploitation of the position so won, resulting in the capture of *c*.400 Spartan citizens and *perioikoi*, was indeed a matter of luck and daring, but it all started from an experienced tactician's evaluation of the site: the trained eye was that of Demosthenes. It was however Kleon's tongue in the Assembly at Athens, and Kleon's hand at Pylos, which first got the task force voted, and then brought the Spartans back prisoner, 'stealing the cake which Demosthenes baked' as Aristophanes put it (*Knights* 54f.). That verdict is tendentious only in as far as it implies imperfect harmony between the two men; but actually this is an early example of a fourth-century phenomenon, a soldier-politician team working in harmony, like the fourth-century 'team' Chares and Aristophon. With the prisoners in her hands, Athens had a strong bargaining lever against Sparta, already hard up for manpower even as early as this. Athens, at Kleon's instance, turned down a Spartan peace proposal which (p. 137) should perhaps have been accepted, or at least flirted with (see *Historical Commentary on Thucydides* note, p. 462), since it involved the betrayal of any thought of liberation and would have angered and alienated Sparta's allies. ('If we', the Spartans say at iv.20, 'Athens and Sparta, stand together, you can be sure that the rest of Hellas, in its inferior position, will show us every possible mark of honour.')

Kleon's hand can also be detected in a measure of this time (425) which is known of only from an inscription (ML 69 = Fornara 136): a massive raising of the allies' tribute (cp. p. 137).

Dazzled by their own success at Pylos, the Athenians punished their generals in Sicily on their return for failing to win the whole island for them (iv.65). This time Sicily — moved by the oratory at the conference of Gela of the Sicilian patriot Hermokrates, a man for whom Thucydides had a great deal of time — united to keep the Athenians out. The capture of the island of Kythera off the Spartan coast (iv.53) also reflects a mood of buoyancy: Thucydides comments on Spartan nervousness at the possibility of mass helot rising (55), a danger which hostile possession of Kythera brought very near to home (cp. Hdt. vii.235 and p. 197 for the 390s). Why Athens did not do more to *promote* servile insurrection in the war is a mystery: she could certainly have won it very quickly if she had.[12] But the facts are clear: what Athens does is to establish bases *to which* (*autose*, vii.26.2) helots could desert; she does little actively to bring about such desertion. It seems that the weapon of the *bellum servile* had yet to be thought of. (Though note Kritias in Thessaly towards the end of the war, 'arming the *penestai*, i.e. serfs, against their masters': Xen. *Hell.* ii.3.36.)

Athens did less well at this time in another theatre, at Megara, where Brasidas on his way north was able to infiltrate the city and abet an oligarchic coup. And more disastrous still was an ambitious Athenian effort to regain control of Boiotia, forfeit as a result of the events of 446 (pp. 45f.). These operations (the Delion campaign of 424, which occupies much of the latter part of Thucydides' book iv) punctured the Athenian euphoria which Pylos had inflated. Delion was fought just over the Attic-Boiotian border on the Boiotian side. It was a severe defeat for the Athenians and one which, like Aitolia but in another respect, anticipates the next century: the Thebans deepened their left wing so as to deliver a hard punch to the enemy *right*, where in a Greek battle the best troops were traditionally stationed. This was how the Thebans were to win at Leuktra in 371. (The more usual concentration of good troops on the right was due to a feature of hoplite warfare noticed by Thucydides (v.71): fear for his unshielded right arm tended to make the second-class hoplite shuffle to the right so as to get the protection of the next man's shield. Hence the need for good troops on the right, to stem this drift. In the normal battle it sometimes happened that the right wing on each side would slide victoriously past the right wing on the other.)

But Athens for her part was not ready to think of peace until to Delion was added the loss of a string of northern places to Brasidas, who as we saw was in the Isthmus area, and thus in a position to act at Megara, only because he was on his way to Chalcidice in the north, a move which begins the truly adventurous period of Spartan strategy for the Archidamian War. Here Brasidas made much use of the 'liberation' doctrine, backed up by genial threats: in an instructive passage (iv.88), Thucydides drily and impartially gives two motives for Acanthus' surrender, the attractiveness of Brasidas' words — and fear for the grape vintage. At Athens, the most serious, or seriously felt, loss was Amphipolis, her obsession with which, not just in the immediately following period but for the whole of the fourth century down to its capture by Philip, seems to us out of proportion and reason. Actually the place had only been finally secured in 437 (p. 46), but its economic value was great and varied (Thuc. iv.108), and perhaps like Singapore in the British Empire this proud site was felt to be symbolic of a farflung imperialism — so that like the fall of

Singapore in 1942 the loss of Amphipolis was felt as a deep wound to the national morale. The Athenian general responsible for the loss was Thucydides the historian, who was exiled in consequence; he was perhaps more unlucky than incompetent: 'not to have been a match for Brasidas', it has been said,[13] 'does not prove him a bad soldier.'

The deaths of Kleon and Brasidas in the course of the same skirmishing (422) removed, Thucydides says, the only obstacles to peace (but the passage (v.16) is highly tendentious and should be read in context). The death in the front line of two commanders is incidentally worth noting as illustrating an essential feature of ancient warfare, the idea that generals should fight as well as think. This was something which, as we shall see in the next chapter, hindered the development of the art of generalship: in order to alter the course of an engagement while it is going on, a commander needs something like a synoptic view and that means physical detachment from the dust and blood. Polybius (x.32–3, about Hannibal and Claudius Marcellus) propounds with an air of conscious novelty the idea that it is a general's job to keep his brains unspilt for another day, though Iphikrates and others are credited with similar reflections even earlier (Plut. *Pelop*.ii). (*Cavalry* fighting is another affair: here personal leadership and *élan* is vital to morale, as witness the best cavalry commanders from Alexander to Rupert of the Rhine.)

Spartan willingness for peace is to be explained not just by Kythera and the Pylos prisoners, but by fear of Argos, with whom a Thirty Year Peace of 451 was to run out in 421.

The Peace of Nikias in 421 ended the First Ten Years War, the Archidamian War, on terms which signify victory for Athens, the existence of whose empire is acknowledged in the phrase used in the treaty documents 'the Athenians and their allies'. She had 'won through' with her *arche* intact. She kept Nisaia, but had to disgorge Kythera, thereby going some way to relieve Sparta from any immediate fear of social revolution. Sparta secured herself positively (v.23) by a written guarantee of Athenian help against her 'slaves', i.e. helots: the asymmetry of this (in that there is no comparable undertaking by Sparta in respect of Athens' numerous slaves) is of interest as proving how peculiarly intense were Sparta's domestic fears. Athens' slaves were an ethnically mixed lot (cp. ML 79 = Fornara 147D) without the Messenian national consciousness of the helots, without a common language to plot in, and — in the case of mining slaves — with a short expectation of life.

We may now return to the questions put earlier: how far did Athens keep to Pericles' policies during the Archidamian War, especially between 429, the year of his death from the plague, and 421? And who was responsible for the non-Periclean features? We have seen that even before 429 Pericles' thinking was not defensive to the exclusion of ravaging expeditions like that to Epidaurus; or of *epiteichismos*, at least in principle (p. 129). To move on to the period after his death: the disciplining of Mytilene was thoroughly Periclean (cp. p. 46 on Samos and p. 138 on 'keeping the allies in hand'. That the Mytilenean revolt was indeed as Kleon had said (iii.40) a piece of well-planned defiance is now shown by some very assertive coins, electrum staters, struck in preparation for the revolt, bearing the legend MYTI-, i.e. they stress their Mytilenean origin; and conforming with the monetary standard of Cyzicus in the approaches to the Black Sea: *Gnomon*, 1982, p.499. Now it was from the Black Sea that Thucydides (iii.2) tells us that the Mytileneans had sent for archers and grain).

Athenian interest in Sicily in the 420s is hard for us to judge without mental contamination from the events of 415–413. It was hard for Thucydides too: *pleoni stoloi*, 'with a greater expedition' (iv.60) is a clear reference to the later expedition. But at the time the response to the appeal from Leontini need not have seemed scandalously out of line with previous policy; for Athens' readiness to make alliances in Sicily, back to the early 450s, see p. 56. Even Pericles (ii.62) had told the Athenians 'there is no power on earth — not the king of Persia nor any people under the sun — which can stop you from sailing where you wish.' This is probably a promise[14] of eventual Sicilian expansion — but not in *wartime*: that was the key to Periclean defensive policy, which meant a temporary 'freeze' on aggressive action, but did not preclude optimistic diplomacy or reconnaissance. Syracuse was growing to be a menace which needed containing. It was only the windfall of the Pylos prisoners, a great psychological stimulus, which made the voters in the Athenian Assembly wish that their generals in Sicily had achieved something more tangible (iv.65); in this they were encouraged by a lobby which does deserve to be stigmatized as unPericlean: it included politicians like Hyperbolus, who thought big, perhaps in terms of attacks on Carthage (Aristophanes *Knights* 1303ff, exaggerated of course with its reference to a hundred ships, but ML 92 = Fornara 165 of the year 410, cp. Thuc. vi.88, shows that overtures were made to Carthage later in the war. And note Livy iv.29.8, on which see p. 89 and p. 141, for Carthaginian encroachment in Sicily at this time). There are always two wings of opinion about Sicily, a conservative and a radical, and therefore two corresponding motives, conservative and radical, are generally given for involvement there (iii.86; 115; vi.6).[15]

Demosthenes' operations in Aitolia look harder to justify on Periclean principles, but if seen as part of a plan to get at Boiotia from the rear (thus anticipating the later attempt on Boiotia which failed at Delion, and which was certainly an attempt to extend the empire in wartime) they can at least be justified as a gamble which could have secured the northern frontiers of Attica, whose land fortifications, as we have seen, were not wholly evacuated by Pericles.

Then there is Pylos: would Pericles have accepted the Spartan peace offer of 425? Thucydides is severe on Kleon for turning it down, but the historian's personal distaste for the man who probably got him exiled has warped his judgement. Actually the Spartans were offering very little, beyond the empty promise of a shared Atheno-Spartan hegemony (see p. 133). But this collaborative mood was not something it was safe for Athens to rely on, as the history of Sparta's highly volatile foreign policy in the pentekontaetea showed. Kleon was right to turn the Spartans away.

Thucydides uses, to describe this episode, the language of *pleonexia*, grasping for more, and it would be tempting but wrong to associate the Sicily policy in its radical aspect with Kleon as well, in view of the very similar language used to describe the mood of the Athenian people who punished the generals on their return from Sicily in 424 (iv.65). But this is a *suggestio falsi*: if the historian could have nailed Sicily definitely on Kleon he would have done so: that he resorts to innuendo is equivalent to an acquittal. And, we can add, nothing in the sources suggests that Aitolia or Delion were Kleon's work: again, silence (where our sources — Aristophanes, see *Knights passim*, as well as Thucydides — are so hostile) is decisive.

It is, however, fair to associate with Kleon the policy of raising the tribute. We have noticed Kleon's marriage link with Thoudippos, the author of the enabling decree (ML 69; p. 123); and Aristophanes (*Knights* 313) has Kleon 'spying out for tribute from the cliff-top like a man watching for shoals of tunny-fish'. Finance was the main area where Pericles' assessment of the future course of the war had proved faulty. He hoped (ii.13) to finance it from 'income', i.e. the tribute of the allies, to which he adds the enumeration of Athens' capital resources more (one feels) as a comfort to morale than because he expected them to be spent. But the accounts of borrowing from Athena (see the charts at the end of *HCT*, vol.ii; ML 72 comm.) — i.e. the spending of capital — show that the siege of Potidaia (2000 talents; ii.70) and the cost of the Mytilene reprisals had put Athens in the red, and Kleon's measures were thus unavoidable. To the extent that this was a 'departure' from Periclean thinking (and Pericles' maxim, ii.13, to 'keep the allies in hand' was a usefully vague phrase) it was a necessary one, a rejection of Pericles' sums rather than his strategy.

The Peace of Nikias was an Athenian victory both retrospectively (in that it recognized Sparta's failure to destroy the Athenian imperial system) and prospectively, in that it began a period of diplomatic difficulties for Sparta;[16] the effectiveness of her allies' anger at her for making an unsatisfactory peace was however cancelled by their failure to act concertedly for long.

Boiotia and Corinth would not sign the peace, and the disorder within the Peloponnesian League encouraged radical strategists at Athens, notably Alcibiades who was now making his debut as a politician, to assemble an anti-Spartan coalition on Sparta's doorstep (see v.47 for the alliance between Athens, Argos, Mantinea and Elis, a concert of *democracies* as v.44 rightly says). This idea — which meant making the war a contest not for the survival of the Athenian Empire but of the Peloponnesian League — was a brilliant turning of the shaft of Sparta's 'liberation' strategy against herself. (Cp. for the general position v.57: 'in the rest of the Peloponnese some states were in revolt and others turning against Sparta', and for *Athens* as liberator vi.87, about Sicily.)

The new factors which made this possible were, first, the release of Argos from her thirty years of enforced inaction imposed by the 451 peace: Diodorus (using Ephorus) speaks of Argive ambitions in this period for the recovery of the 'universal, *holē*, hegemony' (xii.75: *holos* is a favourite expression of Diodorus for *extensive* domination) which she had exercised in the days of 'Temenid' kings, i.e. claimants to descent from Herakles, most notably Pheidon in the seventh century. (Cp. too Thuc. v.28: the Argives 'hoped to gain the leadership of the Peloponnese'.) The second factor was the personality of Alcibiades, who alone, for Thucydides, personifies the 'Argive policy'. There is however reason to think that Hyperbolus was also working for the Argive alignment (perhaps following a lead of Kleon, *Knights* 463ff.); but Thucydides is silent on this point, and on

Hyperbolus' importance generally after 421, either through contempt for the man or because, having 'written up' one archetypal demagogue, Kleon, it was not his method to give comparable coverage to another. (This is true as a generalization despite the space given at vi.35ff. to the Syracusan demagogue Athenagoras.) The evidence connecting Hyperbolus and Argos is epigraphic, a decree standing in Hyperbolus' name (IG i³ 86), which speaks of using the tribute, *phoros*, for 'the war', i.e. the war in the Peloponnese. The novelty here[17] is that the *phoros* is to be regarded as available not just for such obviously 'imperial' purposes as the defence of the Aegean and the cities of the empire, but for the financing of Peloponnesian land operations in time of technical peace. This phase of Athenian activity collapsed, not so much as the result of Hyperbolus' ostracism, probably in 418, but simply because Sparta under King Agis was able to defeat her combined enemies in a straight hoplite battle at Mantinea in the same year. This, says Thucydides, impressed the Greek world with Spartan tenacity, and proved to all that her reverses hitherto had been due to bad luck not loss of nerve (v.75). The victory was the more remarkable if (as is probable, though Thucydides does not say so) Sparta's manpower problems were already growing troublesome.[18]

Athens in this period was also active in another theatre, Persian Asia Minor, where she helped a Persian rebel Amorges, the bastard son of the Sardis satrap Pissouthnes, and heir to his rebellion. This interference in Persian Asia is not mentioned by Thucydides at all before book viii (411) but it is possible that it goes back a few years earlier. Certainly Ktesias (F 15, para. 53) knows of help given by the Athenian Lykon to Pissouthnes, who could have revolted any time after 423. It would be unsafe to dismiss Lykon as a private adventurer: in the fourth century we often find such superficially independent Athenian agents operating in circumstances, and manipulated — however lightly — by controls from home, which make it impossible wholly to exonerate the city from responsibility for them (cp., for example, p. 161 for Chabrias and Chares). And in any case an Athenian inscription from March 414 (ML 77 = Fornara 144, line 79) recording payments to a general at Ephesus, seems to be evidence of official help to Pissouthnes or Amorges.[19] This adventuring with Amorges was, in a phrase of Mahatma Gandhi, a 'Himalayan blunder' by Athens: it destroyed the delicate balance established by the Peace of Kallias, and brought Persia into the war again. (See Andok. iii.29 for Amorges' importance, and for Persia's renewed involvement

Thuc. viii.5: a Persian general called Tissaphernes sent with special powers to extract tribute from places in Asia Minor hitherto under Athenian control.) Although the full implications of this remained only implicit till after the failure in Sicily (cp. p. 144), Thucydides' omission to tell us more about Pissouthnes and Amorges is serious and probably a sign that his work on book v was incomplete.

Whatever the reasons for Thucydides' silence about Amorges, Athens' coercion of the island of Melos in 416 is the last fully described event of Thucydides' 'hollow peace' of 421–415, the *hupoulos eirene*, a phrase which was to be borrowed in the form *pax infida* by Thucydides' admirer Sallust. Like Plataia or the naval techniques of Phormio, Melos occupies the space it does more because of the interest of the issues of unapologetic imperialism which it raises than because possession of this small island mattered in any narrow strategic or territorial sense, or because the action over Melos was productive (contrast Amorges) of important and directly traceable political consequences.

To say so much will perhaps not be controversial. It is less usual to argue, as will be done here, that the whole of Thucydides' next two books, vi and vii, recording the Sicilian Expedition of 415–413, also belong in the category of events inflated by Thucydides, for artistic or other purposes, beyond their true importance *for the outcome of the war*. The problems begin with book vi chapter 1, which asserts that most Athenians were ignorant of the size of the island and of the number of its inhabitants. This is an obvious exaggeration, as one may realize if one simply counts the alliances made by Athens over the previous half-century with Sicilian communities, some (like that with Segesta, ML 37, the earliest in the sequence) showing that Athenian diplomacy stretched far into the non-Greek interior of Sicily. Thucydides has in fact impregnated these opening chapters with a gloom not appropriate to the expedition *as initially conceived*: it is easily forgotten that the original proposal was to send a mere sixty ships, which was no more than the total committed in the operations of the 420s. The irony was that it was the cautious Nikias who raised the stakes to a level (two hundred ships) where failure would be on such a scale that the prestige of the empire would be at risk, and would give opportunities to enemies inside and outside the empire (disaffected east Aegean subjects; Persia). But Thucydides, who liked Nikias, was too charitable to say this.

Nor should we too readily agree with Thucydides' pessimistic assessment of the expedition's military chances. What he does not tell us enough about is the disunity within Syracuse, which is briefly and plausibly alluded to by the otherwise implausible Syracusan speaker Athenagoras (vi.38: our city is rarely in a state of internal peace, *oligakis hesuchazei*), and on which Nikias was still pinning hope at a very late stage (for this fifth column see vii.47, 48). And Livy (iv.29.8; see p. 89) says that the Carthaginian intervention in Sicily, at about the time of the Peloponnesian War, was the consequence of *seditiones Siculorum*. Syracuse, like Sicily as a whole, had in fact a history of population transplants, as we have seen in chapter 4, and it was not too much to hope that this ethnic heterogeneity could be exploited (cp. Polyainos i.43.1 for an uncharacteristic, cp. above, attempt by Athens to stir up servile insurrection at Syracuse during the siege). We should also reckon with Athenian *fears*: Alcibiades is made (vi.18.1) to speak of a possibility of Sicily coming east against Athens. Dionysius' behaviour in 387 was to show this was not ridiculous (p. 189).

Then there is the positive case for regarding the Sicilian expedition as above all a literary construction. Like the Oedipus of Sophocles' *Oedipus the King*, Athens' glamour and arrogance at the outset are insisted on in emphatic language (vi.31), which mirrors the language, equally full of superlatives, in which the eventual annihilation is recorded: 'they remembered' (vii.75) 'the splendour and pride of their setting out and saw how mean and abject was the conclusion. No Hellenic army had ever suffered such a reverse.' But Oedipus had; and so had Troy (whose fall is alluded to in *panolethria*, 'utter destruction', cp. Hdt. ii.120, at the very end of Thuc. vii), and Thucydides' treatment of the Athenian failure in Sicily cannot be understood apart from the techniques of contemporary tragedy, or rather of the Homeric epic to which both Thucydides and the tragedians were the heirs.[20] But Thucydides has more than one register, and the obviously built-up, 'tragic' passages do not exhaust his devices for paining the reader. Even *akribeia*, precision (cp. i.22), may have its emotive function: the captured Athenians are made (vii.82) to turn out their valuable belongings into upturned shields, 'and four were filled'. It would be preposterous to argue that that precise digit four was preserved by Thucydides solely in the interests of factual 'historical' accuracy: the detail adds unsentimental pathos,[21] and it was surely intended to.

In treating the beginning we have anticipated the end, for which the excuse might be offered that, as we have seen, Thucydides – with the dark insinuations of the opening chapters of book vi, a kind of prose counterpart to the sinister awareness of future horror in the first chorus of Aeschylus' *Agamemnon* – has done the same.

Of the three generals sent (Nikias, Alcibiades and Lamachus), Alcibiades was disposed of by the intrigues of his enemies: he was charged with 'profaning the Mysteries', that is the celebration of the rites of Eleusinian Demeter. Unable to get the case heard before his departure (when he would surely have been acquitted), he was recalled when already in Sicily but declined the humiliation of a return under arrest. He escaped his captors and made his way to Sparta where he gave the sensible advice to fortify Decelea in northern Attica. This was taken, though not quite immediately (vii.27:413). In Sicily, Lamachus was killed in action, leaving Nikias in command alone. Thucydides' evaluation of Alcibiades' potential contribution is a famous puzzle. In a passage (ii.65.11) written at the end of the war, as the final paragraph of the chapter shows, he seems (as also at vi.15) to put a very high valuation on Alcibiades, holding his recall to have been fatal to the expedition's success. (That is the meaning — see *HCT* at p. 196 — of the remark that 'the Athenians failed to take the right, *prosphora*, decisions': the whole expedition is said to have been '*not so much an error of initial judgement*' — despite ii.65.7, on which see p. 129 — as marred by that subsequent failure.) But this verdict accords badly with the narrative of book vi, in particular with the chief discussion between the three generals (vi.47ff.): it was Alcibiades' plan (to win Messina and try to 'roll up' Sicily on to Syracuse) which actually prevailed; but Thucydides judged that Lamachus' rejected proposal — an immediate all-out attack on Syracuse — was right (for Thucydides' verdict see vii.42). It seems that the later successes of Alcibiades, between 410 and 407, caused Thucydides to revise his estimate.

Nikias on his own achieved very indifferent results: his attempts to wall off the Syracusans were thwarted by a cross-wall (vii.6). It is a further instance of Thucydides' exaggeration of the 'reversal' of fortune that at the end of book vi he represents Syracuse as on the point of falling, yet the mere providential arrival of Gylippus the Spartan is enough to make Nikias write to the Athenian Assembly in terms of abject depression. (The effect is heightened by having news of Gylippus precede him, borne by one Gongylus of Corinth in a single ship.) Thucydides can even make Alcibiades say — admittedly in a speech, so we should treat it cautiously — that 'if Syracuse falls, all Sicily falls with it' (Thuc. vi.91). This is not self-evidently true: why for instance should the wealthy and powerful Akragas have capitulated?

Nikias's letter, however unnecessary its tone of pessimism, at least secured the sending of the energetic Demosthenes, who as we have seen (p.132) was a man who could learn from experience — that is, from his own mistakes and those of others. In this instance we are told (vii.42) that on his arrival he wanted to avoid the fate of Nikias, who had been formidable at first, but became less so as the initiative passed from him. But the slide was not reversible, and after a theatrically described grand sea-battle in Syracuse harbour, the Athenians in Sicily ceased to exist as a combatant force: this was the greatest action of the war, says Thucydides, summing up at the end of the book, and the most calamitous for the defeated. Their sufferings were on an enormous scale. Few out of many returned.

How correct is this assessment? Probably it is exaggerated. Two books out of a surviving total of eight is a very large proportion to devote to one campaign, and for a number of reasons it seems that Thucydides (writing soon after the events: vi.62 uses the present tense of Himera, which was destroyed in 409) has made the invalid transition from scale of individual human suffering (the enormity of which cannot be denied) to *scale of importance in the war*.

First, we should remember that the eight-book division of the history is not Thucydides' own, being no earlier than hellenistic in date (there was a rival thirteen-book division), and the present arrangement naturally impresses the reader (unduly?) with a feeling of finality as he closes book vii.

This leads to the second point. The opening chapters of book viii emphasize Athenian resilience after Sicily: the Athenians set themselves to build a new fleet, with such success that a careful study of Athenian and Peloponnesian naval totals has concluded[22] that the Athenians had achieved something approaching parity with the Peloponnesians by summer 412 — a staggering achievement.

Third, Thucydides is himself not quite consistent. At the end of book vii he is firm enough about the magnitude of the disaster in Sicily; but later (viii.96) when describing the revolt of Euboia, he says that it caused the greatest panic ever known at Athens (note the characteristic superlatives), greater than that caused by the disaster in Sicily, 'though that had *seemed, doxasa*, great at the time'. The word 'seemed' is curious and implies, if not a revision of the book vii verdict, then at least an awareness that the magnitude of the Sicilian disaster was measurable in the subjective though real enough terms of human suffering, rather than in terms of its influence on the outcome of the war. So too Thucydides comments (ii.65) that despite Sicily, Athens held out for another eight (?) years (the actual numeral in our texts is corrupt).

Fourth and most important is the hard historical fact that in 410, only three years after Sicily, Athens won a sea-battle at Cyzicus as a result of which the *Spartans* sued for peace. This is recorded not by Thucydides (whose narrative breaks off after the battle of Cynossema in 411); nor by Xenophon (whose omissions can however never be taken to prove that what he does not record, did not happen); but by Diodorus (xiii.52ff.), who in this portion of his *Library* (books xiii–xiv) basks in a temporarily high reputation for veracity (the reasons for this are given on p. 7). It is above all this Spartan peace offer after Cyzicus which shows that Sicily should be kept in proportion.

The most serious immediate effect of Sicily was felt by Athens at the other end of the Mediterranean, in a series of revolts of Anatolian cities and offshore islands, abetted by Persia for reasons we have seen — cp. p. 139 on the revolts of Pissouthnes and Amorges. Thucydides says sweepingly (viii.2) that 'the subjects of Athens were all ready to revolt', but this is another of his exaggerations[23] of the consequences of Sicily: book viii as a whole does not give the impression of a spontaneous empire-wide conflagration of revolts (note for example the circumspect behaviour of the oligarchs at Chios who had to reckon with pro-Athenian sentiments on the part of the Chiot *demos*: viii.9). And Persia, despite her anger with Athens over Amorges, was evidently not unconditionally keen to help Sparta, with whom she had technically been at war since 479 (the Peace of Kallias covered only Athens): Persia expected and extorted some very solid guarantees that Sparta, no less than Athens, would abandon claims to Asia (viii.18; 37; 58).

Internally, the most obvious result of the Sicilian disaster was a revulsion of feeling by the Athenians against those regarded as responsible — the democratic leaders, fortune-tellers and so forth, and indeed as Thucydides drily says (viii.1) against everybody but themselves, who were the ones who had actually voted for the expedition. This revulsion took a financial form: ten senior statesmen were appointed as *probouloi* to preside over measures of economic stringency. Though those known to have held the office had impeccably democratic pasts (Sophocles; Hagnon, for whom see v. 11), and though the *probouloi* as satirized in Aristophanes' *Lysistrata* are hardly sinister figures, still it is right to see in these appointments of 413 the beginnings of the anti-democratic movement of 411. The reason for this is that it was the economic effects of Sicily which broke up that remarkable *concordia ordinum* which had prevailed at Athens since Tanagra in 457 — the last time we hear of serious oligarchic disaffection at Athens. The concord between the various economic classes had been built on a shared interest in the survival of the empire: cleruchies and pay for the hoplites and thetes; and for the rich, overseas land-holdings, and exemption from the need to pay for the fleet.[24] But if this economic cushioning was removed, the causes of the class solidarity of the previous decades would go with it. And that is what looked like happening: no proper fleet in being straight after Sicily; allied disaffection which would cut off the tribute from which naval building was usually paid for; and even — after the revolt of Chios — the spending of an 'iron reserve' of a thousand talents which had been set aside by Pericles at the beginning of the war (viii.15, cp. ii.24). (It is, by the way, an indicator of financial stresses to come that there was no ostracism after Hyperbolus in 418: ostracism was too economically gentle for the post-415 democracy, in that it left the accused's property intact.)

Another feature of Athenian economic life which tended to cushion her against *stasis* was the existence of a large *metic* class (p. 7); but metic losses in Sicily had been high among those serving with the fleet, and those (no doubt) more prosperous metics who had stayed back in Athens may have shared upper-class Athenian anger at the irresponsible direction of the war. (It is true, as has been rightly insisted against those who speak crudely of 'economic lobbies' at Athens, especially in the 430s, that metics had no vote in the Assembly and thus no direct influence on decisions made there;[25] but the opening pages of Plato's *Republic* give an idea of the high social esteem which a well-placed metic family like that of Cephalus could enjoy, and that esteem could lead to an influence exerted in less formal ways than Assembly voting.)

The oligarchic revolution of 411 is an episode which features prominently in modern histories, partly because Thucydides covers it at such length in book viii, partly because we have the rare luxury of a rival source, the *Athenian Constitution* (*Ath. Pol.*) of Aristotle. The episode has undeniable interest — as Thucydides says (viii.68), it was not easy to deprive the Athenians of their liberty after a century during most of which they had been accustomed to rule others (a familiar Greek extension of the idea of 'liberty': cp. p. 69). Nevertheless the oligarchic movement at Athens inevitably remained an episode only, since most of the thetes were away from Athens at the time — at Samos, where the oligarchic movement both started and ended earlier than at Athens itself. The oligarchs, that is, were exploiting a supposed political cleavage betwen hoplite and thete which closed up again when the two classes were reunited physically (cp. p. 36).

The movement towards oligarchy was given impetus at first by the belief that a change of government at Athens was the king of Persia's wish: here was a way of atoning for Amorges and (as the oligarchs' delegate from Samos to Athens, Pisander, is made to urge at viii.53) of pulling in Persia on Athens' side, something which Alcibiades (viii.48), hopeful of engineering his own return to Athens, claimed he could bring about.

At Athens an extreme oligarchic coup was pushed through, the old Council of 500 being paid off, in an atmosphere of terror and uncertainty,[26] brilliantly conveyed by Thucydides but wholly absent in the *Ath. Pol.*'s more apologetic account (whose source is probably Androtion, son of one of the oligarchs[27]). In particular Thucydides makes clear (chapters 65–6) the speciousness of the claim of the Four Hundred oligarchs that they proposed to demit power in favour of a larger body of 5000: by contrast the *Ath. Pol.*, hesitating between two sources (Thucydides and the 'apologetic' tradition), both denies and asserts the real existence of the 5000 (chapter 32, para.1: assertion; para. 3: denial). His phrase at para. 3 that the 5000 existed 'in word only' has been recently taken[28] to be compatible after all with the clear implication of para. 1 that the 5000 *did* exist, by a comparison with Thucydides' superficially similar phrase (ii.65) about Periclean democracy which is said to have been a 'democracy in word' but was really one-man rule: here (it is now urged) it is not the existence but the importance of democratic features which is being denied. This view is wrong. The similarity is not complete: had Thucydides said that under Pericles Athens was a democracy in word *only*, he could indeed be said to have denied that it was a democracy at all. The presence or absence of the word 'only' thus destroys the supposed analogy, and we are left with a contradiction in the *Ath. Pol*'s account. Thucydides is thus preferable.

The revolution of the 400 failed because of internal differences between the oligarchs, on two issues, the exact degree of popular participation to be permitted under the new regime, and the attitude to Sparta. On the second point, the original claim of the oligarchs had been (viii.63) that they would fight the war against Sparta more efficiently than the democrats had done; yet as soon as they took power they made overtures to Agis at Decelea (chapter 70), and even fortified a part of the Piraeus called Eetioneia, not with the aim of keeping the Samian democrats out but as their critics said (chapter 90) of letting the Spartans in. Foremost among these critics was Theramenes, son of the Hagnon mentioned above as a *proboulos*; Theramenes also led the opposition on the question of popular participation, taking a more moderate and constitutionalist line than his associates (though he gets no credit for this from Thucydides, whose portrait is hostile (chapter 89), perhaps under the influence of an extreme right-wing oral informant who fled Athens after the fall of the 400[29]; nor from Lysias — xii.65 — who unjustly calls Theramenes the 'man most guilty of the 411 oligarchy'). The evidence for Theramenes' moderate position is to be found partly in the *Ath. Pol.* where at chapter 29 there is preserved a proposal by one Kleitophon to 'seek out the laws of Kleisthenes' and legislate for the new regime according to them — a clear attempt to establish the new order on a more than arbitrary footing. It is in fact an attempt to restrict political voting rights to hoplites, i.e. to establish a 'hoplite franchise', which is the meaning of the phrase used (viii.65) of the 5000: 'the people best qualified to serve the state either in their own proper persons or financially' (Thuc. viii.65). Now there is reason to regard Kleitophon as an associate of Theramenes, with whom he is bracketed not just by the *Ath. Pol.* (chapter 34) but also by Aristophanes (*Frogs* 967), for whom they are both pupils of Euripides, i.e. intellectuals. But the most compelling reason for seeing Theramenes as a convinced and consistent advocate of the hoplite franchise is in the speech given him by Xenophon at his trial in 403, where he is made to use language very like that quoted above from Thucydides (viii.65): Xenophon (*Hell.* ii.3.48, cp. ii.3.17) makes Theramenes say that he has 'never altered his view that the best constitution is that which is in the hands of *those who can serve the state with horse or shield*'. Note that Theramenes in 403 also objected to the attitude of his colleagues to Sparta (cp. Xen.

Hell. ii.3.42, where he singles out the subsidy by Athens of the Spartan garrisons): the parallel with his attitudes in 411 is thus complete — see above on Eetioneia — and shows the injustice of the contemporary charge of political opportunism against Theramenes, who was called the Boot for Both Feet (Xen. *Hell.* ii.3.31). Theramenes, whose later part in the recall of Alcibiades was a disinterested piece of statesmanship as far as we can see, and whose behaviour at the Arginusai trial was as we shall see more creditable than Xenophon allows (p. 151), is one of the most interesting figures of the later fifth century. His search for political compromise makes him unusual in an age of political polarization and extremism, even though he cannot avoid bearing much of the blame[30] for the political divisions which weakened Athens in this last decade of the war.

The fortification of Eetioneia, already mentioned, was the occasion of the fall of the 400: it was a mistake by the oligarchs to allow so many strong hands to assemble in one relatively remote place. The wall was pulled down at the instance of Theramenes and a genuine regime of 5000 was set up instead. ('Theramenes' constitution': Diod. xiii.38.2).

What this short-lived regime amounted to is controversial; since Thucydides, apparently forgetting for the moment his sneers (viii.89) against the individuals such as Theramenes who had propounded it, later (viii.97) praises it as a 'moderate blend of the few and the many', some scholars[31] have been reluctant to admit that, under the 5000, democratic rights to vote in the Assembly and the law-courts (*ekklesiazein kai dikazein*) were denied to the thetes. Thucydides' favourable judgement would, on that view, reflect badly on the radical democracy which came before and after. But this interpretation of the 5000 regime is probably wrong. First, at the beginning of the chapter in question (vii.97) Thucydides speaks of 'affairs', *pragmata*, being handed over to the 5000 and this is most naturally (cp. *pragmata* in the closely comparable Herodes para. 31) to be taken as referring to the rights *ekklesiazein kai dikazein*, rights which were therefore restricted to hoplites; second Thucydides (viii.92.11) draws a distinction between the 5000 and 'outright democracy', i.e. the 5000 regime was less than fully democratic; and third and finally the phrase *metria xunkrasis*, 'moderate blend' (viii.97), should be taken to refer to a 'mixed constitution', and in Greek political life 'mixed constitutions' generally denied the franchise to elements lower than hoplites on the social scale (cp. Aristotle *Politics* 1294a35 on *mixis*). By calling the constitution of the 5000 a blend of the few and the many, Thucydides need not mean that the many enjoyed substantial political *rights*, merely that the constitution was a blend of the *interests*[32] of the few and the many.[33]

Six months after the fall of the 400 Athens won the sea-battle of Cyzicus in the Hellespontine region (March 410). This as we noted earlier restored Athenian morale and induced the Spartans to sue for peace. It also meant the end of the 5000, since it removed the need for *any* form of government tighter than full democracy.[34] Athens was back in the ring, and in the aftermath of Cyzicus was able to re-establish her authority over most of her eastern subjects, some of whom, like Antandros, Miletus and Knidos (viii.108–9) had already and spontaneously expelled their Persian garrisons by about the time of the Athenian victory at Cynossema in 411. (This battle is more or less the last major event described by Thucydides before he breaks off. Cyzicus in 410 is the first major event in Xenophon's *Hellenica*, our chief narrative source, alongside Diodorus Siculus, till the end of the war and down to 362.)

The successes of Alcibiades and the other generals based in the Hellespont created a certain awkwardness in the years 410–407: they were too strong and too successful to be deposed, but they were politically compromised by involvement with the 5000 regime.[35] The solution was to leave them in place — but not to reinforce them or entrust to them the main thrust of the Athenian war effort. Hence their failure to follow up the Cyzicus success immediately: they could not be sure of backing from home. Instead, Thrasyllus was sent to Ionia, further south (409); and it was only when he achieved nothing and the Hellespontine generals were doing obviously better than him — they recovered Byzantium and Chalcedon in 408 — that the tension was resolved and Alcibiades could return to Athens in 407 (Theramenes was behind the original motion of recall in 411; Diod. xiii.38). Alcibiades correctly thought that the key to the war was in the Hellespontine, not the Karian or Ionian region. Hence Pharnabazus, whose satrapal base was at Daskyleion near the Hellespont, predominates in Xenophon's early pages, rather than Tissaphernes who had been so prominent in Thucydides book viii. (Epigraphic evidence that Athens was flirting with Tissaphernes sometime — ?408: IG i³ 113 — is not seriously against this.)

But within months Alcibiades, or rather his second-in-command Antiochus, had lost the sea-battle of Notion (late 407 or early 406) and Alcibiades was now finished. Athens however was not: the new board of Athenian generals was able to defeat Sparta convincingly at sea, at Arginusai in 406.

Sparta had seemed, at the end of Thucydides' narrative (411) to have won the competition for the favour of the satraps: by abandoning her claims to Asia Minor she had secured the financial help which she needed for any naval initiative, in the absence of a proper tributary empire. But since then things had not gone her way and Xenophon (*Hell*. i.4) records two significant moves under the year 407, shortly before the Notion battle: Sparta appeals direct to the Great King, via an envoy called Boiotios, and Cyrus the Younger, son of Darius II (424–404) is given overriding powers in the west of the Persian Empire to wage war on Sparta's behalf. (He got on well with the Spartan commander Lysander and this winning combination is a reminder how important these questions of personality could be: see p. 19 for the Persian-Greek guest-friendships of the fourth century.) Xenophon's reference to Boiotios' mission is brief and cryptic (he merely says it was successful) but it is an attractive modern suggestion[36] that this delegation reopened the issue of the freedom of the Asiatic Greeks (cp. p. 127), closed on the face of it since 411 when they were recognized as Persian property: Darius' alarm at Athenian successes (and his other preoccupations: Media, the Cadusii near the Caspian and troublesome tribes on the Anatolian interior) meant it seemed to him worth making concessions to Sparta about the autonomy of the coastal Greeks.[37] If so, Persia miscalculated: as we noticed at the beginning of this chapter, Alcibiades was right to prophesy that an unconditionally victorious Sparta would one day make life very difficult for Persia in Asia Minor.

The effects of Cyrus' arrival were immediately felt: Notion was a Spartan success — though as much because of the Athenian Antiochus' blundering as because of Cyrus' gold and silver. The Athenian victory at Arginusai in 406, however, showed that all the money in the Persian Empire could not make up for an indifferent commander: in that year the Spartan commander was not Lysander but Kallikratidas, whose defeat is attributable to his own poor generalship not to Spartan seamanship, which Xenophon surprisingly says was superior to the Athenians' (*Hell*. i.4.31).

Arginusai is chiefly memorable for its Athenian aftermath: the generals failed to pick the survivors out of the water; their plea that a storm made that impossible was set aside, and they were condemned to death (see Xen. *Hell*. i.6;7) *en masse* in a notorious demonstration of 'popular sovereignty' (cp. chapter 11, p. 116). In Xenophon's version, Theramenes gratuitously attacks the generals; this is another instance of the malice felt towards him in some quarters: in Diodorus' preferable[38] account Theramenes' speech against the generals is a *counter*-attack, a defence against a denunciatory letter.

Denuded of Alcibiades' services as a result of Notion, and of the victors of Arginusai by the Arginusai trial, Athens, who between 410 and 406 had looked like winning the war, could now hardly fail to lose it: the democracy could not supply limitless strategic talent. Just before the final defeat, which was at Aigospotamoi on the Hellespont in 405, we glimpse Alcibiades for the last time, warning the Athenian generals against recklessly beaching their ships where they would be exposed to attack by Lysander. He was rebuffed; the battle was lost; and Athens now faced starvation. (It was not Aigospotamoi, but the severing of the corn supply, which ended the war.)

The circumstances of Athens' surrender, and the part played in it by Theramenes, rapidly became controversial questions. Xenophon says (ii.2.16) that Theramenes was sent to Lysander's base at Samos and there he culpably delayed for three months; in Lysias however (xiii.10) the delay was at *Sparta*, and since there is evidence for political divisions at Sparta about what should be done with Athens (Xen. *Hell.* ii.4.29), Lysias is probably right (Lysander forwarded Theramenes direct to Sparta). In other words, Theramenes was kept waiting for reasons out of his own control, and was not responsible for any extension of Athenian suffering. A recently discovered papyrus, the 'Theramenes papyrus' in Michigan (*ZPE*, ii, 1968, pp. 161ff.) seems to support the view that Theramenes was sent on his way direct to Sparta by Lysander. A second, more damaging but more easily refuted, charge against Theramenes (Lys. xii.65f) is that he failed to keep a promise to bring back peace terms which would allow Athens to keep her walls and her fleet. The new papyrus echoes Lysias' language down to small details, showing what interest Theramenes continued to generate in the fourth century. Even Xenophon, hostile down to the point (ii.3.10) when he stopped work on the *Hellenica* for a number of years, changed his mind when he came to describe Theramenes' stylish attitude, in the face of imminent execution, to his accuser Kritias (ii.3.11ff.). This allegation fails on the score of commonsense: Theramenes cannot have made any such promises, simply because he must have known he could never have kept them. Theramenes thus stands acquitted on both counts. The real obstacle to the peace was the demagogue Kleophon, but with his removal (Lys. xiii) Athens accepted what she could not resist, the obligation to surrender her fleet (except twelve ships), to pull down the Long Walls, and to join the Peloponnesian League, 'following Sparta wherever she led' (Xen. *Hell.* ii.2.20). The war was over, and the Athenian Empire was ended; no contemporary could have guessed how soon imperial aspirations would revive.

13   The effects of the Peloponnesian War (intellectual activity and treatise-writing; warfare; politics; economic life; religion)

The first discussion, by any historian, of the effects of the Peloponnesian War is near the beginning of book ii of Thucydides, who tells us what it meant to the Athenians to evacuate Attica (ii.14ff.). As we saw in chapter 12, that evacuation is not likely to have been complete; but for many of the inhabitants of the rural demes (and for those with homes in the town but fields to work in the country), the beginning of the war did mean a change in immemorial living habits. This concentration of human beings within the city is perhaps a cause of the more aggressive character which Athenian oratory and politics take on in the age of Kleon (chapter 11). And the war created a captive readership for a profusion of pamphlets of which the *Old Oligarch* is the only fully surviving example (but note the discussion of the merits of different constitutions at Hdt. iii.80ff: 420s?). Even in Thessaly, political life was beginning to intensify — evidently under Athenian intellectual influence, judging from a surviving speech known as the '*peri politeias* of Herodes', a plea to Thessalian Larisa to join Sparta in fighting Archelaus, king of Macedon (404). The vogue for monographs survived the end of the war: in every sphere we find attempts to put down specialist knowledge, or the results of theorizing, in permanent form, on paper. To continue where we have begun, with the political type of treatise: after the *Old Oligarch*, which is a piece of negative analysis by a critic pretending to be impressed by the efficiency with which the Athenian democracy looks after its own interests, we enter in the fourth century a period of system-building in political theory, the most influential work in this sphere being the *Republic* and the *Laws* of Plato.

Plato's aim in the *Republic* was to construct an ideal society immune from change — especially political subversion from within — and strong enough to avoid being overwhelmed from outside.[1] The reason for this is surely that Plato's lifetime had seen extreme examples of both internal *stasis* and external coercion. Corcyra in 427 had shocked Thucydides into an attempt at a general formulation, and in the decades after 404 things got worse as there were now, at the international level, a number of hegemonical rivals, none with the power to impose itself finally. This gave hope of ascendancy to first one then another faction within the various city-states. And the relative decline of the great powers, Athens and Sparta, removed one check on the ability of smaller city-states to coerce and overwhelm each other. (Again, Corcyra had shown the way: the second Athenian commander stood off with the fleet while the blood-letting took place.) Hence an increase in instability both in internal affairs and in foreign relations. An example of each may be given: first, the civil disorder at Argos in 370/69 (Diod. xv.57), known as the *skytalismos* or clubbing to death. The democratic mob, after killing a thousand of the *epiphanestatoi*, i.e. oligarchs, turned on their own leaders, the demagogues, and executed them as well: just as (on a bigger scale) in eighteenth-century France, or Iran of more recent times, this was a revolution which devoured its own children. Then there is coercion from outside: a few chapters later (xv.79), Diodorus recounts how Orchomenos in 364/3 was destroyed by Thebes, the city being occupied, the male citizens killed and the women and children sold into slavery (something rare between Greeks in the fourth century, but practised occasionally by Philip, e.g. at Olynthus in 348.) Hence the changeless theoretical aspirations of Plato, who had moreover witnessed a tyranny at first hand, that at Sicilian Syracuse. It is significant of his dislike of the violent present that Plato's dialogues are always set in the past: the *Theaetetus*, which discusses the concept of knowledge, starts with Theaetetus dying of wounds and dysentery after the battle of Corinth in 369; the dialogue then leaps back in time.[2]

Plato was hostile to the extreme democracy of Athens (the sketch of democratic lawlessness in book ix of the *Republic* could have been inspired by the trial of the generals after Arginusai); and this hostility was shared by his pupil Aristotle, who however in his *Politics* preserved some democratic features, e.g. selection of political office-holders by *sortition* (the lot). But Aristotle, like Theramenes or real-life Boiotia (chapters 7, 12), insisted on a property-qualification as a precondition for full political rights. Part of the justification for this which a contemporary would have given was that it is only when you have some stake in the state to lose, preferably in the form of landed property, that you can responsibly decide about political issues, especially the most important of all, peace and war (because *your* land is at risk from enemy invasion). Hence a link between citizenship and landowning, fundamental to Greek political, not to say social and economic, life.

Disillusionment with democracy affected thinkers less profound than Thucydides (see p. 144 for his treatment of the popular reaction to the news of Sicily), or Plato or Aristotle. Xenophon's *Hiero*[3] discussed tyranny (which for him really means something like benevolent despotism), and shows how it could be compatible with happiness, and even justice — provided that justice is equated with beneficence. This conclusion is curiously like the definition offered at the *beginning* of Plato's *Republic* (332d), where it is suggested that justice is benefiting your friends. Plato's *Republic*, then, starts where Xenophon's *Hiero* leaves off. Again, Xenophon's *Cyropaedia*, idolizing the autocratic founder of the Persian Empire, has elements of romance, and has even been taken[4] as a contribution to *military* theory. But the most obvious reason for choosing such a subject is Xenophon's disenchantment[5] with the democratic ideal (cp. *Hell.* v.2.7 on the 'troublesome demagogues' at Mantinea). It is this disenchantment above all which makes the fourth century an age of monarchic opinion, though we shall see that other alternatives were also found (cp. p. 168 on federalism). Xenophon's *Cyropaedia* is important as the first of the treatises on kingship, *peri basileias*, which were to be so common in the hellenistic period. Xenophon's Cyrus is a leader who rules, not by divine right, or oppression, but by a title conferred by his own exertions (*philoponia, askesis*), which made him a kind of servant of his people: Herakles was the divine model for this conception. 'Glorious servitude' was a slogan used (Aelian *Var. Hist.* ii.20) to describe hellenistic kingship. These doctrines were part of the kingship theory associated especially with the Cynics (a sect of popular philosophy founded in the fourth century by Antisthenes): they believed in renouncing social life — a deep paradox for a Greek, with his developed sense of participation in polis life, and one which shows how in some quarters the idea of the polis was coming to seem bankrupt.

Then there is Isokrates, whose *Philippus*, addressed to Philip II of Macedon, was written relatively late in the century (346), but whose much earlier Cypriot writings (*Nikokles, To Nikokles, Evagoras*) are an admission that the problems, especially the economic problems, of the Greek world are too great for solution by majority decision. An autocrat is required (although in the *Areopagiticus* of the 350s he was also to argue for an oligarchic solution).

The vogue for such writings was not confined to Athens: one Kleon of Halikarnassus wrote a treatise advising Lysander how to set about reforming the kingship at Sparta, making it a 'career open to talent' (*FGrHist*. 583.T 1). Kingship is just another profession.

The fourth century is indeed an age of professionalism in general. This can be demonstrated by the number of technical treatises that were produced. This had already begun in the fifth century, when most of the Hippocratic medical treatises were written down (the name of the great founder of the school of medicine became shorthand for the literary productions of the school as a whole); when Hippodamus of Miletus wrote the first known book on town planning (Ar. *Pol.* 1267bff.); when Damon and Glaucus of Rhegion wrote musical treatises (Plut. *Mor.* 1132e); and when practitioners of the arts like Sophocles (who wrote a monograph on the Chorus), Polykleitos the sculptor, and Parrhasios the painter expounded the theory behind their practice. But it is in the fourth century that the didactic handbooks proliferated exuberantly. Many of their authors are just names to us, like Charetides of Paros and Apollodorus of Lemnos, who wrote (Ar. *Pol.* 1258b40) about the cultivation of vines and olives; and it is only by chance that we know that Androtion, the great mid-fourth-century local historian of Attica, wrote a book on agriculture. As with the elder Cato, this suggests conservative political sentiments, the leisure activity of a landed gentleman. The sculptors of the fourth century, like Pytheos who designed the temple of Athena at Priene, were at least as verbally articulate as their predecessors of the fifth; and so on. The transitional case of the orator Andokides is interesting: he is an amateur still lacking the sophisticated technique of a Gorgias (cp. p. 124 for the influence of Sicilian professionalism in oratory); yet Andokides is forced in his speech *On the Mysteries* to plead like a professional.[6] It may be recalled that Pericles was supposed to have been the first to take a written speech into court (p. 123f.). The turning point is the period of and immediately before the Peloponnesian War.

But the sphere in which the differences between the two periods, before and after the war, is greatest is perhaps that of *military theory and practice*. The fifth century is still the age of the citizen hoplite: Demosthenes in the third Philippic (343) makes the contrast with his own day:

> I am told that in the Peloponnesian War the Spartans and everybody else fought for four or five months in the summer; they would invade, ravage the countryside with a citizen hoplite army and go home again. But now Philip leads an army not just of hoplites but of light-armed troops, cavalry, archers, mercenaries, and he campaigns summer and winter through.

(ix.48ff., cp. already Xen. *Hell.* vi.1.15 on the professionalism of Jason the Thessalian ruler of Pherai, 'using night as well as day ... and rolling morning and evening meal into one'.) The citizen hoplites of the fifth century were not quite universal—Thuc. vii.27, 29 notes the Thracian light-armed soldiers hired by Athens at the time of the Sicilian expedition, and cp. p. 132 on Aitolia—but they were normal; and they evoked no professional literature because they were themselves not professional. Professionalism begins during the Peloponnesian War.

In the 420s we noticed how the relationship between Kleon and the other, i.e. the fifth-century Demosthenes, the demagogue and the *strategos*, foreshadows the fourth-century divide between the military man and the politician in Athens (cp. Lys. xiii.7; Ar. *Pol.* 1305a7 and Isok. viii.54–5 for contemporary awareness of the change). The Peloponnesian War was partly responsible for this: generals now had to think up new methods of fighting. (Phormio towards the end of Thucydides book ii actually *wants* to fight in the open sea because he is confident that his by now highly trained sailors can cope better than the Peloponnesians with choppy conditions; yet only a few years earlier, at Sybota, the fighting is at close quarters and resembles a land battle, *pezomachia*, in its clumsy absence of tactical manoeuvring — just like Salamis in 480 (Thuc. ii.83;89; i.49;74). In other words a year or two of war brought more change than had been seen in the entire *pentekontaetea*. The final sea-battle at Syracuse was another affair that resembled a *pezomachia* (vii.62, etc.), but that was not through the choice of the Athenians.)

Another way in which the Peloponnesian War changed attitudes was by the campaigning demands it made:[7] long periods away from home must inevitably increase professionalism, just as the professional army of Marius naturally resulted from the protracted Spanish Wars of the second century. Xenophon's *Anabasis* has much that is relevant: Tissaphernes (*Anab.* ii.1.7) employs Phalinus, a Greek from Zacynthus, as specialist military adviser, and one Coeratadas of Thebes (vii.1.33) is found at Byzantium at the end of the expedition of the 10,000, 'asking if any city or tribe needed a general'. We find 'tactics' offered as part of the curriculum of the 'sophists', that is, the professional teachers who are so prominent in the semi-philosophical literature of the period; these men arose in answer to a felt need for what would now be called 'vocational' teaching, and professed to make even virtue into an exact science — Plato's *Protagoras* is the key text. Socrates was different from these men because he took no fee, because he was less pretentious — and because he was better. Plato and Xenophon report the claims of sophists to give education in military matters (Plato *Euthydemus* 271d, 273e, 290c; Xen. *Memoirs of Socrates* iii.1.11ff.) though Xenophon shows that the 'art of generalship' which a man like Dionysodorus professed might turn out to be merely 'tactics' in the *Greek* sense of the word, i.e. drawing up troops in formation, not the modern sense of 'how to win a battle'. (Contrast Xen. *Cyrop.* i.6.14, with a sensible plea for the study of topics like medical care, strategy and discipline.) By contrast, Plato's *Laches*, set early in the Peloponnesian War, soon after the battle of Delion in 424, discussed the concept of courage: a simple definition offered early in the dialogue is that a man is courageous when he stays in the battle-line resisting the enemy and disdains flight. No nonsense about theory there. The dialogue begins, it is true, with a discussion of *hoplomachia*, i.e. fencing with hoplite weapons; but this is scornfully dismissed on the grounds that if it were any use the Spartans would go in for it. (This is an interesting point: Spartan citizens, because of their favourable economic position, were for a long time exceptional in going in for single-minded training, being, as Xenophon puts it in a good phrase (*Lakedaimonion Politeia* xiii.5), 'craftsmen of war'. By the time Aristotle wrote the *Politics* (330s), that had changed: 'when the Spartans' (he says) 'were alone in their strenuous military discipline they were superior to everybody, but now they are beaten by everybody: the reason is that in former times they trained and others did not': *Pol.* 1338b.)

The transition from amateur to professional comes with Xenophon himself, who wrote treatises like the *Horsemanship* and the *Cavalry Commander* (not to mention the *Cyropaedia* which covers leadership in its widest sense), which offer solid technical advice — yet their author seeks to avoid the stigma of professionalism. This is shown by his attitude to his only known predecessor in the genre, one Simon 'Hippikos', whom Xenophon looks down on as *hippikos*, horsey, i.e. a professional cavalry man by contrast with Xenophon himself who, as a landed gentleman and amateur, wrote his treatises ostensibly for the instruction of his younger relations. But the fragments of Simon's treatise (see Teubner edn, *de re equestri*) show Xenophon drawing on Simon. This is a warning to us not to distinguish too sharply between 'amateur' and 'professional'. Much depended on social class.

A more comprehensive military handbook was the *Poliorketikos*, 'how to defend yourself under siege against an attack', of Aineias the Tactician, who probably wrote in the 350s. This work, apart from giving detailed practical advice like how to neutralize fire missiles by smearing inflammable objects with bird-lime, and a simple system of code omitting vowels, is also the first collection of stratagems. Many of these are revealing about fourth-century Greek *politics* as much as about warfare: they take it for granted that a standard way for an enemy to take a fortified city is to exploit *internal* subversion.[8] Others are simply the result of improvisation, commonsense and guile: for instance, it is recorded (chapter xl) that in the 360s the people of Sinope dressed up their woman as men, with kitchen crockery for armour, so as to give the enemy (the Persian satrap) the impression that the numbers of the defenders were greater than they really were. Aineias adds that the Sinopeans shrewdly did not allow the women to throw missiles, because, he says, 'even a long way off a woman betrays her sex when she tries to throw' (quite true). The idea that the rusé leader might be admirable goes back to 'guileful Odysseus', and is much in evidence in Xenophon's *Cyropaedia* and *Hellenica* — Agesilaus (*Hell.* iii.4.11;v.4.48f.) sends notice along one line of march demanding that provisions be prepared — and then takes a different direction to throw the enemy off. Economic difficulties lie behind the ideal of the general as 'good at improvising' or 'good at providing' (Xen. *Mem.* iii.1.6; *Hell.* iii.1.8 about Derkyllidas who was nicknamed Sisyphus because of the number of tricks up his sleeve). Even as late as the period after Alexander the Great, Eumenes of Cardia is a good example of the resourceful 'Odysseus' type, and a debt can be traced in his behaviour to Xenophon's writings.[9]

One reason, however, why generalship was slow to develop as a science before the fourth century, and why handbooks did not flourish before then, is that the conditions of ancient warfare placed practical limits on the powers of generals, especialy during the course of a battle, i.e. once an action had been joined. This in its turn had several causes.

First, a conventional classical Greek battle was fought without reserves, by citizen hoplites. After an initial phase of battle (which might be prolonged) of scattered individual combat,[10] opposing groups of heavily armed infantry troops (hoplites) joined ranks and the melée became general. In this second phase solidarity and holding the line counted for everything. This type of fighting was due (in theory at least) by the citizens on behalf of their territory, and this perhaps inhibited the holding back of *part* of the forces available, as a reserve. That attitude was, however, disappearing in the fourth century: Aineias has a special section on reserves (xxxviii) and Diodorus Siculus has much to say about reserves in his accounts of the Greek warfare in Sicily against Carthage (late fifth and early fourth centuries,[11] see e.g. xiii.54, Selinus in about 409). There are plenty of examples in Alexander's day, e.g. his sieges of Halikarnassus, Miletus and Aornus. The relevance of reserves to a general's powers is this: with reserves kept back in his hand, it was possible for him to pick the critical moment to throw in reinforcements, so that more now depended on his judgement and timing. Epaminondas' famous deepening of the phalanx to fifty at Leuktra in 371 was really a deployment of a strategic reserve.[12]

A second reason for the relative impotence of a general during a battle is the essentially democratic expectation, which we have already noticed (chapter 12) in connection with Kleon and Brasidas, that the commander should 'lead from the front'. This meant that a general in the thick of a battle could do little about directing its course. Hence *messages* are very rarely recorded as having reached the commander during a battle; usually something goes wrong, cp., for example, Parmenio's message to Alexander who over-pursued at Gaugamela (p. 280); or there is Demetrius' similar behaviour to Alexander's, at Ipsus in 301.

A third reason why the fifth-century Greek general could not achieve much is political: the powers of a city-state general were limited by the desire to avoid conferring autocratic power on one man. Even in Sparta, the kings could be, and were, called to account for

misdemeanour in the field,[13] although discipline was maintained until
the return home (cp. Thuc. v.63.2–4: King Agis declined battle in
418, causing indignation in his army. The men considered fining him
a huge sum [10,000 drachmai] and demolishing his home, but
relented and merely restricted his powers as commander still further:
he was always to be accompanied by ten 'advisers'). At Athens, as we
have seen, generals were liable to deposition, and though we argued
(chapter 11) that their ability to take strategic initiatives was greater
than is sometimes believed, still they were mostly appointees for one
year only, and were of course a panel not a despot. ('The Athenians',
said Philip, 'can find ten generals every year; I have only ever found
one: Parmenio.') Even Timoleon, who was sent to Sicily from Corinth
as *autokrator* (i.e. with unrestricted powers) in the mid-fourth
century, is in constant touch with the home government (cp. Plut.
Timol. 24.3;16.3 for advisers and reinforcements). Contrast the
methods of the fourth century Age of the Dictators, with the classical
fifth-century Athenian and Spartan position: the *Third Philippic*,
quoted above, correctly represents Philip's position, unimpeded by
committees or campaigning seasons; and for the concentration of
power cp. Demosthenes' *First Olynthiac* (i.4): 'he has entire control
over everything, being at the same time general, master, treasurer.'
Alexander, it is true, discusses problems with his general staff, but
often overrides their advice once elicited. This is only partly the result
of the monarchic character of the Macedonian military tradition (with
which Jason's Thessaly or Dionysius' Syracuse are comparable). Even
the *city-state* commanders of the fourth century were noticeably more
free than their fifth-century predecessors from interference by their
political masters. So Chares in the 350s campaigned recklessly in Asia
Minor, winning victories over the Persian king — till the latter wrote
to the Athenians ordering them to make him desist; and Chabrias in
379 was recalled, as the result of a similar complaint, from service in
Egypt, then in revolt from Persia. These instances show both the
freedom of fourth-century generals, and also — in the rapid
compliance of Athens with requests for their recall — the limits of that
freedom.[14] Such additional freedom as can be detected in this period
is in part the product of sheer lack of money (cp., for example, Dem.
xlix for Timotheus' astonishing financial expedients before his
campaign of 373): this meant that Athenian commanders, not fuelled
in their campaigning by the old tribute of the Delian League, had to
use their wits — like Iphikrates, also in the 370s, who had to put his

soldiers to work on the land at Corcyra for their rations (Xen. *Hell.* vi.2.37). The same Iphikrates had maintained an army for nearly five years at Corinth, twenty years earlier.

We may pass now from theories of generalship and the limitations on generals in practice — the second, as we have seen, impeding the development of the first — to the realities, and especially the novelties, of warfare in the aftermath of the Peloponnesian War.

The first salient feature of the period is the use of mercenary soldiers, the professionals *par excellence*. The idea was hardly new — archaic tyrants like Pisistratus had relied on mercenaries. It is not an accident that the use of mercenaries, common in one *autocratic* phase of Greek history (the archaic) revives in another (the fourth century). Polybius (xi.13.5–8) explicitly makes the connection between tyrants and mercenaries, and Xenophon makes Hiero admit (x) that there is no way in which a tyrant can avoid dependence on mercenaries. This is borne out by real-life Sicilian history: Gelon has 10,000 mercenaries in the early fifth century (Diod. xi.72.3). So, like the increase in the powers of commanders, e.g. Jason of Pherai, this fourth-century phenomenon is in part a product of contemporary monarchism. The big *difference*, however, between archaic and late classical use of mercenaries is this: in the archaic period mercenaries tended to come from a few, always notoriously impoverished parts of the Greek world, e.g. Krete, Arkadia in the northern Peloponnese, Karia in south-west Asia Minor. In these places mercenary service was a kind of alternative to colonization, both being a form of emigration to escape poverty. (The same is true of *piracy*, which persisted as the 'national pastime' in e.g. Krete, Aitolia and Illyria till hellenistic times; for its prevalence in the fourth century cp. p. 214f.) In the fourth century, by contrast, mercenary service has ceased to be the near monopoly of the places just mentioned, because economic problems had now hit the great states of Old Greece as well. A study[15] of perhaps the most famous mercenary army of all time, the 10,000 of Xenophon's *Anabasis* (p. 6) has shown by examining the origins of individual commanders and men that whereas Arkadia and Achaia hold their own as centres for mercenary recruitment —something to which the Arkadian Lykomedes alludes with pride (Xen. *Hell.* vii.1.23, cp., for Krete, Syll.[3] 600 of 200 BC, among much other hellenistic evidence) — still Athens and Sparta provide large percentages of the officers.

Persia's role in all this is very important: near the beginning of the Peloponnesian War Pissouthnes has a mercenary force (Thuc. iii.34.2), a mixture of Arkadians and 'barbarians' (?Karians), and we noticed the mercenary force of the Athenian Lykon a few years later (cp. p. 139). (And Tissaphernes at Thuc. viii.25.2 and Pharnabazus at Diod. xiii.51.1 have mercenaries.) Moreover, references in the *Anabasis* to developed and detailed terms of service — one daric per month for men, four times that for generals — imply a fairly long evolution before 401. But the fourth century is the great age of mercenary service, leading to complaints by Isokrates about the 'roving bands of mercenaries' whom he considers such a menace[16] to orderly civic life (e.g. v.120f., ep. ix.9; iv.168). The most notable achievements of these mercenaries were in foreign service: already in the 390s we hear of the sub-satrap Mania's force of mercenary soldiers (Xen. *Hell.* iii.1.13), but above all it was in the Persian attempts to recover Egypt, in revolt since 404, that mercenaries were indispensable on both sides (Diod. xvi.44: a total of 35,000 on the two sides when Egypt was recovered in 343). It was the activity of Iphikrates of Athens, as well as of Xenophon's 10,000, which made this difference to the nature of warfare: as we saw he kept an army for five years in Corinthian territory and this was subsidized by Persia (Philoch. F 150; Ar. *Plut.* 174). It was not only warfare which was changed, but social attitudes: returning mercenaries helped to dissolve ethnic prejudice:[17] in 401 a soldier is sent packing from Xenophon's army because he 'has pierced ears just like a Lydian' (*Anab.* iii.1.31) — but by the end of the century such racial dislike was being overcome (Menander fragment 612, Koerte's edn: 'the man whose natural beauty is good, is nobly born, though he be an Ethiopian'). There was also a link between mercenary service and the introduction of new foreign cults; these are dealt with at the end of this chapter.

The second salient feature of fourth-century warfare is greater flexibility and lightness of armour. Iphikrates was the innovator here too: his force is described (Xen. *Hell.* iv.4.16) as composed of *peltasts*, i.e. soldiers armed more lightly than hoplites, with a crescent-shaped *pelte* or light shield, which did not have the inside strap that made the hoplite harder to separate from his shield and was perhaps the single piece of equipment most responsible for making the hoplite formation a cohesive force. Iphikrates added light boots (Diod. xv.44) which took his name, 'Iphikratids', like Wellington boots. This kind of light-armed fighter may originally have come from Thrace (cp. p. 157 for the Thracians of Thuc. vii); but we noticed Demosthenes' experience of Akarnanian fighting methods in Aitolia (Thuc. iii.107.3), a lesson learnt by Kleon at Pylos some years later; and (Xen. *Hell.* i.2.1) 5000 sailors are equipped as peltasts by Thrasybulus. The most famous victory won by such troops was the destruction, in combination with Athenian hoplites, of a whole regiment of 600 Spartans at Lechaion (Xen. *Hell.* iv.5.11ff.): it was the *combination* of light and heavy armed that was unbeatable.

There were economic reasons for the growth of peltast fighting: hoplite armour was expensive, and the lighter the armour the cheaper. But it would be wrong to say that hoplite fighting dies out with the arrival of the mercenary and the peltast: the decisive battles of Leuktra (371), Mantinea (362) and Chaironea (338) were all fought with hoplites.

A third feature of fourth-century warfare, related to the other two, is *training*. We saw that Sparta had once been thought peculiar in her dedicated training system. Certainly Athens (as Socrates remarks, Xen. *Mem.* iii.5.15, cp. Thuc. ii.38–9, the Funeral Oration) bothered very little with infantry training (cavalry, as so often, were different: Xenophon's equestrian treatises show, in the complex manoeuvres they describe, that much trouble was taken here; and *naval* training was always at a high pitch, cp. Thuc. ii.84ff.). Some time in the fourth century, Athens introduced the *ephebate*, a compulsory two-year national service, but the first epigraphic evidence for this is to be dated after 330, not (as has been wrongly claimed) in the 360s; although there is some literary evidence — a mention of *sunepheboi* in Aischines (ii.167) — that the institution existed in some form in the mid-century.[18] The Athenian state, it would therefore seem, had until the mid-fourth century neglected military training; but *individuals* like Iphikrates in the early part of the century (Polyain. iii.9.32; Nep. *Iphik.* 2) trained their soldiers in sham manoeuvres, never letting them be idle.

Elsewhere the idea of training was fast catching on — hence the élite corps we find at various places: at Thebes in the 370s (Plut. *Pel.* xix.3); Arkadia in the 360s (Xen. *Hell.* vii.4.22); Argos; and even Syracuse as early as the 460s. But the great exponents of professional training were the autocratic military innovators of Sicily, Thessaly (Xen. *Hell.* vi.1.5ff. for Jason's personally conducted training sessions in full armour) and above all Macedon. Diodorus (xvi.3.1) describes Philip's drilling and manoeuvring which resulted in a proper 'standing army' as Demosthenes calls it (viii.11), and like Scipio Africanus or Marius he is said to have cut down on camp-followers and made his men carry their own provisions.[19]

Sicily's contribution to professionalism was in the field of siege warfare and use of artillery. Generally, Greeks were slow to make technological innovations, partly because as long as slaves could be used to perform routine dreary functions, the impulse towards mechanization was lacking. But the military pressures of the late fifth century — the Peloponnesian War in Greece, the Carthaginian Wars in Sicily — made the combatants more inventive, just as in the First Punic War a new kind of grappling-iron was invented by the Romans before the battle of Mylae (Polyb. i.22), at a time when they were taking to the sea for the first time against an enemy of great financial and intellectual resources. Even at the siege of Plataia in the early 420s, and at Delion (Thuc. iv.100) there is some very ingenious machinery used — pipes for blowing fire, etc. In 399 BC non-torsion field artillery for shooting bolts was invented (Diod. xiv.42.1), and we find artillery-makers in mainland Greece about the same time (Xen. *Hell.* ii.4.27). Torsion artillery comes in at about the middle of the fourth century[20] — the machines with which Philip was repulsed by Onomarchus in the Sacred War (p. 250) were probably torsion-powered stone-throwing devices, which certainly feature in inscriptions not long after (IG ii^{2}1467 B col.ii 48–56, of the 330s/320s, mentioning springs made of hair. Women's hair was best).[21]

The effect of this on the *defenders* of besieged cities was to transform the art of fortification: Aineias Tacticus mentions artillery only once (xxxii.8), where he suggests mining and sapping beneath the ground on which artillery rested. But archaeology shows[22] that the arrival of artillery made far more difference than Aineias implies: city circuits were now greatly strengthened — sprawling, contour-hugging circuits were built to deny the vantage of high ground to the besiegers; crenellations become normal, sally ports are more frequent (with the object of making raids on the siege engines outside), and we find zig-zag 'traces' (a trace is the line a wall follows on the ground), designed to catch the attacking enemy 'on the hip', i.e. on his exposed shieldless side (so-called 'indented trace').

Much of the military change so far reviewed in this chapter is the result of economic difficulties — mercenary service, peltast equipment and methods, and so on, all have partly economic causes. Other specifically fourth-century features of warfare have more general political explanations (cp. above on training and generalship). It is time now to turn from the strictly military results of the Peloponnesian War to its more general effects.

Politically, democracy is everywhere in retreat, apart from a brief period after Leuktra in 371. 446 had been the high point of Athenian democratic influence, for which see generally p. 29. The Athenian fleet, the vehicle of the proselytizing democracy, ceased to exist in 404, and though Athenian maritime ambitions were soon to revive, as we shall see, and though case-histories like Miletus show that strong democratic factions could survive the fall of Athens, still Athens was never again able to export and impose democracy on the old scale. Internally (cp. chapter 11), Athenian democracy becomes less radical, the powers of executive officials (and of the Council) being enhanced at the expense of the Assembly. Theoreticians like Theramenes (chapter 12) and Isokrates, cp. p. 156 on the *Areopagiticus*, found intellectual justifications for welcoming such changes, often by manipulation of the idea of the 'ancestral constitution' which was identified with many a reactionary programme.

Since Athens was less influential abroad than she had been, it was natural that other political systems should be tried. The most obvious is oligarchy, which traditionally Sparta had tended to sponsor (Thuc. i.19). Her victory in 404 brought oligarchic and often Spartan-superintended regimes to power in places like Thasos, the east Aegean and — the best-known example of all — Athens, with its Thirty Tyrants. The Spartan general Lysander was the author of the policy of imposing such regimes, which were often 'decarchies', i.e. ten-man juntas.[23] Spartan imperialism was harsh, though wildly popular with the propertied class in a place like Samos,[24] where Lysander was accorded cultic honours (though perhaps only after his death).[25] The democrats at Samos had been obstinately and heroically loyal to Athens right down to the end of the war (see the Athenian inscription honouring them for this: ML 94) and the gesture now made to Lysander is part of the reaction. But Spartan methods were not generally acceptable; and the dominance, in the Greek world as a whole, of the conservative propertied class had to wait for its final entrenchment until the hellenistic and Roman periods when it found stronger guarantors even than the Sparta of Lysander.

The extreme experiences of Athenian democracy on the one hand and Spartan-sponsored oligarchic regimes on the other, neither wholly satisfactory, led to a search for yet other kinds of political system. One was tyranny of an old-fashioned kind. It had been characteristic of archaic tyranny that it went hand in hand with urbanization, e.g. at Corinth and other cities on the Isthmus. Now, in the late fifth and early fourth centuries, as we have seen in an earlier chapter, we find tyrannies in places like Thessaly which had avoided tyranny earlier: the reason is that Thessaly now contained more *towns* like Pherai, of which Lykophron and later Jason were rulers. Thessaly's fourth-century tyrants were not unique: some of the satraps, like the Karian Mausolus, resemble archaic tyrants like the Athenian Pisistratids in their wealth, their artistic patronage, and in the way they determined the political character of the cities they controlled without necessarily dismantling their self-governing institutions[26] (there were archons at Pisistratid Athens, ML 6 = Fornara 23; and there was an *ekklesia* at Mausolan Iasos, Syll.^{3} 169 which opens 'it seemed good to the council and assembly ... to confiscate the property of the men, who plotted against Mausolus ...). Even in the developed states of mainland Greece there were fourth-century tyrants, like Euphron at Sikyon (a place which had already had a century of tyranny in the archaic age, evidently without having been inoculated). Xenophon's account of this man's funeral honours (*Hell.* vii.3.12) as 'benefactor and founder of the city' shows that tyrants were not automatically detested by classical Greeks: nor can we explain away the phenomenon of Euphron by seeing him as a straightforward champion of the people.[27] The great seminary of tyrants, however, was Sicily, especially Syracuse, which returned to tyrannical rule under Dionysius I in 406, less than a decade after the victory over the Athenian expedition.

But in the long run it was not a mushroom tyranny of the Jason or Euphron type which did most damage to the Athenian democratic ideal, but a fourth type of regime, the traditional hereditary monarchy of Macedon. This was not fortuitous: perhaps Philip succeeded where Jason failed precisely because of the cruder, less urbanized, less developed polis structure of Macedon compared with Thessaly. Philip, a purer type of autocrat, had no civic assemblies to obstruct him (see e.g. Dem. xviii.235). Macedon, then, made few concessions in her internal structure to Greek political forms. In this respect the monarchy in *Epirus*[28] in mountainous north-west Greece seems to have been more progressive. Even before *c.*385, the Molossian tribes had combined with the neighbouring Thesprotians and Chaonians to form a Molossian state with a king and officials called *prostates* (president), *grammateus* (secretary), and tribal representatives called *demiourgoi*; also *hieromnemones*, some kind of cult figure (see for all this e.g. *Sammlung Gr. Dialekt. Inschr.*, 1334f., and SEG xxiii.471, fifteen *sunarchontes*, federal officials. This inscription shows that Orestis was part of the federal organization, that is, the *koinon* or federation was encroaching on what would later be Macedonian territory). So Epirus was a blend of straightforward tribalism, Homeric kingship (the Molossian kings claimed descent from Achilles' son Neoptolemus) and the apparatus of Greek constitutional government. The process was said to have begun with King Tharyps who, in the fifth century, gave the Molossians 'laws, a senate, and annual magistrates' (Justin xvii.3).

The coalition of states represented by the fourth-century Molossian *koinon* or League leads to the fifth regime characteristic of the period after the Peloponnesian War, viz. federalism. Federalism is not much heard of in archaic Greece: the Ionian and Karian Leagues, as such, did something to co-ordinate resistance to Persia, but were religious rather than political entities up to the fifth century. Nor did the Delian or Peloponnesian 'Leagues' — despite their name — contribute much to the development of federalism. The Boiotian League, whose origins we have traced and whose great period we have yet to record, is the earliest and most important of the great *koina*, and we may anticipate discussion of the Theban hegemony by saying that one of its most permanent legacies was the export of the federal principle. (For Arkadia see Xen. *Hell.* vii.4.38, although Xenophon systematically under-reports the Arkadian League, which was directed by Thebes against his beloved Sparta; and for Aitolia see Tod 137 = WV 39. Finally, Tod 160 = WV 60 attests a Boiotian *synedrion* in the 350s modelled on the Second Athenian Confederacy, and including ex-Athenian allies like Byzantium. This league is concrete evidence of the way Thebes, in her Aegean policy of the 360s, capitalized on Athenian unpopularity, stealing her allies — and her institutions: see p. 232.)

The great hegemonical powers disliked and distrusted such federal groupings within their own sphere of influence:[29] the Arkadian League was anti-Spartan, and after Leuktra in 371 Sparta had not the military power to dismantle it as she had dismantled the smaller Arkadian conglomeration of Mantinea in 385 (p. 203). But this policy was not peculiarly Spartan: Athens intervened on the small, federally organized island of Keos in perhaps the 350s, to force them to administer their affairs *kata poleis*, by cities (*BSA*, 1962, pp.1ff.). For federalism as a political advance see p. 236: it was a way of achieving unity without force, and it was, through the representative principle, actually more democratic than many of the primary assemblies of the so-called democracies.

Politically, then, the disillusionment with the 'superpowers' Athens and Sparta, and above all their inability through simple military weakness to impose a uniform political pattern on large parts of the Greek world, as Athens had done in the fifth century, and Sparta was to do after the Peloponnesian War and diminishingly down to about 380, led to a willingness to seek other kinds of political organization and to turn to other, external, saviours. Thus the secessionist states who fought Athens in the Social War[30] (357–355) were *democratic* regimes at the outset: they turned to Persia — and soon ceased to be democratic. But it is important that the Rhodes which turned against democratic Athens was originally itself a democracy.[31] For this paradoxical revulsion an explanation must be sought in terms of Athenian policies (see further p. 242). This is serious evidence of disillusionment, and shows that it was no longer true, if it ever had been, that 'the *demos* everywhere is favourable to Athens' as Diodotus had once claimed in Athens in 427 (Thuc. iii.47). Again, for Polybius, who is concerned to defend collaboration with Macedon, 'those who brought Philip into the Peloponnese, by humbling the Spartans, allowed the Peloponnesians to breathe again' (xviii.14) because relieved of fear of Sparta. This exaggerates Sparta's capacity to damage anybody after the 360s when Thebes deprived her of Messenia; but the psychology of 'Philippising', as of 'medising' (cp. above on Rhodes) cannot be explained unless we grasp how little affection was felt for Sparta and Athens and their methods. Equally, the short-sighted rejoicing in Greece at Alexander's destruction of Thebes was caused not just by traditional dislike of Theban medising in 479 (cp. Tod 204 showing this feeling was still alive in Athens of the fourth century — text of oath with clause vowing to 'tithe the property of the Thebans') but because of the hatred which Theban imperialism had aroused in the mid-fourth century (Isok. v.49ff. for this).

But none of this flirting with different political systems, or with outside kings and satraps, would have been possible if any of the great city-states had been strong enough to stop it at source by imposing a firmly based and permanent imperialism. That they were none of them strong enough to do this requires an explanation in economic terms, and it is to the *economic* effects of the Peloponnesian War that we now turn.

The Peloponnesian War had been won because of Persian money. Without it, neither of the combatant Greek powers could prevail decisively. Economic weakness among the Greek states was, therefore, not simply *caused* by the Peloponnesian War, but was shown up by it: even Athens, with all the human and financial resources listed by Pericles (Thuc. ii.13), could not survive twenty-seven years of war. The contrast with Rome is instructive: what impressed Polybius was inexhaustible Roman citizen manpower, which enabled her to fight Carthage for decades without let-up (vi.52). Polybius neglects, but we should not, to emphasize *Italian* manpower, the result of a policy of integrating subject Italy and recruiting the peoples of Italy for her own war machine. Throughout the Peloponnesian War, Athens did little to integrate her subject allies in this way: only Plataia (Thuc. iii.55) and Samos (ML 94) were granted citizenship on equal terms.[32] As Claudius the Emperor said, contrasting Rome with Athens and Sparta, the Greek states failed as imperial powers because they 'treated their conquered subjects as foreigners' (Tac. *Ann.* xi.24).

We may begin with Athens, and with manpower. We have noticed that Athenians are found serving as mercenaries in the early fourth century (the '10,000'). For Isokrates the mercenary problem was a 'spiral': Greek poverty meant that it was necessary to use mercenaries instead of expensively furnished hoplites, and poverty was the inducement for men to sign up; but these mercenaries themselves exacerbated the problem, creating social unrest and increasing Greek poverty. He was right to think that one cause of the phenomenon of the fourth-century mercenary was *penia*, poverty, and in particular the difficulty which the Greek states of the period found in feeding a large resident population. In Athens' case, imperialism and the search for grain imports had always gone together. In the fifth century she had imported corn, and policed its passage from distant suppliers, at the same time shipping off surplus mouths to the cleruchies. She could no longer do quite that in the fourth century, but we do find her getting rid of mouths in other ways: thus her most unpopular single imperialistic venture of the century, the establishment, maintenance and reinforcement of the cleruchy sent to Samos (365 and after, see p. 233), should probably be seen as in part an old-fashioned

colonizing venture designed to relieve pressure on the food supply at
home (for drought and corn-shortage in this period cp. Dem. 1.61:
361, and xx.33: 357/6).[33] Demades was to call Samos an *aporrox*, an
off-shoot of — or drain on? — the city, *Ath.* 99d. If the latter is the
right sense, there may be a reference to surplus mouths. And an
inscription (Tod 200, of 325/4) shows that Athens sent a colony to the
Adriatic under the sentimentally appropriate leadership of one
Miltiades (the name of the sixth-century founder of the Athenian
colony on the Chersonese) 'in order', as the text revealingly says at
lines 217ff., 'that the people may have trading outlets and may be
provided with corn'. (For acute corn difficulties at just this time,
relevant to the docility of Greece under Alexander, cp. Tod 196:
supplies of grain by Cyrene to the Greek states 'in the corn shortage,'
cp. p. 62.)

Other ways of getting rid of population were by mercenary service,
already noticed; and by other kinds of voluntary emigration. Thus the
collapse of the Athenian Empire, a large-scale employer, led to a
diaspora of sculptors, potters, jobbing architects and builders, and so
forth. (There is no big architectural project in Greece proper between
the end of the Acropolis building programme at Athens, at the end of
the fifth century, and the Temple of Asclepius at Epidaurus in the late
370s.) Some of these men went to Italy and Sicily,[34] others to the
courts of satraps and kings elsewhere[35] (thus contributing to the
diffusion of hellenism in places like Macedon and Anatolia): men like
the Athenians Philistides and Theodorus, whose signatures happen to
survive on statue-bases from Asia Minor. Others switched to
executing private commissions in the Kerameikos, the cemetery
quarter of Athens (this is the great age of the Attic funeral monuments
or *stelai*); still others perhaps returned to working on the land.

The population point is worth dwelling on, because population is
one index of prosperity. But at Athens the graph is not simple, as we
shall see; and in any case the population of a state may diminish
absolutely over fifty years, but if its capacity to feed even those
mouths has diminished even faster, then it may be right to call her
overpopulated at the end of the period but not at the beginning. And
that seems actually to be true of Athens between the late fifth and
mid-fourth centuries.

Thucydides (ii.13) implies that there were perhaps 43,000 adult
males (25,000 hoplites, ?18,000 thetes), which we should multiply by
2¼ to include women and children. But the Peloponnesian War led to

a steep immediate drop: with the 25,000 hoplites above, compare the 9000 hoplites mentioned by Lysias (xx.13), a figure which rises to ?11,000 in the Corinthian War of the 390s (Xen. *Hell.* iv.2.17, not a full turnout). The hoplite population was perhaps back to *c*.14,500 by 322 (Diod. xviii.10) but dropped again with the emigration to Asia in Alexander's time. Figures for corn consumption confirm these population totals in approximate terms: from Eleusis inscriptions we see that 400,000 bushels (*medimnoi*) were produced annually from internal sources in the fourth century, and Demosthenes in the *Leptines* (xx.31ff.) says that another 400,000 came from the Black Sea *alone*, which he says was equal to the total produced from all other outside sources put together. Even assuming that Demosthenes has here exaggerated the importance of the Black Sea say *twice*, that makes a grand total of 1,600,000, i.e. 400,000 + 400,000 + (2 × 400,000) from all sources. At a consumption rate of 6 *medimnoi* per head we might guess at a total population of 258,000 (112,000 citizens — 28,000 adult males plus women and children; 104,000 slaves; 42,000 metics).[36] To sum up, the *pentekontaetea* is a period of great prosperity, and Athens' population reaches its maximum in *c*.432. Then the plague and war casualties caused a heavy drop. In the fourth century it rises again steadily (such post-war demographic recovery can be paralleled from more recent times), hence the need for emigration, of the various kinds we have listed.

If we turn to Athens' economic condition generally, there is an obvious sense in which her citizens are less prosperous now, with no empire, i.e. no overseas possessions for the rich and no cleruchies for the poor (cp. Xen. *Mem.* ii.8.1 or Plato *Euthyphro* 4 for individuals who lost estates in 404). If we understand the strength of the desire, at all social levels, to get all this back, we have the key to Athenian foreign policy in 400–350.

On the other hand, all Attica was now Athenian again, and we have an inscription (Syll.[3] 921) from precisely Decelea — the fort in northern Attica occupied by Sparta for the last ten years of the war — which reflects the physical recovery by Athens of these more distant demes, and their reorganization in the 390s (the inscription is a religious document about the powers of 'phratries', which were religious groups with a family base). But there is evidence that the 390s in particular were a lean time financially, e.g. Lys. xxx.22 which says frankly that when times are hard the Council listens more readily to prosecutions of the rich (for the political implications of this for the power of the Council in times of stringency see chapter 11). And it is significant that ostracism is not heard of after 418 and Hyperbolus: for the reason see p. 145.

But the gloom should not be overdone, as it is by those scholars who speak of a more or less permanent 'crisis' in fourth-century Attica. A favourite Marxist explanation of the economic difficulties of the fourth-century Greek states is that land was being 'grabbed' by *latifondisti*, i.e. big capitalist proprietors who were forcing out the peasants and smallholders. This explanation tends to fasten on Attica, because that is where the evidence is — though it is actually more true of Sparta (below). At Athens, the hypothesis of accumulation of estates was based partly on the number of *horoi* (markers indicating a debt charged on the land), which were thought to show an indebted peasantry. But it has been shown[37] that these encumbrances usually just represent routine raising of money, by *reasonably prosperous people*, for such purposes as raising dowries, leasing out property of children under age, etc. Another supposed piece of evidence is a remark by Dionysius of Halikarnassus who says (in his introduction to Lysias' *Oration* xxxiv) that in 403, five thousand Athenian citizens owned no land; but this does not prove an agricultural crisis, merely that people of hoplite status had slipped to the level of thetes.[38] Finally, it can be proved positively,[39] from the epigraphic record of land sales, that Attica was still very much a land of small estates; such 'accumulation' as did take place was in different demes (cp. Dem. 1.8).

There is also evidence of increased entrepreneurial activity by individuals in the Laurion silver mines by the mid-century — just as Xenophon recommended in his treatise on the *Revenues* (350s): individuals of substance like Diotimos of Euonymon deme, a leading politician and an enemy of Macedon (J. Kirchner, *Prosopographia Attica* 4384; Arr. *Anab.* i.10.4; mining activity: *Hesperia*, xix, 1950, 208f.); or earlier in the century Demosthenes' guardian Therippides (SEG xxviii, 1978, no. 205), also members of the families of Nikias and Kallias, are known to have leased mines, and some of them made fortunes out of it (cp. Hyperides *Euxen.* para. 34: sixty talents). The excavations in recent years by the British School at Athens at Agrileza in the Laurion of a large and handsome fourth-century installation for the washing and processing of silver (*Arch. Reps*, 1979ff.) confirm this picture of well-organized and well- (though privately) subsidized activity in the mining districts. We should not assume that all this was confined to the *second* half of the fourth century.[40]

Turning to Sparta, her economic problems in the period 425–370, expressed in manpower difficulties, are acute and get progressively more acute; but they are dealt with later (chapter 15), because the end of the Peloponnesian War did not immediately worsen them; on the contrary, if we can believe Diodorus (xiv.10), the Spartans after acquiring an empire in 404 'levied tribute upon the peoples they had conquered and ... now collected yearly from the tribute more than a thousand talents'. This is an improbable total (much too high), and in any case Sparta's old problem, how to possess and administer an empire at the same time as holding down her own subject population of helots, jumped back to prominence soon after 400, when a massive revolt, the 'Kinadon affair', was quashed only by brutal repression (Xen. *Hell.* iii.3; cp. p. 191).

In Boiotia the economic effects of the Peloponnesian War were the opposite of those at Athens, the relation being that of two children on a see-saw: Boiotia went up as and because Athens went down. The Oxyrhynchus Historian is explicit about this (xvii Bartoletti): he describes the Boiotians as profiting, not to say profiteering, from the economic difficulties which the Spartan occupation of Decelea brought to Athens; what happened was that the Boiotians bought up refugees, slaves and 'other things to do with the war' at a cheap rate, and looted the evacuated country estates of wealthy Athenians, taking even the tiles from the roofs (for archaeological confirmation of this at one excavated private house see *BSA*, 1957, p.184, n.115: the Dema house). This Boiotian prosperity, due to the war, is one explanation of the Boiotian manpower explosion — see p. 84: 11,000 cavalry, 1100 infantry, on paper — of the late fifth and early fourth centuries; another is the annexation by Thebes of Plataia in 427 (Hell. Ox. xvi Bartoletti). (Cp. also p. 84 on the recent land survey confirming the high density of population in fourth-century Boiotia.)

Corinth, by contrast, suffered from the war: we have noted the dwindling of her navy and the evidence of the fishmonger's shop which perhaps went out of business early in the war as a result of Athenian blockades. The result of this eroding of the middle class was the submerging of Corinth in a — previously unthinkable — *democratic* union with Argos in the late 390s.[41] Corinth was never again a major power after the Peloponnesian War.

Concentration on the city-states of Old Greece may, however, be misleading because there were plenty of other places in the Greek or hellenized world of the first half of the fourth century which were *not* suffering from economic depression: fourth-century Thessaly — which was a fertile and desirable area throughout her history — and Macedon, are treated elsewhere in detail (chapters 7, 16); as is Sicily, in a bad way till the activity of Timoleon in the 340s. In Macedon at least, Archelaus' work of reconstruction (Thuc. ii.100) — roadbuilding, military reorganization, etc. — was possible partly because hostile Athenian and Spartan interference had been largely eliminated from his kingdom by the war, which was therefore much to his advantage. For instance, Athens never got back Amphipolis after 424: Amphipolis is found supplying a Corinthian commander with four triremes for use against Athens in 411 (Hell. Ox. ii Bartoletti) and it eventually passed to Macedon in the 350s (p. 248). We even find Athens *helping* Archelaus to get his hands on Pydna in 410 (Diod. xiii.49, cp. ML 91). Towards the end of the War Archelaus is even in a position to encroach on Thessaly, thus anticipating Philip II (for Archelaus and Larisa, which brought with it control of Perrhaebia, see Herodes *peri politeias*, p. 186, and p. 204 for Sparta's attempts to stem Archelaus' influence here). Archelaus' death in 399 may seem to have ended this energetic phase in Macedonian internal history, and the following decades are certainly anarchic politically; but the human resources available to Philip in 359 must have been steadily growing in just those difficult decades.

In Persian Asia Minor — not a prosperous area in the days of the Athenian Empire[42] — the decline of Greek political influence in the course of the fourth century may have been a disaster from the point of view of admirers (ancient and modern) of democracy (though see p. 199), but it coincides with an improvement in prosperity, manifested in several ways — like expensive monumental building (Nereid Monument and Limyra Caryatids in Lycia, Mausoleum at Halikarnassus in Karia, Priene temple and Ephesus Artemision in Ionia) and the physical transfer of city sites so as to accommodate larger populations — Halikarnassus, Erythrai, Knidos, Kindye were all moved or 'synoikised' (i.e. enlarged by the addition of village populations from round about) in this period, at the instance of wealthy satraps,[43] whose freedom of action is noticeably greater in the fourth century than in the fifth. It has been observed that this patronage, like mercenary service, was to the advantage of *individual* Greeks, in that it created a market for their skills, and offered payment on a scale not available in their impoverished home states.[44] Skilled Athenians, for reasons already reviewed above, gravitated eastwards in numbers after 400, but they were not alone (cp. Steph.Byz. s.v. Monogissa for the activity in Karia of the sculptor Daedalus of Sikyon). The resulting art was often hybrid (as at Karian Labraunda where Doric and Ionic orders were mixed), resembling effects at some half-hellenized Sicilian places (p. 55).

We may end this account of the effects of the Peloponnesian War with the religious changes it brought. A figure who has recurred throughout this chapter is the Greek mercenary, and his impact is felt in this area too (p. 163). Before mentioning innovation in religion, the continuance of conventional beliefs should be stressed, just as a balanced description of hellenistic religion ought to give space to the survival of the old Olympians no less than to the novel and the *outré*. The pious Xenophon, rather than the agnostic and very exceptional Thucydides,[45] is the characteristic figure of the age ('atheism' is freely attributed to men like Kritias or Euripides by their contemporaries but when examined the stories are often worthless concoctions owing their origins to remarks in the mouths of characters invented by these writers,[46] as if one were to impute Mr Squeers' educational theories to Dickens). The prevalence of conventional belief is well illustrated by the Sicilian expedition. Thucydides (vii.50) blames Nikias for superstitiously allowing an eclipse of the moon to persuade him to stay in Sicily longer than was wise. But a good recent study[47] observes that a large number of Athenians (not just Nikias), who presumably would have preferred to save their skins, were actually prevented from doing so by religious scruples, although the interpretation of the eclipse was controversial even among non-scoffers (on one view *ekleipo*, from which derives our 'eclipse', = 'get out', i.e. the eclipse meant 'go' not 'stay'). Again, belief in the Eleusinian Mysteries remains firm, as shown by all the physical attention given to the shrine in the fourth century (Demeter and Athena are the only gods not mocked by Aristophanes); similarly we find an old-fashioned reluctance to steal temple funds — 'borrowing' from the gods was different, much Greek public finance being so organized (cp. ML 72 = Fornara 134) — and abhorrence for those who do it is still strong in the fourth century (Xen. *Hell*. vii.4.33–4: Olympia in the 360s; cp. the indignation in the 350s at the Phokian seizure of Delphi,[48] however much this may have been exploited by interested parties like Philip).

Finally, oracles: Delphi's 'medism' in the Persian Wars did not damage her reputation as much as we would expect: the Spartans approached Delphi as a matter of course at the beginning of the

Peloponnesian War (Thuc. i.118.3). And at the site of the Dodona oracle in Epirus (north-west Greece), ascertainable building activity starts only in the fourth century, though the oracle itself — however humbly housed before 400 BC — was allegedly the oldest in Greece (Hdt. ii.52). Inscribed metal strips found there, asking about marriage, journeys, etc. (N. G. L. Hammond (1967) *Epirus*, p.509; H. W. Parke (1967) *Oracles of Zeus*, appendix 1) mostly date from *c*.500–300 with a noticeable increase in the fourth century: that is to say, oracular activity flourished there in the fourth century as much as, or even more than, in the fifth. The kind of question asked of the oracle at Dodona leaves no doubt that religion for ordinary Greeks of the classical period was no empty form. Here is an example (probably one of the latest in date, but typical of the everyday character of the enquiries put throughout the period): 'Agis asks Zeus, Naos and Dione about the blankets and pillows which he has lost, whether someone from outside may have stolen them' (Parke, p.272, no.27).

Xenophon's belief in divine punishment[49] for wrongdoing (*Hell.* vi.4.3, where he says of the Spartans before the battle of Leuktra, p. 219, that 'the god was leading them on'), and his belief in oracles, are normal.[50] Thus he sacrifices to Zeus 'as Delphi had told him to' (*Anab.* vi.1.22), and he is accused by his men of 'fiddling' the portents (*Anab.* vi.4.14), an accusation at which he is indignant. He records without cynical comment a delightful story (*Hell.* iv.7.2) about an approach by Sparta to Zeus at Olympia in 387 to ask about the religious validity of a quibbling attempt by the Argives to plead a sacred truce. Zeus said that it was invalid, but the Spartans approach Apollo at Delphi to ask him 'if he agreed with his father' (he did). No doubt the reason for seeking a second opinion was that Delphi had greater oracular prestige than Olympia.

Xenophon was not the only upper-class Athenian to be so superstitious: a remarkable set of lead 'cursing tablets', *katadeseis*, the equivalent of the Latin *defixionum tabellae*, has come down to us from fourth-century Athens, mentioning names and families well-known from political history: Phokion, Hipponikos, Kallias the Torchbearer (IG iii.3.24 with *Oest. Jahr.*, vii.1904; cp. now *AJA*, 1974, p.169). Startlingly primitive views, then, on the efficacy of destructive magic, prevailed among the literate upper classes[51] of Demosthenes' Athens: the inscriptions are not crudely *written*, however crude the sentiments. ('Hermes and Persephone, bind the body, soul, tongue, feet, actions and thoughts of Myrrhine wife of Hagnotheos, down to Hell':

Audollent *Tab. Defix.* 50). A recently discovered late fourth-century lead tablet (*Athenische Mitteilungen* 1980, 225ff.) curses a rich batch of Macedonians or their supporters — Pleistarchos, Eupolemos, Kassander, Demetrios of Phaleron. The disgruntled author, having relieved his feelings by inscribing names, then threw the tablet down a well in the Kerameikos where it was found. The well is the route to the underworld.

It is against this conservative background that the religious *innovations* of the period should be seen. The stress of the Peloponnesian War[52] caused intellectuals like Plato and Euripides (in the *Bacchae*) to turn away from rationalism to a less critical religiosity. Plato's *Republic* opens with a description of a torch-race in honour of the new Thracian god Bendis. Bendis has a temple at Athens in the late fifth century (Xen. *Hell.* ii.4.11) and the cult is epigraphically attested in 429 (IG i^3 383 1. 143; cp. i^3 136: c. 413). Note also the proper name Bendiphanes, borne by one of the non-Athenians rewarded for helping free Athens from the Thirty (Tod 100, line 21:401). Such cults begin, in the fifth century, to acquire state recognition, manifested partly in the grant of the unusual right to own land corporately[53] — cp. the rights, mentioned in an inscription (Tod 189), given to Cypriot worshippers of Aphrodite and Egyptian worshippers of Isis — partly in the levying of specially created taxes, the 'drachma' (or 'two drachmas') 'for Bendis' (or Asclepius or whoever: *Hesp.* supp. 1949, 142; *BSA* 1960, 193). The plague led to a great increase in the popularity at Athens of the healing god Asclepius from Epidaurus in the Peloponnese[54] (IG ii^2 4960, showing the cult established by the 420s). Ammon in Egypt is another very popular (oracular) cult (cp. *BSA*, 1962, 5ff., sanctuary at Athens by the 360s): its oracle had been consulted by Kroisos (Hdt. i.46) and Lysander (Plut. *Lys.* 20, 25), and the god was already identified with Zeus by Pindar (cp. Pyth. iv.16). And Greeks in places like Sardis were evidently attracted to *Zoroastrianism*, as we saw (chapter 6, p. 71) when discussing the recently discovered 'Droaphernes' inscription.[55]

What generalization is possible from all this? One comment might be that Athenians in particular had always been innovators in religion — we may recall Pisistratus' promotion of Dionysus, of Artemis Brauronia, Athena Nike, Herakles, etc.[56] But some special explanation seems needed for the *exotic* character of the cults which arrive in and after the Peloponnesian War. One explanation, in terms of a mood of irrationalism in the late fifth century, has already been suggested — the interest in cults of physically distant origins would then be a manifestation of spiritual escapism. Another factor was mercenary and other kinds of overseas military service, which becomes so much commoner in and after the Peloponnesian War. Rome offers a good parallel — the cults of Magna Mater (Cybele), Bacchus and Isis caused problems in the Middle Republic at precisely the period when military service, especially in the east, begins to be required for years at a time (not to mention the psychological strains of the Punic Wars, cp. the Peloponnesian). It is not implausible to connect, as has recently been done,[57] the popularity of, e.g. Ammon and Isis, with the service of Greek mercenaries in Egypt in the fourth century under Chabrias, Iphikrates, Agesilaus, etc; as for Thrace, we know (Dem. xxiii.130ff.) that Iphikrates campaigned here, and see p. 157 for the Thracians at Athens at the time of the Sicilian expedition. Obviously another factor is trade (hence much of the epigraphic evidence at Athens is from Piraeus, the docks area). Intermarriage is less relevant at Athens after Pericles' citizenship law of 451 which restricted citizenship to persons of citizen grandparents on both sides (p. 44); but elsewhere, why not?

Proper discussion of the last new religious contribution of the early fourth century, namely ruler cult or rather benefactor cult, may be postponed for the moment; but we may notice that the first human beings to get such divine or heroic honours, still perhaps only posthumously, are Athenians and Spartans from the time of the Peloponnesian War (Thuc. v.11: the live Athenian Hagnon and the dead Spartan Brasidas, both at Amphipolis, cp. p. 278 for Lysander at Samos). Oikists, i.e. founders of colonies, like Miltiades in the Chersonese or Battus at Cyrene, had traditionally been so honoured after their deaths (as heroes rather than gods, which was a lesser form of cult). Their achievements in establishing Greek settlements in often hostile areas were thought somehow superhuman. And Spartan kings had always received heroic honours after death. That political interference, by powerful representatives of city-states, should be regarded in the same way as the achievements of oikists or kings, by the smaller poleis (Amphipolis, Samos) with which they interfered at the time of the Peloponnesian War, is an expression of the relative powerlessness felt by factions in those poleis, compared to their 'godlike' or 'heroic' liberators. This is a thoroughly hellenistic sentiment, and illustrates the way men like Lysander anticipate the autocratic future and help to make the fourth century the age of the autocrat, of the individual, and of the personality cult;[58] for instance, this is the period in which *portraiture in art* makes strides — Tissaphernes' coins and Mausolus' statue. We must now return to those particular activities of Lysander which caused him to be so treated — that is, to the mainstream of political history after 404.

14   The Corinthian War

After the surrender of Athens in 404, the unanimity of her enemies soon dissolved. Ten years later, Sparta was to be engaged in a war with her former ally Persia (who was now assisted by an Athenian naval commander and crews) fought in the east Aegean from the beginning of the 390s; and in a simultaneous war with a coalition of Boiotia, Corinth, Argos and Athens, fought in mainland Greece from 395: the so-called Corinthian War. This is an astonishingly rapid reversal of fortune, made possible only by, first, singular infirmity of purpose at Sparta — where concessiveness alternated with brutality — leading to, second, general suspicion of her motives among the Greek states and at Persia; in third place there is Athenian imperialistic ambition, which was miraculously quick to recover its strength after an apparently total defeat. Fourth and last there is the element of chance — the accident of death which removed Darius II from the Persian throne in 404, causing dynastic convulsions in which Sparta felt able to interfere (since freed from her dominant preoccupation of nearly three decades, the great war with Athens). This interference incurred the anger of the winning candidate for the Persian throne, Artaxerxes II.

Of these four factors, we are well enough informed about the first and third, because of the biographical interest which attached to Lysander (considered as a figure in domestic Spartan and Athenian politics) and therefore also to the opponents of his methods; and because Athenian internal history is so richly documented in these years (there is much relevant information in the speeches of Lysias as well as the historians and the inscriptions). For the fourth we have Xenophon's *Anabasis*. The second is the problem — how to isolate the precise areas of Spartan penetration which made her seem so threatening to her former friends. Here too Lysander is a crucial figure; but his activity when he moves away from Sparta and Athens is much more elusive, though no less important (hence the qualification, above, that we are well-informed about him '*considered as a figure in*

181

Spartan and Athenian politics'). Yet there is evidence for Spartan expansion in central and northern Greece, and for interference by her in support of Dionysius I in Sicily, and even for some kite-flying in Egypt, all of which though scrappy is just coherent enough, when combined with the source-material for Asia Minor, to show that some people at Sparta had very wide ambitions; probably Lysander was the man responsible for resuming the old policy of central Greek imperialism (p. 132). To understand the years 405–395 it is not enough to accept the restriction of an Athenian viewpoint, if that means neglect of the Asiatic cities (including the strategically vital island of Rhodes), Thessaly, Macedon, Thrace, Syracuse and Egypt.

Suspicion of the Spartans by their former allies does however *begin* with Athens, on whom at the time of her surrender in 404 all eyes were for the moment fixed: would Sparta obliterate Athens now that it was open to her to do so? Boiotia and Corinth pressed for destruction (Xen. *Hell*. ii.2.19); and there were Spartans of that way of thinking too (Polyainos i.45.5). Lysander, however, prevailed and Sparta imposed her traditional solution, an oligarchy — the Thirty Tyrants. Among Sparta's motives, distrust of Thebes predominated,[1] for as we have seen Thebes had already profited by Athenian losses in the war and would have profited still more if Athens had been wiped out, something which would produce what Polyainus calls a 'larger and stronger Thebes'. Thebes and Corinth for their part were not willing (cp. p. 43) to see Athens become a 'faithful satellite' of Sparta.

The eight months which followed (April – end 404) are an ugly period in Athenian history, the regime of the Thirty Tyrants. After a while Sparta was obliged to shore them up with a Spartan garrison of seven hundred men, paid for by Athens (Xen. *Hell*. ii.3.13), with a harmost, Kallibios, in charge. But Athenian democrats in exile had been taken in at Megara, Argos, and above all Thebes (Diod. xiv.6; Dem. xv.22; Xen.*Hell*. ii.4.1, etc.), and there was little Sparta could do to discipline such expatriates. There is no real inconsistency in the Theban attitude (helping citizens of the *polis* she had so recently voted to destroy): the Theban vote for the destruction of Athens had been cast out of desire to prevent Athens becoming a political annex of the Peloponnese; now that that had happened, and the moment for removing Athens from the map of Greece had passed, there remained only the less radical way: to loosen Sparta's grip on Athens by overthrowing her nominees. The democrats under Thrasybulus took Phyle in the north-west of Attica, a fortress only just over the border from Boiotia, but with (on a clear day, and before the pollution of modern times) a heartening view of the Acropolis and even its individual buildings. Thence they moved down to Piraeus and defeated the oligarchs (who advanced from the city to meet them), killing Kritias the leader of the pro-Spartan party (end of 404). Eventually King Pausanias of Sparta intervened, formally overturning Lysander's arrangements and returning the democrats to power (by September 403) — though any oligarch who wanted it was given safe passage to Eleusis where a pocket of them held out till as late as 401. But the period of oligarchic extremism at Athens was over by late 403, as was, for the moment, the period of Lysander's greatest influence. To speak of his fall or even of his eclipse goes too far, but it is certain that after 404 Sparta switched to less harsh methods of control, and not just in Athens either. (Pausanias was tried but acquitted: Paus. v.3.2)

Pausanias' intervention (Xen. *Hell.* ii.4.29) had been pointedly boycotted by the Boiotians and Corinthians — the first open sign of disaffection, and one which Sparta was later to hold against Thebes at least (Xen. *Hell.* iii.5.5). But that same passage is evidence for another grievance against Thebes, also dating from the end of the war: the Thebans had seized a sacred and specially reserved 'tenth part' of the booty collected at Decelea (this was the traditional 'tithe of Apollo' expected from the victors in Greek wars and certainly owed by the Peloponnesians in 404: had not Delphic Apollo promised his help at the very begining? See pp.105, 176). This incident must date from just after the end of the war, i.e. from even earlier than the allies' refusal to march on Attica with Pausanias. As Xenophon, who disliked Thebes, recounts the 'tithe' incident, it is merely intended to show the Thebans as impious and greedy; but it has deeper significance as evidence of early Theban disquiet at the way Sparta was engrossing all decision-making. These two episodes — and the all-important third, the harbouring of the exiles — show how soon feeling began to build up against Sparta.

How rational was this feeling? Here we move to areas less easy for the historian to penetrate (cp. above), the areas, other than the well-documented Athens, where Sparta was applying pressure on a scale sufficient to alarm her former friends.

First, Asia Minor and the Aegean. Diodorus says (xiv.10) that *harmosts* (Spartan military officials) and oligarchic governments were established everywhere in Greece; a little later (xiv.13) he amplifies this a little, distinguishing between the ten-man juntas (decadarchies or decarchies) set up in some places, and the more general 'oligarchies' in others. There is no way, however, in which we can press the distinction, except to say that the decarchies are likely to have been composed of Lysander's personal adherents (cp. xiii.70 for his earlier soliciting of the influential men of Asia Minor at a meeting summoned at Ephesus). Of the eastern cities it is only at Samos (to the reduction of which Lysander had proceeded after the siege of Athens) that a decarchy is firmly attested; here as we have seen (chapter 13, p. 166) Lysander's expulsion of the democrats was viewed with rapture by the oligarchs. Despite the poverty of the evidence, modern doubts about Diodorus' generalizations[2] are misplaced: this whole period 405–395 is so patchily attested in general that silence about other decarchies does not prove they did not exist. In any case Xenophon speaks of Lysander's desire, in 396, to 'restore the decarchies which the ephors had abolished in Asia Minor' (Xen. *Hell*. iii.4.2). This abolition is itself of interest: it marks the end of the phase of tightest control by Lysander, and should be dated to late 403 or early 402,[3] when it is certain that Lysander's influence at Athens gave way to that of the more conciliatory Pausanias. It is in favour of this dating that Lysander's man Sthenelaos had been removed from Byzantium by 402 (Diod. xiv.12ff.; cp. Xen. *Hell*. ii.2.2 for the original appointment in 405), and there is evidence for loss of control by Lysander at his former headquarters of Ephesus in 403/2 (Tod 97 = WV 1, reception of Samian exiles), and at Miletus (Diod. xiii.104, about the same period).

In Asia Minor and the islands, then, Lysander's methods were abandoned before the end of 402. But the Spartan presence in the east Aegean did not, at that moment, cease to give the Persian king and his loyalist satraps cause for irritation. This was because when in 401 Cyrus moved into revolt against the new king Artaxerxes II, his brother, it was with help from precisely Sparta (Xen. *Hell*. iii.1.1ff.). (Cyrus had also built up a force in Thessaly without detection by helping Aristippus, a dynast of Larisa, to collect mercenaries and then calling on him for some of them later: a kind of 'cold storage'.) The expedition against Persia which followed, the *Anabasis*, failed of its object (to replace Artaxerxes by Cyrus) at the battle of Kunaxa, when Cyrus was killed. The Greek force, the 10,000 (p. 6) made its way back to the Black Sea and thence to Greece; but some of Cyrus' mercenaries remained in Asia, to be picked up by an official Spartan commander called Thibron who arrived in Asia Minor in 400 with the aim of liberating the Ionian cities (Xen. *Hell*. iii.1.3–4). How had this mission of Thibron come about? The status of the Ionian cities is crucial in this period. It seems that though Cyrus was satrap of Lydia from 403 to 401 when he revolted, the Ionian cities were somehow exempted from this satrapal arrangement, and they or the revenues from them were allotted to Tissaphernes instead (for this man see p. 140).[4] Now Xenophon tells us, in the context of the beginning of Cyrus' revolt, that at that time the Ionian cities had revolted from Tissaphernes to Cyrus, who was of course Sparta's friend, a friendship which survived Lysander's supersession — necessarily: Cyrus needed mercenaries and could not be too choosy about the exact flavour of regime at Sparta. Hence it was not just Artaxerxes but Tissaphernes who had good reasons for resenting Sparta's behaviour in the last years of the century; for Cyrus had planned with Spartan help to usurp Artaxerxes' throne, but he had also deprived Tissaphernes of the Ionian cities, docking him of prestige and profit. So when the western satrapies were eventually freed from the threat of the 10,000, by their return and partial disbandment, it was natural that Tissaphernes should seek straight away to recover the Ionian cities — and equally natural that it should be to Cyrus' allies the Spartans that they in turn should appeal for help (Xen. *Hell*. iii.1). Hence the mission of Thibron, and the origins of the Sparto-Persian War of 400–390.

We have anticipated a little, in order to make the point that Spartan policy in Asia continued to be dynamic even when not directly determined by Lysander. The relevance of Asia to the enmity felt towards Sparta *in Greece* is this: the presence of Spartan troops in Asia throughout the first half of the 390s (under Thibron, then Derkyllidas in 399–397, and finally, from 396, King Agesilaus, p. 191) was a constant threat not just to Persia but to the Greek states: strategically, any power who controlled the Anatolian seaboard and its harbours could thereby hold down the mainland of Greece with much greater ease[5] (hence Greece caused Alexander little trouble once he had secured the ports of Asia Minor and Phoenicia). The alarm this produced in Greece is one cause of the Corinthian War. (So when Agesilaus tried to imitate Agamemnon by sacrificing at Aulis for his new oriental war in 396, the Boiotarchs disrupted the sacrifice, showing what they thought of Sparta's ambitions in the east (Xen. *Hell*. iii.5.5). As for the coincidence of interests between Persia and the Greeks other than Sparta, this was recognized by the sending, in

396, of the Rhodian Timokrates by Pharnabazus the satrap, to make trouble for Sparta back home, see p. 194.)

But Sparta's oriental policy is not the only cause of the Corinthian War; and we must now move from the first area of Spartan post-war expansion, namely the *east*, to the second, which is *central Greece and the northern Aegean*. Here too it is Lysander's hand which can be detected in the first instance, but here too Sparta kept the pressure on even at times when Lysander was no longer to the front.

Thasos in the north Aegean, like Samos in the east, received Lysander's attentions: he tricked and slaughtered the democrats there (Nep. *Lys.* ii.2; Polyainus i.45.4; Plut. *Lys.* xix, where 'Miletus' is probably an error for 'Thasos').[6] Thasos had been part of the old Athenian Empire, and Spartan reprisals here were perhaps predictable, especially since Thasos, again like Samos, had been conspicuous for its loyalty to Athens (Nep. loc. cit.). But there is evidence that Lysander's northern activities were much more ambitious and geographically extended than this: Plutarch says that he made a journey to *Thrace* and that he laid siege to Aphytis in the Potidaia region of Chalcidice (Plut., *Lys.* xvi; xx. All of this can be put in 405–404). But the most interesting evidence is the speech *peri politeias* of 'Herodes' (actually a speech of the year 404, but falsely attributed to a second-century AD Athenian intellectual, Herodes Atticus; see chapter 13, n.1). This speech urges the citizens of Larisa in *Thessaly* to join Sparta in fighting Archelaus king of Macedon, who (para. 6) 'possesses the land which our fathers handed down to us' (a reference to Perrhaebia, the buffer area between Thessaly and Macedon, usually in classical times an appendage of Larisa, Thuc. iv.78, cp. Strabo 440, but now temporarily Macedonian). The speech also shows (para. 24) that Archelaus, presumably after Aigospotami when his Athenian connections must suddenly have seemed valueless, had applied to join 'the Greeks', i.e. Sparta, but was snubbed although he offered money (something which for a change Sparta did not need).

Sparta, then, was involved in some very high-powered diplomacy in Thessaly and Macedon immediately after the war, and given Lysander's presence in the north at just this moment (above) it is plausible to associate him with it — but again it would be wrong to connect central and north Greek expansion with Lysander exclusively, since in about 400 the Spartan Herippidas was sent to deal with *stasis* at Herakleia in Trachis (the large-scale colony founded by Sparta in 426 (p. 131) to control the southern approaches to Thessaly: Diod.

xiv.38.3–4). In Thessaly proper, a chance reference in, again, Diodorus, reveals (a very surprising and significant item, xiv. 82) that in 395 there was a Spartan garrison at Pharsalus in Thessaly; and Lykophron of Pherai was an ally of Sparta in the late fifth or early fourth century (Xen. *Hell*. vi.4.24). Sparta then, after 405, was resuming her old policy of central Greek, specifically Thessalian, expansion (pp. 81, 132), and was hoping for still more distant pickings in Macedon and Thrace. After the outbreak of the Corinthian War she lost her strong points at Pharsalus (Diod. xiv.82) and Herakleia (to the Boiotians, who inherit Spartan ambitions in Thessaly; cp. Xen. *Hell*. iv.3.3 for Thebes' impressive Thessalian alliances in 394, and see generally p. 204); but in the light of all the above we should not be surprised to find Sparta moving north yet again in the 380s (see p. 207 for the Olynthian operations).

So there were grounds for much Boiotian discontent at what Sparta was up to on Boiotia's northern borders.

The third area of Spartan involvement is in *Sicily*, where an almost incessant warfare with Carthage had directly followed the repulse of the Athenian attack (Diod. xiii.43); here a tyrant, Dionysius I, had established himself at Syracuse since 406, first getting elected as one of the panel of generals, then as sole general, by the Kleon-like device of attacking the competence and integrity of his colleagues and rivals; finally, as Diodorus explicitly says, he imitated an older Athenian, Pisistratus (Diod. xiii.95) and demanded a bodyguard — the familiar old tyrannical tune, as Plato called it (p. 48). But even so Dionysius' position was not firm, so after settling Athens, Sparta sent one Aretes to Syracuse, ostensibly to help the Syracusans recover their liberty, but actually to help consolidate Dionysius in power (Diod. xiv.10, cp. 70). Again, this is not an isolated instance of Spartan–Syracusan involvement: not only is there Gylippus who had saved Syracuse in 414–13, and the Syracusan Hermokrates who fought for Sparta in Ionian waters soon after (Xen. *Hell*. i.1), but late in the Peloponnesian War we hear of one 'Dexippos the Lacedaimonian' who had, remarkably, been 'put in charge of Gela by the Syracusans' (Diod. xiii.93), and whom Dionysius tried to suborn. Dexippos, however, seems to have been a more honest man than Aretes — or else his Spartan masters had not yet seen the advantages of installing a 'faithful satellite' (to adapt Xenophon's phrase about Athens) at Syracuse. He would not co-operate and Dionysius ran him out of Sicily, fearing that he might restore Syracusan liberty; after which we hear no more of Dexippos. Aretes however *was* willing to play the double agent and *agent provocateur*; he incited the opponents of the tyranny and got their confidence — then informed on them to Dionysius. He killed one himself, Nikoteles of Corinth, 'a leader of the Syracusans' (Diod. xiv.10).

This Spartan help to Dionysius came at a difficult moment for the new tyrant: the fighting with Carthage had ended less than gloriously with a negotiated peace (405) under which Carthage retained a strong presence in Sicily and had the right to levy tribute on various Greek cities, for instance Akragas, Gela and Himera. Dionysius still needed to justify his ascendancy by military means, since it was a military crisis which had created that ascendancy, so he started a campaign against the Sikels. But discontent at Syracuse was running too strong and there was a revolt. At one moment the tyrant, under siege in his own citadel, actually agreed to leave with only five ships. But in the end he held out, by a mixture of nerve, concessions and cunning. This was the delicate position which had been reached at the point when we hear of Aretes' activity. It is clear, then, that the survival of Dionysius' tyranny owed something to Sparta; and that here in the west she played out successfully the same hand which was to fail in the east at Kunaxa, when she supported Cyrus' attempt on Artaxerxes' throne. Dionysius did not forget to show gratitude towards, nor did Artaxerxes easily overcome his grudge against, the Spartan government which had authorized these various intrigues (p. 184 for Artaxerxes). Again we may suspect the influence of Lysander, whose diplomacy in this period included a visit to Dionysius (Plut. *Lys.* ii).

Aretes seems to have been sent on his own; but as Dionysius' power grew and he prepared to renew the war with Carthage in the years up to 396, support for him became, from Sparta's point of view, less of a gamble, and we find her sending him solider help: thirty ships under Pharax as admiral (396). Pharax too disappointed the hopes of those Syracusans who associated Sparta with the word 'liberation', but unlike Aretes he did not bother to disguise his mission, announcing that he had come to help Syracuse and Dionysius to fight Carthage, not to overthrow Dionysius (Diod. xiv.63;70). The progression Dexippos, Aretes, Pharax, is interesting: three different kinds of Spartan? Or three stages in Sparta's loss of scruple at this strongest period in the history of her imperialism? Probably the latter, though we do find another Pharax fighting for Dionysius' son Dionysius II later in the century (Plut. *Dion* xlviii–xlix; *Timol.* xi), and

Theopompus said of some Pharax that his lifestyle was more Sicilian and self-indulgent than Spartiate (F 192). All that might suggest that Pharax the admiral had special qualifications or connections to suit him for his Sicilian job.[7]

So Spartan interest in the west was kept up throughout the years after 414, taking more positive form with the end of the Peloponnesian War. Communications between Sicily and Old Greece were fast and frequent in this period, the age of maximum Sicilian involvement in mainland Greek affairs: thus when Persia began to mobilize a fleet against Sparta in 397 it was a Syracusan, Herodas, who brought Sparta the news (Xen. *Hell*. iii.4.1).

From Sparta's point of view, backing Dionysius paid off; we shall see that the King's Peace of 387/6 was brought about by simple Spartan superiority at sea, a superiority to which Persia contributed most obviously — but the Syracusan contribution was twenty ships (Xen. *Hell*. v.1.26), enough to give Sparta a clear numerical margin over Athens. Aretes may, as Diodorus says (xiv.10), have brought Sparta into disrepute, but 387/6 showed that he did well, judged by the usual short-term Spartan criterion 'what is best for Sparta?' — the criterion applied by the Spartans at Plataia in 429 and by Agesilaus at more than one crisis in his reign (Thuc. iii.68; Xen. *Hell*. v.2.32;4.32).

How was all this viewed by the other Greek states? Spartan activity in Sicily is not normally cited as a cause of the Corinthian War, but that is perhaps because Sicily tends to get separate treatment from the modern historian, an arrangement which is more plausible for the mid-fifth century than the late fifth and early fourth. *Athens* was anxious enough to win Dionysius over in this period: an inscription (Tod 108) records honours to him from 393 BC, and Conon had an Athenian embassy sent to Syracuse at about the same time (Lys. xix.19) — all without success, as 387 was to show, when Dionysius (above) repaid the debt incurred through Pharax's mission of 396. Athens did not give up trying: in 368 she succeeded in getting an alliance (Tod 136) with Dionysius (who then died almost immediately). But by that time Athens and Sparta had moved into alliance themselves, against Thebes (after Leuktra, 371) and so Dionysius' new Athenian alignment is not necessarily anti-Spartan. So fear of the old Dorian axis Sparta-Syracuse (chapter 12, p. 141) makes it plausible to add fear or jealousy over Sicily to the reasons which made Athens ready to fight Sparta in 395. Then there is *Corinth*, unmoved perhaps by what was going on in the east Aegean or northern Greece, but never indifferent to the west, especially her colony Syracuse (in 414 Gylippos the Spartan had been preceded in his arrival at Syracuse by Gongylos the Corinthian; and Timoleon who re-established Syracuse in the mid-fourth century was sent out by Corinth). We may recall that one of the men liquidated in 404 in Syracuse was Nikoteles the Corinthian, for whose assassination the Spartan Aretes is explicitly said to be responsible. How did Corinth like this? Corinthian hostility to Sparta in the 390s may well have been fuelled by the activities of Aretes and Pharax.

The fourth and last area of Spartan expansion is the least well documented, namely Egypt. We have only two items of evidence on this, a visit by Lysander to the oracle of Ammon in ?403 (which is suspiciously soon after Egypt fell away from Persia in 404); and material help sent by the rebel Pharaoh to Sparta in 396 for her war with Persia (Diod. xiv.79: equipment for 100 triremes and 500,000 measures of grain. That it went astray does not affect the present argument). It is tempting to connect these two pieces of evidence and to suggest that Lysander's interest in the African continent was not purely religious — in fact that he was investigating possibilities, such as that Sparta might support yet another emergent opportunist, just as she was supporting Dionysius and as she was shortly to support Cyrus who was, like the new ruler of Egypt, a Persian rebel. Lysander's brother was called Libys, which might suggest family ties with Africa (cp. Lichas *son of Arkesilas*, p. 101).

So Sparta was pushing out, with Lysander detectable each time as the driving force, to all four points of the compass, to the east (Samos, etc.), to the north (Thessaly, Macedon, Thasos, Thrace), to the west (Syracuse) and to the south (Egypt). Almost a *Weltpolitik*. Of these directions of penetration, it was the eastern and southern which must have particularly alarmed and annoyed *Persia*. From the point of view of Boiotia, Athens and the other *Greek* states there was another risk, that of encirclement. If Sparta could get through Thessaly, Macedon and Thrace to the Hellespont, at the same time establishing herself in Asia Minor (the Hellespontine Phrygian satrapy was especially important in this respect), working up to the Hellespont from the other side, she could by a pincer movement secure the straits permanently, and would be able to control the food supplies of states which like Athens got their corn by import from the Black Sea. Boiotia was not so dependent; but the purely military threat of a

Sparta so well and widely entrenched was enough to justify Boiotian nervousness (cp. p. 185 for the strategic importance of Asia Minor for control of Greece proper).

These, then, are the 'true causes' of the Corinthian War, the growth of Spartan power in the areas we have discussed, to the point where it 'alarmed the Greeks' (to put things in Thucydidean language) 'and compelled them to war'.[8] But it was Persia who moved against Sparta first.[9]

The mission of Thibron, to help the Ionian cities, was directed against Tissaphernes, now satrap of Lydia; but under Derkyllidas who succeeded Thibron (399–397) the war was broadened out in a northerly direction, as Derkyllidas promptly made a truce with Tissaphernes and attacked the Persian satrap of Hellespontine Phrygia. (For this satrapy and its capital Daskyleion see p. 72.) Derkyllidas' reasons for this were partly personal — a grudge against Pharnabazus dating back to 407 when the satrap had caused him to be punished for some military offence (Xen. *Hell*. iii.1.9). By Xen. *Hell*. iii.2 the two satraps have both suffered enough damage to their territory and have made common cause to 'throw the Greeks out of the King's land'; the king must by now (397) have been getting clear messages of alarm from both of his far western satraps. Full-scale war still need not have happened, though, were it not for the king's own personal hatred for the Spartans, whom the contemporary Dinon says (F 19), he regarded as the 'most shameless of men'. This is an obvious allusion to the Spartan assistance to Cyrus.[10] These anti-Spartan emotions of Artaxerxes were to be an important factor in the years that follow, however irrational those emotions may have been (because sometimes, see p. 197 on the year 392, they were indulged against Persia's own interests).

The Persian king, then, ordered a fleet to be built (397: Diod. xiv. 39.2; for the date Philochorus F 144/5 ; Isok. iv.142) with the Athenian Conon as commander. Since escaping from Aigospotami, Conon had been staying with Evagoras of Cyprus (Isok. ix). This was the fleet of which Herodas the Syracusan brought news to Sparta (Xen. *Hell*. iii.4.1). Sparta for her part now stepped up the war, this time sending the new king Agesilaus, accompanied by Lysander, on what Xenophon represents as a grand crusade against Persia (iii.4.4; but see below for Agesilaus' real intentions, which may have been more modest). In between his accounts of the oriental activities of Derkyllidas and of Agesilaus, Xenophon inserts (iii.3) the Kinadon affair (p. 100), perhaps only because it did actually happen around this time and the accession of Agesilaus offered a suitable pause in the narrative; but perhaps also because the suppression of Kinadon's conspiracy explains how Sparta could safely send a large expedition abroad, something from which fear of helot trouble had always tended to deter her. Fear of helots was to be equally relevant to Sparta's decision, later in the 390s, to abandon Asia after all (p. 197). The Kinadon affair reminds us that Sparta is not a normal imperial power.

The manner of Agesilaus' departure — his solemn sacrifice at Aulis opposite Euboia, in imitation of Agamemnon — provoked an incident whose importance we have already noticed, the disruption of the sacrifice by the Boiotarchs. Were the Boiotarchs right to be so sensitive at just this moment, that is, were Agesilaus' aims really as ambitious as Xenophon makes out? In favour of Xenophon, it is not conceivable that the historical fact of the sacrifice was an invention by the historian and to that extent the symbolism of Aulis is inescapable: it indicates plans for conquest on a grand scale, rivalling the Greek War against Troy. But it is striking that when Agesilaus actually arrives in Asia the first thing he does is to offer Tissaphernes a more realistic deal, mere 'autonomy for the Greeks in Asia' (Xen. *Hell.* iii.4.5). We have seen (chapter 12) that the so-called Treaty of Boiotios of 407 had probably reopened this question of autonomy, and if that view is right it helps explain why neither Xenophon, nor the principals in the affair, show any surprise at what would otherwise be a sudden denial of all the Sparto-Persian diplomacy of Thucydides book viii. What was Agesilaus up to? Perhaps the Aulis incident was mere propaganda for Persian consumption, designed to speed up the diplomacy on the real issue, which was indeed the autonomy of the Greeks on the seaboard: much had happened since Boiotios' mission, including the accession of a new Persian king, and we know from Herodotus (vii.151; Argos checks that her friendship with Persia still subsists; date probably soon after accession of Artaxerxes I) that Persian kings were not necessarily thought to be bound by what their predecessors had done. Or perhaps the actions of Agesilaus, whose true aim was no more than to detach a cordon of rebel satraps from Persia,[11] have misled Xenophon, who was always prone to sentimental 'panhellenism', that is to thoughts of a Greek war against Persia.[12] In favour of the view that Agesilaus wanted the friendship of individual Persians, while posing as champion of hellenism against the Persian Empire as an institution, is the series of 'guest-friendships' and romantic attachments which he formed in Asia — the invitation to Pharnabazus to secede, the relation with the son of the Persian Spithridates (both Xen. *Hell.* iv.1), and the guest-friendship with the young Mausolus of Karia (Xen. *Ages.* ii.26). This ambivalence — one attitude to individuals, another to the institution — also runs through Xenophon's writings; and it anticipates the politics of Alexander, who destroyed the Persian Empire, but promoted its personnel and perpetuated its ruling blood by the marriages of himself and his officers.[13] (Cp. *Hell.* v.1.28: Ariobarzanes and Antalkidas.)

But the deal with Tissaphernes was only temporary (three months' truce according to Xen. *Ages.* i.10); whatever Agesilaus' motives may have been, Tissaphernes' were simply to gain time to send to the Persian king for an army. The result was a smashing Spartan victory, the battle of Sardis (396), which led to Tissaphernes' downfall and death. This is the climax of Spartan land achievement in Asia. But the Persian naval offensive should not be neglected — as it is by Xenophon: it is only from Diodorus (xiv.79.5) that we learn of a vital event in the south-east Aegean, the revolt of Rhodes from Sparta (396), encouraged by the spectacle and prospect of the Atheno-Persian revival by sea. The revolt of Rhodes is highly relevant to Athenian readiness to join the war v. Sparta when the time came, because of Rhodes' advantages of situation: these were both strategic (cp. Dem. xv.12) and economic (see Thuc. viii.35.2 and Dem. lvi for the Egypt-Rhodes-Athens corn route).

Tissaphernes' replacement was a high court official, Tithraustes, who in the king's name offered Agesilaus what he had asked Tissaphernes for, the autonomy of the Greeks — *on condition that Agesilaus sailed home* (Xen. *Hell.* iii.4.25). But Agesilaus, his head perhaps turned by the victory at Sardis, moved on to Pharnabazus' country and there tried to seduce Pharnabazus from his Persian allegiance. Xenophon's account of Agesilaus' movements in Asia ends with the strongest statement in all his writings of Agesilaus' intention to 'go as far east as possible' (spring 394); i.e. he was still planning extensive conquest.

There is no checking the truth of this because Agesilaus was recalled by crisis in Greece, where suspicion of Sparta had developed into war. The news of Sardis can only have strengthened those suspicions.

The *alethestate prophasis*, truest cause, of this war has been discussed at length above. The *aitiai*, the precipitating causes, were as trivial as any believer in Thucydidean theories of causation could wish; they are given by the Oxyrhynchus Historian (xviff.Bart.), and by Xenophon (*Hell*. iii.5), in slightly different versions. Two small central Greek peoples, the Lokrians and the Phokians, had come to blows over some disputed land: the anti-Spartan party in Boiotia, led by Ismenias, incited some Phokian individuals to invade Lokris, and Lokris then complained officially to Boiotia. At Ismenias' instigation help was sent to Lokris. Phokis in her turn appealed to Sparta, who at first tried to get the combatants to accept arbitration, but then moved in on behalf of Phokis. Lysander, back now from Asia ahead of Agesilaus, crossed to Phokis and invaded Boiotia as far as Haliartus. Xenophon says blandly that Sparta was happy to go to war not just because of her grievances against Boiotia (the tithe of Apollo, the refusal to invade Attica in 403, to which add her and Corinth's failure to participate in Sparta's Elis campaign (Xen. *Hell*. iii.2.25) and the Aulis incident) but because *things were going well for her in Asia and she had no other wars on hand* (*Hell*. iii.5.5).

We have seen that for a full understanding of the deep causes of the war we must go much further afield than the superficial account of Xenophon. But there is still the question of how the final coalition (Boiotia, Athens and the others) came about. Here *Hell. Ox.* gives valuable evidence on the state of the internal parties in the various cities, but even he gives too much weight to trivial and personal factors (which is not to deny the importance of personal ambition). For the Oxyrhynchus Historian (vi–vii Bart.) these internal and parochial differences were the key: Timolaos the Spartan sympathizer at Corinth had his enemies whose politics naturally took an anti-Spartan form; similarly at Argos. The Oxyrhynchus Historian is at pains to deny that Persian bribery was a cause. This is a reference to an event which, as we observed earlier, knits together the Sparto-Persian War and the Corinthian War: in 396 Pharnabazus, after and no doubt as a result of the Rhodian revolt, sent a Rhodian called Timokrates to Greece to encourage hostility to Sparta, by spending money in the right places. The Oxyrhynchus Historian is right to say that this money was accepted at Athens, for example (against Xenophon who says it was not: *Hell*. iii.5.2); but right also to say that hostility to Sparta in Greece was longstanding (*palai*, vii.2), so that Timokrates did not simply 'cause' the war. We have examined the causes of that longstanding hostility in the opening pages of this chapter. Our only quarrel with the Oxyrhynchus Historian should be that he rejects the 'Timokrates' explanation, not in favour of a

Thucydidean analysis in terms of Spartan expansion but in favour of a Herodotean account of domestic enmities and impulses in the states concerned. In any case the relevance to the Corinthian War of Persian money can be denied only if we concentrate on Timokrates; the fleet which was building up in the south-east Aegean was commanded by an Athenian — but paid for by Persia.

The main surviving part of the Oxyrhynchus Historian opens in 397, with an account of the atmosphere in Athens. He distinguishes between the propertied classes there, who wanted peace, and the 'many' who (wanted war but) bowed to the opinion of Thrasybulus and his associates that trouble should still be avoided. So officially Athens disowned the trireme which one Demainetos took across the Aegean to Conon (chapter 11, n. 23). By 396 the atmosphere had changed; we saw above that the revolt of Rhodes was a crucial event which must be the explanation why Athens now felt able to compromise herself where she had not felt able in 397. In 395 the Thebans come to Athens to ask them to join the war against Sparta. Athens, as we have seen, was now able, if she wished, to get involved (because Rhodes showed Conon and Persia to be achieving successes by sea, and because of the promise and protection of Theban help by land). But was she willing? The Thebans thought so: in a famous sentence they remark (Xen. *Hell.* iii.5.10) 'everybody knows how anxious you Athenians are to recover your empire'. This was true, and the proofs of it must now be given.

We can go back even before the end of the Peloponnesian War, to the battle of Arginusai in 406, when Diodorus says that the Boiotians, as well as the Euboians and the other Greeks who had fallen away from Athens, fought vigorously for Sparta because they knew that the Athenians 'would take their revenge on them if they should once regain their sovereignty'[14] (xiii.99.6). And there had been a number of incidents and gestures after 404 which showed that imperial ambitions were not dead. At first, Athens had, by the terms of her surrender, to 'follow Sparta by land and sea'. Thus she participated in some Spartan operations against Elis in 402 and 401 (Xen. *Hell.* iii.2.21ff.) and even supplied a cavalry force of three hundred for Thibron's expedition to Asia in 400 (iii.1.4). The latter, however, is not quite straightforward since Xenophon says that the *demos* hoped to be rid of these men, obviously as being oligarchic sympathizers. Two inscriptions attest the revival of an independent spirit: one (Tod 97 of 403/2) honours loyal Samians (cp. p. 184 for the mention of

Ephesus and Notion); and the other (Tod 98, cp. J. Pouilloux (1958) *Thasos*, 145, 196ff.: after 404) renews proxeny grants (v. index) to pro-Athenians from Thasos. So, on Athens' part, half-hearted fulfilment of her military obligations to Sparta, and undisguised gratitude for the services of Athenian democratic sympathizers in other states. The inscription recording rewards for the liberators of the democracy, passed in 401, also fits into this picture (Tod 100 = WV 8): a recently published fragment (*BSA*, 1952, 102ff.) shows that one category of honorand was 'the people who stood by the *demos* in the Piraeus'. But the most revealing text about Athenian ambitions in the 390s is Andokides *On the Peace* (iii.12ff.), delivered in 392, which speaks frankly of Athenian desire to recover 'the cleruchies, and the overseas possessions and debts' (p. 30).

So Athens was willing, as well as able, to respond to the Theban appeal; Thrasybulus, who had played safe at the time of the Demainetos episode in 397, was the man who proposed the Boiotian alliance; this shows that his caution in 397 was due not to some congenital 'moderation' in foreign affairs but to prudence and a weighing of immediate risks[15] (after all, as he remarks at Xen. *Hell.* iii.5.16, the Piraeus was still ungated in 395). That is, he was as keen for war as Conon. Indeed the epigraphic record shows that the aggressiveness of Thrasybulus' Boiotian alliance has been understated by Xenophon, who implies that the alliance was with Thebes only, not Boiotia as a whole (iii.5.16). But the relevant inscription (Tod 101 = WV 5) reveals that it was in fact an alliance between Athens and the *Boiotians*. The importance of this is that, since the inscription records that Athens pledged herself to fight as soon as an enemy attacked Boiotia, Athens was at war with Sparta *by the very fact of concluding the alliance*, since at that moment Lysander was on Boiotian soil (iii.5.17).

Lysander was killed at Haliartus in Boiotia, almost immediately after mounting his invasion. It was high time Agesilaus came home.

Agesilaus' Asiatic policy was near collapse. If he wanted friendly satraps, he had made some personal conquests, but politically he had drawn a blank (Pharnabazus' refusal is courteous but firm: iv.1.37). If, on the other hand, he really wanted to succeed where the 10,000 had failed the chance was denied him because of events at home. Worst of all, the war at sea was now to be decided: the Spartan fleet was crushed at the battle of Knidos by Pharnabazus and Conon in August 394 and the victors, who promised the autonomy for which Sparta had negotiated in vain, were welcomed in the eastern cities and islands as liberators; they then moved into west Aegean waters, occupied Kythera and threatened Sparta's own coastline (393: iv.8.8). Persian money now paid for the refortification of the Piraeus (cp. Tod 107 = WV 10) and for the operations round Corinth (p. 163).

On land, two great hoplite battles were fought in 394, at Nemea (in Agesilaus' absence) and Coronea (after his return: Xen. *Hell*. iv.2;3). Both were strategically indecisive, though technical Spartan victories, and the war in this theatre settled to a stalemate: the anti-Spartan coalition now occupied Corinth, where a democratic revolution led to a political union with Argos (n. 41 to chapter 13). Despite a brief Spartan recapture of Corinth's western port of Lechaion, Iphikrates maintained a strong mercenary and peltast presence at Corinth (p. 163) which Sparta could not dislodge. Though the war took its name from the operations round Corinth it was not here that it was to be decided but at sea, in the south-east Aegean and at the Hellespont.

The occupation of Kythera could not be ignored by a Sparta which had so recently had to cope with Kinadon, for Kythera in hostile hands was a notorious threat to Spartan internal security (Hdt. vii.235; Thuc. vii.26). So Sparta, unable to force a conclusion by land and in grave trouble by sea, sued for peace, offering to clear out of Asia for good: Xen. *Hell*. iv.8.14, 'Sparta will not dispute with Persia for the Asiatic Greek cities.' This offer was made to a new Persian plenipotentiary Tiribazus, whose command is parallel or superior to the ordinary Sardis satrapy held by Tissaphernes, Tithraustes and then Autophradates.[16] These peace terms were negotiated between the Greek powers and Persia, at conferences held at Sardis (Xen. *Hell*. iv.8) and then Sparta (Andok. iii. The date, 392, is secure from Philochorus, F 149). But Artaxerxes, unable to overcome his dislike for Sparta (p. 191), refused, against Tiribazus' advice, to agree to the peace though it gave him everything he wanted, and Tiribazus was replaced by Strouses who was given orders to continue the war against Sparta. Equally, atavistic Athenian hatred for Persia, which could now come back into the open, caused the peace to be rejected there as well: the co-operation between Conon and Persia had been a historical anomaly, for which the Knidos victory had now removed the need. Hence when Evagoras moves into revolt from Persia about this time, he gets help from Persia's nominal allies the Athenians (Xen. *Hell*. iv. 8.24 notes the paradox). There is even evidence from 393, in a new inscription (*Hesp*., 1979, pp.180ff., new fragments of Tod 109 which are not in WV) that Athens sought to represent the Knidos victory as the result of co-operation not with Persia but with *Cyprus* (since Evagoras had helped Conon); that is, the Persian aspect of Knidos was soon felt at Athens to be an embarrassment.

So the war went on. What ended it was Persia's realization that by using Athens to reduce Sparta she had driven out fire with fire. The Theban assessment of Athenian desire for *arche* was now rapidly and sensationally vindicated. Not only did Athens make an alliance with Evagoras but with a far more serious Persian rebel, Egypt (Aristoph. *Plut.* 179); and though initially Pharnabazus and Conon seem to have kept their promises of autonomy (SEG xxvi, 1976/7, no. 1282 with *Cambridge Ancient History*, vol. vi, edn 2, ch. iii), we soon find Thrasybulus laying greedy hands on the *chora*, territory, of Asia Minor (Xen. *Hell.* iv.8.30); and a speech (xxviii) of Lysias shows him taking money from the Asian *polis* of Halikarnassus as well. And an inscription (Tod 114, not in WV, about Ionian Klazomenai) mentions a '5 per cent tax in the time of Thrasybulus'. Finally, Xenophon (*Hell.* iv.8.27) shows that he set up a tithe at Byzantium on traffic coming through the Hellespont — a very fifth-century gesture (cp. ML 58 = Fornara 119 and Xen. *Hell.* i.1.22: Alcibiades after the battle of Cyzicus).

Artaxerxes reacted to this by sending down Tiribazus again, with the opposite brief to Strouses' — that is, the war was now directed against Athens. The war was decided in two areas, both economically important to Athens (to whose corn difficulties in the Corinthian War Lysias xxii attests[17]): first, Rhodes returned to the Spartan side (Diod. xiv.97). Second, the Spartan Antalkidas, with Persian and (as we have noted) Syracusan help, seized the Hellespont (Xen. *Hell.* v. 1.29: this must have brought strong memories of Aigospotami and its aftermath). The result was the King's Peace of 387/6. This document, the text of which is given by Xenophon, decreed (with the preamble 'Artaxerxes thinks it good that') 'the cities of Asia were to be the King's, including the islands Cyprus and Klazomenai' (these two were singled out for special mention because Athens had conspicuously interfered in both places; see pp. 197f. on the help to Evagoras, and on Tod 114). 'The other Greek cities, great and small, are to be autonomous', though Athens was to keep her cleruchies Lemnos, Imbros and Skyros (Xen. *Hell.* v.1.31).

This is a very general and dictatorial document, and it is a likely modern suggestion[18] that a more detailed version spelt out further requirements, such as the dismantling of Athens' navy, the pulling down of the gates of the Piraeus (which were certainly ungated again in the early 370s: Xen. *Hell.* v.4.34), and some more general provisions like a stipulation for the return of exiles (cp. v.1.34: Corinth). We can add perhaps that the provisions about Asia may have been clarified a little:[19] the distinction between 'islands' and 'Asia' was not simple, since many of the bigger islands (Samos, Rhodes, Chios, Lesbos, and even Tenedos; all but Kos[20]) owned *peraiai*, or possessions on the mainland opposite. It is likely that these were now forfeit to Persia; certainly Chios, which had once controlled Atarneus on the mainland near Pergamum, had lost it by the mid-fourth century when it was dynastically ruled by Hermias (p. 254); and J. Pouilloux (1960) *Choix d'inscriptions grecques* 8 attests Samian exiles at Anaia, an old *peraia* site which was thus presumably no longer Samian, since used as a refuge by Samos' enemies.

The King's Peace was a triumph for Sparta;[21] the autonomy clause meant the break-up of the hegemonical organizations which had been building up around Athens (under Thrasybulus: a very recent development) and around Thebes (this was of longer standing:cp. chapter 7 and p. 86 for the centralization of Boiotia upon Thebes). Moreover the union of Corinth and Argos (above) was ended; and Sparta had a free hand to discipline and dismantle anti-Spartan groupings in the Peloponnese which, as we shall see, she immediately did at Mantinea. Her own organization, the Peloponnesian League, counted as a free and voluntary association and was therefore not vulnerable to the autonomy clause. It was not for astonishingly many years that anybody had the obvious idea of interpreting Spartan domination of Messenia as a violation of autonomy and so invoking the clause against her (Xen. *Hell.* vii.1.27, 36:367).

The king of Persia was now free to move against the rebels on Cyprus (Diod. xiv.110), and in Egypt. He was to succeed in the first theatre but fail in the second. Artaxerxes II has been harshly judged by historians, but assessed by the standard of Persian interests he deserves credit[22] for the peace of 387/6, which for fifty years limited mainland Greek interference in Anatolia to the occasional pin-prick. Even from the point of view of the Asiatic Greeks and the islanders of the east Aegean, the years after the King's Peace were a period of greater material prosperity (p. 175). Politically, it is true, Anatolian democracy was increasingly under pressure. Nevertheless oligarchy did not, even in places directly under a satrapal thumb, replace democracy immediately or everywhere (Syll.[3] 169 as we have seen at

p. 167 attests a popular assembly at Mausolan Iasos) and for concessions like this (they are no more), and for the survivals of local autonomy which the inscriptions attest (e.g. *Labraunda* 42 = *Mausolus* M 8: grant of citizenship and tax-immunity by local inland Asiatic community) Persia deserves some credit too.[23]

The third and last of the great powers responsible for the King's Peace, and in some sense included in it (Aristides *Panath.* 172) was the Sicilian Dionysius, who is bracketed with the Persian king — both are barbarians against whom a crusade ought to be declared — in the *Olympic* oration of Lysias, delivered in 384 (Lys. xxxiii, cp. Diod. xiv.109). This piece of 'panhellenic' oratory, very much a product of and reaction to the King's Peace, must have caused pain to Dionysius (whose representatives it seems were physically present at Olympia when it was delivered), for he had cultural pretensions: his death in 367 was to be caused by drinking too much after his play the *Ransoming of Hector* had been awarded first prize by polite or political judges at the Athenian Lenaea. It is easier to say what Persia and Sparta gained from the victory of 387/6 than to see what the other contributor, Dionysius, got out of it, apart from the obloquy of people like Lysias — who, it should be remembered, was himself of Syracusan descent, and so spoke with the rancour of an expatriate. It may indeed be that, as a modern view has it,[24] Dionysius' mainland Greek interventions were no more than megalomania and muscle-flexing; but we have seen that Dionysius had incurred tangible obligations towards Sparta and this too should be allowed weight. After all, for anything Dionysius could foresee the cycle of mutual benefaction could be continued into the future: it would do dissidents at home no harm to be reminded that the tyrant had powerful friends overseas, like the fellow-countrymen of Aretes and Pharax.

Dionysius' subsequent involvement in Old Greece is sporadic but not contemptible: he did something to help the Spartans at Corcyra in 373 (Xen. *Hell.* vi.2.4ff, though that was close to his own sphere of influence — even if we discount, as we probably should, what the sources tell us about his 'Adriatic Empire' as mere unrealized planning[25]). And near the end of his life — about the time of his Athenian alliance, p. 189 — he sent Sparta and Athens a force worth having, for use against Thebes (Xen. *Hell.* vii.1.20ff.; Diod. xv.70). The scale of all this should be judged against Dionysius' other preoccupations: two Carthaginian wars before the King's Peace, in 397/6 (cp. p. 188; this campaign included the capture of the valuable

Motya), and in 392, gave Dionysius more of Sicily than had the treaty of 405. And he extended his power into Italy, taking Rhegion (386). But he did not live to see the Carthaginian problem finally solved: another war of 383–378 was less successful and when he died in 367 fighting had started yet again. His son, though, made a peace which lasted twenty years, and that stability — which was not to be matched by stability in Syracuse's internal affairs — is Dionysius I's most creditable legacy. As a verdict on one who spent so many years fighting what Dionysius himself and no doubt many of his subjects would have regarded as authentic barbarians, Lysias' *Olympic* oration of 384 may, in its Sicilian aspect, strike us as a little unjust. Plato, who visited Syracuse for the first time in the early 380s, did not share Lysias' opinions about Athens or democracy; and perhaps the greatest effect of the Syracusan tyranny on mainland Greece is also the hardest to evaluate exactly,[26] namely the contribution it made to the development of monarchic, or anti-democratic, opinion (cp. chapter 13) among political scientists and thinkers like Plato — and Isokrates, whose *Panegyricus* of 380 is as 'panhellenist' as the Lysias *Olympic* speech, but who was also to address a pamphlet to Dionysius (letter 1: this does not survive complete but probably asked Dionysius to wage war on Persia). The Greek world had to find its saviours where it could.

15 The King's Peace to Leuktra

Xenophon and Isokrates both speak of Sparta as the guardian of the King's Peace (*Hell.* v.1.36; *Paneg.* iv.175), and whether or not this role was explicitly awarded her[1] in some version of the peace itself, it is certain that her prestige was much enhanced after 386. So Xenophon (op. cit.); Diodorus, whose source Ephorus was a native of Asiatic Kyme and so had his mind more on Asia, says that Sparta came into disrepute for her abandonment of the Asiatic Greeks (xv.19, under 383). There is no real contradiction here: the prestige Xenophon had in mind was a matter of power not ideology, a prestige, that is, conferred by purely military hegemony in Greece itself (not just in the Peloponnese but in the north). As for Asia, it ceased to interest Xenophon much after it had been evacuated by his hero Agesilaus. Before examining Sparta's use, in Greece, of her position, we ought to ask how scrupulously the Greeks (that is, the Spartans and Athenians) henceforth kept out of the Persian Empire, as the peace had demanded. Certainly Artaxerxes' agents Tiribazus and Orontes were able to recover Cyprus unimpeded by Greek interference (Diod. xv.8ff.). In Egypt, however, Tithraustes and Pharnabazus failed very badly in a campaign of 385–383, and part of the reason for this was the presence, on the side of the rebel Pharaoh Akoris, of Chabrias the Athenian with a force of mercenaries (Isok. iv.140). He cannot be regarded as wholly independent of the Athenian state, since he was to comply with an order of recall in 380/79 (cp. p. 161). Officially Athens' attitude after 386 to the authors of her brief imperialistic fling of 394–386 was disapproval: Demosthenes (xxiv.134f.) records the trial and condemnation of two of the principals, Agyrrhios and Thrasybulus of Kollytos (not the famous Thrasybulus). But this disapproval is hardly evidence of repentance so much as of anger that things had gone wrong: the language of an inscription (Tod 116, not in WV: honours to a man from the Hellespont who had warned the generals about Antalkidas' movements, but to no avail) implies a belief that the fighting could have turned out differently and indignation that it did not. Whatever the truth, Athens had lost her striking power, and could only work indirectly through men like Chabrias.

During the following decades we do hear of occasional Athenian activity on the Asiatic mainland, and it is worth listing this, although — even after the Athenian naval revival of the 370s — it never adds up to very much. Thus Chabrias seems (*Hesperia*, 1961, pp.79ff.) to have fought at Aianteion in the Hellespont, i.e. in the King's Asia, in perhaps 375; and Timotheus in the mid 360s had some dealings with Ionian Erythrai (IG ii²108, cp. Dem. xv.9 for the occasion). Perhaps that was the kind of thing Demosthenes had in mind (viii.24:341) when he spoke of Athenian generals visiting places like Chios *and Erythrai* looking for money. The reference to Persian Erythrai here is certainly surprising. But Athens observed the 'Asiatic' clause of the King's Peace, more or less (although we shall see that fear of the satraps was highly relevant, at least as relevant as fear of Sparta, to the adhesion of many eastern *islands* to the new Athenian confederacy of the 370s; see p. 211). That formal Athenian observance is illustrated by a recently discovered inscription, in which Erythrai in *c*.386, immediately before the King's Peace, pleads with Athens not to let her 'be handed over to the barbarian', i.e. Persia (SEG xxvi, 1976/7, no. 1282 = CW 262 B). The Athenian answer is lost, since the stone breaks off, but it cannot have been encouraging.

As for Sparta, her only breach of the 'Asiatic' clause of the King's Peace was the help which she supplied to the Persian rebel Glos in Ionia at the end of the 380s, a curious but not incredible episode (Diod. xv.9). But this did not come to anything; and it is not till Agesilaus goes to Egypt in the great Satraps' Revolt of the later 360s that Sparta does anything actively anti-Persian (though see p. 237 on 365).

So Diodorus was not far wrong to speak of the abandonment of Asia (the *political* abandonment, that is; socially and culturally Asia Minor was far from being cut off from Greece);[2] since Athens is temporarily powerless and Spartan aggression is henceforth confined to the Greek mainland.

Here Sparta had used her ascendancy under the peace to move against Arkadian Mantinea, a democracy — and an irritant (Xen. *Hell.* v.2 for the campaign:385/4). Diodorus treats this as a breach of the 'autonomy' clause of the peace, but legalists at Sparta could no doubt have painted Mantinea, which was a concentration of villages, as being herself in violation of the autonomy of those concentrated units. But legalism does not characterize Sparta's behaviour within the Peloponnese: Xenophon gives the Spartan motive as mere desire to punish Mantinea for various past military offences, all of which added up to a demonstration of independence, and this motive, rather than any sincere anxiety to enforce the King's Peace,[3] was surely nearer the truth: Mantinea was to be made an object-lesson. If the peace could be invoked in justification, so much the better. Phlius was also dealt with in this period (Xen. *Hell.* v.3, cp. vii.2); Xenophon records this in a disproportionately long chapter designed, like one of Thucydides' paradigmatic set-piece passages (p. 129) to make a general point; here the point is that disciplined Phlius stayed loyal.

More disturbing to the peace of Greece, both in its implications and its unexpected side-effects, was Sparta's ready reception of an appeal from north Greece, where the death of Archelaus of Macedon without a strong successor (399) had postponed for forty years the unification of the Balkans and Thessaly under a Macedonian king. There follows a rapid series of kings and regents: Orestes son of Archelaus, Aeropus — first as regent for Orestes, then as king — Pausanias, and then (by 392) Amyntas, father of the eventual unifier Philip II. This was a situation which the other interested powers, great and small, Greek and barbarian, could be expected to exploit, and they did. We noted Spartan diplomacy with Thessaly and Macedon in Archelaus' time, and the maintenance of a Spartan presence at Herakleia and Pharsalus till 395. Then, as we saw, the Corinthian War checked Spartan northern expansion, the Spartan garrison at Pharsalus being slaughtered, and Herakleia being taken over by Thebes. But after the King's Peace it seems that Herakleia again fell under Spartan control (Xen. *Hell.* vi.4.9, Herakleiot troops fight for Sparta at Leuktra). In the intervening years, others had begun to test the water: the topic of Theban interest in Thessaly, vital for the understanding of the 360s, will be treated in the next chapter. For the moment we may recall (p. 187) that as early as 394 Boiotia's Thessalian allies had included Larisa, Krannon, Skotoussa and Pharsalus (Xen. *Hell.* iv.3.3). Another beneficiary from Macedonian weakness and the temporary Spartan recoil was the Chalcidic League, centred on Olynthus: an inscription (Tod 111 = WV 12) of perhaps 392 shows that Amyntas signed a fifty-year treaty of alliance with the league, including guarantees of mutual assistance against invasion, and negotiated with it as a commercial equal. Since this book contains many references to inscriptions, it is worth quoting the occasional example in full, and this is a specially interesting one for several different kinds of reason: it illuminates the politics of a very dark period of Macedonian history (and also illuminates the rise of Olynthus, a state which will feature frequently on later pages of this book); it is evidence for the character of the Macedonian monarchy, cp. p. 75, in that 'Amyntas' and 'the Macedonians' are interchangeable: it reminds us of the *phthonos* (chapter 2) felt by Greeks for neighbours, here Amphipolitans, etc.; and it underlines the crucial importance of shipbuilding materials in the lives of the Greeks, most of whom lived only a few miles from the sea and often relied on ships for their livelihood and for their political independence. Here it is:

(Front)

Treaty with Amyntas son of Arrhidaios. Treaty between Amyntas son of Arrhidaios and the Chalcidians. They are to be allies against all comers for fifty years. If anybody proceeds against the territory of Amyntas or of the Chalcidians with warlike intent, the Chalcidians are to help Amyntas and Amyntas the Chalcidians...

(Reverse)

There is to be the right [for the Chalcidians] to export whatever it does not itself require of pitch and timber for shipbuilding, except for fir; fir may also be exported provided, first, that advance notice is given to Amyntas, and, second, that the fixed dues are paid. Other commodities may be exported by the Chalcidians from and through the territory of Macedonia, and by the Macedonians from and through the territory of the Chalcidians, on payment of the dues. Neither Amyntas nor the Chalcidians may make friendship, except by joint decision of both parties, with the Amphipolitans, the Bottiaians, the Akanthians or the Mendians. Oath of alliance: I shall keep the obligations hereby placed on the Chalcidians, and if anyone proceeds against Amyntas' territory with warlike intent...

This agreement was evidence of the weakness, but also of the prudence, of Amyntas, for he was to need Chalcidic help in the early 380s when his kingdom was attacked by another would-be gainer from Macedonian disorders, the barbarian Illyrians (Diod. xiv.92). A pretender arose and Amyntas was actually driven from his kingdom for a while, recovering it with help from 'the Thessalians', and surely also from the Chalcidic League,[4] to whom Diodorus (ibid., cp. xv.19) says he made a grant of valuable land, presumably as a *quid pro quo*. (It

included, remarkably, the site of Pella, the once and future capital.)
This land they refused to give back when Amyntas' position improved
and he asked for it back. The mention of the Thessalians is important
as showing, not only that nobody in Thessaly had an interest in seeing
next-door Macedon fall prey to Illyrians (Livy xxxiii.12. 10 —
Flamininus' reproof to the Aitolians who wanted Philip V destroyed
— is good on Macedon's role as a shock-absorber, keeping Illyrians
and others out of Greece); but also that Thessaly, though often,
certainly, the object of the covetousness of others, nevertheless had
more than passive potential and could sometimes act energetically and
concertedly on her own account. 'The Thessalians' is unsatisfyingly
imprecise, but the career of Jason the tyrant of Pherai — who was to
collide with Sparta as early as 380, on Euboia (see p. 208) — shows
that pan-Thessalian action is indeed conceivable at this time, the early
380s.

The refusal of the Olynthians to return the land which Amyntas had
given them, and the concern of the other Chalcidic cities, notably
Acanthus and Apollonia, at the growth of Olynthian power, caused
them, and him, to appeal to Sparta. Xenophon (v.2) speaks only of an
appeal by the Chalcidic cities while Diodorus (xv.19) speaks only of
Sparta's alliance with Amyntas. Xenophon's account must be true as
far as it goes — he gives a speech by a named Acanthian individual,
Kleigenes. All this looks circumstantial. But Diodorus cannot be
dismissed either: we are told by Xenophon (*Hell.* v.2.15) that Thebes
and Athens were considering allying themselves with Olynthus,
something which they would be much likelier to dare to do if
Olynthus' enemy were, as Diodorus says, a king of Macedon — who
was not a party to the King's Peace — than if Olynthus' prime enemy
were the Greek cities of Acanthus and Apollonia,[5] since in that event
Thebes and Athens would be in breach of the 'autonomy' clause and
would risk Spartan reprisals.

However, the Thebans and Athenians did not get as far as actually
making the Olynthian alliances which Kleigenes (Xen., loc. cit.) had
said they were contemplating: the Atheno–Olynthian alliance (Tod
119, not in WV), which used to be dated 383, is now generally placed
in the 370s; and a hellenistic papyrus fragment (Pap. Ox. i.13 =
*FGrHist.*135), implying alliance between Thebes and Olynthus, is
worthless as historical evidence, being fabricated on the basis of
Xenophon's account rather than being independent evidence in
support of him. (We should note, however, that the Theban *interest* in

Olynthus presages her northern ambitions of the 360s, cp. p. 187 on her Thessalian alliances of 394.)

It was therefore an act of pure and unjustified aggression when the Spartan commander Phoebidas, on his way past Thebes to Olynthus, accepted the invitation of the pro-Spartan faction to seize Thebes by a coup, and throw in a garrison (382). The most justification Sparta could plead (since Thebes had stopped short of alliance with the delinquent Olynthians, the violators of their Chalcidic neighbours' autonomy) was that the Theban government had declared that *no Theban should participate in the Olynthian campaign on the Spartan side* (Xen. *Hell.* v.2.27). But though the Spartans, like the Romans, always took a serious view of their allies' military obligations, this did not amount to a Theban breach of the King's Peace.

In fact, as with Mantinea, Sparta was merely consulting her own interests:[6] even the Sparta-loving Xenophon (v.4.1) regarded the occupation of the Theban citadel, the Kadmeia, as an impiety for which Sparta was later punished by the divine vengeance of Leuktra. But if legalism is out of place, it would be no less wrong to regard the northern expedition as some kind of aberration on the part of 'conservative' Sparta:[7] the preceding chapter has shown that Olynthus was just the latest in a line of northern adventures by her. Diodorus simply and correctly says of the Olynthian campaign that the Spartans 'decided to extend their control to the regions about Thrace' (xv.19, Loeb transl.). We should observe also the evidence (Xen. *Hell.* v.3.9) for *Thessalian* individuals serving as cavalry in the Olynthus campaign out of 'desire to make themselves known to Agesipolis'. Thessaly is never long out of Spartan thoughts (cp. p. 208 on Oreus in Euboia).

The Olynthians were forced to sue for peace in 380, after fighting which had not gone all Sparta's way (*Hell.* v.3.26). The settlement which followed was less harsh than might have been imposed, though there is no special need[8] to see in this a domestic Spartan reaction against the 'hard-line' policies of Agesilaus: Olynthus now had to accept Spartan military leadership and to supply forces when required, a regular settlement for a defeated city outside the Peloponnese (cp. Athens in 404), and one which gave Sparta all she wanted. Sparta did not (p. 219) have so many Spartiates available that she could relish garrisoning two major cities at once, Olynthus as well as Thebes. Agesilaus' whole strategy of control, *philetairia*, i.e. 'support of supporters' (Xen. *Ages.* ii.21) depended on using force economically; Phlius (above) is the text-book example.

It was the occupation of the Theban Kadmeia — the 'side-effect' of Olynthus, of which we spoke earlier — which caused the trouble. To seize and hold down another major Greek *polis* was difficult and rare, cp. chapter 2, p. 15 on boundary-disputes as the commonest causes of war; such disputes did not usually imply any contesting of the right of the enemy *polis* to an independent existence. By that standard Phoebidas' action was an outrage — but though he was fined (Diod. xv.20), Agesilaus insisted that he be judged by the criterion of Spartan interests (Xen. *Hell.* v.2.34, cp. p. 104) and so we find Phoebidas re-employed (v.4.41) as harmost of Thespiai. More important, the Kadmeia was not evacuated; as Plutarch observes (*Pelop.* vi), the Spartans 'punished the offender but approved the offence'.

For Diodorus, 380 was the climax of Spartan power (xv.23.3f.): Thebes was garrisoned, Corinth and Argos cowed, and Athens still unpopular because, Diodorus revealingly says, of her policy of installing cleruchies in the territory of defeated states. (This shows that fifth-century memories were still alive.) We can add as evidence of further buoyancy that the Glos episode (p. 203) falls at about this time, and that the Spartan harmost of Thebes, Herippidas,[9] was even able to check the encroachments on Euboia of a new, Thessalian, power, Jason of Pherai (Diod. xv.30). The point which Sparta had now reached resembles in many respects 395: her military successes were precisely what aroused against her the forces — unpopularity leading to hostile military coalition and war — which were to undo those successes. There is also a parallel with 405/4 (noted by Plutarch, *Pelop.* vi and xiii). On the earlier occasion it was Athens who had needed help from Thebes to get rid of her Spartan garrison and of the oligarchs whom Sparta was maintaining in power; now Thebes was to need and get help from democratic Athens: the famous 'liberation of the Kadmeia'.

Athens' reaction to Spartan expansion in the 380s is generally circumspect: an alliance with Hebryzelmis, king of Thrace, in the mid-380s (Tod 117) perhaps reflects Athenian desire to keep some influence in the north where Sparta was looking so dangerous. An alliance with Chios of 384 (Tod 118) is explicitly framed in accordance with the King's Peace; but it is of interest as showing the mood of the powerful east Aegean islanders: Persian authority on the Asiatic mainland (which is clearly visible from islands like Chios) was now undisputed, and fear of satrapal encroachment was strong enough on the adjacent islands to overcome the suspicion of Athens and memories of the cleruchies of Delian League days (cp. Diod., cited above. And Isokrates (xiv.28) shows that we should add Mytilene and Byzantium to Chios, as Athenian allies who remained loyal after 386). For the moment Athens was not strong enough for her friendship to be worth much, as reckoned by numbers of warships, but that was soon to change. Isokrates in the *Panegyric* of 380 (iv) urges war against Persia under Athenian leadership, and that work explicitly makes the point (para.163) that the eastern islands look to Athens as their protector, and she *must* act or Persia and the satraps will move in. However, the spirit of technical deference to Persia, which had been shown in the Chios treaty, was maintained in 379 when Chabrias was recalled at Persian insistence from Egypt where he had been fighting on the rebel side (Diod. xv.29).

In that year, however, the wheel of Spartan success ceases to revolve. In winter 379/8 a group of Theban exiles, including the young Pelopidas, entered the city and assassinated 'the tyrants' (the Theban protégés of Sparta). This dramatic liberation was achieved with Athenian help (Diod. xv.25.1), which was immediately followed up by a second and larger Athenian expedition. Xenophon implies that Athenian help was given only on a small scale and perhaps unofficially (v.4.10: 'Athenians from the borders' is his only reference), but Diodorus speaks (xv.26.1) of a large and formally voted expedition and this is likely to be right. (Dinarchus (i.39) confirms this, with its mention of a decree of Kephalos, voting help for the liberators of the Kadmeia.) However Xenophon was right to imply that Athens was extremely nervous about the whole affair: the two generals who had participated in the original liberation were tried and condemned (v.4.19). But Sparta had been provoked and Athens had to look to her own safety, which she did by constructing a system of alliances, with Chios, Byzantium and various islands (cp. Tod 121, 122, 123, line 20 = WV 19, 20, 22; Diod. xv.28.3). This is the beginning of the Second Athenian Confederacy,[10] whose origins should thus be placed in 379/8. Xenophon wholly neglects to record the foundation of the confederacy, one of the most celebrated omissions in all his *Hellenica*. But both he and Diodorus, who does record it (xv.28ff.), describe a raid on the Athenian Piraeus by the Spartan Sphodrias at about this time (Xen. *Hell.* v.4.25ff.; Diod. xv.29). Since Xenophon's account is so admittedly lacunose, and since the Sphodrias raid makes sense as a Spartan reaction to the threat of a resurgent Athens (which is preferable to the reverse chronology which would see the Athenian alliances as a response to Sphodrias), it is best to follow Diodorus and put the formation of the new confederacy first and Sphodrias second. This very early chronology for the first stirrings of the new naval confederacy received some epigraphic confirmation in 1972 with the publication (*California Studies in Classical Antiquity*, 1972, 164ff.) of an Athenian alliance dated to 379/8 (archonship of Nikon) with some state whose name is lost (?Methymna: at Tod 122, lines 4–5 the Methymnaeans are *already* allies). This new inscription at the very least rules out attempts to put the beginnings of the new system of alliances as late as winter 378/7.[11]

The formal conclusion — oath-swearing with Byzantium and others — occurred in summer 378 and in February 377 the 'charter' of the confederacy was issued* (Tod 123 = WV 22, 'the most interesting epigraphical legacy of fourth-century Athens'). There is an immediate problem, whether the confederacy was conceived within the framework of the King's Peace: a deliberate erasure early in the text means that the relevant lines cannot be used without circularity of argument. But other evidence has been thought to exist. The charter contains at lines 24–5 a reference to admission to alliance 'on the same terms as the Chians and Thebans'. Similarly a separate alliance with Byzantium (Tod 121 = WV 19) contains the phrase 'as with the Chians'. The obvious assumption is that in both places the reference is to the alliance with Chios of 384 (p. 208, Tod 118 = WV 17), and if that assumption were certain it would follow that the new confederacy, like that alliance, was not intended as a breach of the peace. However the cross-reference to the alliance of 384 is *not* quite certain: the reference could be to another Chian alliance of 378, the stone recording which has not survived.[12]

Despite this minor difficulty about the King's Peace, the charter document is nevertheless highly informative about Athens' fears and aims. There is her attitude to Thebes, the other state which (alongside Chios) is mentioned in the charter as a model for future alliances (cp. IG ii²40 = WV 21 for negotiations involving Thebes in perhaps mid-378). Democratic Athenian goodwill to Thebes was at the root of the new confederacy, and to parade Thebes' name on a manifesto in

---

*This document, following Tod, will be called the 'charter' for convenience, although as has been shown it is not a 'foundation document': the confederacy was already under way by 377.

377 was excellent propaganda. There are, however, some qualifications to be made to this enthusiastic picture, which are ominous for
future Atheno-Theban relations. First, it is notable that in the charter
the Thebans are not called Boiotians. That is, Athens recognizes no
claim by Thebes to suzerainty over Boiotia. Second, the inscription
speaks (lines 72–5) of ambassadors going to Thebes to persuade the
Thebans of whatever good they can, and it is plausible to see here a
reference to what Xenophon darkly calls (v.4.46) the 'rekindling of
the Theban business', i.e. the reunification of Boiotia under Theban
hegemony. In other words the embassy was to tell Thebes to keep her
hands off the rest of Boiotia. If we could believe Isokrates' *Plataikos*
there was yet another cause for Athenian concern in Theban attitudes
after the liberation: not just Theban aggressions in Boiotia but the risk
of a Theban rapprochement with Sparta (xiv.29, attributing to
Thebes after 379 a readiness to show *servility* to Sparta). But this
abusive anti-Theban pamphlet is in other respects unreliable[13] and
dates from a time (373) when an open Athenian breach with Thebes
was much nearer.

There is no darkness or obscurity about the main enemy against
whom the confederacy is directed: the *Spartans* (lines 9ff.) are to allow
the Greeks to be free and autonomous. Sparta had acquitted
Sphodrias just as she had let Phoebidas off lightly (v.4.34) and for the
same reasons. And for Athens the Sphodrias affair meant war
(v.4.63). As for Sparta's reaction to the events at Thebes, this took the
form of an invasion under Kleombrotos (v.4.14) and cp. above: there
is no good evidence that Thebes was inclined to be concessive. The
hostility of Sparta is unproblematic.

This specifically anti-Spartan programme is however more muted
at lines 46–51, which say that 'if *anybody* makes war against signatory
states, the Athenians and their allies will retaliate with all available
force'. Who is here envisaged? Probably not Thebes (despite what was
said above about Athens' desire to limit the consequences of the
liberation): surely, if there is a specific reference at all, *Persia and the
satraps* are meant. Places like Rhodes, Chios and Amorgos, all early
members of the confederacy, had less to fear from Sparta than from
the much closer threat posed by Persian satraps like the Karian
family, the Hekatomnids: a new and aggressive satrap, Mausolus,
succeeded in Karia in precisely 377, and in a threatening or defensive
gesture moved his capital city from inland Mylasa to coastal
Halikarnassus. The question of Athenian deference to Persia (p. 210)

goes beyond the narrow issue of the presence or absence in the charter of formulae about the King's Peace.

So much for the charter in its foreign aspects (though see also p. 214 on pirates). We may now look at the system of representation and guarantees. Athens' aim in both spheres was to avoid the excesses of her fifth-century empire.

In the sphere of *representation* the allies' powers were in theory wide. The old Delian League had only one chamber,[14] which made it easy for Athens to bully the allies separately (p. 27 on Thuc. iii.10–11); so the fourth-century league was to have in effect two chambers: Athens, and the allies. The separate allied chamber, or *synedrion*, could put proposals before the Athenian Assembly, rather as the Council of 500 could (cp. Tod 133, 10ff., about Dionysius of Syracuse; or Tod 144 = WV 46 of 362/1, lines 12ff.). In a decree of 375 BC (Tod 127 = WV 26) the Corcyrans are not to be allowed to make war or peace except in accordance with the wishes of Athens and the majority of the allies.[15] So the first area of competence was the admission of new states to the alliance.

The second area is tribute. From an inscription of the early 330s (Tod 175 = WV 72 from Tenedos) it seems that *syntaxeis*, financial contributions (see p. 214), might even at late dates in the confederacy's history, be fixed by the *synedroi*. However in 346/5 we find the people of Ainos in the north Aegean agreeing their tribute payment with the Athenian general Chares, apparently without reference to the *synedrion* (Dem. lviii.38).

Third, the charter (line 46: certain money to be the common property of the allies) implies a common treasury, and since tribute has not yet been introduced this must mean that the allies were expected to have control of such matters as fines and penalties for the infringement of the guarantees in the charter.

Fourth, the allies had certain judicial powers: infringement of the guarantees are to be judged 'among the Athenians and allies' (lines 57f. of the charter), which probably means, not that there was a joint Athenian and allied court, but that Council, Assembly and *synedrion* participated in treason prosecutions of normal type.[16] An inscription (S. Accame (1941) *Lega*, p.230 = WV 31) — a rare and remarkable decree of the allies — decrees loss of civic rights for the perpetrators of wrongful evictions.

Fifth, presidency of the allied *synedrion* was, logically enough but still worth noting, exercised by a non-Athenian: the inscription just cited attests a Theban president in 372.

What does all this add up to? Some of these duties or privileges diminish on a closer look, e.g. the fourth item, judicial powers, which as we noted probably meant no more than a degree of participation in an essentially Athenian case. (Anyway, in such cases as we do hear of, 'the allies' do not appear at all, for instance in Tod 142 = WV 44, lines 37–8, about Iulis on Keos, it is the Athenian Council of 500 who condemn a man to death for killing an Athenian *proxenos*, though Iulite rebels are said at lines 29–30 to have acted contrary to the interests of the *allies* as well as of the Athenians. We may contrast the League of Corinth formed by Philip in 338/7, which was formally invited to try Kallisthenes and the Chian traitors; Plut. *Alex.* lv.9; Tod 192.) On the second item, tribute, we saw that men like Chares sometimes settled tribute rates themselves — and in any case the levying of tribute was a breach of one of the *guarantees* (see p. 214). The third, the treasury, mattered little once tribute started to be levied, in 373. The fifth — the allied president — looked well enough but Diodorus (xv.28.4) hit the truth more accurately when he said that 'the Athenians were accepted as leaders'. As to the first and most general head of competence, we saw that some texts do show that procedures of consultation were followed in the early years. But not every Athenian ally was also an ally of the confederacy. So the inscribed text of Tod 129, a purely Athenian alliance with Amyntas of Macedon in 375–3, has no mention of the allies, possibly because an alliance with such an autocrat can hardly have been welcome to northern confederacy members like Ainos or Abdera. (Similar considerations may explain a purely Athenian alliance with Thracian kings (Tod 157 = WV 57). And allied opposition to the peace with Philip in 346, the Peace of Philokrates, was brushed aside, though the allies were represented in the negotiations in the person of Aglaokreon of Tenedos.) Or there is Tod 146 = WV 48 — cleruchs are sent to Potidaia. Naturally no 'allies' feature in the preamble since cleruchies contravened the charter. However, this kind of evidence is tricky: thus of two decrees concerning Dionysius from the same period, one does, and the second does not, imply allied involvement (Tod 133, 136 = WV 38). Here the absence of allies in the second cannot be pressed. Again, an alliance with Thessaly (Tod 147) speaks in its opening words of Athens only, but line 12 does mention 'the allies of the Athenians', which has been taken to show they were consulted.[17]

We may turn from the system of representation to the *guarantees* in the charter.

First, there is to be no tribute, *phoros* (Tod 123, lines 21–3). *That* promise was to be kept — in a purely verbal sense. They called it *syntaxis*, contribution, instead (though we shall see that this is not attested before 373). Kallistratos is the politician allegedly responsible for thinking up the euphemism (Theopompus F 98). We shall ask later how far the league's activities justified making the allies 'contribute'.

Second, there are to be no governors or garrisons (ibid.).

Third, possessions in allied territory are to be abandoned (lines 25ff.). Probably most such *private* possessions were lost after 404, but the inscription speaks of public ones as well, and Diodorus (xv.29.8) says specifically that cleruchies were to be restored to their former owners. Since the only existing cleruchies were Lemnos, Imbros and Skyros, which were neither 'restored' nor (surely) ever intended to be, since the original inhabitants had been expelled too long ago to be reassembled, this set of undertakings seems empty, though it no doubt made reassuring reading.

Fourth, no Athenian was to cultivate land in allied territory (Tod 123, lines 35f., preferable to Diodorus' 'outside Attica').

Fifth, 'unfavourable *stelai*' (pillars) 'are to be taken down' (Tod 123, lines 31ff.). What does this mean? It would be tempting to think that these are the boundary markers, set up on e.g. Kos and Samos and delineating the sacred land confiscated for Athens (Hill[2] B 96), but the charter is explicit that the *stelai* were *at Athens*. Perhaps[18] the *stelai* recorded grants to Athenian individuals and their descendants of the right to own land in particular allied states.

Sixth, constitutional freedom and autonomy were guaranteed.

Seventh, a number of freedoms *not* specifically defined were no doubt assumed by the member states; they included freedom from financial, religious and judicial interference.

Many of these guarantees (as we shall see) were to be breached, some of them very soon. We may end with an eighth, last, unspoken and perhaps unbroken undertaking: to guarantee security in the purely physical sense, from the depredations of pirates (for piracy in the early fourth century cp. Isok. iv.115 of 380). An Athenian orator in the 340s (Ps.-Dem. vii.14–15) treats the protection of the freedom of the seas as an Athenian prerogative, and it had been one of the achievements and justifications of the old Delian League to keep down piracy, cp. p. 31. (Though 'piracy' was a matter of definition: Kimon had found it convenient to expel the Dolopian, i.e. indigenous population of Skyros as 'pirates': Plut. *Thes.* xxxvi; *Kim.* viii.) Although the Argolic Gulf and the waters round Aigina were still dangerous in the late 370s and the 360s (Dem. lii.5 and liii.6, and cp. Xen. *Hell.* vi.2.1 for Spartan-sponsored piracy at Aigina), it is possible that things improved in the very early years of the confederacy's existence.[19]

And in general there were few grounds for complaint — in these early years.[20] On land, successive Spartan invasions of Boiotia, first under Kleombrotus (cp. p. 211 for his invasion, Sparta's instant reaction to the liberation), then in 378 and 377 under Agesilaus, made small progress against the joint Theban and Athenian forces: Chabrias gets much of the credit for this (Xen. *Hell.* v.4; Diod. xv.32ff.; cp. *Hesperia*, 1972, 466ff.: Athenian statue honouring Chabrias). Then in 375, at Tegyra, two Spartan detachments were defeated by the Theban élite 'Sacred Band' (Plut. *Pelop.*xvi; Diod. xv.37, cp. 81). This, like the founding of the anti-Spartan confederacy, was something which Xenophon found too painful to record. The significance of Tegyra is that already, four years before Leuktra, Sparta and the Greek world had been given notice that military training and professionalism were no longer a Spartan monopoly (cp. p. 164).

Held to a draw by land, Sparta turned to the sea, but was convincingly defeated at the battle of Naxos in 376, again at the hands of Chabrias, who was showing notable versatility in these years. This was a major event, which won over most of the Cyclades for Athens, including Delos[21] — so important for religious and propagandist reasons. And the Athenian Timotheus, son of Conon, sailed to waters further west and won an equally decisive victory over Sparta at Alyzia in 375. This produced further adherents for the confederacy, including Corcyra (n. 15). And Chabrias added numbers of northern members.

Athens now needed space to breathe since putting together a navy had been a financial effort, especially given Thebes' reluctance to help pay — the first palpable sign of strain in Athens' relations with Thebes. So (Xen. *Hell.* vi.2.1) Athenian ambassadors went to Sparta, as Xenophon has it, and a peace was signed. But the matter cannot be left there, since in Philochorus' (F 151) report of the peace the initiative came from the Persian king (the Athenians *accepted* the *peace of the king*), and Diodorus confirms this (xv.38, in other respects, however, a muddled chapter), emphasizing the king's initiative still more strongly, and plausibly giving him a motive: the desire to end inter-Greek squabbles and so release mercenaries for his own projected reconquest of Egypt. But since Sparta had been so conspicuously the loser from the warfare up to 375 — on land; at Naxos; and at Alyzia — we can go further and suppose that it was the *Spartans* who as early as 376, after Naxos, suggested to Persia that she intervene.[22] In other words the truth is almost exactly the opposite of Xenophon's account: writing for an Athenian readership in the 350s, he suppresses Sparta's close involvement with Persia, the inveterate enemy of Greece.

The Persian king's efforts in Egypt still came to nothing and Pharnabazus was replaced by Datames, who however (?372) was to go into revolt himself, inaugurating a period of prolonged satrapal disaffection which explains why it is not till the 350s that Persia will again be strong and united enough for an assault on Egypt.

In Greece the peace of 375,[23] though short-lived, was not quite as transitory as Xenophon implies (it lasted till 373); and it is an advance in that it reflects the balance of forces of the future: Sparta and Athens, whose maritime hegemony was recognized (Nep. *Timoth.* ii.2) moving closer together in shared alarm at the growth of Thebes. Of the smaller places in Boiotia Thespiai was taken over by Thebes (Xen. *Hell.* v.4.46; vi.3.1ff.) and Plataia actually destroyed. That was in 373 (Isok. xiv; Paus. ix.1.8; Xen. *Hell.* vi.3.1). Moreover the 370s were a discouraging period for any Spartan who still had hopes of central Greek expansion: Xenophon opens his book vi with the response of Sparta to an appeal in early 375 by Phokis against Thebes: though she sent out Kleombrotus with four battalions we must assume that with the peace of 375 this force was withdrawn, unless Xenophon has misplaced the appeal and it really belongs in 371.[24] Still more serious were the implications of another appeal, with which Xenophon continues straight after (vi.1.2ff.), from Polydamas of Pharsalus against the new power in Thessaly: Jason of Pherai. Jason's nominee at Oreus in Euboia had been expelled in 380 without difficulty (p. 208), but since then Sparta had been much weakened: in particular her expulsion from Thebes meant that she no longer had a base from which to act in central Greece. (The Oreus garrison was thrown out in its turn by Thebes in 377: Xen. *Hell.* v.4.56.) Despite Polydamas' alarming report of the spread of Jason's power, of his military reforms (cp. chapter 13) and of his alignment with Boiotia (vi.1.10), Sparta, after examining her own resources, was forced to tell Polydamas candidly that there was nothing she could do (para. 17) and that Polydamas must consult his own interests. So Polydamas submitted to Jason, who now formally became *tagos* (p. 80) over all Thessaly. (He was even briefly enrolled in the Athenian Naval Confederacy, though his name had been erased from the list of members in Tod 123 by 371.)

Sparta's hand, however, was still not quite played out, nor was she yet ready to accept the implications of the Theban menace by holding firm to the Athenian alignment. In 374/3 Sparta sent a force west under Mnasippos, trying to provoke a revolution on Corcyra; Timotheus and a large fleet — sixty triremes — went from Athens in 373, in answer to the Corcyran appeal which followed (Xen. *Hell.* vi.2; Diod. xv.46ff.; Dem. xlix) and the peace was at an end. Timotheus, however, could not repeat his success at Alyzia of 375, and he was recalled to stand trial in disgrace. He was replaced by Iphikrates who 'subdued the cities in Kephallenia' (Xen. *Hell.* vi.2.33). But Thebes had used the interval since the peace of 375 to accelerate the reunification of Boiotia (p. 199) under her leadership, and this yearly turning of the screws by Thebes was alarming enough from both the Athenian and the Spartan viewpoint for peace moves to be once again set on foot (371). Again, Xenophon seeks to conceal the Persian aspect, though he gives himself away when he speaks (vi.3.18) of Sparta's 'acceptance' of the peace, in other words the initiative came from elsewhere; in fact, from Artaxerxes.

It is worth pausing to look at morale within Athens' Naval Confederacy, and in particular to ask how many of the guarantees had been broken. First, the pledge about tribute had been clearly broken by 373: Timotheus' western voyage of that year (above) was subsidized 'from the common *syntaxeis*', i.e. by allied contributions (Dem. xlix.49). There was no great outcry at this, and perhaps, even leaving piracy apart, it had a certain justification: allied appeals required allied money. At least Athens was not yet (contrast the 360s and 350s) using allied funds for territorial adventures on her own account. It was to be different when the chase after Amphipolis began at the beginning of the next decade.

Second, a garrison is clearly attested in Kephallenia in 372 (see the fragmentary inscription *Staatsverträge*, 267), the result of Iphikrates' 'subjugation' of that island. The inscription speaks of 'the garrisons in the islands' and of 'three garrison commanders to be sent to Kephallenia'. Though this garrison was perhaps of no long duration (since all garrisons were outlawed by the peace of 371 and that on Kephallenia was thus presumably withdrawn[25]), this was an ominous precedent; moreover it means that we have no automatic right to assign *undated* garrisons, like that on Amorgos (attested by Tod 152 = WV 54) to the emergency period of the Social War of 357–355 (though *that* garrison is actually best dated to the 360s).

So far, other specific pledges had been kept — the Samos cleruchy was still in the future (366), and Athens was still faithful to the guarantee of autonomy: Xenophon at the end of book v singles out Timotheus' good behaviour on Corcyra in 375 (v.4.64): he *did not* change the constitution, he *did not* enslave or exile anybody. Chares at Corcyra in 361/0 was not to be so scrupulous (p. 242), and this is Xenophon's way of pointing the contrast.

There were grounds, however, at the most general level of all, for allied disquiet. The original *raison d'être* of the confederacy had been democratic dislike of Sparta, and fellow-feeling with newly liberated Thebes. As Athens moves ever closer to Sparta and away from Thebes the confederacy necessarily loses much of its justification. And though Boiotian ships are still found serving in the Athenian fleet as late as 373 (Dem. xlix), Xenophon makes clear that Theban participation was progressively more grudging (vi.2.1). From the allied point of view the shift of alignments was perhaps baffling: an inscription (Tod 131) of 369 records Athenian praise for Mytilene for help in 'the past war', i.e. the Mytileneans have asked what is going on and are politely told that hostility with Sparta is now a thing of the past. On the other hand this same inscription has been taken as evidence of a liberal readiness by Athens to let her allies 'answer back' and criticize her foreign policy.[26]

Again, the introduction into the confederacy of dynasts like Jason and his ally and dependant, Alketas king of the Molossians in Epirus — what has been called a 'looser category of ally'[27] — and Athens' unilateral alliances with people like Amyntas of Macedon, may have been resented: the adhesion of such men was more likely to be in the interests of Athens than of the smaller of her allies. Similarly, there was allied reluctance about the Peace of Philokrates with Philip in 346 (p. 213). This allied feeling was due less to traditional anti-tyrannical prejudice, which was anyway weakening in the fourth century, an age of reviving tyranny (chapter 13, p. 167 on Euphron) than to the justified fear that the inevitably acquisitive and disruptive foreign policies of autocratically run states would tend to disturb the always precarious territorial equilibrium of the Greek *poleis*.

The peace conference of 371 (p. 217) was attended by Sparta, Athens and Thebes. That peace contained a new and interesting clause: those who did not want to fight to defend the peace were not bound to do so (Xen. *Hell.* vi.3.18). That is, Sparta was not to be given *carte blanche* to enforce the peace. But the real historical importance of this conference is its anti-*Theban* aspect. The suspicions of Sparta and Athens at the Boiotian encroachments of Thebes took concrete form in a Spartan attempt to enrol 'Thebes' as such (rather than 'Boiotia') as signatory. At first it looked as if Thebes would acquiesce in this, but after the lapse of a day the Theban Epaminondas announced that, sooner than sign, Thebes would see her name deleted from the document. This, one of the great moments of fourth-century history, meant, in the short perspective, the end of the Theban alliance with Athens and the reopening of war between Thebes and Sparta. On a longer view it set slowly rolling the boulders of a political landslide: it was to bring to an end Sparta's pre-eminence of three centuries (cp. p. 225 for the loss of Messenia), and so deprive Greece of the only power which could have provided both the hoplite strength (unlike Athens), and the ideological magnetism (unlike Thebes), to lead the fight against Philip — and win.

For the moment King Kleombrotus of Sparta invaded Boiotia and reached *Leuktra*. In the battle of Leuktra the deepened Theban phalanx, positioned unusually on the left (p. 134), defeated the Spartan right, 400 of the 700 Spartiates present being killed. The period of Theban hegemony had begun.

To explain Thebes' victory we noted (chapter 13) the deepened phalanx and its importance as a kind of strategic reserve, the weighting of the left and the reasons for this, and the use of a trained élite force, the Sacred Band. But there is a negative half to the explanation: Spartan manpower problems.[28] Even Leuktra need not have been the disaster it was had the pool of surviving Spartiates been larger. As it was, Aristotle was right to say that Sparta was crushed by a 'single blow' (*Pol.* 1270).

The size of the drop in manpower between 479 and 371 is staggering: at Plataia (Hdt. ix.28) Sparta still has 5000 hoplites, and even the losses in the earthquake of 465 were probably made up by natural replacement before long. Thus in 418 (assuming an error at Thuc. v.68) there are still some 6000 (though cp. p. 101). By 394, however (Nemea River, Xen. *Hell.* iv.2.16) the transmitted figure of 6000 must be reduced to allow for liberated helots and others, including the *perioikoi* (see index), now brigaded with Spartiates (perhaps the 6000 or so of 418 should also be reduced to allow for such *perioikoi*). Thereafter, by 371, comes the sensational slump: a mere 1500 (Xen. *Hell.* vi.1.1; vi.4.15 and 17). No wonder Sparta had felt unable to field a force capable of disputing Thessaly with Jason in 375.

Aristotle (*Pol.* 1270a29ff., a crucial text on Sparta's manpower problems) says that 'while Spartan property could have supported 1500 horse and 30,000 foot the number had dwindled by the 360s to less than 1000'. He goes on, remarkably, to attribute Leuktra to Spartan inability to deal with the problem of *property*. *We* should wish to add the simpler point that with manpower troubles on this scale Sparta's (and Agesilaus') policy towards Thebes in the 370s was insane provocation. (An interesting reform of the Peloponnesian League in its military aspect, recorded in Diod. xv.32ff. under the early 370s, shows at least some awareness of the problem, as does the switch from requiring personal service to permitting financial contributions — Xen. *Hell.* v.2.21, which probably belongs after 380 — an attempt to get money for mercenaries?)

Aristotle, though, was right to see the problem as at root economic and social. He lays much blame on 'the women': they (he says) 'managed many things in the time of the Spartan hegemony'. Certainly, Spartan women, unlike Athenian, enjoyed full legal capacity. At Athens a woman was *formally* restricted to transactions involving one *medimnos* of corn or less (Isaios x.10), and though[29] the orators and the inscriptions show that at Athens and in related legal systems women, *de facto*, not only have much prestige and authority within the *oikos* or family, but are found disposing of large sums (loans, payments for dedications, etc.), it is certain that their legal disabilities mattered in one crucial area: women without a living father or brother (*epikleroi*) could not inherit as heiresses in their own right. The position was quite different at Sparta, where women had long been free to marry late, and to marry whom they liked, 'heiresses' in particular being free from property restrictions. So we find a woman like Kyniska, admittedly the sister of a Spartan king, Agesilaus, entering teams for equestrian events at Olympia (Michel 951). The result was, as Aristotle put it (1270a), that two-fifths of the land at Sparta was in the hands of the women: matrimonial freedom meant that money tended to marry money as it always will unless the tendency is artificially checked as it was at Athens by the rules inhibiting *epikleroi*.[30] Estates at Sparta must have tended to get larger, with the result that Spartiates were squeezed off their *kleroi* or lots and forced to become indebted to the larger landowners (the full crisis is reached in the third century cp. Plutarch's *Lives* of the Spartan kings Agis and Kleomenes III).

Spartiates whose estates became smaller in this way would eventually cease to be able to produce the surplus required to pay their 'mess-bills' — these contributions were one of the conditions of Spartan citizenship, the other being success in the educational *agoge*. When that happened they were downgraded out of the Spartiate category and called 'inferiors', *hypomeiones*. Kinadon was one such. Other factors contributed to the thinning out of the Spartiates: late marriages mean fewer children; at Sparta homosexuality was indulged in till late in a warrior's adult life; and Spartiates who exhibited cowardice in battle ('*tresantes*') traditionally forfeited citizenship (Plut. *Ages.* xxx.6; *Mor.* 191c, 214b. But these passages also show that after Leuktra Agesilaus had to suspend the law, cp. Diod. xix.70.5 after the battle of Megalopolis later in the century). Other causes of civic disability are mentioned but are not all equally credible: failure to marry (Xen. *Lak. Pol.* ix.4), late marriage — and even *kakogamia*, making a poor marriage. We are told that Archidamus was fined for marrying too small a wife on the grounds that she would produce 'not kings but kinglets' (Plut. *Ages.* ii). This is solemnly cited in treatises on Spartan constitutional law. The only secure fact is that bachelors were subject to *social* opprobrium, like Derkyllidas who was unmarried and treated ignominiously as a result (Plut. *Lyk.* xv: a young man would not stand up to provide a seat for him because Derkyllidas had not produced a son to stand up for *him* in his old age).

All these are ways of *losing* status; they would not have mattered so much if Spartiate status had been as easy for outsiders to win as it was for its possessors to lose. But after the Persian Wars there is little enfranchisement of foreigners; *neodamodeis* (liberated helots) existed but were objects of deep anxiety to their always very reluctant liberators (cp. p. 21 on Thuc. iv.80); and though there were half-breed categories called e.g. *mothones* or *mothakes*, and though there is evidence that non-Spartiates might receive a Spartan education (cp. Xen. *Hell.* v.3.9 on such persons, 'not without experience of the good things of the Spartan way of life') the barriers were kept high. The surprise is that after Leuktra so many of these excluded groups stayed loyal: Xenophon (*Hell.* vi.5.28) says that 6000 helots were enrolled in the army with a promise of freedom, (cp. vi.5.32, only *some* of the *perioikoi* go over to Thebes and vii.2, above, on the loyalty of Phlius). Myths do not always die instantly. But the truth about the Spartan myth was put with, ironically, a Lakonian simplicity in the Theban epigram for Leuktra (Tod 130 = WV 33): 'the Thebans are mightier in war.'

16 Leuktra to Mantinea and the Revolt of the Satraps

The immediate gainer from the Spartan defeat at Leuktra must have seemed at the time to be Jason of Pherai. He destroyed the fortifications of Herakleia, in order, as Xenophon says, 'to prevent anybody from approaching his domains by that route in future, but also to remove any obstacle to his own passage to Greece' (*Hell.* vi.4.27). This meant the final elimination of Sparta from central Greece. Jason also annexed Perrhaebia to the north of Thessaly (Diod. xv.57): we saw (p. 186) that this frontier area had been in Archelaus' possession at the end of the fifth century, and an inscription of the Roman period (*BSA*, 1910/11, pp. 195ff. = *CW* 321 B) shows that in the last years of his reign Amyntas had authority over part of it at least:[1] he fixed the boundaries of Perrhaebia and Elymiotis. But Amyntas preferred to stay on the right side of Jason: Diodorus (op. cit.) says that Jason made an alliance with Amyntas; later writers were to represent this hyperbolically as Thessalian rule over Macedon, the tail wagging the dog (Isok. v.20; Arr. *Anab.* vii.9.4). How much of all this activity by Jason should be ascribed to the period *after* Leuktra is actually doubtful (from Diodorus' description of him as unpopular at xv.57, surely from Ephorus, but as a 'kindly' ruler a very few chapters later at 60.5, it has been argued[2] that Diodorus has compressed his material and that Jason must be allowed more time to make some friends; but though the conclusion is likely enough the particular argument will not do since xv.60.5 comes from a different source, the 'chronographic source', a hellenistic authority from whom Diodorus drew material such as the dates of the accessions or deaths of rulers).

The second half of Xenophon's account of Herakleia, above, implies that Jason had positive ambitions to meddle in southern Greece. Polydamas the Pharsalian (see chapter 15) had attributed to him even grander designs — a war against Persia. Whatever Jason's plans, they are beyond evaluation since he was assassinated in 370, to be succeeded (after a bloody internecine power-struggle on lines more familiar from Macedonian history) by his nephew Alexander. Xenophon was impressed by Jason (see the whole section *Hell.* vi.4.27ff. where he takes the Pheraian dynastic story down to the 350s), and there is more to this than mere anti-Theban bias (the desire, that is, to direct the focus of his reader's attention away from Epaminondas and Thebes in their day of glory). For a moment after Leuktra Jason had genuinely seemed to hold the balance between the Greek powers to the south of him, when he dissuaded the Thebans from shattering what remained of the Spartan army, urging them to quit (for the moment) while they were ahead of the game (Xen. *Hell.* vi.4.20ff.).

But Jason's death, and that of Amyntas shortly after, opened up the centre and north of Greece once again to foreign intrigue and invasion. This time the struggle was to be between Thebes and Athens, Sparta having retired hurt from the Thessalian ring.

Theban foreign policy in the 360s[3] develops in three theatres: in the south (the Peloponnese); in the north (Thessaly and Macedon); and, after the middle of the decade, in the Aegean Sea — the 'naval policy' of Epaminondas. Of these theatres Xenophon, whose preoccupations are almost entirely Peloponnesian, is interested only in the first, and even there he leaves out some of the biggest events of the age.

In the south, then, a general peace of 371/0,[4] after Leuktra, had been concluded at Athens, from which Thebes was again shut out as in 372/1. The news of Leuktra had been coldly received at Athens (Xen. *Hell.* vi.4.20: the herald was refused even the normal courtesies), and it seems that Athens still hoped to restrain Theban capacity for mischief, while advancing her own interests (the peace contained a pledge to keep the 'decrees of the Athenians and their allies'). That this peace was at Athenian instigation reflects a decline in the influence of Sparta (though it is not necessary to suppose that Sparta actually participated in the peace, thereby acquiescing in her own eclipse). Nevertheless the chief Athenian anxiety continues to be Thebes.

The attitude of Athens is made clearest in an important incident which Xenophon does not mention at all, though he gives the preliminaries. Leuktra was to give encouragement to democratic regimes everywhere (cp. Diod. xv.59: Argos), and the first sign of this was in Arkadia. The scattered Mantineans set about reversing the settlement of 384, repopulating and fortifying their city (*Hell.* vi.5.4).

The process of concentration did not end there: from Diodorus we learn that Lykomedes of Mantinea organized all Arkadia into a federal state, for which over the next few years a federal capital was built, Megalopolis, the Great City (Diod. xv.59). Tegea was coerced into the league, and the Tegean exiles, who had lost the argument and the fighting over the question whether to join, now fled to Sparta. Against the physical intervention of Sparta, which was now a certainty, the Arkadians appealed to Athens, but were turned down (late 370 bc: Diod. xv.62.3; Dem. xvi.12. This is the important incident omitted by Xenophon — as if his failure to report the formation of the Arkadian confederacy were not bad enough). So in a momentous step the Arkadians turned to Thebes, who invaded the Peloponnese in winter 370/69.

This first invasion, under Epaminondas, is painted by Xenophon as a somewhat half-hearted affair (*Hell.* vi.5.24), but Pausanias (ix.14.2ff.) more plausibly represents it as determined action. Its results were concrete enough: not just the consolidation of the Arkadian League as a permanent check on Sparta (and probably also the encouragement of a new league in *Aitolia*: Tod 137 with Diod. xv.57 for the Aitolians as Epaminondas' allies in 370), but the invasion of Lakonia itself, and — most catastrophic of all — the liberation of Messenia after centuries of helotage (Diod. xv.66f.; Paus. ix.14.5). It was the removal of the fertile Messenian *kleroi*, essential for the maintenance of the Spartan lifestyle, which — rather than Leuktra itself, of which it is a consequence — caused the end of Spartan military greatness. Though Athens was roused, by a Spartan appeal, to send help under Iphikrates — at the instance of the leading politician Kallistratos who, in the Athens of these years, leads the anti-Theban reaction after Leuktra— Epaminondas got his army out of the Peloponnese in safety, to the fury of Xenophon who was probably watching from Corinth as the Boiotian army slipped through (*Hell.* vi.5.50f.). Though in the years ahead Arkadian nationalism was to show itself quite as recalcitrant to Thebes as it had ever been to Sparta, there was to be no reversing the damage done at Messene by this first of Epaminondas' invasions. In 369 things went less well for Thebes: Epaminondas again invaded, but withdrew in face of a force which now included help from Dionysius I of Sicily. Moreover this time the Arkadians showed resentment of Thebes; and summer 368 brought another slight lift to Spartan morale: she defeated some Arkadians in the so-called 'Tearless Battle', as predicted by the oracle at Dodona (Xen. *Hell.* vii.1; Diod. xv.72). By 367 Thebes was ready to try to settle things diplomatically by a peace conference at Susa. But we cannot follow Xenophon to Susa without first looking at the north in 371–367.

Epaminondas' first Peloponnesian invasion force had included some Thessalians (Xen. *Hell.* vi.5.23): one of Xenophon's few allusions to Thebes' northern involvement. Then, in the second invasion (Xen. *Hell.* vii.1.28), the Athenians suggested to their Spartan allies that the troops of Dionysius should be used *in Thessaly against the Thebans*. This second passage is thus also important as evidence that Thebes' northern expansion was opposed by Athens. When did this northern policy of Athens revive? On the evidence of Andokides (iii.15) it had never really collapsed: speaking in 392 that orator had referred to Athens' desire to recover *inter alia* the Chersonese (cp. p. 196). But it was not until after Leuktra that Amphipolis and the Chersonese became live issues again (though the alliance with Amyntas, Tod 129 = WV 29 of 375–373, discussed in chapter 15, may be seen as a preliminary). The Athenian claim to Amphipolis (that to the Chersonese is treated below) must have been made in or shortly before 369, since it was recognized by Amyntas (Aischin. ii.32).[5] It is just possible that the claim dates to the 371 peace of Athens which followed Leuktra,[6] if Xenophon's reference there to the 'decrees of the Athenians and their allies' can be pressed to yield a reference to a recognition of Athens' right to recover Amphipolis. But Athens did not actually do anything about this claim until 368, when Iphikrates was dispatched to Amphipolis (Aischin. ii.27; Dem. xxiii.149). She had good cause to pursue the claim energetically, for Pelopidas of Thebes had preceded Iphikrates: a first visit by Pelopidas to Macedon falls in summer 369 in the brief reign of Alexander II[7] (Plut. *Pelop.* xxvi). It is from Plutarch and Diodorus, both using Ephorus, that we derive much of our knowledge of the Thessalian and Macedonian policy of Thebes; that policy, the work of Pelopidas, should be seen as part of a plan complementary to what Epaminondas was doing in the Peloponnese: the one dismantling Spartan power in the south, the other seeking to neutralize Athenian influence and ambitions in the north.

So Pelopidas' northern entanglements are partly to be explained as a response to the change in the direction of Athenian imperialism — which was both a literal, geographical change, and a political departure in that Amphipolis, from the point of view of Athens' allies in her Naval Confederacy, promised nothing but a waste of their resources. But Pelopidas had originally been taken north on a legitimate enough pretext: an appeal by the Thessalian cities against Jason's successor, Alexander of Pherai, and against the other Alexander, the king of Macedon, who had been invited in slightly earlier by the Thessalian Aleuads (p. 80), but had outstayed the invitation, garrisoning Larisa and Krannon (Diod. xv.67.3). Pelopidas, sent to 'arrange things in Thessaly to the advantage of the Boiotians' as Diodorus puts it, took Larisa, obliged the Macedonian Alexander to withdraw from Thessaly and contained, but did not overthrow, the power of Alexander of Pherai. He passed from Thessaly to Macedon and there arbitrated in favour of Alexander against a rival, Ptolemy; thence home to Thebes. Neither the Macedonian nor the Thessalian settlement lasted long: in Macedon Alexander was killed and Ptolemy succeeded (though technically as regent for Amyntas' son Perdikkas); complaints against Ptolemy, and in Thessaly against Alexander of Pherai, brought Pelopidas north again in 368 (Plut. *Pelop.* xxvii; Diod. xv.71. This was after he and Epaminondas had survived attacks on them at home). Some trace of all this survives in the epigraphic record: at Delphi, a metrical statue dedication, standing in the name of 'the Thessalians', honours Pelopidas as 'noble leader of the Boiotians' (*Wien. Jahresh.*, xxxiii, 1941, p. 38 = WV 36, not necessarily a posthumous honour as is almost universally assumed. The statue, by the way, was the work of Lysippos, not a cheap sculptor); and a newly discovered decree of the Boiotian League, dating to the Boiotarchy of, among others, Pelopidas himself, awards the title of *proxenos* and benefactor to one Atheneos *of Macedon* (Roesch at the Epigraphical Congress, 1982).

But in Macedon Ptolemy and Eurydice, the widow of old King Amyntas, had enlisted the help of the Athenian Iphikrates who helped drive out a pretender called Pausanias. So when Pelopidas arrived it must have looked as if Theban influence had been supplanted by Athenian. But surprisingly (since Pelopidas' forces were small) Ptolemy immediately came to terms with Pelopidas, and even surrendered hostages who included the future King Philip II. It is difficult to believe that he did this because he was in awe of Pelopidas' reputation, as Plutarch asserts (*Pelop.* xxvii); a likelier motive is the calculation that Athens would be a more uncomfortable presence in Macedon than would be Thebes, since Athens had concrete territorial ambitions — Amphipolis.[8] It is perhaps also relevant that Iphikrates had been personally close to Amyntas and his children (Aischin. ii.28, who actually says that Amyntas had adopted him), so that Athens' commitment was to the children rather than to the regent. With Thebes, by contrast, Ptolemy could perhaps hope to treat as something more like a ruler in his own right.

Returning to Thessaly, Pelopidas was treacherously seized, during some negotiations, by Alexander of Pherai, and it took two Theban expeditions (368, 367) to get him back; the first failed partly because Alexander had turned to Athens who sent a general, Autokles, with thirty ships and a thousand men (Diod. xv.71, cp. Tod 147, line 39 = WV 49). This is also the moment when Athens tried to have Dionysius' troops sent to Thessaly against Thebes, cp. p. 226 on Xen. *Hell.* vii.1.28. When Pelopidas was eventually released it was at a price: not perhaps any formal recognition of Alexander (for Thebes was to interfere again in 364) but certainly loss of face, leading to three years during which Thebes kept out of the north.

Thebes' Thessalian involvement did not, then, come to much at this stage, but it should not be judged too severely.[9] The original mission of Pelopidas was speculative ('to arrange things to the advantage of the Boiotians') and intended, surely, not so much to make Thessaly into a Boiotian province — Pelopidas never had the manpower with him for that — as to win as many friends and followers as possible and to make sure there was no chance of a second Jason coming south. Anyway the events of 364 were to show that Thebes could still be invoked as a potential check on Alexander, and Pelopidas may have been content to be for the present just a card up the sleeve of his Thessalian well-wishers. We should also remember the Athenian aspect: it is probable that the Theban presence in Macedon, as a third force beside Athens and the various Macedonian kings and pretenders, made it that much harder for Athens to get back Amphipolis (cp. what was said above about Ptolemy's unexpected rapprochement with Pelopidas). In any case, of the various assets which control of Thessaly offered, listed in chapter 7, several were to come Thebes' way after all — but only in 364, pp. 234, 246. In particular we may recall what was said in that chapter about the *religious* advantages of dominating Thessaly, which itself controlled the Amphictyonic Council at Delphi: this control, which Thebes was able to exercise after the middle of the 360s, is important for understanding how she was able to provoke the Sacred War of the 350s.

By 368, Thebes must have been feeling remarkably friendless, with Athens and Alexander of Pherai ranged against her in the north and Arkadia making difficulties in the Peloponnese, where a quarrel between Elis and Arkadia (Xen. *Hell*. vii.1.26) was splitting Sparta's enemies. So we find both Thebes and Sparta (whose need for a respite is too obvious for elaboration) at a peace conference at Delphi in 368, summoned by Philiskos of Abydos, an agent of Ariobarzanes, satrap of Hellespontine Phrygia. This gathering was a diplomatic failure because Sparta was asked to recognize Messenian independence; it did, however, improve Sparta's military position because Philiskos — whose master Ariobarzanes' eye was perhaps already on revolt — provided her with mercenaries. (It may be that, like Cyrus' mercenaries in Thessaly, p. 184, they were to be kept in this way in innocent-looking 'cold storage' till Ariobarzanes was ready to use them himself.) Thus strengthened, Sparta continued to pose a threat to Thebes (the Tearless Battle, already mentioned, was fought shortly after and showed that Sparta was not quite finished militarily), and there was a more serious effort at peace in 367, at Susa (Xen. *Hell*. vii.1.33ff. See p. 226 for this peace conference, very much a Theban–Persian affair.) Pelopidas is the central figure: giving expression to the symmetrical Theban plan he asked that Sparta be forced to acquiesce in the loss of Messenia, and that the Athenian navy be beached: this was Thebes' reply to the actions of Iphikrates and Autokles. And the quarrel between Elis and Arkadia was to be settled in favour of the former. Persia approved the Theban plan, but not surprisingly, in view of the humiliation it held for the traditional great powers, there was no deal. Of the two Athenian delegates, one (Timagoras) who had unwisely agreed to the proposals was condemned and executed on his return; the other, Leon, announced that Athens would now look for friends other than Persia.

But an event on her own northern borders obliged Athens after all to submit to Persian-sponsored diplomacy: in early 366 Thebes seized the disputed territory of Oropus on the Boiotian Attic border in north-east Attica (Diod. xv.76; Xen. *Hell*. vii.4.1; date Σ Aischin. iii.85). This was an indirect result of the secession from the Athenian confederacy of Euboia, soon after Leuktra. Themison, tyrant of Euboian Eretria, was responsible for the original seizure of Oropus and the Thebans then backed him up. This affair produced a revulsion of feeling at Athens: Kallistratos was the man responsible for Athens' anti-Theban stand; he was now tried and in 361 went into exile, and with him the policy of confrontation with Thebes went into eclipse — a policy which had lost Euboia and Oropus without regaining Amphipolis. A different tack was now tried: *concessions* to Thebes, in whose possession of Oropus, and in whose hegemony over Boiotia, Athens now acquiesced, in exchange for recognition 'by the King of Persia and the Greeks' of Athens' right to the Chersonese (Dem. ix.16).[10] This bargain was formalized as a King's Peace of 366/5 (Diod. xv.76.3).

Leon had used threatening words to Persia in 367, and the threat was still good, judging from Athens' next actions: by bowing to a King's Peace on Thebes' terms (terms which, however, were tolerable as those of 367 were not) she had won the right to pursue her claim to the Chersonese; the Amphipolis claim had been recognized for some years now. But acceptance of a King's Peace was by this stage of the fourth century a convenience which did not preclude action against the king. On the contrary, 366 begins a phase of more vigorous Athenian action against Persia, and of a more aggressive style of imperialism within her own league — which enabled Thebes after all to challenge Athens by sea (despite the failure of the crude formula of 367) because of the unpopularity which this tougher Athenian imperialism engendered. (The first step here had been the pursuit as early as 368 of the selfishly territorial claim at Amphipolis.)

The theatre in which Athenian and Persian interest clashed was Samos: Timotheos was sent, perhaps straight after the 366 peace, to help the satrap Ariobarzanes, who was now openly in revolt (Dem. xv.9, where Timotheos is said to have been ordered not to break the King's Peace, i.e. keep his hands off mainland Asia). Timotheos found a Persian garrison installed on Samos; he expelled it and laid siege to the city. When it fell (365), he put in a cleruchy, evicting the Samian inhabitants (Diod. xviii.18). The legality or rather morality of this celebrated action has been much debated[11] and it is worth formally putting the case for and against Athens. In her favour it can be said, first, that Samos was not a member of the Naval Confederacy and therefore not covered by the pledges of the charter; and second that the Persian garrison was itself a breach of the King's Peace by which Persia had undertaken to respect the autonomy of the Greek islands other than Cyprus and Klazomenai. So the initial provocation was on Persia's part, and the brief given to Timotheos, to respect the King's Peace, was not wholly meaningless *as far as Samos goes*, even if the projected help to Ariobarzanes put the peace at risk, and even if the evidence from Erythrai — p. 203 — suggests that Timotheos went beyond his instructions after all. The temporal priority of Persian aggression on Samos is important: Samos is a strategically commanding position for the control of the Aegean crossing (cp. Isok. xv.108),[12] so that the Persian garrison weakened Athens' eastern flank from the military point of view; while politically the Persian presence was a challenge to Athens' ability to protect her island allies from satrapal infiltration (see p. 211 for such protection as part of the programme of the confederacy). It is also relevant to Athens' motives, though hardly to the morality of the affair, that she probably needed the extra land and food (chapter 13, p. 171). On the other side of the argument one may appeal to contemporary Greek opinion: not only the epigraphic evidence which shows that large numbers of states welcomed the evicted Samians, thereby showing what they thought of Athens (ranging from Cardia in the north, *Misc. Acad. Berol.*, ii, 2, 1950, p. 27, via Erythrai, Miletus and Rhodes,[13] to Phaselis in the south-east, SEG i.352); but also the qualms of an Athenian orator called Kydias (Ar. *Rhet.* 1384b32) who warned the Assembly, correctly, what the effect on Greek opinion would be. So, technically unimpeachable though the Samos cleruchy may have been, it was unwise of Athens to excite the old fears associated with the word 'cleruchy', at a time when men like Epaminondas of Thebes (cp. p. 232), and Mausolus of Karia, were ready and able to profit from Athenian mistakes.

   Leon had spoken of Athens looking to 'friends other than Persia', and there is evidence to show that this was not just indignant bravado. An Athenian decree of the mid 360s (Tod 139) honours the Phoenician prince Strato of Sidon who was shortly to be involved in the great Revolt of the Satraps.[14] But Timotheos' involvement with Ariobarzanes is more obviously a blow struck at Artaxerxes — and not just by Athens: from Xenophon's *Agesilaus* we learn that the king of Sparta (and the Persian peace conference of 367 was as offensive to Sparta as to Athens) had also been sent to help Ariobarzanes, who was under siege in the Aeolid, at Assos or Adramyttion, by Mausolus of Karia and Autophradates of Lydia, both still at that time ostensibly loyal to Persia (Xen. *Ages.* ii.26; Polyain. vii.26). But the way the siege ended should make us doubtful about their loyalty:[15] Mausolus and Autophradates abandoned the blockade after Mausolus had given Agesilaus money, and it is a reasonable guess that this joint activity by Timotheos and Agesilaus was part of a deal for Greek mercenaries by satraps who are themselves about to go into revolt — in fact, that the main satraps' revolt, which Diodorus (xv.90) puts under the single year 362, has already begun.

The east Aegean operations of Timotheos, and the cleruchy which resulted, gave Epaminondas and Thebes the opportunity to exploit Athenian unpopularity and rival Athens by sea: as Epaminondas put it, Thebes should 'transfer the *propylaea* of the Athenian Acropolis to the Theban Kadmeia' (Aeschin. ii.105). This Aegean policy is the third of the theatres of Theban activity which were mentioned at the beginning of this chapter. Epaminondas exhorts the Thebans to aim at naval hegemony and they decided to lay down keels for a hundred triremes (Diod. xv.78.4–79.1). Nothing much came of this grand shipbuilding programme, but that does not mean that Thebes' policy of trying to 'rule by land and sea' (as Isok. v.53 was to put it) was altogether a failure: Isokrates speaks of triremes sent to Byzantium, and Justin (xvi.4) of an appeal to Epaminondas from Herakleia on the Black Sea,[16] all of which supports Diodorus who says (xv.79.1) that a sea voyage of Epaminondas 'won over' Athens' allies Rhodes, Chios and Byzantium to Thebes (literally, he made them *idias*, his own: the word means more than just 'friendly' in Diodorus, cp. xix.46.1).[17] An interesting Theban coin should be connected with the overtures to Rhodes: it carries the Theban shield, the name of Epaminondas — and the rose (*rhodos*), the symbol of Rhodes (*Rhodos*): C. Kraay, *Archaic and Classical Greek Coins*, 1976, p. 179, n.1. But though it is remarkable to find Rhodes, Chios and Byzantium already linked in hostility to Athens (as they were to be again in 357 at the prompting not of Epaminondas but of Mausolus), Rhodes and Chios did not secede from the confederacy — yet. Byzantium, however, did; and the seduction of Byzantium stands as the only lasting success of Thebes' whole Aegean venture, because Byzantium's departure from Athens' confederacy was permanent and (because of its situation on the corn-route) damaging. Thus in 362 we find Byzantium harassing the Athenian grain-fleet (Dem. 1.4), and in the next decade Byzantium, now firmly allied to Thebes (cp. Dem. ix.34), is a member of a Theban *synedrion* modelled on the Second Athenian Confederacy (Tod 160, lines 11,21: yet another manifestation of Theban or Theban-inspired federalism (cp. chapter 13, p. 168).

The secession of Byzantium, and the Theban flirtation with Chios and Rhodes, are evidence of disaffection within the Athenian confederacy; and there are other signs of trouble. On Samos, as we saw, prompt action had expelled Persian influence, but the satraps were infiltrating some of the other islands. Kos, for instance, though not a member of the confederacy, was an island and therefore 'autonomous' by the provisions of the King's Peace. Yet Koan coins are now believed to show that the influence of the Karian satraps was already strong in the 360s.[18] And on Keos, very close to Athens, anti-Athenian sentiment took open and violent shape in *c*.363: a revolt with the murder of the Athenian *proxenos* (Tod 142; perhaps cp. comm. on 141 and 142, also to be connected with Epaminondas' voyage).

What had Athens done to deserve this, not yet a secession but certainly a display of imperfect confidence? It is time for another brief review of the way she had been keeping her pledges. By the late 360s her record is much less creditable than a decade earlier. The guarantee about cleruchies had been spectacularly broken in spirit if not formally (and we can add that the Samos cleruchy was reinforced in 362 and 352, Σ Aischin. i.53, Philochoros F 154, and that other cleruchies were sent, to Sestos in 353 and Potidaia in 362: Diod. xvi.34 and Tod 146 = WV 48). Garrisons and *archontes* (governors) are attested for Amorgos and Andros and are best put *c*.364[19] (Tod 152 = WV 54 and Aischin. i.107). And Athens was certainly impinging on the commercial and judicial freedoms which, according to a suggestion of chapter 15, the allies took for granted: Tod 162 = WV 61 (not precisely dateable) shows her interfering with the ruddle trade of Keos in the mid-century, and judicial interference is attested for the same island by Tod 142, line 49 = WV 44 of 362 (cp. IG ii²179:Naxos), which implies that appeals were to be heard at Athens, as in the fifth-century 'Chalkis Decree' ML 52 = Fornara 103; and *syndikoi*, Athenian judges, were sent to Keos on the evidence of IG xii.5.528 and 538, inscriptions recently redated to the fourth century. But more unpopular than anything, perhaps more even than what had happened on Samos, was surely the diversion of both Athenian and league resources to goals in the north (Amphipolis and the Cherso-nese), which could not, even if they were won, profit the league but only Athens, the hegemon. (And in fact the northern war went badly in the 360s: Tod 143 = WV 45 and comm.) Athens could not really complain when in 366 her allies failed, as they did, to help her over Oropus (Xen. *Hell*. vii.4.2, cp. p. 229). What had she done for *them* recently?

The naval programme of Epaminondas in 364 was the result of

ambitious and deliberate calculation; the resumption in the same year of Theban operations in the second main theatre, that is the north, was due to chance: a fresh appeal from Thessaly against Alexander of Pherai. It was Pelopidas' last campaign, for he was killed at the battle of Kynoskephalai in that year. Thebes sent a second and larger army, of 7000 men, who defeated Alexander and forced him to join the Boiotian league, and drastically reduced his territory: Achaia, Phthiotis and Magnesia were not joined to Thessaly but enrolled as separate Boiotian allies (Diod. xv.80). The importance of this was that it gave Thebes a clear majority of votes in the Amphicyonic Council at Delphi (she also, at this time, got the right of consulting the oracle there before anyone else: Syll.[3]176).

But the death of Pelopidas had shaken Theban nerve, and the large force which it took to avenge him, and to cow Alexander, must have stretched Theban resources. So we hear no more of the projected hundred-ship Theban navy. The abiding importance of the Aegean policy lay in two things only: Byzantium; and the example which Epaminondas had offered to the Karian satrap Mausolus, who in 357 is found ranged against Athens with exactly Epaminondas' former allies, Rhodes, Chios and Byzantium, and with exactly the one hundred triremes of which Epaminondas had dreamed (Xen. *Ages.* ii.26). But Mausolus' was no paper fleet.

Another reason[20] for holding back in the Aegean was the situation in the first great Theban theatre, the Peloponnese, with which we began this chapter. Here things had been sliding out of Theban control. We noticed that as early as 368 the Arkadians had been showing a spirit of independence towards Thebes, and the Susa proposal of 367, to award the disputed territory of Triphylia to Elis not Arkadia, is a Theban hit at the latter and an expression of Theban anger. It was a mistake, because it drove Arkadia once again to seek an alliance from Athens; this time it was granted, because Athens considered that the loss of Oropus was due to desertion by her existing allies (Xen. *Hell.* vii.4.2) and was in a mood to welcome new ones. As for Arkadia, her reasons for approaching Athens went beyond the Elis issue: Epaminondas had invaded the Peloponnese a third time in 366, and the Arkadians had been compelled to submit to Theban leadership in, and send troops for, some campaigning by Epaminondas against the Achaians in the north Peloponnese. Thebes had picked a fairly gratuitous quarrel with the Achaians, which had for one of its real motives precisely the aim of calling the Arkadians to order in this very public way (Xen. *Hell*. vii.1.41). Epaminondas' initial settlement of Achaia was mild, but the Theban authorities at home reversed his measures, putting in a garrison and an imposed democratic government. There was a similar story at Sikyon, where Euphron's ambiguous behaviour (p. 167) offered no assurance to Thebes that stable, anti-Spartan policies would be followed.

The war between Arkadia and Elis was resumed in 365; by now Elis had Sparta for an ally and this, together with the absence of the Thebans from the Peloponnese in this campaigning year, must have given heart to the enemies of Arkadian nationalism. But Sparta was too much debilitated: it is a measure of her decline that one must speak now of 'Sparta' not the Peloponnesian League, because that organization had effectively ceased to exist in 366, an important moment and a new 'low' in Spartan history: in that year Sparta permitted Corinth to make a separate peace with Thebes, on terms which included acknowledgement of Messenian freedom (Xen. *Hell*. vii.4.9). This campaigning of 365 ended in humiliation and defeat for Sparta at Kromnos.

It was in 364, the year of Kynoskephalai, and Epaminondas' Aegean voyage, that the Arkadian federal state fell apart. The war with Elis was going badly and some of the Arkadian federal officials, the Tegean faction, started to help themselves to the treasures of Olympia to pay the troops. The Mantineans objected and the Tegean element asked for Theban help; a Theban officer was sent to Tegea with a force of 300 hoplites (Xen. *Hell*. vii.4 is the main source for all this). In 363 the Arkadians (by which term we must understand the Mantinean element) made peace with Elis, without consulting Thebes — an act of independence, not to say defiance. The Theban officer at Tegea locked up a number of leading men from the federal cities, and though he later had qualms and released them, Thebes was now committed to forcible intervention. This is the run-up to the campaign and battle of Mantinea of 362: the Peloponnesian allies of Thebes included Tegea, Megalopolis, Argos and Messene, and of the central Greeks the Euboians, Thessalians and Lokrians; not, however, the Phokians who refused on the grounds that their treaty with Thebes was purely defensive. They were to pay for this later. Ranged against this essentially anti-Spartan coalition were Mantinea, Sparta, Elis and Athens.

Epaminondas' campaign opened with an attack on Sparta itself, an act which was, militarily speaking, impressive rather than productive; it did however have a political point, emphasizing as it did the bond which held the coalition together. That bond, fear and hatred of Sparta, was essentially negative, but nevertheless, after so many centuries of the Spartan myth, it had an irrational power. It is a sign of Epaminondas' political failure, even before the battle of Mantinea, that his Peloponnesian allies fought to reject Sparta rather than because of the positive attractions of Thebes, who was thought to have no cultural ideal to offer (in Ephoran language, neither Spartan *agoge* nor Athenian *paideia*: cp. p. 94f. for Ephorus' views on Thebes). The battle of Mantinea, for all the brilliance of Epaminondas' tactics, was a Theban defeat in that Epaminondas himself was killed. That need not have been fatal to Theban primacy had the name of Thebes been associated in the Greek mind with more amiable values than medism, stupidity and arrogance (Diodorus, i.e. Ephorus again, spoke of 'Leuktran pride', xvi.58; and the conventional Athenian view is put at Isok. v.53 and Dem. xviii.98f. The treatment of Achaia and Sikyon illustrates what they were thinking of, though those incidents were not Epaminondas' fault).

But in all this, Greek opinion, however nearly unanimous, was not quite fair: *federalism* is Thebes' great legacy to fourth-century and hellenistic Greece. The importance of federalism is (as we noted briefly in chapter 13) first, that it is a kind of alternative to imperialism, a way of achieving unity without force (it is no accident that the more brutal Romans were not much interested in federalism, despite the curious tradition that the sixth-century King Servius Tullius was inspired by the Greek Panionion to form the Latin League); and second, that it embodies a representative principle which means that Greek federalism was often more democratic than the often urban-dominated primary assemblies of the city-states. Arkadia itself was democratic in intention at least, witness the sovereign body of Ten Thousand (Tod 132, not in WV).[21] But federalism is an achievement which the modern historian of Thebes and Boiotia has to reconstruct almost entirely from inscriptions (the Oxyrhynchus Historian should however be mentioned, cp. p. 7). Of the positive charges against Thebes, she cannot be acquitted of a thoroughly Spartan arrogance in the Peloponnese which she had entered as a liberator in 370. Stupidity we have discussed already (p. 85); medism is a theme well to the front in Xenophon's treatment of Pelopidas at Susa in 367; but medism was a game which more than one could and did play: thus even the Spartan apologist Xenophon cannot wholly conceal, and alternative traditions explicitly attest, Sparta's participation in virtually every King's Peace in the period covered by the *Hellenica*. Perhaps the answer is simple and cynical: Thebes should have produced her own historian of the 360s (or rather a good enough historian to have survived): somebody who could not only have done justice to her federal creations of Aitolia, Arkadia and the Aegean *synedrion*, but who could have replied in kind both to the charge of imperialistic arrogance — when levelled from the direction of Athens, the evicter of the Samians; and to that of medism — when brought by an apologist of Sparta in her period of Persian-promoted ascendancy.

In fact the policy towards Persia of both Athens and Sparta in the 360s is equivocal: we saw that the peace of 366/5 was a Common Peace, that is, it was sponsored by Artaxerxes of Persia; but Timotheos at Samos and both he and Agesilaus, in their dealings with Ariobarzanes, are found opposing Persian interests at almost the very next instant. The revolt of Ariobarzanes was only the prelude to the great Revolt of the Satraps,[22] which should be thought of as lasting for the whole of the second half of the 360s (see generally Diod. xv.90–2 — all under 362 — and Trogus *Prologue* x). Orontes of Armenia was the leader, but the insurrectionists included Mausolus of Karia, Autophradates of Lydia, and Datames, who had already been holding out in northern Anatolia for almost a decade (see p. 216, and for his career the enjoyable life by Nepos). Agesilaus (Plut. *Ages.* xxxvii) went out to Egypt, and he and the rebel Pharaoh Tachos advanced on Phoenicia where Strato of Sidon was sympathetic (Jerome, *Against Jovinianus* i.45; Xen. *Ages.* ii.30); while Datames pushed over the Euphrates and Orontes moved against Syria. Athens as well as Sparta helped the rebels: Chabrias took a force of mercenaries and was put in command of a rebel fleet (Diod. xv.92, Hicks and Hill, *Greek Historical Inscriptions*, 122). And there is evidence for diplomatic links between Athens and individual rebels: not just Strato (above) but Orontes (IG ii²207a) and Tachos (Hicks and Hill, 121). But this support was to an extent unofficial and back-handed, so that when the revolt failed through treachery, Orontes submitting to the king and Mausolus returning to his allegiance (Diod. xv.91; Tod 138 = WV 40; Datames was killed, Diod. loc. cit.), Athens and the other Greek states could cover themselves by pointing to their official refusal of involvement: the celebrated Reply to the Satraps, recorded in an inscription found at Argos (Tod 145 = WV 47) of 362/1, in which the Greeks say that they have settled their differences and will abstain from war against the king if he respects the peace they have made.

This is a reference to a peace concluded, in an atmosphere of general exhaustion, after the battle of Mantinea (Diod. xv.89).

For Xenophon, who ends his *Hellenica* at this point, the outcome of Mantinea was 'uncertainty and confusion' in Greece (*Hell*. vii.5.27) but in fact by guaranteeing that each state should keep *what it held* (rather than 'what belonged to it' which is a formula opening the way to litigiousness) this peace at last gave general recognition to the existence and right to statehood of the Messenians. (The Spartans of course stayed out of the peace for precisely that reason.) Xenophon's judgement is no more than an expression of gloom at the demise of Sparta, who as a result of the events of 371–362 had two new, strong and hostile neighbours in Messene and Megalopolis. There was no 'uncertainty or confusion' about that. Nor could Xenophon, had he wished to do so, have extended his remark from Greece to the Persian Empire with any greater truth: Persian authority looked stronger than ever. 'Uncertainty and confusion' would have been aptest, around 360, as a description of Macedon, the power to which within thirty years both Greece and the Persian Empire were to succumb.

17 Philip

Ptolemy, regent in Macedon for Perdikkas, died in 365 and Perdikkas succeeded in his own right. The achievements of Perdikkas, which include keeping Athens out of Amphipolis (cp. Aischin. ii.29), and the reorganization of Macedonian harbour-dues in 361/0 through the agency of the Athenian exile Kallistratos (Ps.-Arist. *Oecon.* ii.22, cp. p. 229) are overshadowed by the disaster in 359 in which he lost his life and 4000 men to the invading Illyrians under King Bardylis (Diod xvi.2). The new king was Philip II.

For contemporaries, the success of Philip was due to the personal greatness of Philip himself: Theopompus, who said that 'Europe had never produced a man like Philip son of Amyntas' (F 27) gave the title *Philippika* to his history of the period, thereby acknowledging the importance of the king's personality. Such a title could scarcely have been given to a history of any earlier period. No modern historian need shrink from following Theopompus in recognizing that Philip did what he did, and what his predecessors had been unable to do, because Philip was Philip. There is, however, a negative side to the explanation of Philip's rise, namely the absence or ineffectiveness of early opposition to him. It has been said that 'it is arguable that Caesar [in 60 BC] would not have made such an immediate impact on Roman politics had the state been [in Ciceronian language] less "wretched" and "unstable".'[1] Something similar can be said about Philip in his relation to the traditional Greek powers. Each of them was in deep trouble in the 350s: *Thebes*, because of the protracted, bitter and useless Sacred War of 355–346 (the first diplomatic shots of which were fired in 357); *Sparta*, because of her loss of Messenia and her problems inside the Peloponnese; and *Athens* because of the 'Social War', i.e. the war against her seceding allies, of 357–355. Each of these will be treated in turn in the pages that follow; it will be shown, moreover, that they are interconnected: thus (to give one illustration) it was safe for Phokis' enemies to declare Sacred War against her only after the point in 355 when Phokis' strongest potential ally Athens suddenly looked certain to lose her own 'Social War'.[2] So each state helped to make the problems of the others worse.

So much for the powers of mainland Greece (and it should be added that the death of Alexander of Pherai in 358 ends *Thessaly*'s phase of interventionism abroad, and from now on her independence progressively dwindles: at any rate Alexander's successors initially moved closer to Thebes: Σ Aristid. *Panath.* 179.6). What, though, of those powers *outside* Greece proper which had determined Greek destinies earlier in the century? *Persia* was strong again after 360, and especially after 359 when a new king Artaxerxes III succeeded; he ordered the disbandment of satrapal mercenary armies (Σ Dem. iv.19), a measure that completed the disciplining of the satraps which had largely been achieved by his predecessor (p. 237). But Persia shared an interest with Philip in limiting Athenian sea-power; hence Mausolus was to help the rebels against Athens in 357 and Artaxerxes was to order Chares out of Asia Minor in 355 with the threat that otherwise he would supply the rebels with further Persian help. It is not till 346 that there is any evidence of designs by Philip *against* Persia, and thus before then there was no reason for Persia to do anything about Macedon. On the contrary, Macedon was doing useful work.

The other power outside Greece proper which, as will be recalled, had helped to bring about the first King's Peace of 386, had been *Syracuse*. But Syracuse was in no condition to intervene in Greek affairs, even in the sporadic way characteristic of Dionysius I, after the death of that ruler in 367. The circumstances of Syracuse's collapse as a great power, and of the reconstruction of Sicily in the 340s by Timoleon of Corinth, are recorded for us very fully in Diodorus' Sicilian narrative in books xv–xvi, and in Plutarch's *Lives* of Dion and Timoleon (there is also the problematic evidence of the Seventh Letter of Plato).[3] But even the impressively reconstructed Sicily of Timoleon was not strong enough, or interested enough, to involve itself in affairs in Greece. After Dionysius' death in 367 his son Dionysius II had quarrelled with his father's adviser Dion, a relative by marriage twice over of the old tyrant, and Dion went into exile (366). In 357 Dion returned from his exile in Greece, and made an attempt to 'liberate' Syracuse; but his own motives were suspect or at least suspected. He did force Dionysius to leave Syracuse for south Italy, but in 354 Dion was himself assassinated and by 346 Dionysius was back. An appeal against him to Corinth, the city which had founded Syracuse back in the eighth century, led to the mission of the

Corinthian Timoleon, who landed in 344, expelled Dionysius, defeated the Carthaginians at the Krimisos River, and began to rebuild the prosperity not just of Syracuse but of much of Greek Sicily (Diod. xvi.83 — the difficulties of excavating Syracuse, due to modern settlement, mean that a clearer archaeological picture is to be had from places — Tindari, Heraclea Minoa, Morgantina, Megara Hyblaea — *other* than Timoleon's main centre of activity).[4]

Politically, Timoleon's settlement shows him to be a child of his oligarchic home-city, since he established what, despite loose encomiastic talk of 'democracy' in the literary sources, should certainly be counted as an oligarchic constitution; and a child of his monarchic age: all that distinguishes his own position from that of the conventional 'tyrant' is his eventual abdication and his good fortune in having favourably disposed historians to write about him.[5] He was certainly not doctrinaire in suppressing *other* tyrannies in Sicily: most of them went, but not all: some were too loyal, and too useful.[6] The military forces which Timoleon had taken with him numbered some 3000 all told (his first landing was with only 700 men); these are not large forces for doing what Timoleon did (it is surprising that Carthage held her hand for so long) and they imply an impoverishment and depopulation in Sicily which in turn helps explain why in the mid-century Syracuse counts for so little in the outside world. As in the eighth century she now became a receptacle for a colonizing influx (Plut. *Timol.* xxiii speaks of 60,000 immigrants in all), rather than, as in the fifth and early fourth centuries, an aggressive force to be feared by mainland Greeks — let alone Macedonian kings. The Greek exodus to Sicily in the 340s and afterwards has been plausibly enough connected[7] with the material debilitation of the old city-states and the imminence of the new order in Greece which Philip looked set to establish; for instance, Plutarch records (*Timol.* xxx) that some of his hero's mercenaries had served in the Sacred War on the Phokian side, enlisting with him only after 'roaming round the Peloponnese for some time'. So Sicily was at most a refuge from, not a weapon against, the new power in Macedon.

We may now return to the problems of the mainland Greek states in the 350s — Athens, Sparta and Thebes.

Athens in the late 360s and early 350s was no more successful than she had ever been in the north, where every general was prosecuted on his return, a normal Athenian reaction to failure in the field[8] (the defection of Byzantium did not help); inside the confederacy, the

Aegean islands of Peparethos and Tenos were attacked by Alexander of Pherai (Diod. xv.95; Dem. 1.4), and at Corcyra, Chares supported an *oligarchic* coup (Aen. Tact. xi.13; Diod. loc. cit.). That was not the kind of thing the allies had expected of Athens back in the early 370s when they joined the new, democratic, anti-Spartan, confederacy. There were a few compensating successes — Pydna and Methone had been won in the late 360s, but were to be lost to Philip early in his reign (Dem. i.5); and on Euboia in 357, Theban influence was expelled and replaced by Athenian, with a speed which shows that pro-Athenian feelings on the island were general (Diod. xvi.7, cp. Tod 153). But Athens' breaches of pledge, her chase after northern territories, her failure to police her Aegean allies against a ruffian like Alexander of Pherai, all offered formidable grounds for discontent. The underlying cause of the Social War is given by Demosthenes (xv.3; 15) as resentment by the allies of what they regarded as Athens' 'plotting' (i.e. increasingly high-handed imperialism) and at her 'recovery of what was her own' (i.e. Amphipolis?). But Demosthenes is also helpful on the precipitating cause, which he identifies as the intriguing and incitement of the Persian satrap Mausolus. Mausolus had surely digested the example of Epaminondas a very few years before (see chapter 16); and by the early 350s, after the checking of whatever precisely had been his eastward aspirations in the Satraps' Revolt, he was ready to enlarge his influence westwards at the expense of Athens' disaffected Aegean flank. Demosthenes' evidence is up to a point suspect in that the political context of the Rhodian speech (xv, of 351) gave him every motive to minimize Athens' own culpability for the war and to magnify that of the scapegoat satrap, who had no votes in the Ekklesia; but fortunately there is external evidence to corroborate him: Diodorus (i.e. Ephorus) attests concrete naval help given by Mausolus to the rebel allies (xvi.7.3), and recently published coins of Rhodes and Chios[9] prove that Mausolan or Hekatomnid influence on those islands was strong (cp. p. 233 for Kos).

The war broke out in 357, and Athens lost one of her best commanders, Chabrias, at almost the first blow. This left Chares alone in command for the moment. The rebels ravaged Athens' three cleruchies Lemnos, Imbros and Samos (Diod. xvi.21) — perhaps a way of making a political point against a detested institution as well as a sound strategic move (cleruchs traditionally had duties of defence). At Embata, off Erythrai, Chares wanted to engage the rebel fleet but was not backed up by his new colleagues, Iphikrates and Timotheos, who had recently reinforced him with sixty ships. Denouncing the other two in a letter to the Assembly at home, Chares got sole command (Diod. xvi.22) and then, short of money, hired himself out to a Persian satrap Artabazus. This man was satrap of Hellespontine Phrygia, and his revolt in the 350s is the last main phase of satrapal insurrection in the mid-century (though it should be kept distinct from the great revolt of the 360s, in which Artabazus had stayed loyal). At first Chares gained brilliant successes (including a 'Second Marathon' — but on Persian soil, unlike the First: Σ Dem. iv.19), and ravaged the territory of a Hellespontine Phrygian feudatory called Tithraustes (*FGrHist.* 105, no.4). But in mid-355, in a decisive diplomatic intervention, the Persian king wrote to Athens ordering her to recall Chares, or he would help the rebels with three hundred ships (Diod. xvi.22). Athens complied, and that was the humiliating end to the war. The *Peace* of Isokrates (Isok. viii) and the *Revenues* of Xenophon, a set of proposals for financial reconstruction, both reflect the depressed mood of this time. One feature of the military narrative in particular bears out Xenophon's essentially economic diagnosis of Athens' difficulties, namely the lack of money which had forced Chares to sell his services to a rebel satrap, thus taking the war out of the domestic Athenian sphere and risking Persian reprisals.

The problem with the Athenian navy was not so much lack of ships as lack of properly equipped ships:[10] she had 349 in 353/2 (IG ii[2] 1613 1.302). Part of the trouble was that the 'trierarchs', rich persons appointed to pay for the equipping for one year of a trireme or part share of a trireme as a kind of income tax (such a duty was one kind of 'liturgy' or compulsory state service) were reluctant to carry out more than the minimum demanded of them.[11] (We saw in chapter 13 why there was a change by the fourth century in the formerly expansive attitudes of upper-class Athenians, no longer cushioned by allied tribute on the old fifth-century scale.) Thus in the late 360s there is evidence that trierarchic obligations were being hired out (*misthosis*). This is attested by a speech of Demosthenes (li) entitled *On the Trierarchic Crown*. Similarly there were difficulties in operating the system of *proeisphora*, that is, payment in advance of *eisphorai*, or capital levies, by three hundred rich individuals on behalf of their taxation groups or 'symmories', from whom they then had to recoup. This system is as old as 377 (Isaios vi.60) but had evidently broken down by the time of Demosthenes' Fiftieth Oration (362/1) when we hear of an old-fashioned system of deme-based collection. It seems[12] that *proeispherontes*, people liable to pay the *eisphora*, sought exemption from trierarchies on the grounds that *proeisphora* was a liturgy and you could not be liable to more than one liturgy at a time.

There were attempts to reorganize the system, but the size of the propertied class could not be increased by simple legal or administrative *fiat*: the so-called law of Periander in 357/6 (Dem. xlvii.21, 44) tried to spread the burden of the *eisphora* load over as many as twelve hundred persons, but this seems to have been unrealistically many, as we can see both from Demosthenes' unsuccessful proposals of the later 350s in speech xiv (*On the Symmories*) and from his successful ones of 340/39 (Dem. xviii.102–8), because in 340/39 the old figure of three hundred was reverted to (Hyperides F 159 OCT).

What was lacking was elementary goodwill among the rich, cp. above. Nor was it only the rich who were short of goodwill: Dem. 1.6–7 of 362 is the first mention of *conscription*. It is also relevant that although the orators attest to a very active commerce, much of it was in metic hands, and though metics were liable to the eisphora (Lys. xxii.13; Dem. xxii.61, etc.), and some other liturgies, they were exempt from the vital trierarchy (Dem. xx.10–21). Xenophon in the *Revenues* (ii.1f.) makes suggestions for the exploitation of metic wealth and this idea was to some extent acted on. But only later.

Such were some of the background difficulties in the organizing of the trierarchy system. At the level of detail, that is, the manning and equipping of individual triremes, too much depended, here too, on individual initiative. The state was supposed to supply equipment (Dem. li.5), but if you were experienced (and rich) enough you provided your own, to avoid troublesome dealings (*pragmata*) with the polis (Dem. xlvii.23). In any case we are told that in 357 all equipment was in such short supply that everything in private hands was commandeered by the state (Dem. xlvii.20, 44). (There were also problems about manning: some trierarchs provided their own *skilled* crews: Dem. 1.7, 12; ordinary sailors were state-provided by the 340s: Dem. xxi. 155; but if Dem.1.7 can be trusted, a trierarch in 362 actually had to provide his own ordinary crew. Not all trierarchs can have enjoyed borrowing large sums to pay their crews in advance, like Timotheos in 373: Dem. xlix.11, 14f.)

No wonder that in 357 'there was no equipment in the dockyards' (Dem. xlvii.20). Immediate steps were taken, it is true, when and even before the Social War broke out. Arrears of *eisphora* had already been collected in some year after 377 by Androtion (*FGrHist.* 324

Androtion T 6). And at the beginning of the Social War itself, in 357, the superintendent of the dockyards, one Satyros, collected thirty-four talents which was spent on equipment for a fleet (Dem. xxii.63). So too the 'nationalization' of private equipment, mentioned above, belongs now. And after 355 Eubulus improved finances generally.

All these leisurely methods were well enough suited to campaigns in which Athens herself decided when and how to strike. Demosthenes saw the danger: in an extravagant passage in the First Philippic (iv.36) he was to claim that the city's reaction if any crisis occurred was then — and only then — to appoint trierarchs, embark on legal proceedings for the exchange of liturgical obligations (so-called *antidosis* suits) and so forth. That is too fantastic to be true as it stands. But it *is* clearly true that the Athenian system was poorly suited to a war in which the initiative lay in hands other than Athens' own. In 357 she was subjected, for the first time in many years, to the test of such a war, and her methods were shown up as inadequate: hence Chares' involvement with Artabazus, and the inglorious end to the war. Demosthenes was to say in the speech *On the Crown* of 330 (xviii.234) that Athens had to face Macedon with small totals of tribute in hand, and without the help of her largest island allies. The orator was quite right to make this causal connection between Athens' Social War and the rise of Philip.

Next there is *Sparta*. The causes of her weakness after 370 have already been reviewed. The battle of Mantinea did not even bring her the consolation of seeing the back of the Thebans in the Peloponnese, for we hear of an invasion by Pammenes of Thebes in 361 (Diod. xv.94), who forcibly prevented the break-up of Megalopolis, which was being attempted by secessionists within the city. In the 350s Sparta's foreign policy, no longer piloted by Agesilaus who had died in 360, is very restricted: Demosthenes in the speech *For the Megalopolitans* of 353 (Dem. xvi), urging an Athenian expedition on behalf of Megalopolis, greatly exaggerates Sparta's aggressive power at that time: it is true that she had provided help for her ally Phokis against Thebes in 355 (Diod. xvi.24), and had got into a war with Argos and fought a winning battle at Orneai in the north-west Argolid in 353 (xvi.34). But the help to Phokis in 355 was moral (and financial) rather than active; as to Sparta's position inside the Peloponnese, a bigger war in 352 against Argos and Megalopolis (ibid.) seems to have been prompted by the sheerest opportunism at a time when the Phokians under Onomarchus looked much stronger than Thebes, but

Thebes against the probabilities not only invaded the Peloponnese in aid of her allies there but forced Sparta to a draw. Demosthenes' opponents were thus vindicated in their policy of non-intervention: Sparta could not prevail even over a Thebes so conspicuously weakened as she was by the Sacred War.

It is to the Sacred War itself, that is to *Thebes'* difficulties in this period, that we must now turn. The importance of this war (355–346) can hardly be exaggerated, for it was what brought Philip into Greece proper in the first instance, in the later 350s; and because he was the victor in 346 instead of the thoroughly exhausted Thebans, he, rather than they, took the prize for which they had provoked the war originally, namely the undisputed first place among the Greek states.

The expulsion of Theban influence from Euboia in 357 was a blow to Theban prestige as well as to her power in central Greece, and the Theban decision to attack Phokis, the recalcitrant ally who had refused military help to Thebes in the Mantinea campaign, seems to have been prompted by the mere desire on Thebes' part to assert herself at the expense of a conveniently situated neighbour. Theban preponderance in the Delphic Amphictyony had been assured since her settlement of Thessaly in 364: by her alliances with the Magnesians and Phthiotic Achaians, now split off from the rest of Thessaly, Thebes controlled 16 of the 24 votes in the Amphictyony. Moreover Thebes, acting through the Thessalian president Andronikos, had in perhaps 363 suppressed a movement against her at Delphi, the evidence for which is an Athenian inscription (Syll.^{3} 175); and the anti-Theban elements responsible had fled to Athens. ('Since Andronikos the Thessalian has exiled Astykrates contrary to the Amphictyonic laws and those of Delphi...' the Athenians passed measures favourable to Astykrates and his associates.) So it was not difficult for Thebes to persuade the Amphictyony to condemn Phokis to a large fine, ostensibly for 'cultivating sacred land' (Diod. xvi.23: Diodorus' sixteenth book[13] is the main source for the Sacred War), in the expectation that Thebes would herself be given the leadership of the war which would follow if, as was likely, Phokis was unable to pay. The condemnation of Phokis was in autumn 357. But Phokis did indeed refuse to pay, and the Phokians under their leader Philomelus took everybody by surprise and seized Delphi itself with its treasure (spring 356). However it was not until a year and a half later, in fact in autumn 355, that the Amphictyony actually declared war against Phokis: we have seen that the reason for this was that Phokis had powerful friends, notably Athens, and it was not until Athens had clearly lost the war against her naval ex-allies (something far from inevitable before Persia demanded Chares' recall) that Phokis' enemies dared to act. This is true of the Thessalians in particular, despite earlier Thessalian readiness to follow Thebes when it was a question of merely uttering condemnations of Thebes, a painless matter. So at first the Phokians, fortified by the funds of the Delphic treasury, kept the initiative: Philomelus invaded Ozolian Lokris in 356, and by self-justifying embassies in the same year was able to turn his Athenian and Spartan friendships into formal alliances. But then came the end of the Social War in the Aegean, and the Thessalians were now ready to support Thebes positively.

In the fighting of 354, the first proper year of the war, Philomelus, despite some initial success against the Lokrians and Thessalians was decisively defeated by the Boiotians at Neon in Phokis; Philomelus threw himself over a cliff, and though his colleague Onomarchus took over the remains of the army, it must have seemed that the war was more or less over. That seems to have been the Theban view at any rate, for when Artabazus, now deprived of his Athenian support asked for Theban help, he got it: 5000 men under Pammenes (Diod. xvi.34). This loan of perhaps a third of the Theban army could only have happened in the optimistic aftermath of Neon. But it was a mistake, for when Onomarchus resumed the war the Theban force in Asia found itself stranded for various reasons (Phokian successes in Thessaly, and the establishment of Athenian influence at Sestos in the Hellespont, including the cleruchy mentioned on p. 233, both contributed to block Pammenes' passage home), and so when Artabazus was defeated, the Thebans in Asia probably simply hired themselves out to Artabazus' enemy the king of Persia for a projected recapture of Egypt. In any case they were never again available to Thebes for use in Greece.

Onomarchus helped himself to more of Apollo's money, and made alliances with Lykophron and Peitholaus, who now ruled in Thessalian Pherai in Alexander's place; there was now for the first time, on the assumption that the tyrants in Pherai could carry or drag the rest of Thessaly with them, a chance for Phokis to end the war by legitimate means: rescission, at Thessalian initiative, of the original condemnatory decree. For their part the tyrants of Pherai could hope with Phokian help to expel Theban influence from Thessaly: Philomelus' Thessalian victory of 354, and Onomarchus' suddenly acquired wealth, seems to have convinced Lykophron and Peitholaus that there was, after all, an alternative to tame acceptance of Theban control.

But for the other Thessalian cities there was an alternative too: namely, the traditional recourse of free Thessaly against the tyrannical house of Pherai: Macedon. So in 353 the Aleuads of Larisa called in Philip II. The principle of using Macedon as a stick to hit their enemies may have been the same as that applied in the 360s and even early 350s (see p. 227), but the concrete results were certain to be very different given the strength of Philip's position after a mere six years of rule.

Those six years had begun with the programme of military reorganization discussed in chapter 13 (p. 165): after some initial temporizing diplomacy he had crushed the Paionians and then the Illyrians who had defeated his brother Perdikkas (Diod. xvi.5ff.). Then, by a series of political marriages, he ensured that Macedon was encircled by friendly powers or loyal cantons: Phila of Elymiotis, Audata of Illyria and Alexander's mother Olympias of Epirus (357). Next, he probed down beyond Elymiotis into Thessaly (358: Justin vii.6.8, cp. 'returning to Thessaly' at Diod. xvi. 14.2 under a later year).[14] In this first intervention Philip, who was probably as anxious at this stage to avoid trouble from as to make trouble in Thessaly, laid no heavy hand on Thessaly, but perhaps gave brief and unspectacular help to Larisa against Alexander in the last days of that tyrant's rule.

The Greek world at large may have missed the significance of Philip's Illyrian campaign, and it may reasonably have viewed his first Thessalian adventure as a resumption of established Macedonian policy; but in 357 it was, one would have thought, given clear enough notice at Amphipolis that Macedon now had a ruler of a different and incalculably more dangerous type, militarily and diplomatically, than any before him. In that year Philip, having opened his dealings with Athens in 359 by an ostensible abandonment of designs on Amphipolis (Diod. xvi.4.1), suddenly struck at the city, which he captured after a siege (cp. Tod 150 = WV 50), thus achieving within months what Athens had failed to do in eleven years, to go no further back. That the Amphipolitans themselves had a clear idea what they were faced with is shown by the remarkable and despairing direction to which they turned for help: Athens. But Athens could not[15] or would not fight Philip for Amphipolis, and actually declined a proffered alliance with Amphipolis' neighbour Olynthus at this time

(Dem. ii.6). The explanation for Athens' attitude may indeed lie in the celebrated 'secret diplomacy', involving the Athenian Council (see p. 117), by which Philip purported to bargain Amphipolis for Pydna. But Philip's next move was simply to attack and take Pydna (Dem. i.9), not bothering to wait for the place to be delivered to him by virtue of any diplomatic undertaking by Athens. Now at last Athens was obliged to regard herself as at war with Philip (Aischin. ii.70). All this, as we have said, was clear notice, and the Athenian reaction is explicable only if we grasp the strength and blindness of her desire for Amphipolis, the quest for which had not only helped to lose her the goodwill of her allies and bring down on her the disastrous Social War, but had now led her to rebuff Olynthus, whose Chalcidic Confederation was the strongest Greek power in the north still independent of Philip. In 355 Olynthus made an alliance with Philip instead (Tod 158 = WV 58), and this helped Philip to take Potidaia in 356 and Methone in 354 (siege began 355, ended 354. It cost Philip an eye). He was also greatly strengthened economically when he annexed the rich mining area of Krenides (Diod. xvi.8.6: earlier than 356, cp. Tod 157 = WV 57).

Athens was no more astute, or fortunate, in her dealings with the non-Greek powers in the north, than with Olynthus. An inscription (Tod 151 = WV 51, of 357) records an alliance between Athens and the three kings of Thrace, and another (Tod 157 = WV 57, cp. Diod. xvi.22.3) gives the terms of a grand quadrangular Athenian alliance with the kings of Thrace, Paionia and Illyria. All this looks very sensible. But very different thinking is attested in Demosthenes' Oration xxiii, the *Aristokrateia*, a problematic speech, apparently written early in the 350s and then touched up: some parts at least (e.g. 124, Sacred War events of 352) certainly belong late in the 350s, but other passages (cp. 107) assume that the three Thracian kings are still independent, which they had ceased to be by 355.[16] The curiosity of this speech is that it recommends that Thrace be kept disunited in Athens' interests — a very short-sighted view of those interests at a time when Athens needed all possible assistance against Philip. But even if we try to retrieve some of Demosthenes' credit by pushing back his advocacy of so mistaken a policy to, say, 356, the *Aristokrateia* is an interesting commentary on the epigraphic record, from which otherwise a more single-minded Thracian policy at Athens could reasonably have been inferred. In any case Philip was able to deal with the northern members of the quadrangular alliance one by one — and there is no sign that any of them received help from Athens, who was by now heavily committed in the Social War. In 356 Grabos of Illyria was defeated (Plut. *Alex*.iii); a defeat of the Paionians must be assumed though it is not explicitly attested; and in 353, after the final surrender of Methone (354), Philip turned against the most defiant of the Thracian kings, Amadokos, and reduced him to vassalage (Σ Aischin. ii.81. Another, Ketriporis, had probably submitted a year or two before; the final reckoning with the third and last, Kersebleptes, was to be delayed for ten years, partly because in 352 Kersebleptes acquired a friendly neighbour when Athens under Chares took Sestos and established a cleruchy on the Chersonese: p. 247).

Such then was the position Philip had reached when the invitation of 353 arrived from Thessaly: he had secured Macedon against Illyria, Paionia and Thrace and then reduced their rulers to vassalage or impotence; he had already done something to neutralize Thessalian Pherai in 358; he had a marriage tie with Epirus; he had taken Amphipolis, Pydna, Potidaia and Methone, thus rectifying an age-old weakness of Macedon, its lack of outlets to the north Aegean sea as a result of the Greek colonizing scramble; with the remaining Greek power in that area, Olynthus and the Chalcidic League, he was already on terms of alliance; and to make all this possible he had a fine, professionally trained army and enviable resources in precious metal from Krenides, by now renamed Philippi. Moreover this great access of power had so far called forth no more than protests and inept diplomacy from any of the southern Greek states, tied up as they were with their own problems. With Philip's involvement in the Sacred War that was to change; but Philip was already formidably strong. That being so, it was not likely that his invitation into Thessaly, whatever its immediate outcome, would result in a polite withdrawal from Greece. With hindsight, we can say that the Aleuads of Larisa have a good deal to answer for.

The terms of Onomarchus' alliance with the Pheraian tyrants required that Onomarchus send help when called upon; so now (Diod. xvi.35) he sent his brother Phayllus to Thessaly against Philip, and when that did not work Onomarchus himself engaged Philip —and won (ibid., and Polyain. ii.38.2, showing that this victory, the only military defeat of Philip's entire career, was achieved by artillery, which is thought to have been the newly invented torsion catapults).[17] It was at this moment, when things looked so black for Phokis' enemies the Thebans, that Sparta tried, unsuccessfully as we saw, to reassert herself in the Peloponnese.

But in 352 Philip returned to Thessaly where he was probably now elected *tagos* or *archon* of Thessaly (a gesture of alarm by the Thessalians at the successes of the Pherai-Phokis coalition), and he utterly destroyed Onomarchus and much of his army at the battle of the Crocus Field before Athenian help could reach the Phokians. The Crocus Field had given Philip final mastery of most of Thessaly and its resources: as Diodorus says, he 'settled the affairs of Thessaly' (38.1); he suppressed the tyranny at Pherai and took the port of Pagasai (Dem. i.9), thus acquiring the valuable Thessalian harbour revenues to which Demosthenes alludes (i.22). Philip now had absolute title to the material Thessalian resources — cavalry, harbours, revenues — which, as we have seen in the preceding chapters, the Greek states had so long coveted, back to Kleomenes of Sparta in the sixth century and Sparta's foundation at Herakleia in the fifth, through the period of Theban-Spartan rivalry in the Corinthian War and after, and the succeeding phase of Theban-Athenian rivalry in the 360s. We have almost reached the end of the Thessalian theme which has run through much of this book. Religious primacy in the Amphictyony would be formally Philip's, just as soon as he had settled the Sacred War. Actually he had it already, measured by Amphictyonic votes, but with Delphi in hostile Phokian occupation, votes meant nothing. As to the last of Thessaly's advantages, its strategic control of the land-passage linking Greece and the north, Philip displayed his awareness of the importance of this by moving straight to Thermopylai, the correctly named 'Gates'. But here he was checked: Athens had finally exerted herself to send a task force of 5000, which kept Philip out of the Gates (Diod. xvi.37.3, 38.1; Dem. xix.319).

We next hear of Philip in Thrace. (It is an annoying characteristic of our sources for Philip's reign that we know so much more about his dealings with the Greeks, especially Athens, than about his other preoccupations; yet he had to balance the former against the latter when calculating, for instance, whether to try to force or besiege the Gates, or to answer whatever summons had reached him from the Thraceward region.) In November 352, as we learn from Demosthenes (iii.4), he was besieging Heraion Teichos in eastern Thrace — part of the grinding down of Kersebleptes (Σ Aischin. ii.81). But this campaign menaced Athens too, as did any hostile activity near the Hellespontine corn-route (and there was now the Chersonese cleruchy not far away, newly established and vulnerable). So she decided to mobilize forty triremes and levy a war-tax of sixty talents (Dem. iii.4). They never sailed, Philip was reported ill, or dead, and the mood of crisis at Athens passed. (A small force was sent in September 351.)

In 349 it was the turn of Olynthus (Dem. i.5ff.); in the *First Philippic*, of 351 (Dem. iv.17), Demosthenes had already spoken of Philip's lightning wars against (among other places) Olynthus, and this allusion has caused some scholars to down-date the speech to 349. But the argument defeats itself: the very casualness of the allusion shows that Olynthus is not yet under serious attack.[18] Another reason for questioning the 351 dating, for a speech whose general recommend-ation is all-out war against Philip, has been found in the Rhodian speech (Dem. xv), which is certainly from 351, and which barely touches on Philip (only at para. 24), urging instead an intervention in the south-eastern Aegean: that, however, would have been a piece of diversionary folly not at all consistent with the single-minded opposition to Philip which is the theme of the *First Philippic*. But the truth is that Demosthenes was not yet so obsessed with Philip that he was incapable, even after delivering the First Philippic, of the short-sightedness of the Rhodian speech — compare what was said above about the equally short-sighted *Aristokrateia* which in its final version also belongs at the end of this decade. Three appeals to Athens led to three Olynthian expeditions from Athens (Philochorus frags 49–51); but the city fell in 348. Philip razed the site and enslaved the inhabitants (Tod 166 = WV 64; Dem. ix.26). Part of the reason for Athens' failure to do more was the need to deal with a revolt on Euboia, which even if not actually sponsored by Philip[19] (at Aischin. iii.87 the reading 'Philip' may be corrupt) would certainly be to Macedonian advantage. The island was however lost (Plut. *Phok.* xiif.) so that Athens lost twice over: on Euboia itself, and by the diversion of her resources away from Olynthus at a critical time.

In his *Olynthiacs* (Orations i-iii), Demosthenes had repeatedly urged strong action to help the Olynthians, including the suggestion that Festival Pay be diverted to military purposes; he planned thereby to finance a general northern task-force, or rather two, one for Olynthus and one to ravage Philip's territory. Demosthenes' idea was to jab at Philip *in the north* at whatever point he looked weakest. His opponents preferred to meet Philip, or try to pre-empt him, on the *Greek* doorstep (Thermopylai, Euboia). That was certainly a cheaper policy than Demosthenes', and perhaps also the sounder of the two;

but in favour of Demosthenes there was something to be said for keeping Philip on his toes[20] — barbarian neighbours, as we see from the better documented career of Philip V a century and a half later, might at any moment force a Macedonian king to modify his foreign policy, or (to put it more bluntly) to drop everything and march to some threatened frontier. It was also true, as Demosthenes observed (iv.8), that Philip was not immortal: his assassination in, say, 349 (rather than 336 when it did happen) would scarcely have surprised any contemporary who knew some Macedonian history.

With Olynthus gone, the chances of Athens ever taking Amphipolis receded to invisibility, and the talk began to be of peace. The evidence for the Peace of Philokrates of 346, and the run-up to it, has to be retrieved from Aischines ii and iii and Demosthenes xviii and xix, all speeches written years after the events, and full of the most amazing lies, especially — since the peace later became very unpopular — on the central issue of individual responsibility, or culpability, for the peace.

For the immediate background we must return to the Sacred War. After Onomarchus' defeat, the command of the remaining Phokian forces was taken by Phayllus and then (after his death from illness) by Phalaecus. (All three men were related.) By now both Thebes, from whom Phokis had succeeded in stripping much Boiotian territory, and Phokis, whose money was running out and whose allies Sparta and Athens were wholly absorbed with their own difficulties, were in very low water. Phokis formally removed Phalaecus from the generalship on a charge of embezzlement (*actually* removing him was another matter since he still had part of the army) and appointed three new generals who ravaged Boiotia (347). The Boiotians for their part now called in Philip. This was Philip's cue to return to the heart of Greece, but at first he sent only a small force, enough to meet his obligations and check the Phokians, but not enough to allow the war to be ended without his personal intervention. The Phokians, that is the Phokians other than Phalaecus, learning that Philip was himself on his way south, as indeed he was, appealed to Sparta and Athens for help, and for a moment it looked as if there would be a re-run of Thermopylai in 352 (Aischin. ii.36f. for Athens' vote to mobilize a fifty-ship fleet, which does not seem to have come to anything). Then suddenly everything collapsed; Phalaecus, who may now have seen in Philip his only saviour, refused to hand over Thermopylai to the Athenians, and Philip's way into southern Greece lay wide open. It was this which finally drove Athens seriously to seek peace with Philip (February 346).

From the favourable Athenian response to the Phokian appeal, a response which was not insincere though it was in the event insubstantial, and from an Athenian summons to the Greek world at large, early in 346,[21] organized by Eubulus, to 'deliberate about the freedom of the Hellenes' (Aischin. ii.60; Dem. xix.303), it is clear that the final crumbling of Athenian resistance to the peace was dramatically sudden. What caused it to crumble was first, news of the change in Phokian, or more precisely in Phalaecus' intentions (cp. Aischin. ii.132); and second the failure of the 'freedom of the Hellenes' mission (Aischin. ii.79: perhaps the negative attitude of the Arkadians in particular was decisive). In March a first, and in May-July a second Athenian embassy went to Macedon to negotiate peace. Phalaecus and the Phokians surrendered to Philip; the two Phokian votes in the Amphictyony were given to Philip and Phokis was broken up into villages (cp. Dem. xix.65). A last-minute attempt by Athens to get Phokis included in the peace had been firmly resisted by Philip (Dem. xix. 159). The Sacred War between Phokis and the Theban coalition was over, with an immeasurably strengthened Philip as its only victor, not only militarily supreme in central Greece, but through his new Amphicytonic membership, a barbarian no longer.

The Athenian Peace of Philokrates had for its main clause the Athenian abandonment of Amphipolis (Dem. v.25). But Philip wanted more from Athens than that — in fact, an alliance. Why? There would be an obvious answer if we could accept Diodorus who claims that Philip was already planning a Persian War (xvi.60). In that case the Athenian fleet would be very useful. Isokrates in the *Philippus* of the same year (Isok. v) was to urge Philip to attack and colonize the Persian Empire, but that proves nothing about Philip's *actual* intentions. There is not much concrete evidence for a few years yet: by the end of the 340s, Philip was in communication with Hermias who ruled an Asiatic pocket dynasty at Atarneus (Diod. xvi.54 and Tod 165 for this man, and for Atarneus p. 199); by 341 Hermias was in open defiance of Persia and was suppressed by the king's agents, the main charge against him being correspondence with Philip (Dem. x.32 and Σ on p. 202 Dindorf). Another well-informed friend was the Persian Artabazus, who had been given Macedonian hospitality *c*.350 when he fled from Asia after his revolt (Diod.

xvi.52.3). And it is possible that there were pro-Macedonian factions in some Ionian cities by the end of the 340s (cp. the statue to Philip at Ephesus, Arr. *Anab*. i.17).[22]

But how feasible would an outright attack on Persia have been in 346? The Persians had failed to recover Egypt in the late 350s (cp. Diod. xvi.40.3; 44) and in the early 340s Phoenicia and Cyprus revolted as well (Diod. xvi.42.5). Cyprus was still in revolt in 346 because Isokrates (v.103) speaks in that year of Idrieus satrap of Karia (brother of Mausolus who had died in 353) as a potential rebel; yet we know from Diodorus that Idrieus helped to suppress the Cyprus revolt, which was to make Isokrates' language about Idrieus look foolish. This proves that the disciplining of Cyprus was still in the future when Isokrates said what he did. So Persia certainly had her hands full in the year of the Peace of Philokrates. But before 344 (when Idrieus died) Cyprus had been recovered, as was Phoenicia not long after, leaving Artaxerxes to proceed against Egypt which, with Greek mercenary help (cp. p. 163), he conquered in 343 (Diod. xvi.51, and for the date see *FGrHist.* 69 T 1, para. 14). Then there was some mopping up in Asia Minor: the Hermias affair, already mentioned. The reduction of Cyprus, Phoenicia, Egypt, and Atarneus, was an impressive show of strength: if Philip did have designs on Persia's western satrapies as early as 346, admittedly a black year for Artaxerxes, they cannot be *proved* to have gone beyond the employment or encouragement of spies, double agents and dissidents, and perhaps that was the limit of what was feasible. But if we want to know where Philip, and Alexander after him, got the idea of a religious war against Persia, we need look no further than the Greek Sacred War which ended in 346: if the Phokians were temple-robbers, were not the Persians of 480 temple-burners? The religious card could be played more than once.

There is another, more immediate, problem about Philip's aims in 346: Demosthenes more than once implies that, as late as 346, a view was current that Philip was genuinely keeping his options open in Greece, and that he contemplated saving Phokis and coming down hard on *Thebes* instead, breaking her up into villages and handing over Oropus to Athens (Dem. xix. 21, v.10). That is a surprising claim, and though taken seriously in modern times[23] it is emphatically to be rejected: Thessaly hated the Phokians as only Greek neighbours could hate (p. 15), and Greece generally execrated them as temple-robbers, so that Philip would have been mad to risk alienating his Thessalian supporters, or affronting Greek opinion, by such a volte-face in favour of Phokis. Perhaps something on those lines was put about by Philip's agents — but if so its purpose was simply to gull Athens into inactivity: this was necessary because, as we have seen, she was still contemplating a fight for Phokis early in 346.

After the Peace of Philokrates there was trouble with the Illyrians (345: Diod. xvi.69.7),[24] which Philip dealt with successfully, at the price of a serious thigh-wound. In 344 he reorganized Thessaly into its ancient system of *tetrarchies* (Dem. ix.26, cp. p. 80), and in 342 he finally moved against Thrace: this is the reckoning with Kersebleptes, postponed a decade earlier (Diod. xvi.71, cp. Dem. xii.10). Here the reorganization was perhaps more ambitious, looking not back in time, as in Thessaly, but sideways to Persia: we hear at the beginning of Alexander's reign of a 'general in Thrace' (Arr. *Anab.* i.25; Diod. xvii.62.5), and this has been taken as evidence that Philip now turned Thrace into something like a satrapy on a Persian model — interesting evidence if true that Philip was indeed starting to look east (cp. p. 254). But the case would be stronger if the office of general over Thrace were firmly attested before the end of Philip's reign, which it is not.[25]

As in 352, operations in Thrace brought Philip close enough to Athens' vital interests to provoke panic there. The atmosphere in the Athens of the second half of the 340s was highly volatile, policy towards Philip, who was at least potentially dangerous to Athens, being complicated by hostility to the king of Persia, who was not (anti-Greek activity by Persia in this century takes the form of infiltration of the islands). In 346–344 Philip had done little of which Demosthenes or anybody else could reasonably complain (for one thing his wound may have incapacitated him); but there is hard evidence that he interfered in the Peloponnese on behalf of Argos and Messene against renewed Spartan aggression (Dem. vi.15), and that was enough for Demosthenes, whose real concern of course was not technical delicts by Philip but the constant growth of Macedonian power: from now on, despite his undoubted advocacy of the original peace with Philip in 346, Demosthenes seeks to bring the peace to an end by convicting Philip of breaking it. In 344 he made a start by prevailing on the Assembly to rebuff an offer by Philip to renew the peace (Dem. vii.21, xviii.136). The problem in the years that follow is to determine whether Philip was genuinely in breach of the peace or whether the 'breaches' are merely the inventions of a provocative

Demosthenes. The crux is Euboia: in the *Third Philippic* of 341 Demosthenes denounces Philip for his interference on Euboia (paras 57ff., and cp. xix.204 spoken in the year 343); but the alleged 343 interference is not mentioned in another nearly contemporary speech (Dem. vii, delivered in 342) and the detail of the 341 allegations gets no support from the *Chersonese* speech of a few months earlier (Oration viii). On an extreme view this is proof of Demosthenes' mendacity:[26] 'Philip was not breaking the peace: he did not need to' (because, the argument runs, he had plenty of supporters, in Euboia as elsewhere). But if we accept, as we probably must, that there were limits to what even an Athenian orator could expect to get away with when describing events of very recent memory,[27] we must also accept that Philip was heavily involved, and not just diplomatically either, in the accession to power of his friends in Euboia.

Philip's Thracian campaigns brought him further and further east, till in mid-340 he attacked Perinthos in the Propontis (Diod. xvi.74; Philoc. F 54 for date). This should still be regarded as a continuation of the Thracian operations rather than as an act of aggression against Athens, whose ties with Perinthos were not particularly close; though Demosthenes vaguely and tendentiously gives Philip's motives generally at this time as the desire to starve Athens by interrupting her corn-supply (xviii.87).[28] The Perinthos siege was a failure, despite the best efforts of Philip's military technology, partly because the Persian king sent help to the city via his satraps of the western Anatolian coast: this is of interest as the first overt clash between Philip and Persia. When Philip switched attention to Byzantium, Athenian grain was truly threatened, and they sent help (Diod. xvi.77; Plut. *Phok.* xiv). That, at last, meant war.

Philip took the initiative by seizing 230 corn ships assembled near the entrance to the Bosporus (Philoch. F 54, 162): Demosthenes again distorts the sequence by representing this as the final provocation which compelled Athens to war (xviii.73, 139), but this is belied by the dates: the capture of the merchantmen was a consequence not a cause of the renewal of hostilities.[29] But after a few months Philip broke off the siege, and in 339 he moved south and was at Elatea in Phokis before the end of the year (Dem. xviii.169). There was now an interval of ineffective diplomacy during which Philip tried to lure the Thebans onto his side. In vain: Demosthenes (op. cit.) arranged a last-minute alliance with the old enemies, the Thebans, and this, despite the absence of Sparta who stood aloof, gave the Greek hoplites something like numerical parity with the Macedonian phalanx ranged against them in the decisive battle of Chaironeia fought in August 338. This battle[30] was won by a feigned withdrawal (Polyain. iv.2.2) by Philip, who then re-gathered and routed the over-pursuing Athenians; Diodorus' account adds that Philip's son Alexander led the Macedonian cavalry to victory, presumably on the left (xvi.86). The only other certainty about the battle is that Philip did not pursue the defeated Greek forces far, or at all. He wanted the co-operation of the Greeks and Chaironeia was a means to that end.

Philip, in his political settlement of Greece,[31] did not impose pro-Macedonian regimes generally; an exception is Thebes, which was garrisoned and forced to take back its political exiles, i.e. Macedonian partisans were returned to power (Justin ix.4). But in general Philip did not intervene positively in individual cities: he did not need to, because his victory brought 'his' men to power naturally. At Athens, for instance, there is evidence of a right-wing reaction in an inscription (SEG xii.87) found in the early 1950s, dated to 336, which warns potential 'tyrants' not to try to attack the democracy. That this decree should have been necessary (i.e. that subversion of democracy was a danger in the post-Chaironeia atmosphere), that the constitutionalists should have issued their warning to anybody thinking of making trouble in this way, and that the stone should then have been thrown down (as the archaeological evidence shows it was, within a short time), are all evidence of a vigorous political tussle. Even at Sparta, Philip stopped short of overturning the constitution, though he invaded Spartan territory (Paus. iii.24.6). Isyllos of Epidaurus, a slightly later poet, was to say that Philip entered Sparta in order to 'deprive her of her kingly honour' (IG iv^2 1.128): this does not refer to any proposed abolition of the old dual kingship but is a flowery way of saying he eroded still further Sparta's position of dominance in the Peloponnese; this he did by awarding the Dentheliatis, a frontier area, to Messene (Tac. *Ann.* iv.43).

Such territorial alterations were one way of achieving the balance at which Philip seems to have aimed — thus, for instance, Sparta was to be isolated in the southern Peloponnese. They were also a handy punitive device: so Thebes forfeited Oropus, which she had held since 366 (see p. 229); but though Philip threatened to restore Orchomenos, Thespiai and Plataia, which would have weakened Thebes yet further (Paus. i.9.8), he evidently did not do so (Arr. *Anab.* i.7.11, showing that they had not been restored by Alexander's time). Philip did not, however, break up the great federations, although Athens lost most of her naval league (retaining, however, the cleruchies still outstanding, including Samos): even the Boiotian confederacy stayed intact (there are federal 'Boiotarchs' at Arr. *Anab.* i.7.11) and so did the Euboian,[32] Arkadian and Achaian leagues (Hyp. *Dem.* 18). The exception was perhaps the Aitolian League, which was arguably suppressed for a time,[33] perhaps as a punishment for seizing Naupaktos from the Achaians: if so, this is a rare instance of such treatment by Philip, who was generally concerned to build up the federations as a counter-weight to the traditional *poleis*.

Much of this was negative and preparatory: the positive institution was the League of Corinth, set up in 337. We have the stone (Tod 177 = WV 74; A. J. Heisserer, *Alexander the Great and the Greeks*, 1980, chapter i) recording the terms of the general Greek peace with Philip, with the oaths of the participants and a list of the member states with some mysterious numbers attached to the names. These numbers have been taken as evidence that voting in the new league was organized on a proportional principle, but the suggested analogies — Boiotia, the Delphic Amphictyony — are not convincing, being much more compact organizations than the new league which had a huge geographical extension; and the better view[34] is that the numbers indicate the *military* turnout which each state was expected to furnish. For the rest, the stone, which is in two small fragments in the Epigraphic Museum in Athens, both very difficult to read, can be restored with the help of Demosthenes xvii, *On the Treaty with Alexander*, a speech of 331/0 which deals with supposed infractions of the treaty by Macedon. (This procedure of restoration is justified in view of various close correspondences, e.g. Tod 177, line 14 = Dem. xvii.10, but it must be admitted that the texts of the inscription usually printed are optimistic.)

The league guaranteed existing constitutions; this ban on political change was of course in Macedon's interest given that, as we have already noticed, pro-Macedonian regimes had taken power in the aftermath of Chaironeia even without Philip's direct interference. Demosthenes (xvii.10) speaks of 'freedom and autonomy' — slogans reminiscent of and evidently borrowed from the old charter of the Second Athenian Confederacy — but those are flexible terms and in the new edition of the political dictionary their definition seems not to have excluded the posting of Macedonian garrisons in Greece proper, at Thebes (above), Ambracia, and at the 'handcuffs of Greece',

Chalkis and Corinth (Dem. xvii.3; Polyb. xxxviii.3; Plut. *Arat.* xxiii). The alternative solution is to see these garrisons as a 'peace-keeping force'[35] maintained in the interest of the general security (cp. Dem. xvii.15), but that view perhaps concedes too much to Macedonian benevolence. Finally, the actually anti-democratic character of the settlement is made clear at Dem. xvii.15, with its ban on 'cancellation of debts and redistribution of land'. Although a similar ban had been included in the oath taken at *democratic* Athens, when democracy was restored in 404 (Andok. i.88), the phrase was conventional shorthand for radical discontent (cp. Plato *Rep.* 566 on the programme of the demagogue in his passage to the popular tyrant) and here the ban has undemocratic connotations.

Modern historians have unreasonably doubted whether there was an alliance as well as a peace. It is true that the very fragmentary stone does not mention the word alliance; but literary evidence (Arr. *Anab.* iii.24.5, and Plut. *Phokion* xvi, a neglected passage) implies it. More important, all precedent — such as the peace of Philokrates — suggests that such would have been the general expectation; it is certain that by this time Philip wanted a Greek war against Persia (cp. Diod. xvi. 89.3; Justin ix.4), and that he was soon chosen as 'general with full powers' (Diod. loc. cit.). Diodorus goes on (chapter 91) to describe the first moves in the war: Attalus and Parmenio, the most experienced Macedonian general, crossed to Asia with an advance force. In the words of the Delphic oracle, 'the crown had been put on the sacrificial victim, and the sacrificer was at hand' (ibid.). But this turned out to be the kind of two-edged oracle so dear to the Greeks (and not necessarily to be set aside on that account):[36] the 'victim' of 336 was not the Persian Empire but Philip himself, who was stabbed to death at the moment of his greatest glory, after walking in a procession in which he himself was represented as a thirteenth Olympian god (Diod. 92.5); this was an astonishing departure from what Greeks or Macedonians thought of as religiously acceptable. The assassin, Pausanias, was (as far as we can see) not a political agent, nor a champion of outraged piety; he was a homosexual psychopath with an old grievance.[37] It was the kind of thing that could have happened at any time in the past twenty years, as Demosthenes had commented years ago (p. 253) when urging that the pressure on Philip be kept up. But Alexander was now old enough (he was twenty) and capable enough to assume the succession smoothly, and it was too late for Greek pressure to be of the slightest use.

18 Alexander[1]

To say of any Macedonian accession that it was 'smooth' is to use a relative term: Alexander's was without challenge, but it was accompanied by the shedding of noble Macedonian blood, and it precipitated a major insurrection, that of Thebes. There was also the predictable Illyrian rising.

The noble casualties of the beginning of Alexander's reign are bracketed together by Plutarch, who says (*Mor.* 327) that Macedonia after Philip's assassination was 'seething' and that 'all eyes in Macedon were on Amyntas and the sons of Aeropus of Lynkestis'. This is probably exaggerated, not just because Alexander's grip was firm from the outset, but because it is doubtful if the Lynkestian princely house, from upper Macedonia, was as closely related to the Temenid, i.e. established Macedonian royal family, as a modern theory would have it:[2] they could no doubt be said to have 'royal blood' in a more parochial sense, referring to their own princely line of Lynkestis, but that kind of thing was true of others too. Thus Perdikkas is called 'born of royal stock' (QC x.7.8), but no one claims that he was a candidate for the throne. The 'sons of Aeropus' were called Heromenes, Arrabaios and Alexander; the first two were done away with immediately (AA i.25.1; Diod. xvii.2); the third, 'Alexander the Lynkestian', was arrested later, in 334/3 near Phaselis in Pamphylia, when King Alexander's Asian expedition was well advanced, and he was executed later still, in 330 (AA loc.cit.; QC vii.1). He had escaped death when his brothers died because he was quick to do the new king homage (which presumably explains why *they* were killed — for not doing homage); it may also be relevant that he was son-in-law to the influential senior general Antipater. Alexander the Lynkestian went on, after 336, to hold the high office of 'general in Thrace', for which see p. 256. His arrest is mysteriously connected in our sources with tales of Persian espionage; his death three years later in the aftermath of a collision with the disaffected Macedonian nobility, the 'Philotas Affair' (p. 284) suggests that the original pretext for the arrest was insubstantial and that the real trouble with Alexander the Lynkestian were his connections, or supposed connections, with *Macedonian* dissidents.

The other 'candidate' mentioned by Plutarch is Amyntas, whose dynastic claims were more serious. He was the son of Philip II's brother Perdikkas, and though Justin actually says that Philip was initially regent for Amyntas, this author loses our credit because he says the regency was lengthy, 'diu' (vii.5.9–10).

But the coins show that Philip posed as king from the first,[3] and there is no good evidence that Amyntas was ever regarded as king: a Boiotian inscription (IG vii.3055, from Lebadeia) does call him 'king of the Macedonians' and this has been thought to be an insurrectionist declaration from the year 335, when another Boiotian city, Thebes, revolted. But this cannot be right because Amyntas' wife Kynna was already available for remarriage, and so a widow, by 335 (AA i.5).[4] The 'seething' of Macedonia was therefore short-lived: it is to be dated to 336, straight after Philip's death.

The final death was Karanos, a child (male, cp. 'aemulus imperii') of Philip by Phila (Justin ix.2.3, cp. xi.7.3). We can add here that before setting out for the Persian expedition he killed the relatives of Philip's last wife, Kleopatra (xi.5.1).

In 335 Alexander marched against the Triballi and Illyrians (AA i.1–6),[5] in some campaigning described very fully by Arrian, whose source Ptolemy took part: the motive given is that Alexander wished to forestall their revolt, of which he had wind, but the additional consideration given in Arrian, 'that it would do them no harm to be humbled' on the eve of the planned Asiatic expedition, suggests that this fighting could be thought gratuitous. Most of Alexander's fighting was, and this is one of his most obvious differences from his father, who was no less of an expansionist, but who was happy to act through diplomacy and what his enemies called bribes. Certainly there was no Illyrian threat in 336 comparable to 359, though the news of Alexander's march may have *provoked* the Illyrian revolt, which has become a fact by AA i.5. The ascription, in Arrian, of an official and more creditable motive, emphasized at the expense of the other, is a good introductory warning that the 'main sources' are at least as anxious to do their hero credit as the 'vulgate' (for the terms in inverted commas, see n.1). The rapid campaigning which followed took Alexander to the Danube, which he crossed out of *pothos*, longing, to go beyond (AA i.3.6). This, in its turn, introduces us to a word and theme frequently used of Alexander, for which mystical and ambitious claims have been made in modern times; but when all has been said in sober qualification, the strong 'natural curiosity', which the word denotes at its lowest, was surely an important part of Alexander's motivation throughout his short life.[6] The Illyrians were crushed by superior Macedonian drill and Alexander's own speed of attack: the one his legacy from Philip, the other his own most impressive military quality — but one which all successful Macedonian kings needed (Philip V being especially noted for his *celeritas*), given the proneness of any one neighbour to capitalize on damage inflicted on Macedon by another.

Thus the Theban rising of 335 (AA i.7ff.) was excited not just by desire for 'liberty', i.e. their own return to power on the part of the Theban exiles, but by a popular rumour that Alexander had been killed in Illyria: we may recall that in 352 a similar rumour had circulated about Philip, and had also conditioned Greek foreign policy. At Alexander's accession the Greek states had voted him the hegemony of the Corinthian League (AA i.1) and he had been recognized as *archon* or *tagos* of Thessaly (Justin xi.3.1–2; Diod. xvii.4.1). Alexander reached Boiotia within five days and overran the Theban resistance. The sack of Thebes which followed stuck awkwardly in Greek minds for many years: Aischines (iii.159) describes the influx of refugees into Attica — those who had not been enslaved — and the restoration of the once hated Thebes by Kassander in 316, after Alexander's death, attracted subscriptions from many of the Greek states (Syll.[3] 337 and Diod. xix.54).

This uneasiness is reflected in a divergence in the Alexander-historians: the 'main sources' exonerate Alexander and the Macedonians, putting the blame on Thebes' Greek enemies, AA i.8.8, but Diodorus xvii.13, from the 'vulgate', is a corrective. The moral responsibility was certainly Alexander's since he could have stopped the massacre, though the actual decision on Thebes' fate was left to the League of Corinth: but Diodorus (xvii.14) is right to give Alexander the initiative here as well. He spared the house of the poet Pindar, a sop to Greek sentiment which reminds us that cultural philhellenism is not the same thing as political (thus he was to have Greek taught to Darius' children after their capture at Issos). In any case Pindar, who had written an encomium for the Macedonian king Alexander I the 'Philhellene', had ancestral claims on Macedonian generosity. Alexander was never to make much use of the League of Corinth

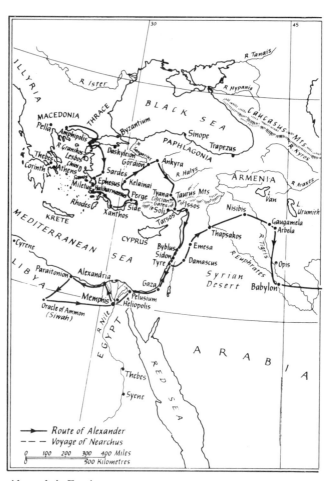

Alexander's Empire

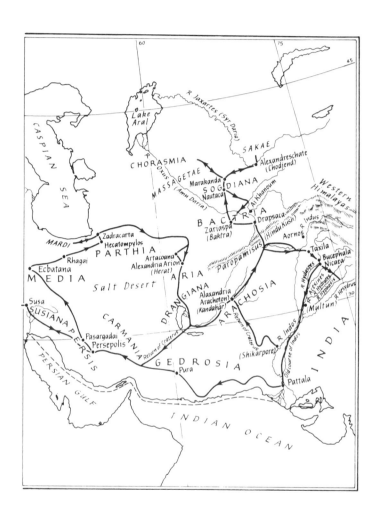

machinery, which he seems to have viewed as a way of making Greeks punish each other (cp. p. 213 for the Chiot prisoners and Kallisthenes, and note AA i.16.6, invoking the 'common decrees' of the Greeks when he sentenced the Greek prisoners taken at the Granikos to hard labour). In Kallisthenes' history, Alexander was evidently made to stress the *Greek* motif — as at the battle of Gaugamela (Plut. xxxiii.1) where Zeus is urged to help the *Greeks*, and there is similarly propagandist 'panhellenism' in Alexander's letter to Darius (AA ii.14.4); this is all part of the attempt to represent the crusade against Persia as punishment for Xerxes' burning of the Athenian temples. Polybius, in a celebrated passage, rightly dismissed this (iii.6) as a mere pretext, but some Greeks may have enjoyed the flattery implied.

After the 'settlement' of Thebes the Athenians, who had shown at least sympathy with the Theban cause, were told to surrender a number of leading politicians, and though this order was rescinded after an appeal for mercy, the mistrust remained, on Alexander's part as well as the Greeks'. It is striking how few Greeks from the old city-states — especially Athens, Sparta, Thebes — were ever employed by Alexander in any capacity; those who were tend always to have one or both of two qualifications: first, they come from outlying Greek districts or places strongly under Macedonian influence; and second they have some skill not possessed by Macedonians.

In the first category should be put the Thessalians with their cavalry (Diod. xvii.17.3). Ordinary Greek troops tended to be used, on the Persian campaign, for line-of-communication purposes only: an example is the garrisoning of Sardis (AA i.24.3). With Alexander's policy towards the ordinary Greek contingents one might compare the way in which Soviet Russia uses its politically unreliable Muslim troops, who 'tend to be relegated to service in rear battalions, construction divisions and farm troops'. Nevertheless, some Boiotian cavalry are attested by inscriptions (Tod 197 and F. Hiller (1926) *Historische Griechische Epigramme*, no. 79: Thespians).

There was, however, a good political reason for retaining Greek fighting units (rather than just not using them at all, as one might have expected Alexander to do): they were hostages for the good behaviour of the Greeks at home. Thus Alexander kept back twenty ships out of the large but politically suspect Athenian navy (Diod. xvii.22.5). And the disbandment of the fleet in the first winter of the campaign should be explained similarly (AA i.20.1; cp. ii.2.3 for its reassembly the following spring). Arrian gives the reason for the disbandment as shortage of money, but that is implausible since Alexander now possessed the treasure of Sardis, a rich Persian satrapal capital (i.17.3).

Individually, as well as collectively, the Greeks employed by Alexander can be sorted into the same two categories. Like the Thessalian cavalry, Thessalian engineers and siege-technicians such as Diades and Charias belong in the first category,[7] though their special aptitudes put them in the second category too, and the same is true of a man like Eumenes of Cardia with his secretarial skills — but Cardia had always hated Athens (Dem. v.25, viii.58) and such a man was politically safe. The literary man and philosopher Kallisthenes came from Olynthus, now in the Macedonian orbit, and his gifts would have been hard for any Macedonian to match (Ptolemy is the only Macedonian in Alexander's entourage who took to the writing of history). There are also odd individuals like Deinokrates the Rhodian town-planner (the new city of Rhodes had been laid out in the late fifth century on the principles of the creator of theoretical town-planning, Hippodamus of Miletus), or the 'bematists' (surveyors) Diognetos and Philonides from Asian Erythrai and Krete respectively; another man from Krete, which is very much out of the Greek political mainstream, was Nearchos, Alexander's admiral (p. 288). But his naval skills, like those of Onesikritos from the Greek island of Astypalaia, put him in the second category too: Macedon for all her timber had long been hampered, by Greek colonies, from access to the nearest sea. The only Greek *hetairoi*, the privileged class of Alexander's 'companions', were Demaratos of Corinth and Eriguios and Laomedon of Mytilene, though mention should be made of Medius of Thessalian Larisa, politically reliable and perhaps a man with a special skill — the throwing of parties, for which Thessalians were famous (Xen. *Hell.* vi.1; for Medius see also B. Helly (ed.) *Inscriptions of Gonnoi*, (1973) no.1). It was the wild drinking at a party given by this man which cost Alexander his life. There is an occasional Greek satrap in Alexander's empire like Nearchos the Kretan (Lycia), Thoas from Magnesia on the Maiander, satrap of Gedrosia, or Stasanor of Cypriot Soli (Areia). These men bear out the general conclusion of this survey, that the central places of old Greece are barely represented among Alexander's appointees and staff. One final purpose for which Alexander has been thought to have tried to use specifically Greek talent is in colonization and the diffusion of Greek culture, *paideia*, but if this was a serious aim of Alexander's it failed (cp. Diod. xviii.7 on the unhappiness of the Greek settlers in central Asia, with p. 286). All this is evidence for recognition of specially Greek talents, but little respect for Greek freedom.

So when Alexander — Illyrian and Greek resistance now crushed — planned his Asian campaign in earnest, the man left behind was in effect appointed satrap of Greece: Antipater, to whom he 'handed over' Greece (AA i.11.3). The description of this man's job (and that of his eventually designated successor Krateros) as including looking after 'the freedom of the Greeks' (AA vii.12.4) is of course the merest euphemism, an early instance of the abuse of the term 'freedom of the Greeks' which was to run through hellenistic history till its most brilliant exploitation by the Roman Flamininus in the early second century BC.

In spring 334 Alexander crossed the Hellespont, throwing a spear into Asian soil before landing (Diod. xvii.17), thereby claiming Asia as 'spear-won territory', *doriktetos chora*,[8] a Homeric idea which had played little part in the foreign relations of the Greek city-states, whose warfare had been for strips of frontier land or for 'hegemony' (cp. Dem. xv.17, quoted p. 15. But Dem. xii.23 shows *Philip* had already in the 350s claimed Amphipolis by right of conquest). Homeric reminiscences abound in both of our two literary traditions about Alexander,[9] and it is clear that this reflects not just a literary reworking of the facts but the facts themselves, in that Alexander genuinely modelled his behaviour on the Homeric heroes, notably Achilles (he could claim descent from Achilles' son Neoptolemos through his mother Olympias of Epirus; Thucydides' *Archaeology* shows that even sophisticated Greeks drew no absolute line between such 'mythical' figures and the subject-matter of 'history'). Thus Alexander dishonoured the corpse of Batis at Gaza (QC iv.6.29), just as Achilles had dishonoured Hector; he 'fought with a river' (the Indos) as Achilles had done (Diod. xvii.96); and at the death of his beloved companion Hephaistion he imitated the mourning of Achilles for Patroklos (AA vii.14.4). There are plenty of other examples of 'heroic' imitation (at AA iii.3.2 the journey to Ammon is in imitation of Perseus and Herakles; it was from Herakles that the *Macedonian* royal line ultimately descended via Temenos — just as Perseus on one account ranked as the eponymous founder of the *Persian* empire: Hdt. vii.150). Such emulation[10] (which is how we should see it, rather than as literary imitation by the historians; though the influence flowed both ways) shaped much of the behaviour of the great figures of the ancient world, and should not be minimized.

Close to the Hellespont, Alexander fought the first of his three set-piece battles against the Persians, the battle of the River Granikos.[11] Here the 'main sources' and the vulgate are more strikingly discrepant than on perhaps any other single issue, for whereas Arrian (AA i.13ff. for his account) makes Alexander, in daytime, confront the massed Persian cavalry drawn up on the opposite bank of the river, the vulgate version of Diodorus (xvii.19ff.) has Alexander attack the unopposing Persians at *dawn*, that is, Alexander follows the advice of Parmenio which Arrian says he rejected. The vulgate must be wrong, not only because the idea of an attack 'under cover of dawn' is militarily implausible (it would have been chaotic to organize) but because the 'main source' account presumably goes back via Ptolemy and Aristobulus to Kallisthenes, and it is not conceivable that any of those writers could have hoped to get away with such a bold falsification. The Persian strategy, on Arrian's account, is admittedly not easy to understand, but it seems that they hoped to repel the Macedonian cavalry, whose efficiency they may have underrated (cp. Polyain. v.44 for earlier Persian successes against Philip's advance force), by simply pushing it down into the river-bed.

The description of the battle in all our sources is thoroughly 'Homeric', with a good deal of prowess being shown in single combat; but, as we have seen, that is not ground for scepticism. The Persian cavalry were routed; Alexander's way into Asia Minor had been opened up. The Granikos was not a David and Goliath contest with Alexander as David; on the contrary it was, as Arrian calls it in a later context (vii.9.7), a 'satraps' battle', hastily mounted from local levies; and the Persians were outnumbered in total (the Persian strategy at i.12 implies numerical inferiority at least in infantry: Alexander had perhaps 40,000+ foot and 6000+ horse;[12] the Persians are said to have had 20,000 of each but the Persian cavalry figures are hard to believe).

Alexander's political settlement in Asia Minor, the western part of which he now overran, takes two simultaneous and apparently contradictory forms: he appoints satraps in the old Persian way (AA i.17: Kalas made satrap of Hellespontine Phrygia, Asander satrap of Lydia, the old Sardis satrapy; both men were Macedonians); but he proclaimed democracy and the restoration of laws (AA i.17.10; 18.2;

cp. Plut. *Al.* xxxiv.2 with comm.). The puzzle is only apparent: back in the 390s, there had been a satrap of Ionia, Strouses (Tod 113), but the Ionian cities could still regard themselves as in some sense free from control by 'the barbarian', at least till the King's Peace (see p. 203 on SEG xxvi.1282). Part of the explanation of the 390s evidence was to be sought in the Persian distinction between 'cities' and 'territory': the latter enjoyed fewer rights and was exploited more directly (cp. *Labraunda* 42 where the distinction is already made at the end of the Achaemenid period, in the satrapy of Pixodaros). And exactly this distinction is formally perpetuated by Alexander in his settlement at Ionian Priene: he remits the *syntaxis* payable by the city — but makes clear that the territory, *chora*, is 'mine' and must go on paying *phoros*, tribute (Tod 185).[13]

The inscription from Priene also raises the question whether the Greek islands and cities of the western Asiatic coast were now made members of the League of Corinth.[14] The question matters because it should help us to decide whether Alexander regarded the new Greek possessions, which he had prised away from Persia, as being fully Greek or not.

Of the *islands*, Tenedos was clearly a member (cp. AA ii.2.2 on the agreement of Tenedos with Alexander and the Greeks);[15] so was Mytilene on Lesbos (ii.1.4, where the different wording — agreement with Alexander only — is not significant). Eresos on Lesbos was a member on the evidence of the speech *On the Treaty with Alexander*, para. 7;[16] this curious production, mentioned in chapter 17, p. 259, is unreliable in many details, but a fact of this kind can hardly be an invention. (The speech talks of Macedonian-sponsored 'tyrannies' in e.g. Messene, Pellene and Sikyon, paras 7,10,16; though this is exaggerated language, it does underline the contrast with the treatment of Asia Minor, see further p. 271.) Chios was a member as is proved by an inscription (Tod 192), which contains a reference to Chiot traitors being dealt with according to 'the decree of the Hellenes' (but see AA iii.2 for what really happened: Alexander dealt with them autocratically). When these places had joined is a problem; recent attempts have been made to put the enrolment, into the league, of Chios and Eresos as early as 336 or even 340,[17] in Philip's lifetime; but despite the mention of altars to Zeus Philippios in the Eresos inscription (Tod 191), these honours to Philip do not prove membership of the League of Corinth for Eresos in his lifetime. And as for Chios, it is probable[18] that she remained garrisoned by the Karian (i.e. Persian) satraps down to well after 340 when Persian-controlled Chios helped Perinthos and the Athenians against Philip (Diod. xvi.77, probably confirmed by IG ii^2 234, cp. Tod 175 = WV 72). Rhodes had a Macedonian garrison till after Alexander's death (Diod. xviii.8.1), and though this does not exclude membership — cp. p. 260 — there is no other good evidence of any kind.

For the mainland of Asia Minor there is less evidence; the mention of *syntaxis*, 'contribution', in the Priene text has usually[19] been taken to prove membership, since that was the term used by the Second Athenian Confederacy, an organization on which as we saw Philip's League of Corinth was modelled in certain respects. But though probable, this argument from analogy is not decisive, especially if we adopt a rival interpretation of the Priene *syntaxis* as bearing its hellenistic sense — see n.13 — of a once-for-all payment (and it must be admitted that the letter forms of the inscription look third century rather than fourth: so a rephrasing could have gone along with the recarving). Other places further south and east, like Aspendos (AA i.27) were treated more harshly; but, as their coinage shows, they were not fully Greek and Alexander may have felt less compunction here than when settling the ancient Ionian cities of the west coast.

Alexander's treatment of Asia Minor may seem inconsistent not only in that he treated cities and territory in different ways, something we have already discussed and explained above, but in the different treatment accorded to Asia Minor, where democracy and liberation are the themes, compared with mainland Greece, where a hostile critic could speak of 'tyranny' (Dem. xvii) which, even allowing for exaggeration, suggests a less liberal approach than in Asia Minor. But here again there is no real inconsistency, provided we accept that Alexander was indifferent to particular *forms* of government, something for which Greeks were prepared to die before and after his day. His real 'principle' is pragmatic reversal of the previous *status quo*: Persia had supported oligarchies on the whole, so in Asia Minor Alexander set up democracies. In Greece, by contrast, opposition to Macedon had tended to be democratic, so we find Macedon supporting more right-wing regimes.

His passage down the western Anatolian coast saw the first of the 'Alexander foundations' — refoundations of Smyrna and Priene,[20] two old cities which were in low water by the mid-fourth century.

Here he seems to have been taking a leaf out of the book of satraps like Mausolus, who had moved or refounded cities like Halikarnassos, Erythrai and Knidos earlier in the century.

The conquest of the western Anatolian coast was easy except for the siege of the exceptionally well-defended Halikarnassos, a satrapal Persian capital, the siege of which held Alexander up for several months in the summer of 334. In Pamphylia at Mt Climax the sea is said (Kallisthenes F 31) to have receded, as if doing him obeisance (i.e. as a god); whether the gloss about 'doing obeisance' is from Kallisthenes himself or is the addition of the later writer who is quoting him, is strictly uncertain, but this incident is probably the first evidence of literary efforts to 'deify' Alexander (see p. 277).

He then struck north into the plateau of inner Anatolia, and visited the old Phrygian capital of Midas at Gordion, not far (fifty miles) from modern Ankara. Here, by cutting the 'Gordian knot' by which the yoke of the shepherd Gordius' chariot was secured (AA ii.3), Alexander won the 'lordship of Asia' which an old legend promised. This raises the question of Alexander's early aims: the Hellespont incident (p. 268), and the Gordian knot, help explain how he could call himself Lord of Asia after the battle of Issos (ii.14.7, in a letter to Darius which is usable evidence).[21] The scope of the ancient term 'Asia' was elastic, but here it surely denotes the whole Persian Empire (as at Diod. xvii.17).[22] Arrian (iv.11.7, in a speech of Kallisthenes which is fictitious but based on near-contemporary material, cp. n.21) writes of an original intention merely to 'add Asia to Europe', which might be thought to refer just to a plan to strip away western Anatolia (that would perhaps mean something like Agesilaus' more limited objectives, p. 192); but there is no reason to think that Philip, the great opportunist, would ever have stopped at that if the way east lay open, and still less reason to think it of Alexander. Alexander's strategy, as put into his mouth by Arrian before the siege of Tyre (ii.17), is defensive (but note the phrase 'expedition *to Babylon*'); and in a letter (ii.14.9) he tells Darius that he regards himself as owning everything that had been his. Stand your ground, he tells Darius, because I shall pursue you wherever you are. (For Darius — III — see index.)

Alexander swept south again, to Cilicia, and left the Anatolian subcontinent — to find that Darius and the full Persian army, now mobilized at last, had got in his *rear*. This is the prelude to his second great battle, Issos (November 333),[23] fought by the gulf of Alexandretta which forms the right-angle between the Anatolian subcontinent and the Phoenician coast. For this battle we have not only Arrian's account (ii.6ff.), which goes back via the 'main sources' to Kallisthenes, but detailed criticisms of Kallisthenes' original version. These criticisms are in Polybius' polemical twelfth book (chapters 17ff.), which though as pedantic and often foolish as many ancient 'corrections' of a predecessor (one thinks of Thucydides' specific strictures on Herodotus) are useful to us in that they enable us to get closer to what Kallisthenes actually wrote. (The 'vulgate' of Diodorus is of no value on Issos; Curtius is however a little better.)[24] Darius, like Xerxes at Salamis, forfeited his advantages in numbers by allowing the battle to take place in a narrow space between the shore line and the Amanus mountains (although Kallisthenes exaggerated both numbers and narrowness). Alexander won by what was to become his classic tactic of piercing a hole in the enemy left with the cutting edge of the 'Companion Cavalry', whom he led on the far Macedonian right, then wheeling towards the enemy centre, where by Persian tradition the king was posted. This was a kind of 'hammer and anvil' manoeuvre which relied on Parmenio holding firm with the Macedonian left, and on the infantry phalanx standing its ground in the centre. Darius fled, and his womenfolk fell into Alexander's hands; his chivalrous treatment of them prompted Diodorus (xvii.38) to contrast the *tyche*, fortune, which wins battles with the self-restraint of true virtue.[25]

After Issos Alexander had the choice of pursuing Darius or moving south, thus giving his opponent time to regroup. That he chose the second, apparently risky course, which took him via Phoenicia towards Egypt, may — note the *pothos* to visit Ammon (AA iii.3.1) — have something to do with the pull which Egypt exercised on all ancient Greeks (cp. Hdt. ii). But there were also, as correctly expounded in his speech at ii.14 (from the main sources) sound strategic reasons: the Aegean Sea, where an energetic Persian counter-offensive was still going on, would never be safe for Macedon while the Phoenician ports were in hostile possession, and that, with a disaffected Greece in his rear (where the Spartan king Agis III was to lead a serious revolt in 331) would have cut off Alexander's communications in both directions (money, supplies, reinforcements, intelligence).[26] Like Agesilaus in 394 he would have had to scuttle back home.

But Alexander's great advantage over Agesilaus, thanks to men like Diades (p. 267), lay in his ability to take fortified cities by siege — not just Halikarnassus in 334 but, after the battle of Issos, the great Phoenician maritime states of Tyre and Gaza. With these places in his control (AA ii.15ff. for the elaborate sieges) he could indeed claim to have 'conquered the Persian fleet on dry land' (cp. AA i.20.1). The stubbornness of the resistance to Alexander in those three places is due not just to their fortifications but to the long tradition of Persian tolerance to their native, client rulers, the Hekatomnids of Karia (whose last representative, Ada, Alexander wisely reinstated) and the Semitic rulers of the Phoenician coastal states. Such men had no reason to hope for Persia's defeat (the rulers of Sidon and Halikarnassos had taken part in the Satraps' Revolt, it is true, but perhaps only to increase their holdings). In this they were unlike, say, the Ionian Greek democrats, or the native population of Egypt.

In Egypt, Curtius says, the Persians had governed 'avariciously' (iv.7.1, cp. Diod. xvii.59) and this misrule — which in any case goes back immediately no further than 343, cp. p. 255, not to mention a possible revolt in the early 330s — is given as the reason why Alexander was welcomed (November 332). But in the past seventy-five odd years several Persian armies had failed to penetrate past Pelusium and the Nile Delta, and the lack of resistance to Alexander proves that the Persian high command had decided not to try to hold Egypt, and this, as much as Persian unpopularity, explains why Alexander had no trouble.[27]

Alexander now gave instructions for the first of the great city-foundations named after him, Alexandria in Egypt, which was to be the 'first city' of the hellenistic, and the 'second city' of the Roman world. Like so many of his achievements, the colonizing activity of Alexander was inherited from his father: we saw that after gaining control of Krenides (by 356) Philip renamed it Philippi, and this should really rank as the first of the eponymous city-foundations of the hellenistic age. But Philip also founded Bylazora (cp. Polyb. v.97: 'the largest city in Paionia and very favourably situated in relation to the pass from Dardania into Macedonia') and perhaps a Herakleia Lynkestis (358); he also colonized the Hebros basin in Thrace with *inter alia* another eponymous foundation, Philippopolis.[28] Like for instance the Athenian colony at Brea in the same area (ML 49), a garrisoning function was no doubt combined with another aim: to dispose of unwanted and (from the Macedonian point of view) undesirable population. We may compare Antipater who, after the crushing of the Athenian revolt which took place after Alexander's death, shipped off some five-figure number of Athenians, whose status was below the 'hoplite' census, to Thrace (Diod. xviii.18.5).

Another influence was Persia: we noted the analogy between Mausolus' refoundations in Ionia and Alexander's; and it is certain that Alexandreschate, 'Furthest Alexandria', was deliberately intended to imitate Cyrus the Great, a great city founder (cp. Strabo 517 for Alexander as a 'lover of Cyrus', and for Alexandreschate see p. 285). Increasingly, as at Ai Khanoum in north Afghanistan, archaeology is revealing that Alexander chose existing Achaemenid settlement centres for his new Alexandrias (though Ai Khanoum itself cannot certainly be identified with any attested Alexandria, it is the best excavated and richest central Asiatic *polis*, see below): there is Achaemenid irrigation in the Ai Khanoum area, and epigraphic proof of resident Persians (SEG xxviii, 1978, 1327 for the good Iranian name Oxybazos: hellenistic, but doubtless a descendant of an earlier settler). Again, at Kandahar[29] = Alexandria in Arachosia, there is Achaemenid-type pottery and a tablet inscribed in Elamite, the Persian bureaucratic script in which the Persepolis records were kept.

Plutarch (*Mor.* 328) credited Alexander with seventy city-foundations, a gross exaggeration (comparable to the traditions about archaic Miletus which was supposed to have been the mother of seventy-five or ninety cities). It needs to be interpreted against the background of Plutarch's view that Alexander's activity as a founder of cities was part of his hellenizing greatness. Plutarch's remark that Alexander changed the nature of the savage tribes among which these cities were founded is untrue, as is the statement (328e) that Alexander sowed all Asia with Greek magistracies (see further p. 286). It is part of the picture of Alexander the philosopher and man of practical virtue (cp. above for Diodorus on his behaviour after Issos).

Modern scholars[30] have followed Plutarch till very recent times, when there has been a reaction and a tendency to see most of Alexander's foundations as repressive devices with little cultural intention behind them, instruments for holding down the natives whose participation was enforced. No doubt many of the eastern city-foundations were bleak places, like Alexandria in Margiane, which according to Pliny was refounded in the hellenistic period after it had been overrun and destroyed by barbarians (*Natural History* vi. 46–7). But it was possible to enjoy the forms of city life in the back of Asiatic beyond: at the early hellenistic city of Ai Khanoum on the Oxus in north Afghanistan,[31] excavations since the 1960s have revealed dedications to Hermes and Herakles the patron gods of athletics, i.e. there was a gymnasium, and there was a theatre.

Pausanias (x.4.1) was to regard these two buildings as the emblems of Greek city life. Leaving aside Alexander's success and considering only his motives, it is clear that he wanted to give his new cities a characteristically hellenic send-off:[32] after the foundation of Alexandreschate in 329 BC he held a cavalry and athletic contest (AA iv.4.1). But such inaugural ceremonies do not take us very far; we shall see that the practical difficulties of survival could be acute. Self-defence came first, *paideia* and self-government afterwards.

Nevertheless gestures like that of 329 show that the gloomy, minimalist picture of Alexander's aims does not account for all the evidence; and it certainly does not work for Alexandria in Egypt, whose foundation Arrian describes in terms which show that he hoped for the city's commercial[33] and civic success. Arrian (iii.1.5) describes how Alexander personally marked out the site of the *agora* and the future temples (cp. also the food omen at Plut. *Al.* xxvi, and see Diod. xvii.52); the site certainly had superb natural advantages. (The actual act of foundation is dealt with further below.)

One approach to the problem of Alexander's foundations is to make some distinction between *types* of foundation: first, the *poleis*, civic communities with magistracies, Assembly and perhaps Council (though even at Egyptian Alexandria the existence of a Council is doubtful):[34] Plutarch tendentiously assimilates *all* Alexander's foundations to this type (the Ionian refoundations certainly belong here). Second, the *katoikiai*, military settlements: these are a common feature of the hellenistic, particularly the Seleucid, world, e.g. Dura Europus on the Euphrates. Third, the *phrouria*, essentially movable garrisons (cp. AA iv.27.7, Bazira = ?Birkot,[35] Ora, Massaga, places in the territory of Musicanus, Pattala or the *phrouria* against Spitamenes at AA iv.28.4: central Asia). Those modern scholars who take a minimalist view tend to be thinking of the second and third types.

Egyptian Alexandria was founded soon after Alexander's arrival in Egypt (before the visit to Ammon at Siwah oasis, as Ptolemy believed, not, as in QC iv.8.1, on his return).[36] The commercial motives for the foundation have already been given above; but hellenistic and Roman history (particularly the accession of Vespasian) show that possession of Alexandria was always of great military value too, though one aspect of this importance, its control of the grain outlet from Egypt, can hardly be distinguished from the commercial. The original settlement was more than just a military camp for time-expired troops, since

able-bodied Macedonians and Greeks were surely encouraged to settle
in Egypt — a newly discovered Greek order on papyrus from the
military governor Peukestas son of Makartatos (AA iii.5.5. for this
man) has recently been discovered, putting a temple at Memphis out
of bounds (*JEA*, 1974, pp.239ff.). However, when Strabo (797)
speaks of natives, mercenaries and Greeks, he is quoting from
Polybius and thus reflects second-century conditions, and cannot be
read back[37] automatically to the *very* beginning of Alexandrian
history. Alexandria in Egypt resembled other of the Alexandrias and
other early hellenistic foundations in that the site was not quite virgin
(see p. 275 on the Achaemenid prehistory of Kandahar and Ai
Khanoum): Pseudo-Callisthenes, the 'Alexander Romance', a hellenistic novel which now and then contains some circumstantial detail,
says (i.31.2) that Alexandria was formed by a *synoikism* or concentration of a number of named native Egyptian villages. But the names are
not reliable, except Rhakotis (cp. Strabo 792).

Alexander now travelled across the desert to visit the oracle of
Ammon at Siwah: we have seen that the cult of 'Zeus Ammon' was
already well established in the Greek world of the fourth century
(chapter 13, p. 178), and this visit does not prove that Alexander is
already 'going native' in any very novel way. The visit is, however, of
profound importance as the most dramatic evidence for Alexander's
belief in his own 'divinity'[38] in the sense of divine filiation from Zeus.
It is not quite the first piece of evidence: as we noted, in Pamphylia the
sea had 'done him obeisance', an incident possibly 'written up' by
Kallisthenes, and suggested by a passage in Xenophon's *Anabasis*
(i.4.18) where the Euphrates makes way for Cyrus the younger, thus
(incorrectly) predicting that he would be king. (Cp. too Homer, *Iliad*
xxiv.96, where the sea divides to make way for the god.) And even
earlier, as the sober Alexandrian scholar Erastosthenes records (Plut.
Al. iii), Olympias had told Alexander the 'secret of his paternity', i.e.
his divine filiation.

But it is with Alexander's real father Philip that any treatment must
begin, for Alexander's 'divinity' or 'divine filiation' have their origins
not in Persian or other Oriental conceptions but in the Greece and
Macedon that he had left behind him.

The Persian kings did *not* regard themselves as gods: Darius I in
the Behistun inscription smites armies by the will and under the
protection of Ahura Mazda, with whom he was in no sense identified.
Greek misunderstandings of Persian belief and practice are another

matter: in Aeschylus' *Persai* the chorus address Atossa as a wife and mother of gods (line 157), and Longinus' *On the Sublime* (iii.2) quotes Gorgias (in the 420s BC) as saying that Xerxes was the Persians' Zeus. But this is a mere distortion of a piece of gross flattery in Herodotus (vii.56) where a man from the Hellespont suggests that Xerxes is Zeus who has taken on the shape of a man. What contributed to Greek notions was undoubtedly the ceremony of *proskynesis* before the Persian king (see p. 287), which in one of its forms required total prostration, something which Greeks reserved for the gods (cp. Hdt. vii.136; Xen. *Anab.* iii.2.13; Isok. iv Paneg. 151).

In Greece the hero-cult of city-founders and leaders of colonies was longstanding (p. 179), and these are of course aspects of Alexander's activity too, as of Philip's (founding a city like Philippi, named after oneself, could be regarded as a kind of *hubris*); we noted also such benefactor cults as that of Lysander at Samos and Euphron at Sikyon, though whether Lysander received cult *in his life* has recently been questioned.[39]

But the most important, though for us elusive, precedent for Alexander was his father Philip[40] (just as he is the precedent for Alexander the city-founder, cp. above). This, superficially, is a paradox, since Alexander's own beliefs, which seem to have gone deep, implied at one level a denial that Philip was his father at all.

In the theatre at Aigai just before his death Philip had been represented as a 'thirteenth Olympian god' (see p. 260 on Diod. xvi.92.5). This remarkable statement is the solidest evidence for Philip's intended apotheosis and it is tantalizing that we do not know who was Diodorus' source for the four years between 340 (when Ephorus stopped) and the beginning of Alexander's reign,[41] which makes it hard to assess the truth of the story. The altars to Zeus Philippios at Eresos on Lesbos (Tod 191) may signify 'Zeus Protector of Philip' rather than 'Philip who is Zeus',[42] but they are still an unusual religious manifestation in the prehellenistic world (cp. the statue of Philip in the temple at Ephesus, AA i.17.1). There is also some archaeological evidence, but interpretation is difficult and likely to be circular: the 'Philippeion' at Olympia (cp. Paus. v.20.9f.), which contained statues of Philip and his family but which may have been altered after Philip's death so any 'cult' may have been posthumous;[43] and the finds at Vergina, which are still too recent and incompletely published for proper assessment (it was at first claimed that the great tomb found in 1977 had a temple attached which if true would curiously confirm a statement in the Alexander Romance, Ps.–Call. i.24.11).[44]

There is enough here to have stimulated Alexander in the same direction, though we must remember that in the Greco-Macedonian world it was *personal* merit which secured divine or heroic honours:[45] Philip's 'divinity' could not be inherited; nor should we speak of Alexander's role as 'son of Ammon' as some kind of *ex officio* title acquired by him as Pharaoh.[46]

Arrian (iii.3–4) provides the vital evidence for the visit to Ammon, which has to be supplemented by Kallisthenes (F 14a = Strabo 88); Arrian and Kallisthenes are in basic agreement. The vulgate (see especially Diod. xvii.49–51) is significantly different. Arrian's account is however extremely reticent. He says that Alexander went to Ammon because of a *pothos* to consult the infallible oracle; Kallisthenes adds the motive of love of glory; both agree that Alexander wished to rival the two heroes Perseus and Herakles (for the significance of these two, see p. 268). Arrian says that Alexander *was seeking* to trace his birth to Ammon, in other words the idea of his sonship from Ammon was already in his head before he set out[47] — we are reminded of the Pamphylian *proskynesis*; what he wanted now was 'more certain knowledge' (*atrekesteron*) from an infallible oracle. This is interesting, but if it were just Arrian's own comment it would not be worth much; Curtius however (iv.7.8) confirms Arrian. Then, still on Arrian's version, he made his enquiry and received the answer his heart desired, as he said. That is all. Kallisthenes adds some detail such as that only Alexander was allowed to enter the temple, while the rest had to listen to the priest's responses from outside. The responses were not given in words but in nods and symbols, and the priest interpreted the god. Kallisthenes is, however, very important in that he shows that the responses included the declaration of Alexander's divine filiation: he goes on to describe how Ammon was promptly confirmed on the subject of the 'birth from Zeus' by the deliverances of the Ionian oracles at Branchidai and Erythrai, seat of a prophesying sibyl. This is the crucial response of Ammon and it seems to have changed Alexander's conception of himself. But since the better sources are so reticent we cannot go much further than that. Alexander himself was in no doubts: at Gaugamela he prayed (Plut. *Al.* xxxiii) for Zeus' help 'since', *eiper* (not 'if', cp. Homer, *Odyssey* ix.529–30), 'he was the son of Zeus'. And for Kleitos (Plut. l. 6.) and the Opis mutineers at the end of his life (AA vii.8.3, see p. 291), his 'filiation from Ammon' was common knowledge. (This is relevant to the clashes with Macedonians, individually and collectively, described on p. 284.)

The vulgate is different, fuller and more dramatic: 'son of Zeus' was here a public salutation by the priest, not a private or semi-private response, and Alexander was told, in answer to a question, that he *had* punished all his father's (i.e. Philip's!) murderers, and that he would be invincible and rule over the whole earth. These traditions are not necessarily baseless (AA vi.19.4, where it is said that Alexander 'sacrificed to the gods Ammon had told him to', shows that not *everything* the god said was kept secret). But we may doubt whether Alexander's 'world-rule' and 'invincibility' were as central to, and pervasive in, Kleitarchos' original book as has recently been claimed.[48]

In spring of 331 Alexander left Egypt and, returning through Phoenicia, was in Mesopotamia by mid-summer; the final great battle with Darius was fought at Gaugamela[49] on 1 Oct. (Plut. *Camillus* xix). The course of the battle is even more obscure than most ancient battles, because of the tendency of the sources to disparage Parmenio at Alexander's expense (though on the enemy side the good performance of the Indian and Persian cavalry emerges clearly enough). Again, as at Issos, Alexander's tactic on the right was to wheel and charge leftwards at the critical second, towards Darius himself. Parmenio on the Macedonian left is, however, supposed to have sent a message to Alexander, who was already in pursuit of Darius; the message was an appeal for help. This story creates great difficulties (how could any messenger have located and reached galloping cavalry?) and the most recent accounts either rationalize it (e.g. by turning the message *during* the battle into a prearrangement),[50] or else distort Arrian's text (by rendering Arrian's 'Alexander turned back from *further* pursuit' at iii.15.1 as 'Alexander was just on the brink of pursuit'),[51] or else treat the whole incident as an anachronism lifted from the later battle of Ipsus in 301 and designed to make a propaganda point about that battle instead.[52] It is better simply to reject the story as evidence of malice towards Parmenio, and to admit ignorance: all we can say is that Alexander did not in the end overpursue ruinously; Darius did, again, get away; and perhaps Parmenio could safely be blamed for this. None of his family or friends survived to write history.

Darius rode in flight towards Media; Alexander turned south to Babylon, and then Susa. Possession of these great cities of the old eastern world was, as Arrian rightly says, the 'prize of the war' (iii.16.2); that is a reference to the Persian treasure — a huge access of wealth for Alexander, even though the Achaemenids may not have gone in for economically unproductive 'hoarding' on the insane and extreme scale that was once thought.[53]

These last weeks of 331[54] were a political, as well as a military and financial, turning-point, for at Babylon Alexander reappointed Mazaeus, a Persian, as satrap of Babylon, though with a Macedonian, Apollodorus of Amphipolis (Amphipolis refers to location of fief, not Greek origin) as garrison commander, and another Macedonian, Asklepiodoros, to collect the taxes. This division of responsibility reproduced that which Alexander had imposed at Sardis in 334 (AA i.17.7), which was itself possibly modelled on Achaemenid practice at, precisely, Sardis (cp. Hdt. i.153, describing Cyrus the Great's arrangements). However, Alexander learnt from Cyrus' experience, which had not been wholly happy, and did not leave a native in charge of funds, either at Sardis or Babylon.

Mazaeus had been satrap of Syria under Darius, and commanded the Persian right at Gaugamela; it used to be thought that Alexander now gave him special privileges of issuing coinage with his own name on, but this is a numismatists' conjecture with no real foundation.[55] But that Alexander, both at Babylon and a little later at Susa, where he appointed Abulites, should have appointed Persians to major satrapies is politically a departure, though of course he showed straight after Granikos that he planned to perpetuate Persian *institutions*, by appointing Kalas as satrap. (Ada, the reinstated satrap of Karia, p. 274, belonged to a *native*, i.e. non-Iranian, dynasty and is anyway a special case: here Alexander was exploiting a division within the dynasty by backing her against her usurper brother Pixodaros. The only other possible Persian appointee before Mazaeus is Sabiktas, appointed satrap of Cappadocia (AA ii.4.2), but there is no proof that this man is a Persian.) In part Alexander's attitude can be explained by mere expediency: he hoped to weaken resistance in advance by thus announcing to the upper cadres of the Persian administration that by coming over to him they could get their old jobs back. But this is too negative: in the reaction against too idealistic views current earlier in the present century about Alexander's policies of 'harmony', *homonoia*, with Persia and Persians, the recent move has been to deny too completely that Alexander had a policy of fusion, as opposed to repression, towards the Persians.[56] But we have seen in earlier chapters of this book that satraps like Ariobarzanes and Mausolus had got on very well with individual Greeks (Agesilaus, Antalkidas); and though the views of Alexander's tutor Aristotle on barbarians were not enlightened, it has sensibly been said that[57] Alexander is not likely to have regarded Pharnabazus' son Artabazus, who as we saw had spent time at Philip's court, as a natural slave.

In addition to the Babylon and Susa appointments, we hear of Phrataphernes, appointed to Parthia, Atropates (Media) and Satibarzanes (Areia). The latter rebelled and was replaced, but by Arsakes, another Persian — and another unsatisfactory appointment. An old friend, Artabazus (above) got Baktria, until he retired in 328; Alexander even had a liaison with Artabazus' daughter and a son Herakles was the result (Diod. xx.20).[58]

Subsequently, after Alexander went down the Hindu Kush, he reverted to appointing Macedonians. Nikanor got the 'land this side of the Indos' (AA iv.28.6), Philippos son of Machatas the land east of the Indos and Peithon son of Agenor the area from the lower Indos to the sea. But it is significant that these were not 'Iranian' territories.

Alexander regarded the Persian Empire with the feelings of one who saw himself as the heir to the Achaemenids: though he destroyed the possessions (p. 283) of the unworthy Darius III, he did give Darius a royal burial (AA iii.22). And Alexander took care to cultivate the memory of Cyrus the Great, the founder of the Persian Empire, being, as Strabo calls him, a 'lover of Cyrus'.[59] Again, a people known as the Euergetai (benefactors) were honoured by Alexander because of the assistance which they had given to Cyrus (AA iii.27), and Alexander restored Cyrus' tomb (AA vi.29f. Cp. QC vii.6.20). Cyrus may even (AA iv.11.9) have been Alexander's precedent and model for the introduction of the 'prostration' ritual, *proskynesis*, on which see p. 287.

That he punished Iranians after his return from India does not prove that his attitude had changed: at AA vi.30, towards the end of his life, he honoured Peukestas, the Macedonian satrap of Persis, for his adoption of Persian habits (nor was Peukestas alone in knowing Persian, cp. Laomedon who was put in charge of barbarian captives as being bilingual: AA iii.6.6); and he was planning further measures of integration before his death: for instance (AA vii.23.3) Persians and Macedonians were to be assimilated to the same infantry formation. But perhaps this should be seen neither (as on one extreme view) as idealistic integration at the political level, nor (as on the other extreme)[60] as repression, but as a training device. Certainly military considerations alone are enough to explain the use, very soon after Gaugamela, of Iranian horse-javelin men (AA iii.24.1; iv.17.3; v.11.3); it has been correctly noted (Loeb, Arrian intro. lxxv discussing iv.4) that the Companion Cavalry on their own were no match for Scythian tactics. But as we shall see this had its political consequences in the unpopularity it generated among the Macedonians.

For the moment, however, Darius still lived, and though Alexander could appoint Persians as satraps his own personal position does not change — King of the Macedonians into Great King of Persia — until after Darius had been hunted down and had died at the hands of his Persian noble followers in August 330. This helps explain Alexander's next actions after passing from Susa to Persepolis (forcing the 'Persian Gates' en route): he set fire to the palace of Persepolis at the end of his stay (January–May 330, AA iii.18 and all sources). Whether interpreted as a deliberate (the main sources), or as a drunken and unpremeditated (the vulgate), act of revenge — or whether explained on a choice of modern rationalizations[61] — this was a hostile act: Alexander did not yet think of himself as destroying his own property. (Arrian makes Parmenio ineffectively urge this point of view, which resembles the — effective — advice given by Kroisos to Cyrus the Great at Hdt. i.88.)

But after Darius' death Alexander was at last entitled to assume the 'upright tiara', the symbol of Persian kingship (Kleitarchos F 5, and Arrian says he did assume it (iv.7.4), but see below). It was certainly also assumed at about this time by Bessus the murderer of Darius. It was to be some time — see p. 285 — before Alexander settled things with this man. In any case, Alexander now unquestionably started to change his personal image. The dress he now adopted was, however, a mixture (Plut. *Al.* xlv, cp. Eratosthenes F 30. Date: after leaving Zadrakarta for Parthia, cp. AA iii.25; i.e. only weeks after Darius' death): he *did not* wear the Persian trousers which Greeks found ridiculous, nor the *kandys* (gold or purple cloak), nor, Plutarch says, the tiara:[62] these were the 'weird and theatrical items of barbarian costume', as Eratosthenes says. Arrian's judgement (vii.29) was that this new dress was partly a 'sophism' designed for non-Macedonian consumption — Persian clothes-consciousness was known to Aeschylus who makes much of the symbolism of the rags of Xerxes in defeat[63] — but we know that it gave great offence to the Macedonians (AA vii.8.2): it helped to precipitate the Opis mutiny.

As Alexander's career continued, his preference for such 'oriental-izing' became more marked. His friend Hephaistion approved, others did not, and Alexander chose to make a personal issue of this: Hephaistion was, in Alexander's phrase, a 'lover of Alexander' whereas men like Krateros were merely 'lovers of the king' (Plut. *Al.* xlvii).

Alexander could draw on great reserves of Macedonian loyalty — Antipater, whose goodwill was vital for getting reinforcements (cp., for example, AA iii.11.10), remained steady till very late, though the Suda, a Byzantine lexicon, preserves the suggestion that he disapproved of Alexander's deification.

But the Ammon episode, and the new personal style which Alexander was now adopting, tested that loyalty, and the first great collision, the Philotas affair, came in the autumn of the year 330, after Alexander had moved further east across Iran via Hyrkania and Parthia and into modern Afghanistan passing Herat (where he founded an Alexandria 'in Areia'). At modern Farah (due south of Herat), in the ancient Persian satrapy or sub-satrapy of the Drangaeans, Philotas was arraigned on a 'conspiracy charge'[64] (AA iii.26; QC vi.7ff.). The actual evidence against Philotas was slight: he was supposed to have failed to report the (genuine) plot of one Dimnos, but if so he was, as Curtius makes him say (vi.10.20f.), careless to have allowed Kebalinos, an informer, to go around for two days without disposing of him. The real issue was the relationship between the more intransigent Macedonian nobility (note Philotas' *onkos*, pride, at Plut. *Al.* xlvii) and the new Alexander: Curtius (vi.10.28), who refers to Ammon, may explain Arrian's curious reference to a 'previous' report about Philotas conspiring *in Egypt*. (That is, Philotas disliked the claim to be 'son of Ammon', and said so.)

The execution of Philotas was followed straight away by that of his father Parmenio, now in Media: he had been ordered to go to Hyrkania instead (AA iii.19.7), but there is nothing sinister in this: some twist in the story has probably been omitted by Arrian. Certainly a posting to Media, with its large troop concentrations on the Mediterranean land-route, was no relegation. But Parmenio was too dangerous to live: the elucidation of his family's control of senior jobs is one of the most convincing results of applying the study of family ties, the so-called 'prosopographical' method, to Alexander's reign. Parmenio himself commanded the whole Macedonian left wing, and had personal command of the Thessalian cavalry (AA iii.11.10, cp. Diod. xvii.17.3). Of his sons, Philotas commanded the Companion Cavalry, and Nikanor the *hypaspists* (AA iii.8;9). Other connections included leaders of infantry brigades like the sons of Andromenes, and Hegelochus the commander of the Scouts (AA iii.27.1; i.13.1 with QC vi.11.22): whether this man was the nephew of Philip's last wife Kleopatra, and was therefore seen as an additional threat, is doubtful.[65] (For *hypaspists* see index.)

In early 329[66] Alexander, following the great southward arc which still connects western to eastern Afghanistan, passed into the satrapy of Arachosia, where he founded (or rather refounded) a city at modern Kandahar.[67] The recent British excavations at the site of Old Kandahar properly belong in the hellenistic volume in this series, but a newly discovered Greek metrical inscription from the third century BC must be mentioned here, because it appears to include the phrase 'among the citizens of Alexandria' and this greatly strengthens (though it does not quite clinch) the identification of Old Kandahar as the site of Alexandria in Arachosia (which is the twelfth in Stephanus of Byzantium's list of the Alexandrias, see n.30). From Arachosia he moved north towards Baktria.

The next two years saw some of Alexander's most demanding warfare, the campaigns in Baktria and Sogdiana against Bessus and (after Bessus had been betrayed to him, and executed, mid-329) against Bessus' successor as resistance leader, Spitamenes. At Begram not far from Kabul he founded another great Alexandria, Alexandria ad Caucasum (AA iii.28.4,[68] cp. Strabo 514 and Pliny *NH* vi.61), on an important intersection of routes from further Asia in the east towards the west (Iran) and north (Baktria). Another showpiece foundation was Alexandreschate (Alexandria on the Tanais/Jaxartes), the eighteenth Alexandria in Stephanus' list. This gives further insight into Alexander's founding motives. The imitation of Cyrus is important, for the city was to replace Cyropolis, one of the furthest Achaemenid outposts to this point of the compass. Arrian says that Alexander was planning (iv.1.3) to found a city on the Jaxartes and give it his own name; the site was suited to rise to greatness; it would be well placed for the eventual invasion of Scythia; and it would provide protection against the incursions of the barbarians who lived across the river. So we have three motives, prosperity, offence and security. Greek mercenaries, time-expired or otherwise militarily unfit Macedonians, and natives were settled there. Arrian says the natives were volunteers but other evidence suggests they were pressganged (Justin xii.5.12 and QC vii.6.27, cp.vii.1.1 on Sogdians distributed as slaves to the settlers). This evidence is a main weapon in the hands of those scholars who refuse to allow Alexander high-minded cultural intentions as a proselytizing hellenist.[69]

Other foundations firmly attributable to Alexander in this part of the world[70] were really part of a purely military policy of containment (AA iv.17.4 (*phrouria*), cp. ibid.16.3). Such Greeks as were settled here were certainly held down by fear (cp. QC ix.7.1–11 and Diod. xvii.99.5f.; xviii.7). They were discontented and tried to get home again after Alexander's death because they missed their Greek lifestyle — although the Ai Khanoum finds have, as we saw, shown that that lifestyle could be reconstructed on the banks of the Oxus. As to the forms of government, despite the large claims of Plutarch, the colonists were actually governed by *strategoi* or *episkopoi*, both military titles (cp. AA iv.22.5: Nikanor and iii.28.4: Neiloxenos). (As with the archaic Greek colonies, with their militarily autocratic *oikists*, this made sense: survival, and the repelling of hostile natives, were the first considerations.) And Arrian's narrative (vii.6.1) is revealing, with its mention of 'satraps' of the newly founded cities; this does not imply much self-government. As to the locals, the overrunning of Alexandria in Margiane (p. 275) was an often-repeated story (cp. AA v.29.5 for monsoon damage to some of Alexander's Indian found-ations). If Alexander's aims included a desire to replace nomadic by agricultural habits, as Arrian (*Indike* xl.8) asserts (cp. Pliny *NH* vi.95 on Alexander forbidding the Gedrosian fish-eaters to eat fish), he failed, at least in central Asia — where all governments have failed to contain the Kutchi (gypsy-like nomads) or their equivalents. These people still move at will, covering great distances, whether Afghans or Russians hold power at Kabul. It was and is hard to alter the timeless nomadic habits of central Asia.

Mention of the military policy of containment is a reminder that the early 320s were years of fierce campaigning of an entirely new type against enemies whose ancestors had killed Cyrus the Great. Eventual success was won by the *phrouria* system (AA iv.17.4); this was how Alexander solved the problem of bringing an elusive enemy to bay — and holding down the countryside after that enemy's defeat. Spitamenes was captured by mid-winter 328/7. But before this difficult phase was concluded there had been some serious blunders, and one in particular had an importance beyond the strictly military, because it caused more trouble with traditionalist Macedonians: the Kleitos affair (late 328).

The precipitating incident was a defeat by Spitamenes of a Macedonian force which Alexander had put under the command of a Lycian interpreter called Pharnouches. From this we may infer that Alexander had underestimated the opposition (AA iv.3.7ff.) and it was therefore largely his fault when the force was cut to pieces. A Greek poet at court produced a song (Plut. *Al*.1 is the best source for the episode; cp. too AA iv.8) jeering at the Macedonians; that enraged Kleitos, the commander of the Royal Squadron of the Companions. He reacted by taking advantage and more than advantage of traditional Macedonian freedom of speech towards the king, quoting Euripides:[71] 'A bad custom has grown up in Greece: the soldiers get the sweat, the generals the glory.' The lines signify an objection to personal kingship and the personality cult, which, at the end of chapter 13, we traced back to the time of Brasidas and Lysander (and note that Kleitos' remarks to Alexander also included a reference to *Ammon*); Alexander, equally enraged, got hold of a pike; and *ran Kleitos through*.

From now on, Alexander's orientalizing tendencies and conciliation of Iranian sensibilities develop without the Macedonian nobility taking an open stand against them: the next departure, the attempt to introduce the ceremony of *proskynesis*, obeisance, was primarily opposed by a Greek, Kallisthenes (though the Macedonian Leonnatus is said to have burst out laughing, if that counts as an 'open stand'); and the troubles later in the reign, culminating in the Opis mutiny, lay with the rank and file.

In early 327, at Baktra (Balkh), Alexander tried to introduce the old practice of *proskynesis*, obeisance, before the Persian king, i.e. himself, and on the likelier of the two versions of the episode given by Arrian (iv.10ff.)[72] Kallisthenes opposed this head on: *proskynesis* may indeed have been no more than shorthand for a graded set of social approaches (cp. Hdt. i.134ff.), as suited to a highly stratified society like the Persian (which for instance, as we can now see from the Persepolis tablets, dispensed rations to great dignitaries according to an elaborately differentiated tariff). Hence *proskynesis* might involve no more than the exchange of kisses, which obstinately features in our sources, perhaps as part of an official attempt to minimize the implications of *proskynesis* at a time when it was no more than a failed experiment. But to Greeks, *proskynesis* meant prostration (which indeed is probably what Alexander, as Great King of Persia, had in mind); and *that* meant impiety (see references given on p. 278). Kallisthenes, who had on an earlier occasion represented Alexander as the son of a god (Ammon), was not, despite confusion on the subject later in antiquity (contrast T 20,21), being inconsistent in resisting an apparent claim by Alexander, at Baktra, actually to *be* a god: this and other such distinctions, e.g. that between god and hero, mattered; cp. the speech given to Kallisthenes by Arrian (iv.11). The attempt to introduce *proskynesis* was dropped, but Kallisthenes' moral victory was very temporarily his to enjoy, for he fell soon after, allegedly implicated in a conspiracy.

It is probable that Alexander's aims in trying to introduce *proskynesis* had been mixed: he must have been aware of its religious implications to Greek and Macedonian minds, but there is the Persian aspect too — emulation of Cyrus and a desire to conciliate and attract loyalty from his Iranian subjects. His marriage to the Sogdian princess Roxane should certainly be seen in this light, despite a recent denial:[73] Curtius says explicitly (viii.4.25) that this was designed to bind and consolidate his Persian and Macedonian empires, to 'take shame from the conquered and arrogance from the conquerors'.

In 326 Alexander began the 'conquest of India', as this phase is conventionally called, though in post-partition language most of his activity was in modern Pakistan, where he subdued the Punjab. The going here was much easier, politically and militarily, in terms of the external opposition he had to face. (There was only one great battle, on the Hydaspes[74] = Jhelum, against Porus and his elephants: AA v.9ff.) Partly this was because Alexander exploited the fragmentation of the Indian states and the jealousies of their rulers, just as, years before, he had profited from the divisions in the Karian satrapal house. It was *internal* opposition which defeated him: his troops, depressed by the rains and not sharing Alexander's *pothos* for infinite novelty and conquest, mutinied on the River Hyphasis (Beas), a little way inside the frontier of modern India; and he turned back, down the Indos to the Arabian Sea.

His own march back to Persis via the poorly provisioned satrapy of Gedrosia (Beluchistan) was a logistical error which cost many lives (325); the fleet went separately, commanded by Nearchus, whose account, written in Herodotean style and manner, survives in the *Indike* of Arrian. This is the first tangible manifestation of the great stimulus to the hellenistic science and literature of *geography* given by Alexander's campaigns.[75]

After returning from India, Alexander, Arrian says, became 'harsher', *oxyteros*, and out of the disciplining at this period (324) of satraps and generals (who thought that Alexander would never return from India), modern scholarship has reconstructed a reign of terror[76] (see AA vii.4.1–3 for Arrian's judgements). But though it is certainly true that delinquents were now brutally punished or called to order, not all aspects of Alexander's behaviour at this time are equally sinister; for instance Peukestas was indeed summoned to the king's presence, but there was evidently nothing alarming about that because he was only to be congratulated for his orientalizing (AA vii.23.1–3). Other 'detainees' arrive — but bringing reinforcements (Atropates, Philoxenos, Menander). This looks like normal administration. However, Alexander's growing impatience (an idea present in the Greek word *oxys*) is well illustrated by his treatment of his boyhood friend Harpalus, a Macedonian with high financial responsibilities, who had deserted once before but been forgiven; this time, guilty of peculation on an impressive scale, he decamped to Greece taking large sums of money with him; before his death he was to help provoke the anti-Macedonian resistance whose most serious phase falls after Alexander's death (and is therefore reserved for the next volume in this series. See Diod. xvii.108 for Harpalus. There is an annoying gap at the relevant point in the manuscripts of Arrian).

At Opis, not far from Babylon, Alexander faced more mutiny in 324, which as we shall see he overcame by some theatrical gestures of reconciliation including a famous banquet. The great grievance this time was Alexander's 'orientalizing', and the importance of the Opis affair is that it shows that the grievance was felt not only by the Macedonian officer class but by the rank and file (AA vii.6ff).

It was not only Macedonians who were moved to resentment. Near the end of his life Alexander took two actions which alienated the *Greek* world also. First, in August 324, in an announcement relayed by Nikanor (not the son of Parmenio, but a different man, a relative of Aristotle) Alexander ordered the Greek cities to take back their exiles (Diod. xviii.8; Tod 202, from Tegea in Arkadia). This was not formally connected with another decree, ordering the disbandment of satrapal mercenary armies (Diod. xvii.106.3, cp. p. 240 for the similar measure of Artaxerxes III in the 350s), but the latter decree must in fact have exacerbated the 'exiles problem'. For Athens the exiles decree meant evacuating Samos which they had held since Timotheus had installed the cleruchy in 365 (p. 230), a cleruchy more than once reinforced since then, and it is not surprising that, faced with a refugee problem on this scale, the Athenians prepared to go to war (*FGrHist*. 126 Ephippus F 5; for the specific decision about Samos see Syll.³ 312). What were Alexander's motives? Isokrates' writings show that the numbers of expatriates were indeed regarded with alarm, at least by the settled citizens for whom Isokrates speaks (p. 170); but what is interesting is that Alexander thought he could resolve the difficulty at a stroke, indifferent both to opposition (Athens) and to the sheer complexity of the operation (as the Tegea inscription shows, the decree cut clean across established or prescriptively acquired property rights and was thus against Macedonian interests in that the League of Corinth arrangements of 337 had generally protected the possessing classes, p. 260 on Dem. xvii.15). It seems that Alexander now saw himself in a superhuman role, imposing global solutions — like a god: it is Zeus who makes men exiles, 'wandering driven by the gadfly over the earth' (*Iliad* xxiv, 531f.), and who but a god can reverse the process on the necessary scale?

That leads to the second affront to Greek feeling, the demand for deification sent to the Greek cities in winter 324/3. This is discussed further below.

The consequences of all these actions of the final phase were felt well beyond 323; but the immediate story ends abruptly in 323 with Alexander's death in Babylon, aged thirty-two, from illness after heavy drinking in the company of Medius of Larisa (p. 267). The problem of Alexander's final aims has to be answered from his last acts and reliably recorded intentions, since a fabulous list of 'Last Plans' at the beginning of Diodorus' book xviii has recently been shown[77] to emanate, not from the trustworthy source whom Diodorus was to follow for the early hellenisitic period, Hieronymus of Cardia, but from his much more sensational source for the previous book (that on Alexander), namely Kleitarchos. They are certainly more in his manner. As given by Diodorus (xviii.4) the Plans included the building of a fleet of a thousand ships larger than triremes for a campaign against the Carthaginians; the building of seven great temples, three in Greece, three in Macedon and one at Troy; population transfers between Europe and Asia; and the erection of a pyramid to Philip as large as any in Egypt. Nothing much can be made of this, though it is hard to prove that any one of the Plans is downright impossible (and one, in the form of the seeking of Phoenician settlers for transplant to the Persian Gulf, is soberly attested: cp. AA vii.19 for the mission of Mikkalos of Klazomenai). To take an analogy from the Peloponnesian War, the Athenian demagogue Hyperbolus' proposal of a hundred-ship armada against Carthage would be dismissed as complete fantasy if we had only Aristophanes' word for it. But an Athenian inscription happens to attest Athenian diplomatic dealings with Carthage a few years later (ML 92, cp. p. 136). Aristophanes has given us — not the truth, but a grain of it. Perhaps that holds for Kleitarchos too. But isolated grains are not very nutritious. Instead we are forced back to a closer look at Alexander's *last acts and reliably recorded intentions*, as already briefly described above.

That Alexander issued some kind of formal demand to the Greek cities for his own deification is known to us only from some dubious historical sources (Aelian Varia Historia v.12; Ath.251b), but the balance is just in favour of belief rather than scepticism:[78] the evidence of the orators is characteristically confusing but points in this direction. Hyperides says that Demosthenes 'agreed that Alexander could be the son of Zeus — and of Poseidon if he wants, as well' (against Demosthenes column 31), and again speaks of the Athenians 'being forced to witness sacrifice being offered to mortal men ... and to see their servants (Hephaistion?) being honoured as heroes' (Funeral Oration).

This demand is more extreme, and in Greek terms more indefensible, than almost anything that Alexander had done so far — the claim to be son of Ammon was to some extent a private affair, and *proskynesis* had its positive political aspect as a way of accommodating to Persian practice. Yet the supreme self-confidence breathed by the exiles decree is of a piece with an explicit request by a man for his own deification.

Then there are the actions which alienated the *Macedonians* in the final phase. Macedonian sentiment was moving away from Alexander, it is clear, on some of his most cherished policies: by the time of the Opis mutiny the enrolment of orientals in the cavalry had become a special grievance (AA vii.6.3); a new fifth hipparchy, partially composed of barbarians,[79] was taken in very bad part. At the political level, the banquet in the *aftermath* of the Opis mutiny is crucial evidence (AA vii.11.8ff.):[80] Alexander prayed for partnership in rule between Macedonians and Persians. This picked up a phrase of Thucydides' Alcibiades (viii.46.3, *koinonoi arches*), used to make a cynical proposal to Tissaphernes for a joint Atheno-Persian rule over the Greek world; and was in turn picked up, in its thought rather than its language, by Plutarch (*Mor.* 329e). In Plutarch's account, Alexander mixes the lives and customs of men 'as in a loving-cup'; there is embroidery here but comparison with Strabo (66), who draws on Eratosthenes, shows that both Strabo and Plutarch go back to the great third-century scholar Eratosthenes (both talk of distinguishing between people by whether they are virtuous or vicious, in preference to asking whether they are barbarians or not). If so, that enhances the value of the passage: Eratosthenes is not easily to be dismissed. And we have seen that such desire for upper-class (note the qualification) *homonoia*, harmony, between Persians and Greeks/Macedonians has parallels earlier in the fourth century. Persian and Macedonian institutions were not dissimilar, for instance the 'royal kin' are an important feudal notion common to both empires.[81]

Immediately, Alexander undoubtedly planned to go on fighting — he offers his men 'dangers and hardships' (AA vii.8.1), which is a euphemism for something military. Arrian (vii.16.2) also speaks of voyages to explore the Caspian Sea and circumnavigate Arabia; for Aristobulus (Strabo 741, cp. AA vii.19.6) he simply wanted to be 'lord of all', and perhaps this was true. We certainly have not the evidence to refute it.

The final assessment of Alexander's aims must await the hellenistic volume of this series, which will explore the limits of hellenization in the east. But one, backward-looking, point may be made here: the hellenization which Alexander's conquests undoubtedly promoted in *fact* (however central or peripheral an *intention* of his we judge it to have been) had already taken swift steps in the last decades of Achaemenid Persian rule. For this, satraps like Mausolus had been responsible.

Or take a client-kingdom of Persia, like fifth- and fourth-century *Cyprus*. Cyprus is a good historical test-tube, sealed off in the simple physical sense by the sea, and containing a strong racial mix from the first. Here we can trace the progress of hellenization between 500 and 300 as the native element advanced and receded. In the mid-fifth century, sculpture like the 'Chatsworth Head' of Apollo argue a high degree of Greek penetration; this fell back as the century continued and Athenian influence diminished in face of Phoenician. But then in the fourth century a series of forceful native dynasts, the Cypriot equivalents of Mausolus, actively diffused Greek culture again (Isok. ix, *Evagoras*, 47):

> He (Evagoras of Cypriot Salamis) inherited a thoroughly barbarized city which, because of Phoenician rule, had neither been visited by Greeks nor acquired cultural skills, having neither market nor harbour. He put all that to rights: he extended Salaminian territory, threw walls around the city, built triremes, and put up civic buildings. In this way he advanced its power so that it was generally viewed with fear rather than, as formerly, with contempt.

A little later we find a Cypriot ruler, Nikokreon, making benefactions at Argos, Delos and Delphi (Tod 194, time of Alexander, with commentary): the Argive dedication includes the metrical Greek lines: 'I am Nikokreon, whom the sea-surrounded land of Cyprus bore; I am a king descended from a divine lineage.'

But like Mausolus in Karia (after whose time the native Karian script dies out), such Cypriot rulers were also positively concerned to preserve the native cultural element: a recently discovered dedication to Aphrodite at Cypriot Amathous, from the end of the fourth century, stands in the name of Androkles the last king of the place, and is *bilingual*: it is inscribed both in the Cypriote syllabary and in the Greek alphabet (*Arch. Reps*, 1980–1, p.64).

Men like Evagoras, Nikokreon and Androkles look forward to the philhellenes of the hellenistic world, a category for which Sir W. Tarn coined the phrase 'culture-Greeks'. But that idea is already implicitly present in a decree which we have discussed earlier in another context, a recently discovered Athenian decree of the 390s (*Hesperia*, 1979, pp.180ff. = *SEG* xxix.no.86 cp. p. 197): Evagoras, the same man for whom Isokrates wrote the panegyric just quoted, is there called *huper Hellados Hellen*, a 'Greek benefactor of Greece'.[82]

Notes

ABBREVIATIONS OF PERIODICALS

AJA = *American Journal of Archeology*
AJAH = *American Journal of Ancient History*
AJP = *American Journal of Philology*
BCH = *Bulletin de correspondance hellénique*
BSA = *Annual of the British School at Athens*
Cal. Studies Cl. Ant. = *California Studies in Classical Antiquity*
CJ = *Classical Journal*
CP = *Classical Philology*
CQ = *Classical Quarterly*
CR = *Classical Review*
GRBS = *Greek, Roman and Byzantine Studies*
HSCP = *Harvard Studies in Classical Philology*
JEA = *Journal of Egyptian Archaeology*
JHS = *Journal of Hellenic Studies*
JRS = *Journal of Roman Studies*
PCPhS = *Proceedings of the Cambridge Philological Society*
REG = *Revue des études grecques*
TAPA = *Transactions of the American Philological Association*
ZPE = *Zeitschrift für Papyrologie und Epigraphik*

1 XERXES' LEGACY

1. E. N. Gardiner (1930) *Athletics of the Ancient World*, Oxford, reprinted 1955, at p.43 for the 476 games; see generally for the Olympic Games the readable account of M. Finley and H. Pleket (1976) *The Olympic Games, the First Thousand Years*, London; for Olympic victors, L. Moretti (1957) *Olympionikai*, Rome. For the way the Athenian richest class ceased, after 400, to spend big money on horse-racing at e.g. Olympia see J. Davies (1981) *Wealth and the Power of Wealth in Classical Athens*, London, pp.102ff. Whatever the reasons for the more grudging attitude to expenditure on the part of the Athenian propertied class in the fourth century (and they are discussed by Davies; see also p. 243), such changed attitudes must have weakened the spirit of 'internationalism' in this one major city at any rate. Victors *post* 336: Gardiner 45f.
2. See K. J. Dover (1976) *Talanta*, vii, 51.
3. Persepolis: E. Pemberton (1976) *AJA*, 123, n.92. Marathon dead: J. Boardman (1977) in *Frank Brommer Festschrift* Mainz/Rhein, pp.39ff., showing that horses are linked with hero-cult.

294

4. W. H. Plommer (1979) *JHS*, xcix, 100.
5. V. Shevoroshkin (1963) *Nestor*, pp.282f.
6. For all this see A. Snodgrass (1980) *Archaic Greece*, London, chapter 6, stating (and overstating) the case against 480/79 as a cultural divide.
7. M. I. Finley (1980) *Ancient Slavery and Modern Ideology*, London. (But see review by P. Brunt (1981) *CR*, xxxi, 70.)
8. Cp. A. Toynbee (1965) *Hannibal's Legacy*, Oxford.
9. D. Lewis (1976) *AJA*, 311, reviewing J. Traill (1975) 'Political organization of Attica', *Hesperia*, supplement xiv.
10. L. Robert (1969) *Opera Minora Selecta*, i, Amsterdam, p.384 (= *Revue de Philologie*, 1957, 16).

2 PHTHONOS (ENVY) AND THE ORIGIN OF THE DELIAN LEAGUE

1. Because metics (resident foreigners) conducted much trade but could not own land; hence an economically unhealthy divorce between commerce and property. See M. I. Finley (1952) *Studies in Land and Credit in Ancient Athens 500–200 BC*, New Brunswick, N.J., p.78, and consult index under entry 'Land, monopoly of by citizens'.
2. See D. Magie (1950) *Roman Rule in Asia Minor*, Princeton, N.J. pp.892f., n.99; R. Meiggs (1972) *The Athenian Empire* (henceforth *AE*), endnote 14. On causes of Greek wars note G. E. M. de ste Croix (1972) *Origins of the Peloponnesian War* (henceforth *OPW*), pp.218ff.
3. L. Robert (1969) *Opera Minora Selecta*, i, p.393 (against earlier views).
4. Illustrations of this: M. I. Finley (1960) *Revue internationale des droits de l'antiquité*, vii, p.189 = *Economy and Society in Ancient Greece* (1981) London, p.149; W. Wyse (1904) *The Speeches of Isaeus*, Cambridge, pp.351f.
5. P. Gauthier (1973) in M. I. Finley (ed.) *Problèmes de la terre dans la Grèce ancienne*, Paris, pp.163ff.
6. C. Kraay and V. Emeleus (1962) *The Composition of Greek Silver Coins: Analysis by Neutron Activation*, Oxford, p.34.
7. A. Momigliano (1979) in A. Ryan (ed.) *The Idea of Freedom: Essays in Honour of Isaiah Berlin*, Oxford, p.140. A. J. Holladay (1978) *Greece and Rome*, xxv, p.177 less plausibly denies the attractions of the Persian way of life.
8. Unpublished paper by E. L. Hussey.
9. Strabo 629 'Hyrkanian Plain' in Lydia, with Diod. xvii. 19 — Hyrkanians at the battle of the Granikos: two passages first connected by Domaszewski. For the Gongylids, Demaratids and Hermias see S. Hornblower in *CAH²*, vi, chapter xi[a], forthcoming.
10. W. Connor (1971) *The New Politicians of Fifth-Century Athens*, Princeton, N.J., p.149 and n.28.
11. Pausanias' youth is stressed by A. W. Gomme (1945) *Historical Commentary on Thucydides* (henceforth *HCT*), i, p.270.
12. Contra Gomme, p.272, followed by de ste Croix, Meiggs and the authors of *The Athenian Tribute Lists*.
13. See Meiggs, *AE*, p.454.

14. See (accepting it) G. Cawkwell (1971) *Blaiklock Studies*, p.53 and de ste Croix *OPW*, p.172. Gomme's note on the passage is right, as is A. Andrewes (1978) in P. Garnsey and C. Whittaker (eds) *Imperialism in the Ancient World* (henceforth *Imperialism*), p.303, n.11.

15. See P. Cartledge (1979) *Sparta and Lakonia*, London, p.228.

16. See C. Kraay (1976) *Archaic and Classical Greek Coins*, London, (henceforth *ACGC*), p.97, drawing on R. Williams (1965) *Numismatic Notes and Monographs*, 115, especially p.7.

17. See A. Andrewes (1970) *HCT*, vol.iv, p.60.

18. See my *Mausolus*, pp.79ff.

19. W. G. Forrest (1960) *CQ*, x, pp.221ff. (contra M. Wörrle (1964) *Untersuchungen zur Verfassungsgeschichte von Argos in 5 Jhdt*, pp.120ff. For the Mantinea synoikism see S. and H. Hodkinson (1981) *BSA*, lxxvi, pp.260f. (contra J. O'Neil (1981) *CQ*, 335ff.).

20. Allies: Gomme. Sparta: P. S. Derow, unpublished paper. Pretext: H. Rawlings (1977) *Phoenix*, xxxi, pp.1ff., rightly protesting against translations of *proschema* as, e.g., 'announced intention' (Meiggs, Gomme). See also A. French (1979) *Phoenix*, xxxiii, pp.134ff., and N. Robertson (1980) *AJAH*, v, pp.64ff. and 110ff.

21. M. Chambers (1958) *CP*, liii, pp.56ff.

22. See Meiggs, *AE*, endnote 12. On the 'harshness of Kleon fallacy' see Finley in *Imperialism*, extreme expression of impatience with problems of dating. (No mention of the terminological point mentioned in the text.) On the Finley approach see Meiggs (1966) *JHS*, lxxxvi, p.98: 'Finley has made a molehill out of a mountain', the mountain being dating of decrees by their letter-forms.

23. G. E. M. de ste Croix's views (1954/5) on the popularity of the Athenian Empire, *Historia*, iii, 1ff., are challenged by D. Bradeen (1960) *Historia*, ix, 257. Athens hated and feared in the north: N. G. L. Hammond (1979) *History of Macedonia*, ii, p.142, n.3. See now de ste Croix (1981) *The Class Struggle in the Ancient Greek World*, chapter 5 but cp. the present writer in *CR*, xxxii, 1982, pp.236, 238.

24. See C. Fornara (1979) *CQ*, xxix, pp.49ff.

25. See the present writer's comments in the revised and amplified LACTOR source-book on *The Athenian Empire*, edn 3, 1983. For bibliography on the Athenian Empire since 1972 see the end of that work.

26. See Finley, *Imperialism*; Gauthier, op. cit. at n.5 above.

3 ATHENS IMPOSES HER WILL

1. ML 26 = Fornara 51; H. T. Wade Gery (1933) *JHS*, liii, 71ff. (but see W. Peek (1940) *HSCP* supplement i, 97ff.).

2. D. Francis and M. Vickers (1983) *CQ*, xxxiii.

3. J. Boardman (1977) in *Frank Brommer Festschrift*.

4. See A. J. Holladay (1977) *JHS*, xcvii, p.55, n.6 to p.54.

5. Contra C. Macleod (1982) *JHS*, cii, pp.124ff. Themistokles 'preparing the ground': contra, P. J. Rhodes (1981) *Ath. Pol. Comm.*, p.274 and

notes on chapter xxiii. This commentary is now fundamental on Ephialtes, and much else.

6. As is wrongly claimed by G. E. M. de ste Croix (1972) *OPW* , p.213; cp. Holladay, op. cit. under n.4 above.

7. D. M. Lewis (1981) 'The origins of the First Peloponnesian War', *Classical Contributions, McGregor Studies*, pp.71ff., especially pp.74ff.

8. G. R. Driver (1957) *Aramaic Documents of the Fifth Century BC*, Oxford.

9. R. Hopper (1979) *Trade and Industry in Classical Greece*, London, p.72.

10. R. Meiggs (1982) *Trees and Timber in the Ancient Mediterranean World*, Oxford, p.124 (cp. app. 6 generally); note also his pp.131 and 139 for *Sicilian* timber.

11. B. M. Mitchell (1966) *JHS*, lxxxvi, p.112; F. Chamoux (1953) *Cyrène sous les Battiades*, Paris, pp.203ff.

11. G. T. Griffith in N. G. L. Hammond and G. T. Griffith (1979) *History of Macedonia*, ii, Oxford, p.454. See chapter 17 below.

13. de ste Croix, *OPW*, app.x is wrong.

14. R. Meiggs *AE*, pp.121ff.

15. M. McGregor (1967) *Athenian Policy at Home and Abroad*, Semple Lecture, part 1; J. K. Davies (1977) *Classical Journal (CJ)*, lxxiii, pp.105ff. (see chapter 13, n. 32 below for full title of this).

16. R. Meiggs (1972) *The Athenian Empire*, pp.125.

17. Contra P. A. Brunt (1966) *Ancient Society and Institutions, Studies presented to Victor Ehrenberg*, Oxford, p.81, cp. pp.87f.

18. F. Adcock and D. Mosley (1975) *Diplomacy in Ancient Greece*, London, p.40.

4 ITALY AND SICILY IN THE 'FIFTY YEARS'

1. See 'Les mariages des tyrans' in L. Gernet (1968) *L'anthropologie de la grèce antique*, Paris, pp.344ff. (This book is now translated into English by J. Hamilton and B. Nagy (1981) *The Anthropology of Ancient Greece*, Baltimore, Ma.) A. Griffin (1982) *Sikyon*, Oxford, pp.53, 55ff. is disappointing on the Agariste affair — no mention of the aspects to which Gernet drew attention.

2. On Simonides see Mary Renault's novel (1978) *The Praise Singer*, Harmondsworth, Mdx; also G. L. Huxley (1978) 'Simonides and his world', *Proc. Roy. Irish Acad.*, c, 9, pp.231ff.

3. On the historians of Greek Sicily see the useful short survey by F. W. Walbank (1968/9) in *Kokalos*, 476ff.

4. The modern extreme: C. R. Whittaker (1978) 'Carthaginian imperialism' in P. Garnsey and C. R. Whittaker (eds) *Imperialism in the Ancient World*; Whittaker here follows the line taken in M. I. Finley's (1980) *Ancient Sicily*, which is a reaction against the 'Pindaric' view of Carthage as a would-be enslaver to be found in e.g. T. Dunbabin's (1948) *Western Greeks*, Oxford.

5. The comparison is due to Mr G. Cawkwell.

6. See P. Veyne (1976) *Le Pain et le cirque*, Paris.

7. For Thurii and literature about it see A. Andrewes (1978) *JHS* at pp.

5ff. Thurii and timber: R. Meiggs (1982) *Trees and Timber in the Ancient Mediterranean World*, p.124.

8. N. Demand (1982) *Thebes in the Fifth Century BC*, London, chapter 5; P. Leveque and P. Vidal-Naquet (1960) 'Epaminondas pythagoricien', *Historia*, ix, 294ff.

9. A. Andrewes (1962) in *The Greeks*, ed. H. Lloyd-Jones, pp.16f.

5 CYRENE, AFRICA AND EGYPT IN THE FIFTH CENTURY

1. See F. Chamoux (1953) *Cyrène sous la monarchie des Battiades*, Paris.

2. S. Applebaum (1979) *Jews and Greeks in Ancient Cyrene* (henceforth *Cyrene*), p.18, is right to take *perioikoi* at 161 in the sense of natives, in view of 159.4 where it certainly means that. G. E. M. de ste Croix (1981) *Class Struggle in the Ancient Greek World*, p.534, follows Chamoux and denies this, but seems unaware of Applebaum.

3. Applebaum, *Cyrene*, p.32.

4. A. N. Sherwin–White (1973) *The Roman Citizenship*, edn 2, p.390 and n.1; de ste Croix, op. cit. under n.2.

5. For the date of the fall see B. M. Mitchell (1966) 'Cyrene and Persia', *JHS*, lxxxvi, pp.99ff.; at pp.110ff. arguing against Chamoux's low (439) date.

6. Mitchell, ibid., p.112.

7. There is a graphic fictional reconstruction of the fall of the Battiads of Cyrene in Naomi Mitchison (1928) *Black Sparta*, London, chapter 5.

8. C. H. Coster (1951) 'The economic position of Cyrenaica' in *Studies in Roman Economic and Social History presented to A. C. Johnson*, Princeton, N.J., at p.16; contains other useful material; but Applebaum is now fuller on Cyrene's economic life. Horses, *pyrgoi*: Walbank, *HCP* iii 488.

9. J. Boardman et al. (1973) *Tocra*, ii, p.91 (finer pottery Attic, some southern Italian).

10. For all this para. see S. Hornblower, *Mausolus*, app.1. For the Ammon oracle see H. Parke (1967) *Oracles of Zeus*, Oxford, chapter ix, and see p. 178.

6 PERSIA AND ASIA MINOR

1. The best book by far on the Persian Empire is now J. M. Cook (1983) *The Persian Empire*, a great improvement on A. T. Olmstead's (1948) *History of the Persian Empire*, Chicago, which is however more copiously documented than Cook and so still needs to be consulted on the political side. See especially Cook's chapter 16 on satraps, hyparchs and fief-holders with much of relevance to the Persian presence in Asia Minor: note his map on p.179, marking known fiefs. This should be taken with pp. 71f. of the present work, on the social penetration of Iranians in Asia Minor. G. L. Cawkwell says (Penguin Xenophon *Anabasis*, 1973, p.33) that 'All the evidence we have suggests that many a Greek city of Asia hardly saw a Persian...' which is an extraordinary remark even if 'city' be emphasized. He goes on to say '...let alone a Persian garrison in normal

times', which *is* true: the Persian military presence was not obtrusive.

Two other recent books should be mentioned, D. M. Lewis (1977) *Sparta and Persia*, an extremely acute and interesting account of the diplomacy between Sparta and Persia in the late fifth and early fourth centuries, and containing excellent introductory chapters on Spartan and Persian institutions; second, Pierre Briant (1982) *Rois, Tributs et Paysans*, Paris, a collection of articles, mostly on Achaemenid Persia, from a Marxist standpoint; full of useful insights.

The present writer has discussed Persian history and institutions in chapter vi of *Mausolus* (1982), Oxford, and in two chapters in the forthcoming second edition of the *Cambridge Ancient History* (*CAH*), vol.vi (chapters iii and xi(a)). From a desire to avoid duplication this chapter is shorter than it otherwise would have been; and reference is hereby made to those places, where fuller documentation is provided for statements made in the present chapter.

2. See Lewis, *Sparta and Persia*, pp.148ff.
3. As implied by A. Momigliano (1975) *Alien Wisdom*; see the present writer's review *TLS*, 20, viii. 1976.
4. See chapter 13, n. 42.
5. W. Childs (1981) *Anatolian Studies*, xxxi, p.75, n.122.
6. Lewis, *Sparta and Persia*, p.62.

7 MACEDON, THESSALY AND BOIOTIA

1. The basic study is now E. Badian (1982) 'Greeks and Macedonians' in *Studies in the History of Art*, vol.10, Symposium Series 1, *Macedonia and Greece in Late Classical and Early Hellenistic Times*, Washington, pp.33ff.
2. See N. G. L. Hammond (1979) *History of Macedonia*, ii (volume written with G. T. Griffith); also Hammond's (1973) *History of Macedonia*, i. A third, hellenistic, volume, by Hammond and F. W. Walbank, is in preparation.
3. Hammond, ii, p.102. A. W. Gomme, followed now by E. D. Francis and M. Vickers (1981) *PCPhS*, 207, 105, denies that all 10,000 were killed, but that is what the Greek of Thuc. iv.102 plainly says.
4. R. Meiggs (1982) *Trees and Timber in the Ancient Mediterranean World*, Oxford, p.127.
5. Hammond, ii, p.105.
6. See M. Andronikos' chapter in M. B. Hatzopoulos and L. D. Loukopoulos (1980) *Philip of Macedon*, for plates.
7. N. Mitchison (1928) *Black Sparta*, chapter 2, well evokes the atmosphere of Thorax's Thessaly. (It was for Thorax that Pindar wrote Pyth. x.)
8. M. Sordi (1958) *La lega tessala*, Rome, p.68, n.5 to p.67.
9. W. G. G. Forrest (1982) *CAH*, edn 2, vol.iii(3), p.297.
10. A. Andrewes (1971) *Phoenix*, xxv, p.219 and n.28 to p.221. J. S. Morrison (1942) 'Meno of Pharsalus, Polykrates and Ismenias', *CQ*, xxxvi, pp.57ff., is also useful on fifth-century Thessalian history, as is H. Westlake, *Thessaly in the Fourth Century BC*, which ranges more widely than its title suggests. Note also L. H. Jeffery (1965), *BSA*, lx, 52, n.49.

On Sordi's 'revolution of 457' Andrewes' dismissal, p.219, n.25, seems justified.

11. See A. W. Gomme (1911/12) 'The topography of Boeotia and the theories of M. Bérard', *BSA*, xviii, pp.202ff., reprinted in *Essays in Greek History and Literature* (1937) Oxford. The question is still debated, cp. N. Demand (1982) *Thebes in the Fifth Century: Herakles Resurgent*, London, pp.10f.
   For the political history of classical Thebes P. Cloché (1952) *Thèbes de Béotie*, remains standard. For other works see also chapter 16, notes, p. 311, n.3.

12. P. M. Fraser and T. Rönne (1957) *Boiotian and West Greek Tombstones*, Lund, pp.102, 90. (Note their supplement (1971) 'Some More Boiotian and West Greek Tombstones' in *Opuscula Atheniensia*, x, 8.)

13. Demand, op. cit. above at n.11, p.118.

14. Demand, chapter 7.

15. Demand, chapter 5, on the Phaedo, etc. Adventurous.

16. R. Buck (1979) *A History of Boiotia*, Edmonton, Alberta, chapters 8–9. Contra, Demand, p.18, with references to a dissertation by C. Dull (*non vidi*: not in Bodleian). As given by Demand the case is not overwhelming.

17. D. Reece (1950) *JHS*, lxx, p.76. Contra, L. H. Jeffery (1965) *BSA*, lx, 55, n.58.

18. See I. Bruce's commentary (1967), Cambridge, on the Oxyrhynchus Historian, with appendixes.

8 THE EVE OF WAR

1. R. Meiggs (1972) *The Athenian Empire*, p.528, following *The Athenian Tribute List*'s assumption of a stone-cutter's error. See also *OPW* app. xiv.

2. C. Tuplin (1979) *CQ*, xxix, 301ff. holds to 460.

3. Contra G. E. M. de ste Croix (1972) *Origins of the Peloponnesian War*, on which see G. L. Cawkwell's review (1975) in *CR*; R. P. Legon (1981) *Megara*, Ithaca, N.Y., especially p.214; and R. C. T. Parker (1983) *Miasma*, Oxford. For Thucydides' view of the cause of the war see now K. J. Dover (1980) *Historical Commentary on Thucydides*, v, on book viii, app. 2(7).

4. S. Hornblower, *Mausolus*, p.255, n.251.

9 CORINTH

1. For the *diolkos*, the artificial stone track for haulage of ships — or just merchandise? — see R. Cook (1979) *JHS*, p.152; photo in B. Ashmole (1973) *Architect and Sculptor in Classical Greece*, London, p.21.

2. See F. Walbank (1933) *Aratos of Sikyon*, Cambridge, pp.45ff.

3. J. Wiseman (1979) *The Land of the Ancient Corinthians*, Göteborg.

4. D. Lewis (1981) *Classical Contributions (McGregor Studies)*, p.78.

5. R. Stroud (1968) 'Tribal Boundary Markers at ... Corinth', *Cal. Studies in Class. Ant.*, i, 233ff.

6. G. Griffith (1950) *Historia*, i, p.241.

7. A. Andrewes (1980) *Historical Commentary on Thucydides*, v, on book viii, p.10.

10 SPARTA

1. Cp. Forrest (1969) *GRBS*, x, p.281, n.7, for the *anti*-Spartan foreign policy of the tyrants at Athens.
2. G. E. M. de ste Croix (1972) *Origins of the Peloponnesian War* for the Peloponnesian League and Spartan foreign policy; and A. Andrewes' excellent (1978) 'Spartan imperialism?' in P. Garnsey and C. R. Whittaker (eds) *Imperialism in the Ancient World*.
3. A. N. Sherwin–White (1980) *JRS*, p.178.
4. P. Brunt (1965) *Phoenix*, xix, pp.255ff. On Sparta and Samos see now P. Cartledge (1982) *CQ*, xxxii, 243ff.
5. Contra R. Seager and C. Tuplin (1980) *JHS*, c, 141ff. See p. 127.
6. On the government of classical Sparta see A. Andrewes (1966) in *Ancient Society and Institutions, Studies presented to Victor Ehrenberg*, chapter i; also D. M. Lewis (1977) *Sparta and Persia*, chapter 2 (both stressing the Assembly's importance; de ste Croix op. cit. under n.2 stresses the importance of the *gerousia*, especially in political trials, but is answered by Lewis).
7. So Lewis.
8. See M. Finley (1975) 'Sparta' in *Use and Abuse of History*, London.
9. A. Andrewes, op. cit. above at n.6, at his p.17. P. Cartledge (1979) *Sparta and Lakonia*, discusses the physical environment in detail; but see the present writer's review in *TLS*, 15, ii, 1980.

11 ATHENS

1. A. French (1965) *The Growth of the Athenian Economy*, London, p.1.
2. R. Wycherley (1978) *The Stones of Athens*, Princeton, N.J., p.16.
3. E. Vanderpool (1979) 'Roads and forts in north-west Attica', *Cal. Studs Class Ant.*, xi, pp.227ff.; U. Wilamowitz, (1893) *Aristoteles und Athen*, Berlin, i, p.199.
4. C. Mee (1978) *Anatolian Studies*, pp.121ff; S. Hornblower, *Mausolus*, pp.14ff.
5. See S. Hornblower in the new and amplified (1983) LACTOR sourcebook on *The Athenian Empire*, introduction.
6. E. J. A. Kenny (1947) *BSA*, xlii, pp.194ff.
7. See D. M. Lewis (1975) *AJA*, p.311, reviewing J. Traill (1975) *Political Organization of Attica, Hesperia*, supp. xiv (on which see also M. I. Finley, 1983, *Politics in the Ancient World*, p. 74); note too C. W. J. Eliot (1962) *Coastal Demes of Attica = Phoenix*, supplement, vol.v.
8. On the Asia Minor formula about control of taxes see S. Hornblower, *Mausolus*, p.161, n.197. IG xii.8.2. (Lemnos) may similarly be an acknowledgement of Athenian control. Piraeus demarch: see D. Whitehead (1982) *ZPE*, xlvii, pp.37ff., 'Notes on Athenian demarchs', at end (also discussing Oropos, which like Eleutherai in ML 48, another

frontier site, was part of Attica but not a normal deme).

9. J. Mikalson (1977) *AJP*, xcviii, pp.42ff. Thorikos as one of the old twelve cities of Kodros: Philochoros F 94 with *HCT*, v, p.317.

10. Best discussion of demarchs in B. Haussoullier (1884) *La vie municipale en Attique*, part i, chapter 3. On the demarch in the Clouds see, however, J. K. Davies (1981) *Wealth and the Power of Wealth in Classical Athens*, London, p.147 (perhaps the debt a deme not a state debt); demarchs and *eisphora*: Davies, ibid.

11. J. E. Jones, A. J. Graham, L. H. Sackett (1973) *BSA*, pp.355ff.; cp. J. Young (1941) *Hesperia*, pp.163ff.; D. Hunt (1947) *JHS*, pp.68ff.

12. See P. Siewert (1982) *Die Trittyen von Attika*, Munich. The argument of the book can be grasped, by those who have no German, just by studying the maps at the end.

13. See E. T. Salmon (1982) *The Making of Roman Italy*, London, chapter 5.

14. R. Duncan–Jones (1980) 'Metic numbers in Periclean Athens', *Chiron*, x, pp.101ff.

15. I owe this whole interpretation of the temples to Hector Catling.

16. See James Morris (1973) *Heaven's Command: an Imperial Progress* (= vol.i of *Pax Britannica*) Harmondsworth, Mdx, chapter 10.

17. Thuc. iii.104, with S. Hornblower (1982) *Historia*, xxxi, pp.241ff.

18. See M. H. Hansen (1976) 'How many Athenians attended the Ecclesia?' *GRBS*, xvii, pp.115ff. (Thuc. viii.72, which speaks of five thousand as the largest total which ever actually gathered (a) is a report of a speech designed to make a point and (b) refers to an abnormal period of wartime absenteeism).

19. See M. H. Hansen (1977) 'How did the Athenian Assembly vote?' *GRBS*, xviii, pp.123ff. with P. Rhodes (1981) 'Notes on voting at Athens', *GRBS*, xxii, pp.125ff.

20. Thuc. i.87.2; Ar. *Pol.* 1270b27 with G. E. M. de ste Croix (1972) *Origins of the Peloponnesian War*, app.xxiv and D. M. Lewis (1977) *Sparta and Persia*, p.41. Note '*relatively* orderly' in the text: for disorder see R. de Laix (1973) *Probouleusis at Athens*, California, p.83, n.43.

21. C. Hignett (1952) *History of the Athenian Constitution*, Oxford, p.233, and J. W. Headlam (1933) *Election by Lot*, Cambridge, edn 2, p.31, write as if the passage said that the demos *was* a monarchos. At 1292a he says that the people become *monarchos* when the laws are not supreme, but that in democracies which are subject to the law the best citizens hold first place: Periclean Athens?

22. A conservative view in P. Rhodes (1972) *The Athenian Boule*; but W. R. Connor (1974) 'The Athenian Council: method and focus in recent scholarship', *CJ*, lxxvii, pp.32ff., argues that the Council was much more than a rubber stamp for the Assembly.

23. Against the scepticism of G. E. M. de ste Croix (1963) 'The alleged secret pact between Athens and Philip II concerning Amphipolis and Pydna', *CQ*, xiii, pp.110ff. (reprinted in S. Perlman (1973) *Philip and Athens*, Cambridge, pp.110ff.), see W. R. Connor, op. cit. under n.22 above and R. de Laix (1973) *Probouleusis at Athens*, pp.78ff. (also citing Andok. iii.33: the demos has to be deceived for its own good sometimes. The new

Michigan papyrus about Theramenes, *ZPE*, ii, 1968, p.166, is however indignant about his negotiating in secret from the Assembly). Demainetos' vessel was a state trireme, which suggests official authorization but not necessarily by the Assembly.

24. J. D. Mikalson (1975) *The Sacred and Civil Calendar of the Athenian Year*, Princeton, N.J., pp.196ff.; P. Rhodes (1982) *Comm. on Ath. Pol.*, Oxford, on xliii, 3, at p.521.

25. M. H. Hansen (1977) *GRBS*, xviii, pp.43ff.; P. Rhodes, op. cit. under n.24 above, is not persuaded, p.522, because the frequent trial of *eisangeliai* by the Assembly (treason trials) is incompatible with a limit to the number of meetings.

26. P. Rhodes, *Athenian Boule*, p.5.

27. A. Zimmern (1931) *Greek Commonwealth*, Oxford, edn 5, p.162, lacks foundation (but is worth reading generally on demes).

28. Carpet-baggers: A. H. M. Jones, *Athenian Democracy*, p.106. Epilachontes: P. Rhodes, *Comm. on Ath. Pol.*, p.518. Tension between Council and Assembly in Roman period: R. Macmullen (1974) *Roman Social Relations*, London and New Haven, p.187, n.18.

29. Jones, op. cit. pp.125f., minimizes the power of the generals unduly. For depositions see the equally conservative C. W. Fornara (1971) *Athenian Board of Generals*, Wiesbaden, p.37f. On this topic I am indebted to a paper by D. M. Lewis read in 1980, and remarks on it by Professor A. Andrewes (see the latter in *Ehrenberg Studies*, p. 11).

30. Contra W. Connor (1971) *The New Politicians of Fifth-Century Athens*. Princeton, N.J. On which see J. K. Davies (1975) *Gnomon*, xlvii, pp.374ff.; D. M. Lewis (1975) *CR*, xxv, pp.87ff.

31. J. K. Davies (1971) *Athenian Propertied Families*: entry under Dikaiogenes. But see now F. Bourriot (1982) *Historia*, xxxi, pp.404ff.

32. See M. I. Finley (1974) 'Athenian Demagogues' in *Studies in Ancient Society*, London, chapter 1, and A. Andrewes (1962) *Phoenix*, xvi, pp.64ff., at end, for the functional importance of demagogues.

33. See A. Andrewes (1981) *Historical Commentary on Thucydides*, v, pp.258ff.

34. See P. Rhodes (1979/80) 'Athenian democracy after 403 BC', *CJ*, lxxiv, pp.305ff.

35. M. H. Hansen (1979) *Symbolae Osloenses*, liv, pp.5ff., and (1979–80) *Classica et Medievalia*, xxxii, pp.105ff., with D. M. Lewis (1982) *JHS*, cii, p.269.

12 THE PELOPONNESIAN WAR

1. P. A. Brunt (1965) 'Spartan policy and strategy in the Archidamian War', *Phoenix*, xix, pp.255ff., at p.259; G. E. M. de ste Croix (1972) *Origins of the Peloponnesian War*, p.208.

2. R. Seager and C. Tuplin (1980) 'The freedom of the Greeks of Asia', *JHS*, c, pp.141ff. (but see p. 102 above).

3. A. J. Holladay and J. Poole (1979) 'Thucydides and the plague at Athens', *CQ*, xxix, pp.282ff. (But E. L. Hussey believes that contagion

is at least compatible with Hippocratic thinking about disease, even if the extant treatises do not make their awareness explicit.)

4. G. L. Cawkwell, see n.5 below.

5. The best accounts are G. L. Cawkwell (1975) 'Thucydides' account of Periclean strategy', *Yale Class. Studs*, xxiv, pp.53ff. (against Wade Gery in the *Oxford Classical Dictionary*[2] and A. J. Holladay (1979) 'Athenian strategy in the Archidamian War', *Historia*, xxviii, pp.399ff. The chapter (7) on the war in J. K. Davies (1978) *Democracy and Classical Greece*, London, is full of interest.

6. L. H. Chandler (1926) *JHS*, xlvi, pp.1ff.

7. ML 53 comm.

8. So Classen-Steup's note on this chapter, preferable to Gomme's, who thinks only the 'sacred precinct' was inviolate, and that because the Spartans deliberately 'spared' it. Certainly there is no break in the record of building at Eleusis, cp. G. Mylonas (1961) *Eleusis*, Princeton, N.J.. Thuc. ii.24.1, 'they established guard posts', probably refers to positions outside Attica, cp. *HCT*.

9. See S. Hornblower, *Thucydides*, London, forthcoming.

10. See A. Andrewes (1978) 'Spartan imperialism?' in P. Garnsey and C. R. Whittaker (eds) *Imperialism in the Ancient World*, at pp.95ff. Cp. A. Andrewes (1971) 'Two Notes on Lysander', *Phoenix*, xxv, pp.206ff.

11. Andrewes, *HCT*, v, on book viii, p.9.

12. D. M. Lewis (1977) *Sparta and Persia*, p.28.

13. H. T. Wade Gery, *Oxford Classical Dictionary*[2], s.v. Thucydides at p.1067.

14. So Mr G. L. Cawkwell at a seminar in March 1981 on the Sicilian Expedition held at Harrow School and addressed by Mr Cawkwell and the present writer.

15. H. D. Westlake (1969) 'Athenian aims in Sicily 427–424 BC', *Essays on the Greek Historians and Greek History*, Manchester, chapter 6, pp.101ff.

16. On this period see R. Seager (1976) 'After the Peace of Nikias: diplomacy and policy', *CQ*, xxvi, pp.249ff.

17. Andrewes, *HCT*, v, on book viii at pp.261ff. for this inscription. On Argive aspirations generally in this period see R. A. Tomlinson (1972) *Argos and the Argolid*, London, chapter xi.

18. Andrewes, *HCT*, iv, pp.111ff. on the Spartan numbers. It seems that Thucydides' totals should be doubled. See below p. 219 for the manpower problem generally.

19. For Amorges' revolt see S. Hornblower, *Mausolus*, p.31f., with references.

20. See above all C. W. Macleod's paper 'Thucydides and tragedy', originally delivered at a seminar on Thucydides and the Sophists, organized by E. L. Hussey and the present writer in 1981, to be printed in O. Taplin (ed.) (1983) *Classical Papers*, Oxford. See also Macleod's (1975) 'Rhetoric and history' in *Quaderni di Storia*, ii, pp.39ff. (and in *Classical Papers*) — an examination of the tendentious rhetoric and literary artifices used in Alcibiades' speech, vi.16–18.

21. S. Hornblower, *Thucydides*, for this point, and for 'tragic *akribeia*' generally.
22. Andrewes, *HCT*, v, on book viii, p.66 and generally pp.27ff.
23. Andrewes, ibid. On Thucydides and Sicily see K. J. Dover (1981) *Proc. Roy. Irish. Acad*, lxxxi, c.8, pp.231ff.
24. S. Hornblower, in LACTOR sourcebook on *Athenian Empire*, edn 3, Excursus: 'The Athenian upper class and the Empire'.
25. Cp., for example, de ste Croix, *OPW*, p.216, against F. Cornford (1907) *Thucydides Mythistoricus*, London.
26. Andrewes, *HCT*, v, on book viii, including a comm. on *Ath. Pol.* xxix-xxxii. See also P. Rhodes' *Ath. Pol.* comm.
27. Rhodes, *Ath. Pol.* comm., introduction for discussion. Scepticism about Androtion can be taken too far, as by P. Harding (1974) 'The Theramenes myth', *Phoenix*, xxviii, pp.101ff.
28. Andrewes, *HCT*, v, pp.238ff.
29. Andrewes, *HCT*, v, p.253.
30. A. Andrewes, *OCD²*, s.v. Theramenes.
31. G. E. M. de ste Croix (1956) 'The constitution of the five thousand', *Historia*, v, pp.1ff.
32. Andrewes, *HCT*, v, p.325, dealing with a difficulty pointed out by de ste Croix, op. cit. under n.31 above.
33. For other problems about Thuc. viii.97, cp. the present writer's review of *HCT*, v, in *TLS*, 3, iv, 1981.
34. For the connection between Cyzicus and the fall of the five thousand see A. Andrewes (1953) *JHS*, lxxiii, p.4: Cyzicus 'relieved the mass of Athenians from that pressing sense of military insecurity which alone induced them to accept the constitution of the 5000'.
35. See for this paragraph Andrewes' article (1953) 'The generals in the Hellespont 410–407 BC', *JHS*, pp.2ff. cited in n.34 above. On the battles of Notion and Kyzikos see Andrewes (1982) *JHS*, cii, pp.15ff.
36. D. M. Lewis (1977) *Sparta and Persia*, p.124. Lewis' whole chapter is very important on the Ionian War. Lewis actually thinks that the third treaty of 411 was *de facto* a dead letter soon after it was agreed.
37. Lewis, ibid., chapter 5, end.
38. A. Andrewes (1974) 'The Arginusai trial', *Phoenix*, xxviii, pp.112ff.

13 The effects of the Peloponnesian War (intellectual activity and treatise-writing; warfare; politics; economic life; religion)

1. See Dover in K. J. Dover (ed.) (1980) *Ancient Greek Literature*, Oxford, p. 119. For Herodes see H. T. Wade Gery (1958) *Essays in Greek History*, pp.271ff.; A. Andrewes (1971) *Phoenix*, xxv, pp.218ff.; S. Hornblower, *Thucydides* (forthcoming). Text: ed. E. Drerup (1908), U. Albini (1968), or in Ed. Meyer (1909) *Theopomps Hellenika*, Halle, pp.202ff. Note that Thrasymachus and Kritias both wrote pamphlets on Thessaly; Wade Gery thinks Kritias wrote 'Herodes'.

2. See Iris Murdoch (1977) *The Fire and the Sun, Why Plato Banished the Artists*, Oxford, pp.77, 68.
3. See L. Strauss (1963) *On Tyranny*, London, on Xenophon's *Hiero*.
4. J. K. Anderson (1970) *Military Theory and Practice in the Age of Xenophon*, California, *passim*.
5. E. K. Goodenough (1928) 'The political philosophy of hellenistic kingship', *Yale Classical Studs*, i, pp.55ff.
6. See D. Macdowall (1962) *Andokides on the Mysteries*, Oxford, pp.18ff.
7. See Jane Hornblower (1981) *Hieronymus of Cardia*, Oxford, pp.207 and ff.
8. P. Brunt (1969) *CQ*, xix, pp.245–7 especially p.246, n.1, listing passages.
9. J. Hornblower, op. cit. under n.7 above, pp.207ff.
10. See G. L. Cawkwell (1978) *Philip of Macedon*, chapter x, contra, A. J. Holladay (1982) *JHS*, cii, pp.94ff.
11. R. K. Sinclair (1966) 'Diodorus Siculus and fighting in relays', *CQ*, xvi, 249 ff.
12. G. L. Cawkwell (1972) 'Epaminondas and Thebes', *CQ*, xxii, at p.261.
13. D. M. Lewis (1977) *Sparta and Persia*, p.39.
14. W. K. Pritchett (1974) *Greek State at War*, California, ii, pp.113ff.
15. J. Roy (1967) 'The mercenaries of Cyrus', *Historia*, xvi, pp.287ff.
16. A. Fuks (1972) 'Isokrates and the social-economic situation in Greece', *Ancient Society*, iii, pp.7ff; cp. ibid., v, 1974, pp.51ff.
17. See S. Hornblower, *CAH*, edn 2, VI, chapter iii.
18. D. M. Lewis (1973) *CR*, p.254; P. Rhodes comm. on *Ath. Pol.*, p.496.
19. D. Engels (1977) *Alexander the Great and the Logistics of the Macedonian Army*, California, pp.12, 16 (but QC vi.8.23 with N. G. L. Hammond and G. T. Griffith (1979) *Macedonia*, ii, Oxford, p.161, n., shows such camp-followers still numerous in Alexander's time).

    Corps d'élite: W. K. Pritchett (1974) *Greek State at War*, California, ii, pp.221ff.
20. E. W. Marsden (1969–71) *Greek and Roman Artillery*, 2 vols, Oxford.
21. W. W. Tarn (1930) *Hellenistic Military and Naval Developments*, Cambridge, pp.114ff.
22. S. Hornblower, *Mausolus*, chapter xi, *passim*.
23. H. W. Parke (1930) 'The development of the Second Spartan Empire', *JHS*, 1, pp.37ff. On Lysander's methods see also J. K. Davies (1978) *Democracy and Classical Greece*, pp. 156ff. The significance of the Milesian democrats: D. Lotze (1964) *Lysander*, Berlin, p.18.
24. G. E. M. de ste Croix (1981) *The Class Struggle in the Ancient Greek World*, pp.74, 395.
25. See E. Badian (1981) in *Macedonian Studies presented to Edson*, pp.33ff. (p. 319, n. 38).
26. For this analogy see S. Hornblower, *Mausolus*, p.77.
27. For a rosy view of Euphron, de ste Croix, *Class Struggle* pp.297f.; but cp. A. Griffin (1982) *Sikyon*, p.73.
28. N. G. L. Hammond (1967) *Epirus*, Oxford, pp.525ff.
29. T. T. B. Ryder (1965) *Koine Eirene*, chapter 1.

30. J. Cargill (1981) *The Second Athenian League*.
31. See S. Hornblower (1982) *CR*, xxxii, review of Cargill at p.238.
32. S. Hornblower, ibid.; J. K. Davies (1977) 'Athenian citizenship: the descent group and the alternatives', *CJ*, lxxiii, pp.105ff.
33. S. Hornblower, *Mausolus*, chapter vii; G. T. Griffith (1978) in P. Garnsey and C. R. Whittaker (eds) *Imperialism in the Ancient World*, p.140. Demades: Hicks and Hill, *Greek Historical Inscriptions*, p.227.
34. B. Macdonald (1981) 'The emigration of potters from Athens in the late fifth century and its effects on the Attic pottery industry', *AJA*, lxxxv, pp.157ff.
35. See S. Hornblower, *CAH* vol.vi, edn 2, chapter xi(a), and *Mausolus*, chapter ix for particular known individuals.
36. A. W. Gomme (1933) *Population of Athens*, Oxford, and in *JHS*, 1959; A. H. M. Jones (1957) *Athenian Democracy*, Oxford, appendix on population; Ch. Pélékidis (1962) *Histoire de l'ephébie attique*, Paris, app.1.
37. M. I. Finley (1952) *Studies in Land and Credit in Ancient Athens*, New Brunswick, N.J., M. I. Finley (1982) *Economy and Society in Ancient Greece*, chapter 4.
38. C. Mossé, 'La vie économique d'Athènes au iv siècle', *Raccolta Sartori = Praelectiones Patavinae*, reprinted at the back of Arno reprint (1979) of her *Fin de la démocratie Athénienne*, Paris.
39. V. Andreyev (1974) *Eirene*, xii, pp.5ff. (cp. de ste Croix (1966) in *Ehrenberg Studies*, pp.109ff., on the Phainippos estate in Dem. xlii).
40. R. Hopper (1979) *Trade and Industry in Classical Greece*, 170ff.; but see e.g. *Arch. Reps*, 1979–80, p.19 (Thorikos) for mining activity apparently late fifth/early fourth centuries.
41. G. T. Griffith (1950) 'The Union of Corinth and Argos', *Historia*, i, pp.236ff. for the economic background; contra, though only on chronology, C. Tuplin (1982) *CQ*, xxxii, pp.75ff.
42. J. M. Cook (1961) 'The problem of Classical Ionia', *PCPhS*, cclxxxvii, pp.9ff.
43. S. Hornblower, *Mausolus*, chapter iv. Cp. too S. Hornblower in *CAH*, edn 2, vol.vi, chapter xi(a).
44. J. M. Cook (1983) *The Persian Empire*, chapter xviii, p.219, who speaks of Greek mercenaries enjoying a prosperity out of proportion to their 'productivity'.
45. N. Marinatos (1981) *Thucydides and Religion*, Königstein, confuses Thucydides' allowance for the irrational in human affairs with religious belief. See S. Hornblower, *Thucydides*, forthcoming.
46. K. J. Dover (1976) 'The freedom of the intellectual in Greek society', *Talanta*, vii, pp.24ff.
47. C. Powell (1979) 'Religion and the Sicilian expedition', *Historia*, xxviii, pp.15ff.
48. G. L. Cawkwell (1976) *CQ*, p.102. P. Brunt (1965) *Phoenix*, p.261 (as also Beloch before him) observed that it is the more 'enlightened' Corinthians, not the traditionalist Spartans, who in Thuc. i.121 suggest that the Peloponnesians should help themselves to temple treasures at e.g. Olympia.

49. K. J. Dover (1974) *Greek Popular Morality*, especially p.259, against Adkins' idea that fourth-century Greeks did not believe the Gods punish injustice; cp., for example, Lys. vi.20.
50. A. D. Nock (1972) 'Religious attitudes of the ancient Greeks' in Z. Stewart (ed.) *Arthur Darby Nock* (Collected Papers), vol.ii, Oxford, pp.534ff.
51. M. Nilsson (1972) *Greek Folk Religion*, Pennsylvania, pp.114ff.
52. K. Popper (1966) *Open Society and its Enemies*, London, edn 5, i, pp.169ff.
53. W. Ferguson (1949) *Hesperia*, supplement viii, pp.130ff.; M. I. Finley, *Studies in Land...*, p.89.
54. A. Burford (1966) *Greek Temple-Builders at Epidaurus*, Liverpool.
55. Cp. S. Hornblower, *CAH*, edn 2, vol.vi., chapter xi(a).
56. A. Andrewes (1982) *CAH*, edn 2, vol.iii(3), pp.410ff.
57. H. W. Parke (1977) *Festivals of the Athenians*, London, p.152.
58. Who also break with tradition by putting up assertive dedications in Greek sanctuaries, the tradition being that which required decent anonymity in such matters. See S. Hornblower, *Mausolus*, chapter x, discussing Brasidas, Lysander, the Hekatomnids and Alexander. On fourth-century and later civic benefactions of an assertive, individualistic type see P. Veyne (1976) *Le Pain et le cirque*. Boastful fourth-century 'choregic' monuments (i.e. monuments celebrating victories by choruses, etc., trained and paid for by wealthy citizens) at Athens, like the famous choregic monument of Lysikrates, are socially significant in ways discussed in *Mausolus*, ibid.: city-state 'corporatism' giving way to a personality cult of a hellenistic type.

  Portraiture: *Mausolus*, pp.272ff. and references; M. Robertson (1975) *History of Greek Art*, Cambridge, pp.504ff. Tissaphernes' coins: see e.g. C. Kraay (1976) *Archaic and Classical Greek Coins*, no.206.

14 THE CORINTHIAN WAR

1. G. E. M. de ste Croix (1972) *Origins of the Peloponnesian War*, app. xxi. D. Lotze (1964) *Lysander*, Berlin, p.46, thinks that some of the more emancipated Spartans may have felt gratitude to Athens as the source of the liberal and liberating ideas which had changed their own lives.
2. H. W. Parke (1930) 'The development of the second Spartan Empire', *JHS*, 1, pp.37ff.
3. A. Andrewes (1971) 'Two notes on Lysander', I, 'The abolition of the decarchies', *Phoenix*, xxv, pp.206ff.
4. D. M. Lewis (1977) *Sparta and Persia*, pp.120f. against Andrewes op.cit. under n.3 above, p.208.
5. S. Perlman (1964) 'The causes and the outbreak of the Corinthian War', *CQ*, xiv, pp.64ff.
6. A. Andrewes, op.cit. under n.3 above, p.217 and n.20, who is followed for much of this paragraph. See also J. S. Morrison (1942) 'Meno of Pharsalus, Polycrates, and Ismenias', *CQ*, xxxvi, pp.57ff.

7. L. Pareti, *Studi*, i, pp.93ff. is here followed on the identification of Diodorus' 'Pharakides' with the well-known Pharax. Jacoby thinks that Theopompus is describing the younger Pharax, Pareti assumes the elder.

8. Cp. Andrewes, op.cit. under n.3 above, p.224.

9. See *CAH* edn 2, vol.vi, chapter iii, 'Persia', where the present writer treats the Sparto-Persian warfare of this period in detail.

10. Lewis, *Sparta and Persia*, pp.26, 138.

11. R. Seager (1977) 'Agesilaus in Asia: propaganda and objectives', *Liverpool Classical Monthly*, ii, pp.183ff.

12. G. L. Cawkwell (1976) 'Agesilaus and Sparta', *CQ*, xxvi, pp.62ff.; and S. Hornblower, *CAH*, edn 2, vol.vi, chapter iii.

13. S. Hornblower, *Mausolus*, p.105 and n.209, p.220 and n.5; also *CAH*, edn 2, vol.vi, chapter iii, all on the early fourth-century background to Alexander's *homonoia* or fusion policies towards the Iranians. For a fictional sketch of the complexity of the attitudes of mainland Greeks to Persia and Persians in Asia in the 390s see Naomi Mitchison (1928) *Black Sparta*, London, chapter 10.

14. S. Accame (1951) *Ricerche intorno alla guerra corinzia*, Naples, p.23.

15. R. Seager (1967) 'Thrasybulus, Conon and Athenian imperialism', *JHS*, lxxxvii, pp.95ff.; G. L. Cawkwell (1976) 'The imperialism of Thrasybulus', *CQ*, xxvi, pp.270ff. Note that the somewhat high-handed Tod 110 (Karpathos), which has often been used to illustrate the aggressiveness of 'Thrasybulan' policies in this period, is now thought to be fifth-century.

16. See *CAH*, edn 2, vol.vi, chapter iii, for the satrapal dispositions of this period.

17. R. Seager (1966) 'Lysias and the corn-dealers', *Historia*, xv, pp.172ff.

18. G. L. Cawkwell (1981) 'The King's Peace', *CQ*, xxxi, pp.69ff.

19. S. Hornblower, *Mausolus*, p.128; *CAH*, edn 2, vol.vi, chapter iii; the full argument is there given.

20. L. Robert (1951) *Études de numismatique grecque*, p.11, n.1.

21. See G. Underhill's good note on Xen. *Hell.* v.1.31.

22. But see J. M. Cook (1983) *The Persian Empire*, p. 218f.

23. See *CAH*, edn 2, vol.vi, chapters iii and especially xi(a) for this whole topic, where M. I. Finley (1980) *Ancient Sicily*, p.98, is quoted for the comment that 'assemblies have often continued to meet under tyrannies, in Sicily as elsewhere'.

24. M. I. Finley, *Ancient Sicily*, p. 85.

25. A. G. Woodhead (1970) 'The "Adriatic Empire" of Dionysius I of Syracuse', *Klio*, lii, pp.503ff.

26. Finley, op. cit. under n. 23 above, chapter 7, for a sceptical view.

15   THE KING'S PEACE TO LEUKTRA

1. G. L. Cawkwell (1981) *CQ*, p.77 and n.3 against earlier views and criticisms.

2. S. Hornblower, *CAH*, edn 2, vi chapter iii.

3. R. Seager (1974) 'The King's Peace and the balance of power in Greece 386–362 BC', *Athenaeum*, lii, pp.36ff.

4. As assumed by K. J. Beloch, *Griechische Geschichte*, iii² 1, p.102.
5. G. L. Cawkwell (1976) *CQ*, p.77.
6. R. Seager, op.cit. under n.3 above, p.41.
7. So wrongly T. T. B. Ryder (1965) *Koine Eirene*, p.45; who writes of Sparta's Olynthian intervention that it 'constituted a quite remarkable course of action for a state that had been traditionally conservative'. The last few words hardly do justice to Spartan policies generally in 405–395, nor does 'remarkable' take account of the specifically northern aspect to those policies.
8. With Cawkwell (1976) *CQ*, p.78.
9. Cp. H. W. Parke (1927) 'Herippidas harmost at Thebes', *CQ*, xxi, pp.162ff.
10. G. L. Cawkwell (1973) 'The foundation of the Second Athenian Confederacy', *CQ*, xxiii, pp.47ff.: generally accepted here.
11. Cp., for example, N. G. L. Hammond (1967) *History of Greece*, edn 2, p.485: '378/7'.
12. S. Accame (1941) *Lega ateniese*, Rome, p.34.
13. Cp. J. Buckler (1979) 'The re-establishment of the *Boiotarchia* (378 BC)', *AJAH*, iv, pp.50ff., at p.52; and J. Buckler (1980) 'The alleged Theban-Spartan alliance of 386 BC', *Eranos*, lxxviii, pp.179ff.
14. S. Hornblower, in LACTOR sourcebook on *Athenian Empire*, edn 3, p. 28.
15. J. Cargill (1981) *The Second Athenian League*, denies that Corcyra was a member but see G. L. Cawkwell (1981), *JHS*, p.42, and S. Hornblower (1982) *CR*, pp.236ff. (review of J. Cargill).
16. D. M. Lewis (1974) *Phoros for Meritt*, Locust Valley, N.Y., p.89, n.39.
17. G. L. Cawkwell (1981) *JHS*, ci, p.50.
18. P. A. Brunt (1966) *Ehrenberg Studies*, p.86.
19. H. Ormerod (1924) *Piracy in the Ancient World*, Liverpool, p.114; G. L. Cawkwell (1981) *JHS*, p.48, n.32; S. Hornblower, *Mausolus*, p.204.
20. See generally for a favourable view G. L. Cawkwell (1981) 'Notes on the failure of the Second Athenian Confederacy', *JHS*, ci, pp.40ff.; and G. T. Griffith (1978) 'Athens in the fourth century' in P. Garnsey and C. R. Whittaker (eds.) *Imperialism in the Ancient World*, at pp.127ff.; J. Cargill, op.cit. under n.15 above; and G. de ste Croix (1981) *Class Struggle in the Ancient Greek World*, chapter 5, who defends Athens uncritically; see review of Cargill cited in n.15.
21. S. Hornblower, *Mausolus*, p.190 and n.60.
22. G. L. Cawkwell (1963) *Historia*, p.90, cp. Cawkwell, Penguin *Hellenica* (*A History of My Times*), revised transl. p.297 n.
23. For which see G. L. Cawkwell (1963) 'Notes on the peace of 375/4', *Historia*, xii, pp. 84ff.
24. G. L. Cawkwell (1981) *JHS*, p.44, n.23.
25. ibid., p.46, where it is also suggested that not all Kephallenian communities had joined the confederacy, i.e. there was no necessary breach of the charter; Cawkwell is also right to stress that Amphipolis is not yet an issue so that Athens was not yet unpopular with her allies on that account. For the date of the Amorgos garrison see his p.51.

26. G. T. Griffith, op.cit. under n.20 above, p.136.
27. A. G. Woodhead (1957) *AJA*, lxi, p.373; cp. G. T. Griffith, op.cit. under n.20 above, p.136, for Athens' 'alliances on the side'. See too J. Cargill, op.cit. under n.15 above, pp.84–7.
28. G. E. M. de ste Croix (1972) *Origins of the Peloponnesian War*, pp.331ff.; P. Cartledge (1979) *Sparta and Lakonia*, London, chapters 12,14; A. Andrewes, *Historical Commentary on Thucydides*, vol.iv on Mantinea in 418.
29. D. Schaps (1979) *Economic Rights of Women in Ancient Greece*, Edinburgh; J. Gould (1980) 'Law, custom and myth: aspects of the social position of women in classical Athens', *JHS*, c, pp.38ff.
30. G. E. M. de ste Croix (1970) 'Some observations on the property rights of Athenian women', *CR*, xx, pp.273ff.; P. Cartledge (1981) 'Spartan wives: liberation or licence', *CQ*, xxxi, pp.84ff. For women 'competing' (i.e. as owners not participants) at Olympia see A. Cameron (1976) *Circus Factions*, Oxford p.204, n.1; M. I. Finley and H. W. Pleket (1976) *The Olympic Games, the First Thousand Years*, pp.30ff.

16   Leuktra to Mantinea and the Revolt of the Satraps

1. N. G. L. Hammond (1979) *History of Macedonia*, vol. ii, pp.178ff., thinks Amyntas acted as impartial arbitrator, but this is unlikely: Macedonian power had included Perrhaibia only decades before, and this would have given Amyntas an interest. The same applies *a fortiori* to Elymiotis to the north.
2. H. D. Westlake (1935) *Thessaly in the Fourth Century BC*, p.84, n.2. (This book is still essential reading on Jason.)
3. On this decade see generally J. Buckler (1980) *The Theban Hegemony 371–362 BC*, but above all G. L. Cawkwell (1972) 'Epaminondas and Thebes', *CQ*, xxii, pp.254ff. Cp. too S. Hornblower, *Mausolus*, p.195.
4. For this peace see T. T. B. Ryder (1965) *Koine Eirene*, pp.71ff. and app.iv; G. L. Cawkwell, Penguin *Hellenica* (*A History of My Times*) pp.280, 295, and *CQ*, 1972, p.266, n.1. Both think that Sparta participated. For the opposite view I am indebted to lecture-notes by D. M. Lewis (pointing out that *pantes hēmeis* at vi.5.37 should mean not 'all of us who have come now' but 'all of us who came then').
5. *Mausolus*, p.195.
6. See now G. L. Cawkwell, Penguin *Hellenica*, p.280, apparently favouring the conference of 371/0. At *CQ*, 1961, p.81 and n.2 he had preferred 369.
7. N. G. L. Hammond in Hammond-Griffith, *Macedonia*, vol.ii, at p.181 prefers 368, but Griffith at p.219 of the same volume has the usual date 369. Hammond's late dating is to be rejected. See Buckler, *Theban Hegemony*, app. 1.
8. Buckler, ibid., p.122.
9. As by Buckler, chapter 5; cp.his p.152 on Thebes' 'recent blundering and humiliation in Thessaly'.

10. G. L. Cawkwell (1961) 'The common peace of 366/5 BC', *CQ*, xi, pp.80ff.
11. *Mausolus*, 197ff., with references.
12. Cp. J. M. Cook (1961) *JHS*, lxxxi, p.70, n.81.
13. *Mausolus*, chapter 5, where each city is treated in turn.
14. R. Moysey (1976) 'The date of the Strato of Sidon Decree (IG ii^2 141)', *AJAH*, i, pp.182ff.
15. *Mausolus*, pp.174, 201.
16. See S. Burstein (1974) *Outpost of Hellenism*, California, p.49.
17. G. L. Cawkwell (1972) *CQ*, pp.270ff.; his translation of *idias* as 'attached' on p.271 is better than his 'friendly' on p.270. *Mausolus*, p.200, n.137.
18. S. Sherwin-White (1978) *Ancient Cos*, Göttingen, pp.70ff.; cp. *Mausolus*, p.134.
19. G. L. Cawkwell (1981) *JHS*, pp.51f.
20. G. L. Cawkwell (1961) *CQ*, p.273. Perhaps add to the factors he adduces the obscure internal Boiotian trouble, involving men from Orchomenus, described under 364 by Diod. xv.79.
21. J. Larsen (1968) *Greek Federal States*, Oxford, pp.180–95, especially p.195.
22. S. Hornblower, *CAH*, edn 2, vol.vi, chapter iii; *Mausolus*, chapter vi(2). The present work assumes the correctness of the views there argued for.

17 PHILIP

1. James Sabben-Clare (1971) *Caesar and Roman Politics 60–50 BC*, Oxford, p.7.
2. This point is well made in what is easily the best account of the Third Sacred War, the 1961 Oxford B.Litt. thesis (unpublished) of that title by C.Ehrhardt. The results of that work are drawn on in the pages that follow.
3. See Mary Renault's admirable novel *The Mask of Apollo* for a reconstruction of this period of Sicilian history, down to the death of Dion.
4. R. Talbert (1974) *Timoleon and the Revival of Greek Sicily*, Cambridge, and cp. C. Mossé (1979) *Fin de la démocratie Athénienne*, pp.340ff.
5. M. I. Finley (1980) *Ancient Sicily*, chapter 8.
6. H. D. Westlake (1952) *Timoleon and his Relations with Tyrants*, Manchester.
7. Finley, *Ancient Sicily*, p.95.
8. S. Hornblower, *Mausolus*, p.203 and n.167, and pp.206ff. for the Social War generally.
9. *Mausolus*, plate 36.
10. G. L. Cawkwell (1962) 'Notes on the Social War', *Classica et Medievalia*, xxiii, pp.38ff.
11. J. K. Davies (1981) *Wealth and the Power of Wealth in Classical Athens*, last chapter, and cp. C. Mossé, *Fin*, p.168 (liturgies).

12. A. H. M. Jones (1957), *Athenian Democracy*, p.27.
13. See N. G. L. Hammond (1937) *CQ*, xxxi, p.79 (arguing against the idea of a 'doublet' in Diodorus).
14. G. T. Griffith (1979) *Macedonia*, vol.ii, pp.218ff., 226f.; and Griffith (1970) *CQ*, xx, pp.67ff., against C. Ehrhardt (1967) *CQ*, xvii, pp.298ff. More suggestions in T. Martin (1981) *CP*, lxxvi, pp.188ff.; *HSCP*, lxxxvi, 1982, pp.181ff.
15. G. L. Cawkwell (1978) *Philip of Macedon*, p.74, for the possibility that the northerly winds at the relevant time actually made it impossible for Athens to help Amphipolis, even if she had wanted to. Cp. Dem. iv.31.
16. I am indebted here to an unpublished paper by P. A. Brunt on Athens' relations with Kersebleptes. Brunt thinks Tod 151 may represent not the agreement of Dem. xxiii.173 but the earlier agreement made by Athenodorus, ibid., 8, 170.
17. E. W. Marsden, *Greek and Roman Artillery*, i, pp.59f.
18. G. L. Cawkwell (1962) 'The defence of Olynthus', *CQ*, xii, pp.122ff. (reprinted in S. Perlman (ed.) (1973) *Philip and Athens*, Cambridge).
19. G. L. Cawkwell (1978) 'Euboia in the late 340s', *Phoenix*, xxxii, pp.42ff. Cp. *Philip of Macedon*, pp.88ff.
20. P. Brunt (1969) 'Euboia in the time of Philip II', *CQ*, xix, pp.245ff., at p.250, n.3, against Cawkwell, op.cit. under n.18 above.
21. G. L. Cawkwell (1960) 'Aeschines and the Peace of Philokrates', *REG*, lxxxiii, pp.416ff.; and Cawkwell (1978) 'The Peace of Philokrates Again', *CQ*, xxviii, pp.93ff., followed here on the question of the summons. An excellent general account of the peace of Philokrates is in A. W. Pickard-Cambridge (1914) *Demosthenes and the Last Days of Greek Freedom*, London and New York. The excellent Penguin *Demosthenes and Aeschines*, translated by A. N. W. Saunders (1975) has a valuable introduction and notes by T. T. B. Ryder. Note also J. Ellis and R. Minas (1970) *The Spectre of Philip* (translated source book).
22. *CAH*, vi, edn 2, chapter iii for this para. See however R. M. Errington (1981) *AJAH*, v, pp.74ff., who is sceptical about attempts to argue that Philip was thinking of proceeding against Persia as early as 346.
23. M. Markle (1974) 'The strategy of Philip in 346 BC', *CQ*, xxiv, pp.253ff. Contra, rightly, Cawkwell, op.cit. (*CQ*, 1978) at n.21 above.
24. For the date Cawkwell (1963) *CQ*, xiii, p.126f. (in S. Perlman, *Philip and Athens*).
25. G. T. Griffith, *Macedonia*, chapter xvi (Thessaly), p.558 (Thrace), curiously not citing Arr. *Anab*. i.25. Cp. also Cawkwell, *Philip*, p.117 and n.9.
26. Cawkwell (1963) *CQ*; cp. *Philip*, pp.127, 132.
27. Griffith, *Macedonia*, ii, p.502 and n.3; pp.544ff.
28. J. R. Ellis (1976) *Philip II and Macedonian Imperialism*, p.125; Cawkwell, *Philip*, pp.117, 186, and *CR*, 1979, pp.214ff. at p.216 (review of H. Wankel, edn of Demosthenes' *De Corona*).
29. Cawkwell, *Philip*, p.138, and *CR*, op. cit. under n.28 above.
30. N. G. L. Hammond (1973) *Studies in Greek History*, Oxford, pp.34ff.
31. C. Roebuck (1948) 'The settlements of Philip II with the Greek states in

　　　338 BC', *CP*, xliii, pp.73ff., reprinted in S. Perlman, *Philip and Athens*.
32. Cawkwell (1978) *Phoenix*, pp.42f.
33. A. B. Bosworth (1976) 'Early relations between Aitolia and Macedon', *AJAH*, i, pp.164ff.
34. Cawkwell, *Philip*, chapter xi.
35. Cawkwell, *Philip*, p.172.
36. J. Fontenrose (1978) *The Delphic Oracle*, California, p.337 puts this oracle in the 'not genuine' category; characteristic of that sceptical book.
37. On the death of Philip see Griffith, *Macedonia*, chapter xx; A. B. Bosworth (1971) 'Philip II and Upper Macedonia', *CQ*, xxi, pp.93ff.; P. Brunt (1976) Loeb *Arrian*, i, pp.lviii ff; N. G. L. Hammond (1978) *GRBS*, xix, pp.331ff. (contra P.Parsons (1979) 'The burial of Philip II', *AJAH*, iv, pp.97ff.).

18　ALEXANDER

1. The surviving accounts of Alexander's reign were all written down centuries after the events they describe. The essential narrative is the *Anabasis* of Arrian, a Greek from the Bithynia of the second century AD who held high office in the Roman Empire (he governed provinces in Anatolia and Spain), and modelled his literary output on that of Xenophon P. Stadter (1980) *Arrian of Nicomedia*, Chapel Hill, N. Carolina, is a good account of the man and his writings, and see now R. Syme (1982) 'The career of Arrian', *HSCP*, lxxxvi, pp.181ff. There is a full and first-rate commentary on books i–iii of the *Anabasis* by A. B. Bosworth (1980) Oxford; P. A. Brunt's (1976) Loeb Arrian vol.i (books i–iv) London and Cambridge, Mass., is also invaluable and more approachable for the beginner — has excellent introduction and appendixes — and J. R. Hamilton's 1976 revision of the Penguin Arrian *Campaigns of Alexander* (= Anabasis) should also be noted. Arrian's account (abbreviated as AA in the present chapter) goes back to the nearly contemporary writings of Ptolemy, later king Ptolemy I Soter of Egypt, and of Aristobulus of Kassandreia, both eye-witnesses; these and the other 'primary sources' (i.e. in this context, sources surviving only in extracts or quotations by later writers) are collected in F. Jacoby's *Die Fragmente der griechischen Historiker* (*FGrHist.*), Leiden, nos 117ff.; there is a two-volume translation by C. A. Robinson (1953) Providence, Rhode Is., of the Alexander historians from Jacoby. The 'primary sources' are discussed, chapter by chapter, in L. Pearson (1960) *The Lost Historians of Alexander the Great*, Oxford. Ptolemy and Aristobulus themselves drew on the account of Kallisthenes, the nephew of Aristotle, until that ceased (cp. p. 288 for Kallisthenes' death).

　　The other main strand of the literary tradition is more rhetorical and flamboyant; it goes back to Kleitarchos, a writer about whom personally little is known; he lived in the Alexandria (Egypt) of Ptolemy I in the late fourth or early third centuries BC. This tradition has come down to us in the writings of Diodorus (book xvii; on the debt to Kleitarchos see most recently and sensibly J. R. Hamilton (1977) *Schachermeyr Studies* = *Greece and the Near East*, K. Kinzl and of Quintus Curtius Rufus (abbreviated QC in the present chapter; commentary on books iii–iv by J. Atkinson (1980), Amsterdam. Books i–ii are lost, books iii–x survive). There are Loeb translations of both authors; the Diodorus volume by C. B Welles (1963) (vol.viii) is particularly good. In the jargon of Alexander scholarship this second tradition is called the 'vulgate', Aristobulus and Ptolemy the 'main sources', i.e. the main sources behind Arrian, to distinguish them from the vulgate, of which Arrian is also aware, though he introduces material from it with formulae like 'it is said' rather than *citing* Kleitarchos, whom he never mentions.

Plutarch's *Life* of Alexander is long and valuable, eclectic in its use of source-material (and so has to be treated separately from the two great strands mentioned above). Useful comm. by J. R. Hamilton, Oxford, 1969.

The relevant inscriptions are gathered by Tod in *GHI*, ii, nos 183-202; A. J. Heisserer (1980) *Alexander the Great and the Greeks: the Epigraphic Evidence*, Oklahoma, offers some new interpretations but is much longer than Tod, and much less helpful for the student.

For the coins see A. R. Bellinger (1963) *Essays on the Coinage of Alexander the Great*, New York, with O. Zervos and M. J. Price (1982) *Numismatic Chronicle*, pp.166ff., 180ff., with references to more recent literature.

Modern books on Alexander are numerous. U. Wilcken, *Alexander the Great*, translated by G. C. Richards in 1932, and reprinted in paperback (New York), is still perhaps the best, though rather sparsely documented. W. W. Tarn (1948) *Alexander the Great*, 2 vols, Cambridge, is no longer as influential as it once was, chiefly owing to the series of articles published since 1958 by E. Badian; these are cited below at the appropriate moment. Tarn's vol.ii — vol.i is a narrative, reprinted from *Cambridge Ancient History*, vol.vi, edn.1 — is still good on the foundations and on military matters, but not reliable on the sources or on Alexander's policies. Badian has deflated many of Tarn's more exalted theories, and on the positive side has fruitfully used techniques of prosopography (i.e. the study of careers and family connections) more familiar from Roman history, to examine the interrelations of the Macedonian office-holding nobility — a technique which has its limitations given the poverty of Macedonian nomenclature. But Badian's work has revolutionized Alexander-studies. Of recent monographs, J. R. Hamilton (1973) *Alexander the Great*, London, though not exciting, can be recommended as giving an account of Alexander updated to the post-Badian era; more meaty and enjoyable is Peter Green (1974) *Alexander of Macedon*, Harmondsworth, Mdx. R. Lane Fox (1973) *Alexander the Great*, London, is very readable but unsatisfactory footnote arrangement means controversial statements are never properly argued for. N. G. L. Hammond (1981) *Alexander the Great, King, Commander and Statesman*, London, is specially valuable on Macedonian and military topics but has an old-fashioned, pre-Bosworth, attitude to source-criticism. Chapters 2, 4 and 5 of F. Walbank (1980) *The Hellenistic World*, London, are admirable on Alexander and his legacy. But the reader who is really interested in Alexander is recommended to read Arrian in a good translation (Brunt's Loeb; Penguin; or the old Bohn Library version by E. Chinnock) and to work through Brunt's introduction and appendices. Note that his vol.ii, containing *Anab*. v–vii and *Indike*, 1983, contains very valuable material on Indian topics and deeper examination of the source-problems. (Serious students will also consult Bosworth's comm. where possible for major difficulties.) He should then read Diod. xvii in Welles' Loeb.

A good monograph on the city-foundations of Alexander is badly needed. See meanwhile Brunt's appendixes, Tarn's app.8 (reprinted in G. T. Griffith (1966) *Alexander the Great: the Main Problems*, Cambridge, henceforth Griffith, *Problems*), and P. M. Fraser in *Afghan Studies*, ii, 1979 (see n.67 below).

Prosopographic material is gathered in H. Berve (1926) *Alexanderreich auf prosopographischer Grundlage*, vol.ii; though this is in German, very little German is needed to use it as much of the material is in the form of references to ancient authorities.

D. Engels (1977) *Alexander the Great and the Logistics of the Macedonian Army*, California, is of interest beyond the immediate scope of its title; see the review by G. L. Cawkwell (1980) *CR*, pp.244ff.

Mention should also be made of the fictional reconstructions by Mary Renault, *Fire From Heaven*, Harmondsworth, Mdx (on the early years; drawing on Plutarch and Diodorus), and *The Persian Boy*, Harmondsworth, Mdx (relying heavily on Curtius). Her *Funeral Games* (1981) Harmondsworth, Mdx, covers events in the years after Alexander's death, and uses Diod. xviii–xx, which comes from a splendid source, Hieronymus of Cardia. See also the same author's *The Nature of Alexander* (1975) New York; reprinted in different format 1983, Harmondsworth, Mdx.

The present writer has reviewed a number of the above books, and discussed some of the topics they raise: see *TLS*, 17, ix, 1976 (review of Brunt Loeb *Arrian*, vol.i); *CR*, 1981 (reviews of Bosworth's comm. vol.i and of Stadter's *Arrian*); *CR*, 1982 (review of Hammond's *Alexander*); *JHS*, 1982 (reviews of Atkinson's Curtius *commentary* and of Heisserer's *Alexander … the epigraphic evidence*).

2. N. G. L. Hammond (1980) *CQ*, pp.457ff., and in his (1981) book *Alexander the Great, King, Commander and Statesman*; but see *CR*, 1982, p.65. For the Macedonian kings and their relations P. Green, *Alexander of Macedon*, has a very helpful tree.

3. See J. R. Ellis (1976) *Philip II and Macedonian Imperialism*, app. at p.235ff. (with an unfortunate misprint at the vital point: for 349 read 359); G. Le Rider, *Le monnayage d'argent et d'or de Philippe II, frappé en Macédoine de 359 à 294*, Paris, at pp.386ff. Ellis refers to Le Rider's work in advance of publication; Le Rider then refers to the 'brilliant' work of Ellis! (referring to op.cit in n.4 below, a view soon attacked). E. Badian 'Macedonians and Greeks' (see chapter 7, n.1), p.47, n.26, thinks there must be something behind Justin.

4. J. R. Ellis (1971) *JHS*, xci, p.21; contra R. Errington (1974) *JHS*, xciv, pp.20ff. Cp. Bosworth comm. p.160, and P. Brunt Loeb *Arrian*, i, introduction, p.lxi, for the point about Kynna (both scholars assume, probably rightly, that Kynna could not have been betrothed while Amyntas lived; although Macedon was not quite a monogamous society and a disgraced Amyntas' claims could conceivably have been set aside. Arr. *Successors* i.22 just says that Amyntas was killed before Alexander crossed to Asia. Green, *Alexander of Macedon*, p.141, thinks Amyntas *was* still alive at the time of AA i.5; contra, W. Heckel (1982) *Rheinisches Museum*, p.78, n.1).

5. N. G. L. Hammond (1974) 'Alexander's campaign in Illyria', *JHS*, xciv, pp.66ff.; cp. also Hammond (1977). 'The campaign of Alexander against Cleitus and Glaucias', APX. MAK. (= *Archaia Makedonia*), ii, pp.503ff.

6. See Brunt Loeb *Arrian*, i, p.469f., discussing earlier views; cp. too Bosworth comm. p.62 — perhaps *too* sober.

7. E. W. Marsden (1977) 'Macedonian military machinery and its designers under Philip and Alexander', APX. MAK., ii, pp.211ff. Cp. Tarn, *Alexander*, ii, pp.39–45. Badian in 'Macedonians and Greeks' (see chapter 7, n.1) at pp.39ff.; P. Green, *Alexander*, pp.157–8. Muslims: Edward Mortimer (1982) *Faith and Power, The Politics of Islam*, London, p.394.

8. W. Schmitthenner (1968) 'Uber eine Formveränderung der Monarchie seit Al.d.Gr.', *Saeculum*, xix, pp.31ff., shows that the phrase and the concept of 'spear-won-territory' gets much commoner in books xvii onwards of Diodorus. Qualifications are made in A. Mehl (1980/81 (1982)) 'ΔΟΡΙΚΤΗΤΟΣ ΧΩΡΑ ...', *Ancient Society*, xi/xii, pp.173ff., but he is wrong to think that the concept was a fiction for Hieronymus: at e.g. xviii.39 the word *hoionei* doriktetos means 'in effect' spear-won, cp. Polyb. iii.87.9, xvi.34, and A. Mauersberger's *Polybius Lexicon* under *hoios* III; it does not imply a denial.

Cp. also F. Walbank (1950) *JHS*, p.79f. (but contra F. Walbank and E. Badian (1965) *Greece and Rome*, p.66, n.1, Roman fetial practice, which was concerned with the demanding of reparations, is surely not an influence here).

9. P. Goukowsky (1978) *Le Mythe d'Alexandre*, Nancy, i, p.139 (on which book see the deflationary review by P. Fraser (1980) *CR*) thinks that the idea of Alexander as hero was central to Kleitarchos' book (for which generally he makes very large claims; see further under n.48); this is no doubt true but the 'hero' theme was equally prominent in the 'main sources', see Brunt Loeb *Arrian*, app. IV, 'Alexander and the heroes', and L. Edmunds (1971) *GRBS*, xii, pp.363ff. There is now a vol.ii of P. Goukowsky: (1981) *Alexandre et Dionysos*, Nancy.

10. P. Green (1978) 'Caesar and Alexander: aemulatio, imitatio, comparatio', *AJAH*, iii, pp.1ff., a very interesting article. For the idea that such influences could flow both ways see J. Griffin (1977) 'Propertius and Antony', *JRS*, lxvii, pp.17ff., showing that life may imitate literature as well as vice versa.

11. N. G. L. Hammond (1980) 'The battle of the Granicus River', *JHS*, c, pp.73ff., and E. Badian (1977) 'The battle of the Granicus: a new look', APX. MAK., ii, pp.271ff. (cp. C. Foss, ibid., pp.495ff.); also Bosworth in comm. and Brunt Loeb *Arrian*, app.1. Except for Bosworth (and see Green, app.) all rightly follow Arrian not Diodorus; on Bosworth see *CR*, 1981, p.186.

12. Brunt, apps i, xiii, and introduction section 56; also Brunt (1963) 'Alexander's Macedonian cavalry', *JHS*, lxxxiii, pp.27ff. (though he takes too seriously the 10,000 of Polyain. v.44: this is a round figure for the Parmenio-Attalus advance force, which anyway suffered heavily in Asia, as Polyain says, and cannot be assumed to have been available in numbers to supplement Alexander's army in 334).

13. See Badian in *Ehrenberg Studies* (1966); S. Hornblower, *Mausolus*, pp.161ff. On *syntaxis* Bosworth comm. p.281 has a different interpretation — a once-for-all contribution (a sense attested for Seleucid Lydia).

14. V. Ehrenberg (1938) *Alexander and the Greeks*, Oxford, chapter 1; Badian, op.cit. under n.13; Bosworth, op.cit. and pp.183ff.

15. *Mausolus*, p.128, on the strange references to the King's Peace.

16. G. L. Cawkwell (1961) 'A note on Ps.-Dem.17.20', *Phoenix*, xv, pp.74ff.

17. Heisserer, *Al. the Gt and the Greeks* (but see (1982) *JHS*, p.271f., review) and Bosworth, comm. p.178.

18. Hornblower, *CAH*, edn 2, vol.vi, chap. iii.

19. E.g. by A. H. M. Jones (1949), *CR*, p.123, reviewing Tarn. Aspendos: D. M. Lewis (1977) *Sparta and Persia*, p.144, n.55 to previous page.

20. Smyrna: J. M. Cook (1958/9) *BSA*, liii, p.34; Priene: D. van Berchem (1970) *Museum Helveticum*, xxvii, pp.178ff., Hornblower, *Mausolus*, pp.323ff.; for Mausolus' activity, see ibid., chapters iv, xi.

21. See Brunt, Loeb *Arrian*, vol.ii forthcoming, app. xxvii.

22. P. Brunt (1965) *Greece and Rome*, p.208, citing Isok. v.76. Brunt, Loeb *Arrian*, vol.i, app.xv, points out that India had ceased to be part of the Persian Empire by Darius I's time; for the elasticity of the term Asia see ibid., intro., n.64 on p.liii.

23. Good discussion in Brunt, Loeb *Arrian*, i, app.iii; Hammond, *Alexander*, chapter 5; Walbank, *Historical Commentary on Polybius*, vol.ii, 1967, on Pol. xii.17ff. (the last two with helpful maps). Some of the worst problems are of topography, especially the identification of the River Pinaros; these are passed over in the present book.

24. E.g. Bosworth, p.199, uses it to reconstruct strategy; he thinks, on Curtius' evidence, that Alexander intended to fight a defensive battle and that Darius was forced to meet Alexander on unfavourable terrain. Bosworth's acceptance (210) of Curtius on Darius' position (left not centre) is less convincing.

25. S. Hornblower (1983) *Liverpool Classical Monthly*, viii, p.43, showing that this passage has been wrongly translated in modern edn (Loeb and Budé): translate *ta pleiona e* as 'more than' not 'for the most part either'. The whole passage is Diodoran not Kleitarchan, cp. the language of the Main Proem at Diod. i.2.3 with 'weakness of human nature' at xvii.38. This matters because much has been said, especially by F. Jacoby, on

tyche, fortune, in Diod. xvii, and if chapter 38 is Diodorus it limits what can be said about *Kleitarchos* and *tyche*, since this is easily the most striking passage in the book.

26. See A. R. Burn (1952) *JHS*, lxxii, pp.81ff., for the Persian counter-offensive; for Agis' revolt see Brunt, Loeb *Arrian*, i, app.vi, with bibliography.

27. See Bosworth on AA iii.1. (Note however QC iv.1.30–1.)

28. For Philip's city-foundations see G. L. Cawkwell (1978) *Philip of Macedon*, pp. 39–40; Herakleia Lynkestis: Hammond-Griffith, *History of Macedonia*, ii, pp.660, 558f.; J. R. Ellis (1976) *Philip II and Macedonian Imperialism*, 168.

29. For Kandahar see D. Whitehead and S. Helms (1978–9) *Afghan Studies*, i–ii; D. MacDowall and M. Taddei (1978) 'The early historic period: Achaemenids and Greeks', chapter 4 in F. Allchin and N. Hammond (eds) *The Archaeology of Afghanistan*, London, New York, San Francisco; J. M. Cook (1983) *The Persian Empire*, pp.192ff. Ai Khanoum: see n.31 below. Cp. now Helms (1982) *Afghan Studies*, iii/iv, 1ff.

30. Cp. U. Wilcken, *Alexander the Great*, p.259, but contrast C. B. Welles (1965) *Greece and Rome*, p.225, and P. Briant, op. cit. at n.69 below.
    For general bibliography about Alexander's foundations see above n.1. The basic lists are in Stephanus of Byzantium s.v. Alexandria, and Ps.-Call. (the Alexander Romance), ii.35.

31. For Ai Khanoum see P. Bernard (1967) *Proc. Brit. Acad.*; (1973); *Fouilles d'Ai Khanoum*; R. Lane Fox (1980) *Search for Alexander*, London, last chapter (excellent photos). On the irrigation, etc. from the Achaemenid period see J. Gardin (1980) *CRAI*, pp.480ff., and P. Briant (1982) *Rois, Tributs et Paysans*, pp.475ff.

32. A. H. M. Jones (1940) *The Greek City*, Oxford, p.305, n.4.

33. P. Fraser (1972) *Ptolemaic Alexandria*, Oxford, p.1.

34. ibid., pp.94ff. and nn.

35. Cp. A. Stein (1929) *On Alexander's Track to the Indus*, London, for this identification.

36. Date: P. Fraser (1967) *Opuscula Atheniensia*, Lund, p.30, n.27, cp. *Ptol.Alex.*, ii, p.3, n.9, preferable to C. B. Welles (1962) *Historia*, xi, pp.271ff., who puts it *after* the Siwah visit. See also A. B. Bosworth (1976) *CQ*, xxvi, pp.136–8 and comm., but note *CR*, 1981, p.187.

37. Used by Brunt, p.224 of Loeb *Arrian*, i, note on iii.1.5.

38. See now the excellent long article by E. Badian (1981) 'The deification of Alexander the Great', *Macedonian Studies presented to C. Edson*, pp.27ff., henceforth *Deification*, giving bibliography (of the older items note especially J. P. V. D. Balsdon (1950) 'The "divinity" of Alexander', *Historia*, i, pp.364ff., reprinted in Griffith, *Problems*, pp.179ff. D. G. Hogarth (1887) 'The deification of Alexander the Great', *Eng. Hist. Rev.*, ii, pp.317ff. is still of interest). On the Ammon visit in particular see Brunt, Loeb *Arrian*, i, app.v, and Bosworth's notes on AA iii.3–4, also Bosworth (1977) 'Alexander and Ammon' in *Schachermeyr Studies* (cp.n.1 above for this volume).

39. See Badian, *Deification*.
40. See most recently E. Fredricksmeyer (1979) 'Divine honours for Philip II', *TAPA*, cix, pp.39ff., discussed, and, in its new suggestions, rejected, by Badian, in and especially at the end of his *Deification*. See also Griffith, *Macedonia*, ii, chapter xxi, and cp. app.6. Philippi as hubris: Fredricksmeyer, p.52.
41. Diyllos: Hammond (1937) *CQ*; Theopompus: Welles, Loeb *Diod.*, vol.viii, intro.; Duris: R. Kebric (1977) *In the Shadow of Macedon*, Wiesbaden, pp.62ff. Jacoby, comm. on *FGrHist*. 328 F 56 wisely calls the source unknown.
42. Badian, *Deification*, p.41.
43. Ellis, *Philip*, p.307, against E. Gardiner (1925) *Olympia*, Oxford, p.134.
44. See M. Andronikos (1980) in Hatzopoulos and L. D. Loukopoulos (eds), *Philip of Macedon*, pp.18ff. (cp. Badian, *Deification*, p.71, where for 226 read 228). The original 'temple' report: *The Times*, 15, xi, 1977, p.7.
45. Fraser, *Ptol. Alex.*, i, pp.213ff.; ii, p.362f.
46. Badian, *Deification*, p.45 (contra e.g. P. Green, *Alex.*, p.274).
47. I.e. Wilcken, *Alex.*, p.127, is wrong to say that Alexander received enlightenment 'like a flash of lightning'. Arrian's own comment: Badian, *Deification*, p.44, but for Curtius see Bosworth, 'Alexander and Ammon', p.72 (see under n.38 above).
48. P. Goukowsky (1978) *Le Mythe d'Alexandre*, i, pp.136ff., 149ff. But see P. Fraser (1980) *CR*, p.247 (world rule). Invincibility: actually quite a favourite word and thought of Diod. e.g. used of pre-Leuktra Sparta and of the Argyraspids in xix.
49. Brunt, Loeb *Arrian*, i, app.ix, and Bosworth on AA iii.7ff.; Hammond, *Alexander*, chapter 6; Tarn, ii, 182ff.; Griffith (1947) 'Alexander's generalship at Gaugamela', *JHS*, lxvii, pp.77ff.; E. W. Marsden (1965) *The Campaign of Gaugamela*, Liverpool.
50. Brunt, Loeb *Arrian*, p.514.
51. So Hammond, p.146.
52. So Bosworth. But see *CR*, 1982.
53. Cp. P. Briant, *Rois, Tributs et Paysans*, p.489, citing Stolper's dissertation on Achaemenid Babylonia, against A. T. Olmstead (1948) *History of the Persian Empire*, chapter xxi.
54. Brunt, Loeb *Arrian*, i, app.viii (chronology and topography).
55. Bosworth, p.318.
56. Against Bosworth (1980) 'Alexander and the Iranians', *JHS*, c, pp.1ff., see S. Hornblower, *Mausolus*, pp.105, 220, and *CR*, 1981, p.187; also *CAH*, edn 2, vol.vi, chapter iii. Bosworth takes much further the views of E. Badian (1958) 'Alexander the Great and the unity of mankind', *Historia*, vii, pp.425ff. = Griffith, *Problems*, pp.287ff.
57. D. M. Lewis (1977) *Sparta and Persia*, p.152, n.114.
58. Brunt (1975) 'Alexander, Barsine and Herakles', *Rivista di Filologia*, ciii, pp.22ff. For Satibarzanes and Arsakes see Bosworth (1981) *JHS*, ci, pp.20f.
59. The Loeb Strabo mistranslates *philokuros*; the word refers here to Alexander.

60. Bosworth (1980) *JHS*, c, p.18. His views on the *hippokontistai* are here rejected, cp. *CR*, 1981, p.187.
61. Bosworth comm. pp. 331f., giving the modern views and suggesting that, although the palace had been 'picked clean' =? evidence of premeditation, Alexander's remorse points the other way.
62. Cp. Bosworth (1980) *JHS*, p.5, n.30.
63. *Mausolus*, p.157 and n.159.
64. Brunt, app.xi (Farah: his pp.501f.), and Bosworth on AA iii.26f. with references, among which note especially E. Badian (1960) 'The death of Parmenio', *TAPA*, xci, pp.324ff. Cp. W. Heckel (1977) 'The conspiracy *against* Philotas', *Phoenix*, xxxi, pp.9ff., but that Coenus and Hephaestion ganged up against a doomed man is explicable enough psychologically for reasons other than a 'plot of the nobility' against Philotas: Coenus needed to dissociate himself, cp. QC vi.9.30 for Coenus' marriage links with Philotas. Badian op.cit. above may be right to think that Hephaestion, Perdikkas, Krateros and Coenus were advanced because they had shown themselves Alexander's men in the decisive test; but in qualification QC vi.8.17 shows Perdikkas *already* a somatophylax, and cp. AA iii.25.6: Krateros left in command of the whole army (before the Philotas affair).
65. W. Heckel (1982) 'Who was Hegelochus?', *Rh. Mus.*, cxxv, pp.78f., reviving an old idea.
66. For the years 329–327 (especially on chronology and satrapal appointments) see Bosworth (1981) 'A missing year in the history of Alexander the Great', *JHS*, ci, pp.17ff.
67. See M. Wheeler (1968) *Flames Over Persepolis*, London, pp.65ff. (contra W. Tarn (1951) *Greeks in Bactria and India*, edn 2, Cambridge, pp.469ff.); Brunt, pp.502–3. New finds: P. Fraser (1980) 'The son of Aristonax at Kandahar', *Afghan Studies*, ii, pp.9ff., with good general discussion of Alexander's foundations in this area, occasioned by the inscription he publishes.
68. Tarn, *Greeks in Bactria and India*, app.vi; Brunt, p.503.
69. P. Briant (1978) *Klio*, lx, pp.74ff., reprinted in his *Rois, Tributs et Paysans*, 1982; Bosworth (1981) *JHS*, p.26 and n.60. For the site see the Russian publications cited in *CR*, 1982, p.66.
70. Attempts to locate the Alexandrias in Sogdiana and Oxiana mentioned in later sources are very conjectural; Goukowsky, *Mythe*, i, apps xxv–xxvi, Tarn (1940) *JHS*, lx, pp.90ff. Ai Khanoum, though a settlement centre both before (above) and after Alexander, cannot be certainly identified as an Alexandria though Bosworth (1981) *JHS*, p.29, now suggests that Alexander crossed the Oxus very close to this site. Further evidence of hellenization in this area continues to emerge: see Fraser, op.cit. under n.67 above, and more fully B.Litvinskij and I. Pitchikjan (1981) *Rev. Arch.*, pp.195ff., for hellenistic Greek dedication to the River Oxus by one Atrosok. (English version: *Journal, Royal Asiatic Soc.*, 1981, pp.133ff.)
71. A. Aymard (1967) *Études d'histoire ancienne*, Paris, pp.53ff.; Goukowsky, *Mythe*, pp.44ff.; E. Carney (1981) 'The death of Clitus',

GRBS, xxii, pp.149ff. (speculative).

72. E. Bikerman (1963) 'À propos d'un passage de Chares de Mytilene', *Parola del Passato*, xvii, pp.241ff.; Brunt, app.xiv; Badian, *Deification* (above, n.38), pp.48–54 (rejecting Chares' version).

73. Bosworth (1981) *JHS*, p.11.

74. J. R. Hamilton (1956) 'The cavalry battle at the Hydaspes', *JHS*, lxxvi, pp.26ff.

75. Cp. O. Murray (1972) 'Herodotus and hellenistic culture', *CQ*, xxii, pp.200ff.

76. Badian (1961) 'Harpalus', *JHS*, lxxxi, pp.16ff. with the qualifications in W. Higgins (1980) 'Aspects of Alexander's administration', *Athenaeum*, lviii, pp.129ff. Harpalus' first flight: Badian (1960) *Historia*, ix, pp.245ff.; W. Heckel (1977) *CP*, lxxii, pp.133ff.

77. J. Hornblower (1981) *Hieronymus of Cardia*, pp.87–97. Alexander's final aims: P. A. Brunt (1965) *Greece and Rome*, pp.205ff.

78. See the works cited under n.38 above and add P. Fraser (1958) *CR*, p.153; K.M.T. Atkinson (1973) 'Demosthenes, Alexander and *Asebeia*', *Athenaeum*, li, pp.310ff.; E. Fredricksmeyer (1979) 'Three notes on Alexander's deification', *AJAH*, iv, pp.1ff.

79. Brunt (1963) *JHS*, pp.42f. (but he will withdraw suggestions about emendation in Loeb, ii); Griffith, pp.68ff.; Badian (1965) *JHS*, pp.160ff. Bosworth (1980) *JHS*, pp.20f. does too much violence to the text; anyway it is clear that Arrian thought there were five and only five hipparchies, four of them Macedonian (*not*, as Bosworth says, 10 Macedonian ones, 4 Iranian, one mixed).

80. Badian (1958) *Historia*, vii, pp.425ff. = Griffith, *Problems*, pp.287ff., perhaps unduly sceptical on the Eratosthenic origin of Plutarch here. See also Badian (1976) in Fondation Hardt vol. on *Alexandre le Grand*, p.268.

81. A point made by Hammond, *History of Greece*, edn 2, p.268.

82. Fifth-century Cypriot hellenization: R. Meiggs (1972) *Athenian Empire*, app.7. On fourth-century Cyprus see G. F. Hill (1940) *History of Cyprus*, i, Cambridge; V. Karageorghis (1982) *Cyprus*, London. 'Culture-Greeks': W. W. Tarn and G. T. Griffith (1951) *Hellenistic Civilization*, edn 3, London, p.160.

For hellenization by the satraps in Asia Minor see the present writer in *CAH*, edn 2, vol.vi, chapter xi(a), and *Mausolus*.

Additional note (to p. 72, about Persians in Asia Minor)
Since the present book was printed, another, very interesting, Greco-Persian stele from Daskyleion has been published, in the new periodical *Epigraphica Anatolica* (vol. i, 1983, 1ff.). I should also have mentioned the remarkable tomb-painting of a Persian dignitary found at Karaburun near Elmali in N. Lycia (early fifth century; see J. Cook, 1983, *The Persian Empire*, plate 30 and pp. 165, 258, n.32). See also the discussion at J. and L. Robert, 1983, *Fouilles d'Amyzon* i, p. 168, cp. 154 no.15B, of the Persian name of the father of the Lycian Tlepolemos son of Artapates (early 2nd century BC).

Select critical bibliography (abbreviations given in brackets)

On Athens and the Athenian Empire in the *pentekontaetea*, vol.1 of A. W. Gomme (1945) *Historical Commentary on Thucydides* (= *HCT*), Oxford (5 vols, vols 4 and 5 completed by A. Andrewes and K. J. Dover, 1970 and 1981) is still indispensable, despite its date; note that in the appendices to the new vol.5 (on book viii) there is much material relevant to book i also. On the Athenian Empire see above all R. Meiggs (1972) *The Athenian Empire* (= *AE*), Oxford, paperback reprint 1979; the opposing viewpoint of M. I. Finley (1978) is in 'The fifth-century Athenian Empire: a balance-sheet', in P. Garnsey and C. R. Whittaker (eds) *Imperialism in the Ancient World* (= *Imperialism*), Cambridge, pp. 103ff., reprinted in M. I. Finley (1982) *Economy and Society in Ancient Greece*, London, pp. 41ff. I have discussed many of the issues raised by the Athenian Empire, including the Finley-Meiggs argument and the question of the archaic background to the fifth-century empire, in the new material which I have contributed to a new and amplified (1983) LACTOR translated sourcebook on *The Athenian Empire*, edn 3.

On Sicily, M. I. Finley (1980) *Ancient Sicily*, London, edn 2, is both readable and scholarly (the first edn was not annotated).

On Cyrene, F. Chamoux (1953) *Cyrène sous la monarchie des Battiades*, Paris, is excellent but does not take the story beyond the mid-fifth century; S. Applebaum (1979) *Jews and Greeks in Ancient Cyrene* (= *Cyrene*), Leiden, goes down to Roman times; the title is misleading in that there is much of great value on the period *before* the hellenistic age when the Jews begin to be relevant.

On Persian Egypt see Cook and Hornblower (app.1) cited under chapter 6; also M. I. Rostovtzeff (1953) *Social and Economic History of the Hellenistic World*, Oxford, chapter 2.

CHAPTER 6

J. M. Cook (1983) *The Persian Empire*, London, is now fundamental, equally masterly in its handling of historical and of archaeological evidence, a distinction which that author's writings have helped to dissolve; for some interesting Marxist studies on Achaemenid Persia see P. Briant (1982) *Rois, Tributs et Paysans*, Annales de l'Université de Besançon, no.269, Paris. D. M. Lewis (1977) *Sparta and Persia*, Leiden, chapter 1, is a brilliant attempt to exploit the new archival material from Persepolis.

On both Persia generally and on Asia Minor specifically I have drawn on my (1982) *Mausolus*, Oxford, chapter vi for the Persian satrapal system and my chapters for the revised *Cambridge Ancient History* (= *CAH*), edn 2, vol.vi forthcoming.

CHAPTER 7

On Macedon see especially N. G. L. Hammond's (1972) comprehensive and impressive *History of Macedonia*, Oxford, vol.i by Hammond alone (a historical geography), vol.ii (1979) with G. T. Griffith, who contributes in effect a separate monograph on Philip II; vol.iii with F. W. Walbank is announced.

On Boiotia and Thebes P. Cloché (1953) *Thèbes de Béotie*, Namur, is still standard; note also J. Buckler (1980) *The Theban Hegemony 371–362 BC*, Cambridge, Mass., who however fails to grasp the importance of Boiotian federalism and its export to other parts of Greece; for this subject see J. Larsen (1968) *Greek Federal States*, Oxford, or his shorter and more readable (1955) *Representative Government*, California.

On Thessaly, H. D. Westlake (1935) *Thessaly in the Fourth Century BC*, London, is admirable, and relevant to the fifth century as well as the fourth.

CHAPTER 8

G. E. M. de ste Croix (1972) *The Origins of the Peloponnesian War*, London, is a masterpiece whose main contribution lies in the background material it provides on topics like Spartan foreign policy and the Peloponnesian League; the book's main thesis, about the importance of the Megarian decree, is not accepted in the present book.

CHAPTER 9

There is no good modern monograph on Corinth; one is expected from J. Salmon. J. Wiseman (1979) *Land of the Ancient Corinthians*, Göteborg, is unsystematic but full of interest. Meanwhile see reports in *Arch. Reps*.

CHAPTER 10

The best book on Sparta is W. G. G. Forrest (1980) *History of Sparta 950–192 BC*, London, edn 2; sparsely documented but extremely acute. See also D.

M. Lewis' *Sparta and Persia*, chapter 2 (cited under chapter 6) and M. I. Finley, *Economy and Society*, pp. 24ff. (cited under chapters 1–3). See also G. E. M. de ste Croix, cited under chapter 8.

CHAPTER 11

On the Athenian constitution see P. J. Rhodes' (1981) magisterial commentary on the *Ath. Pol.*, Oxford, also the same author's (1972) *The Athenian Boule*, Oxford. On the *deme* system and representation of demes on the Council of 500 see J. S. Traill (1975) *Hesperia*, supplement xv, *The Political Organization of Attica*. On the character of Athenian political life W. R. Connor (1971) *The New Politicians of Fifth-Century Athens*, Princeton, N. J., uses documentary evidence (inscriptions, etc.) to reassess the demagogues vilified by Aristophanes and this has rightly led to revisions of judgements on e.g. Kleon, but see also the reviews of Connor cited in the text-notes. For all individual politicians see the entries in J. K. Davies' superb (1971) *Athenian Propertied Families* (= *APF*), Oxford; an introductory volume has now been published as *Wealth and the Power of Wealth in Classical Athens* (1981) London.

CHAPTER 12

On the Peloponnesian War A. W. Gomme's commentary (cited under chapters 1–3) on Thucydides is all that is needed. Some good insights in J. K. Davies (1978) *Democracy and Classical Greece*, London, chapter 7, and in A. Andrewes, 'Spartan imperialism?' in P. Garnsey and C. Whittaker, *Imperialism* (cited under chapters 1–3).

CHAPTER 13

Too many topics are touched on in this chapter for an itemized bibliography to be feasible. See text-notes at p. 305.

CHAPTER 14

See R. Seager's forthcoming chapter on the Corinthian War in *CAH*; on the Thessalian and central Greek aspect A. Andrewes (1971) *Phoenix*, xxv (cited in text-notes, p. 308). The 'Sicilian' angle argued for in the present book is new.

CHAPTER 15

T. T. B. Ryder (1965) *Koine Eirene*, Oxford, contains sensible discussion of the peace agreements between the Greek states sponsored by Persia in this period. On the Second Athenian Confederacy J. Cargill (1981) *The Second Athenian League*, California, is the most recent discussion, but he unduly minimizes Athenian misbehaviour, cp. my review in *CR*, 1982. For the other topics in this and following chapters it is more often necessary to cite articles than books; since the 1950s many of the issues have been clarified in articles by G. L. Cawkwell, which are cited in the text-notes where appropriate, rather than in the present bibliography.

CHAPTER 16

On the Boiotian hegemony see J. Buckler (cited under chapter 7, with remarks there made). For Athenian and Persian aspects to the 360s see my *Mausolus*, chapter vii.

CHAPTER 17

There have been several good recent accounts of Philip; G. L. Cawkwell's (1978) *Philip of Macedon*, London, summarizes views he has propounded over the years in articles, with ancient but scarcely any modern documentation; this is a first-rate and original picture. J. R. Ellis (1976) *Philip II and Macedonian Imperialism*, London, is longer and more densely written; specially good on topics (e.g. the Sacred War) involving Delphic evidence. For Griffith's contribution see above under chapter 7. M. B. Hatzopoulos and L. D. Loukopoulos (1980) *Philip of Macedon*, Athens, is a 'coffee-table' book with chapters by a number of distinguished scholars (Hammond, Griffith, Cawkwell, Andronikos, etc); note especially the illustrated account of the new Vergina finds including the (?) tomb of Philip II. R. Errington (1981) *AJAH* discusses all four new Philip books.

CHAPTER 18

The Alexander literature is dealt with in n.1 to this chapter because of the special problems presented by the sources.

ADDITIONAL NOTE

A number of important modern books are cited or drawn on in the present work but not listed in the above bibliography because they do not relate exclusively to any one chapter. Specially to be noted are G. E. M. de ste Croix (1981) *The Class Struggle in the Ancient Greek World*, London, a Marxist account of Greek history through to the Roman period; for the period covered by the present book chapter v is particularly important (discussion of the 'destruction of democracy' in the Greek world after the waning of Athenian influence). Also A. W. Lintott (1982) *Violence, Revolution and Civil Strife in the Classical City*, London, a thoughtful and perceptive contribution to the history of many of the states dealt with in this book; this book is shorter, but at the same time less breathless on its chosen period, than de ste Croix. Another book on social history which should be mentioned is D. Whitehead (1977) *The Ideology of the Athenian Metic*, Cambridge Philological Society supplementary paper no.4, containing *inter alia* valuable discussions of e.g. the citizenship law of 451. M. I. Finley's (1973) *The Ancient Economy*, London, is not a comprehensive ancient 'economic history' but a combative argument for several theses, e.g. that economic policies as such were not pursued by ancient states who cared only about securing grain and precious metal for coinage; on slavery Finley, rejecting a Marxist view in terms of class, prefers to speak of a 'spectrum' of different 'statuses' of unfreedom. The jargon here is less important than the valid point that 'chattel' slaves (see my chapter 1) were not the only kind of dependent labourer; this is relevant to a number of groups discussed in the present book — Thessalian *penestai*, Sikels, Anatolian peasant workers closely attached to the Greek cities, etc. (see further my chapter 1).

Finally, some valuable studies of special topics of social, economic or cultural history:

W. K. Lacey (1968) *The Family in Classical Greece*, London.

K. J. Dover (1974) *Greek Popular Morality*, Oxford.

K. J. Dover (1978) *Greek Homosexuality*, London.

H. Marrou (1956) *History of Education in Antiquity*, translated G. Lamb, London.

A. Momigliano (1975) *Alien Wisdom*, Cambridge (on Greek perceptions of foreign cultures like the Jews, Iranians, etc), with O. Murray's (1977) review, *JRS*, p.177.

D. Macdowall (1978) *The Law in Classical Athens*, London.

H. W. Parke (1933) *Greek Mercenary Soldiers*, Oxford.

M. M. Austin and P. Vidal-Naquet (1977) *Economic and Social History of Ancient Greece*, London (confined despite title to classical Greece; introductory discussion followed by translated sources).

M. I. Finley (1980) *Ancient Slavery and Modern Ideology*, London; (Penguin edn 1983).

Index

Note: (i) 'esp.' before an entry indicates a more considerable discussion. (ii) This index occasionally functions as an extra glossary (see e.g. entries under *archons, harmosts, perioikoi, proxeny*); also, space (date-charts, etc.) has been saved by often giving *dates* of battles, peaces and reigns under the appropriate entry.

munities; free, unlike the helots, but politically subjects of Sparta), 220, 222

Perrhaebia, 175, 186, 223, 311

Persephone, 177

Persepolis, Persepolis Tablets, 10, 67, esp. 283, 287, 321, 324

Perseus, 268, 279

Persia, Persians, esp. chaps 6 and 18, also ix, 10, 40, 45, 59ff., 102, 127, 136, esp. 139f., 144, 146, 161, 163, 169f., 181, 184ff., 190ff., 199f., 208f., 211f., 216, 223, esp. 230ff., 240, 247, esp. 254ff., 260, 275, esp. 298f., esp. 324; *see also under* medism, satraps

Persian Gulf, 291

Persian Wars, 9, 13, 15, 17, 23, 33, 76, 85, 95, 97, 108, 113

Persis (Persian satrapy), 282, 288

Personality, personality cult, 49, 180, 239, 284, 287

'Petalism', 54

Peukestas (satrap of Persis), 282, 289

Peukestas son of Makartatos, 64, 277

Phalaecus, 253f.

Phalanx, 160, 219, 258; *see also under* hoplites

Phaleron, 12, 108

Phalinus of Zacynthus, 158

Pharakides, 309

Pharaoh, 190, 279; *see also under* Akoris, Tachos

Pharax, 101, 188ff., 200, 309

Pharnabazos, 149, 163, 186, 194, 196, 198, 202, 216, 282

Pharnakes (Parnaka), 67

Pharnouches, 287

Pharsalos, 80, 82f., 187, 204, 216f., 223

Phaselis, 37, 231, 261

Phayllus, 253

Pherai, 82, 157, 162, 187, 206, 208, 223f., 234, 240, 242, 247, 250f.

Phidias (Athenian fifth-century sculptor), 59, 125

Phila, 248

philetairia, 207

Philhellene, philhellenism, 74, 76, 263, 293

philia (friendship), *philoi*, 123

Philip II (king of Macedon 359–336), esp. chap. 17, and 4, 17, 43, 74, 117, esp. 156f., 161, 165, 169, 175f., 204, 213, 219, 227, 261, 270, esp. 278f., 280, 285, 288, 312ff., 319f., 326

Philip V (king of Macedon 221–179 BC), 253, 263

'Philippeion' at Olympia, 278

Philippi, 108, 250, 278

Philippopolis, 274

Philippos son of Machatas, 282

Philiskos of Abydos, 229

Philistus of Syracuse, 52

Philochorus, 191, 197, 216, 233, 252, 257

philoi: *see under philia*

Philokrates, Peace of (346), 118, 213, 218, esp. 253ff., 260, 313

Philomelus, 247

Philonides, 267

Philosophy, philosophers, 8, 18, esp. 57f., esp. 153ff., 267, 275, 306; *see also under* Aristotle, Cynics, Eleatics, Lysis, *paideia*, Plato, Pythagoras, Stoicism

Philotas (son of Parmenio), 261, 284f.

Philoxenos, 289

Phlius, 204, 207, 222

Phoebidas, 104, 207f., 211

Phoenicia, 185, 231, 255, 273f., 280, 291ff.

Phokion, 177

Phokis, Phokians, 15, 42f., 45, 85, 176, 194, 216, 239f., 241, 245ff., 251, 253ff., 256f.

Phormio, 89, 121f., 130, 140, 157

phoros, xi, 139, 214; *see also under* Athenian Tribute Lists, *syntaxis*, tribute

Phrataphernes, 282